The Future Security Environment in the Middle East

Conflict, Stability, and Political Change

Edited by Nora Bensahel and Daniel L. Byman

Prepared for the

United States Air Force

RAND

Project AIR FORCE

The research reported here was sponsored by the United States Air Force under Contract F49642-01-C-0003. Further information may be obtained from the Strategic Planning Division, Directorate of Plans, Hq USAF.

Library of Congress Cataloging-in-Publication Data

Bensahel, Nora, 1971–
    The future security environment in the Middle East : conflict, stability, and
political change / Nora Bensahel, Daniel L. Byman.
        p. cm.
    Includes bibliographical references.
    "MR-1640."
    ISBN 0-8330-3290-9 (pbk. : alk. paper)
    1. Middle East—Strategic aspects. 2. United States—Military policy. I.
Byman, Daniel, 1967– II.Title.

UA832.B45 2003
355' 033056—dc22

                                                                    2003020980

The RAND Corporation is a nonprofit research organization providing objective analysis and effective solutions that address the challenges facing the public and private sectors around the world. RAND's publications do not necessarily reflect the opinions of its research clients and sponsors.

RAND® is a registered trademark.

Cover design by Stephen Bloodsworth

Published 2004 by the RAND Corporation
1700 Main Street, P.O. Box 2138, Santa Monica, CA 90407-2138
1200 South Hayes Street, Arlington, VA 22202-5050
201 North Craig Street, Suite 202, Pittsburgh, PA 15213-1516
RAND URL: http://www.rand.org/
To order RAND documents or to obtain additional information, contact
Distribution Services: Telephone: (310) 451-7002;
Fax: (310) 451-6915; Email: order@rand.org

PREFACE

This collection of papers examines emerging security trends that will shape the Persian Gulf in the coming years. The authors address a number of topics that will affect regional security, including prospects for economic and political reform, civil-military relations, regime change, energy security, the spread of new information technologies, and the proliferation of weapons of mass destruction. The volume aims to help policymakers and the public develop a better understanding of the underlying issues at work in a region at the forefront of concern today.

Readers of this report may also be interested in a related publication: Daniel Byman and John R. Wise, *The Persian Gulf in the Coming Decade: Trends, Threats, and Opportunities*, RAND Corporation, MR-1528-AF, 2002. This volume examines likely challenges to U.S. interests in the Persian Gulf region in the next decade, with principal focus on the conventional military strength of Iran and Iraq, the potential for subversion, and the social and economic weaknesses of the regional states. (Research for MR-1528-AF was completed before the September 11, 2001, attacks.)

The research reported here was sponsored by the Director of Operational Plans, Office of the Deputy Chief of Staff for Air and Space Operations (HQ USAF/XOX), and conducted within the Strategy and Doctrine Program of RAND Project AIR FORCE. Comments are welcomed and may be addressed to the acting Program Director, Alan Vick.

RAND PROJECT AIR FORCE

RAND Project AIR FORCE (PAF), a division of the RAND Corporation, is the U.S. Air Force's federally funded research and development center for studies and analyses. PAF provides the Air Force with independent analyses of policy alternatives affecting the development, employment, combat readiness, and support of current and future aerospace forces. Research is conducted in four programs: Aerospace Force Development; Manpower, Personnel, and Training; Resource Management; and Strategy and Doctrine.

Additional information about PAF is available on our web site at http://www.rand.org/paf.

CONTENTS

TABLES

SUMMARY

Since the end of the 1991 Gulf War, threats to political security in the Middle East have increased. Tensions between states have long threatened to destabilize the region. At times these tensions have resulted in open warfare, disrupting political and economic security and creating humanitarian crises. Today, the threat of interstate aggression is manifested in new and more dangerous ways. The collapse of the Arab-Israeli peace process and the subsequent outbreak of violence have inflamed anti-Western sentiment throughout the region. The proliferation of weapons of mass destruction (WMD) has also raised the potential for conflict between rival countries. The exportation of Middle East terrorism around the world has contributed to the political and economic isolation of the region.

Domestic developments over the past decade could also contribute to the destabilization of the region. A new generation of leaders has begun to take power with untested leadership skills and uncertain bases of support. Education among women has increased, presenting a challenge to traditional social hierarchies. Information technologies such as satellite television have become more available, providing populations with diverse views on political and social issues. Together these developments could bring about major political, social, and economic changes. The long-term effects of such changes may be positive from the perspectives of democratization and the advance of human rights. However, the short-term effects could spell political and economic turmoil, increased threat of conflict, and unpredictable shifts in policy and behavior by individual states.

POLITICAL INSTABILITY IN THE MIDDLE EAST COULD HAVE SERIOUS CONSEQUENCES FOR THE UNITED STATES

Since the terrorist attacks of September 11, 2001, the Middle East has played a more prominent role in U.S. policy than ever before. The United States relies on Middle Eastern partners such as Israel, Saudi Arabia, Qatar, Egypt, and others to fight terrorism and to halt the proliferation of WMD by rogue states. The loss of key partners due to hostile regime changes or increasing anti-Americanism could limit the United States' ability to fight terrorism within the region. In addition, the United States has an interest in maintaining stable energy prices and reliable supplies. Given the West's dependence on Middle East oil, political instability in the region could hurt economies around the world.

EMERGING TRENDS WILL INCREASE THE POTENTIAL FOR DESTABILIZATION

What are the prospects for political security in the Middle East in the foreseeable future? RAND Project AIR FORCE studied current political, economic, and social trends in the Middle East to forecast future threats to regional security and their potential impact on the United States. Key findings include the following:

- *Liberalization will advance slowly and democratization will be even more limited.* Middle East states are typically controlled by authoritarian, nondemocratic regimes. In recent years, these regimes have come under pressure to reform the political system and to relax government controls over the media and other forms of public expression. Some states have responded to this pressure by allowing *liberalization*—the introduction of civil liberties such as free speech and freedom of assembly—but have limited *democratization*—the development of democratic institutions such as elections and representative legislature. For example, some states allow citizens to participate in civic organizations that remain tied to the state and do not represent grassroots interests. Despite these limitations, however, continued liberalization may fuel the public appetite for political reform and may lead to more long-term democratic change. (See pages 15–55.)

- *Declining economies will likely increase popular dissatisfaction with governments.* Recent economic reform efforts have failed to create jobs or to attract foreign investment to the Middle East. Heavy debt, overtaxation, and government corruption have prevented economic growth. The region currently suffers from unemployment, poverty, and heavy demands on both clean water and domestic food supplies. High population growth will exacerbate these problems in the coming years. Countries will need to import more food and will have to invest in expensive water reclamation technologies. Continued economic decline will erode public confidence in leaders and will increase the potential for unrest. Moreover, the surplus of educated youths without jobs will provide fertile ground for radical fundamentalism to grow. At the same time, the reforms that would need to take place to improve economies—such as fewer government regulations and greater accountability—could destabilize regimes by alienating special-interest constituencies. (See pages 57–128.)

- *Militaries will be more devoted to internal control than to external defense.* Many Middle East states have "dual mandate" militaries responsible for protecting their regimes from internal challenges as well as defending their countries from external dangers. As economic and social pressures cause domestic threats to increase, militaries will have to commit their best resources to internal police functions such as suppressing demonstrations. Regimes will seek to consolidate control and will be less willing to grant power to frontline commanders. As a result, military forces will become less effective at external defense. This trend will have mixed implications for the United States. The persistence of civil control over the military will mean that U.S. allies in the region will possess the means to suppress terrorist groups within their borders. At the same time, these partners will be less effective in combat operations. (See pages 129–162.)

- *New leaders may be weaker and less likely to cooperate with the United States.* Since 1997, new leaders have come to power in Iran, Algeria, Bahrain, Jordan, Morocco, and Syria. Further leadership changes are expected in Saudi Arabia and Egypt in the near future. Incoming leaders will need to concentrate on building popular support for their regimes. They may therefore be less willing to continue unpopular policies such as cooperat-

ing with the U.S. war on terrorism or supporting Arab concessions to Israel in future peace negotiations. Furthermore, inexperienced leaders will be more likely to make mistakes in foreign
policy, whether by overestimating their countries' military
strength, by believing that they can intimidate their adversaries,
or by trusting in international support that proves to be unreli-
able. These political miscalculations could lead to increased
tensions between states. (See pages 163–195.)

- *Changing patterns in the energy market will strengthen Middle
  East ties to Asia.* The Middle East dominates the global energy
  market with roughly 70 percent of the world's proven oil reserves.
  The region is expected to maintain its preeminence through new
  exploration and increases in production capacity. However, the
  United States and Europe are expected to shift the majority of
  their consumption from Middle Eastern oil to Russian oil in the
  coming years. Asia will become the leading consumer of oil from
  the Middle East. This shift could have important political
  implications for the West. China, North Korea, and Russia are
  among the leading suppliers of WMD and missile technologies.
  As Asian energy demands increase, the defense trade between
  Asia and the Middle East is likely to grow. As a result, the United
  States will find it more difficult to pressure Asian governments
  not to export arms to hostile Middle East regimes. (See pages
  197–225.)

- *Communications technologies may increase the demand for
  public participation in government.* Advanced technologies
  such as the Internet are primarily limited to the wealthier and
  more educated echelons of Middle Eastern society. However,
  mid-level technologies such as satellite television, videocassettes, fax machines, and photocopiers have become widespread
  among the general population. These technologies could have a
  profound impact on the political landscape. They permit the
  quick and inexpensive circulation of printed materials that are
  beyond the control of government media and publishing monopolies. Satellite television gives people access to Western media. These innovations provide the population with diverse
  views on politics and world events. They also provide forums for
  greater discussion and debate. One possible outcome of this
  change is that Middle Eastern governments will be compelled to

take greater steps to eradicate corruption, to bring transparency to the government process, and to increase standards of living. However, it is equally possible that governments will respond by becoming more authoritarian. Regimes may attempt to silence dissenting voices through intimidation or force. They may also attempt to limit popular access to certain technologies. (See pages 227–251.)

- *Middle East states will continue to develop and acquire WMD.* WMD capabilities in the region have increased in recent decades, though not at the rate originally feared by Western analysts. Nevertheless, many regimes seek to develop or acquire chemical, biological, radiological, or nuclear weapons and advanced delivery systems. It is possible that states such as Iran will develop nuclear weapons capabilities within the next decade. Continued proliferation of WMD in the Middle East would have serious implications both within the region and around the world. The geographical distance between adversaries in the Middle East is very short. States would not need long-range delivery systems to inflict sudden and catastrophic damage upon each other. The expansion of WMD capability in the Middle East would also constrain U.S. freedom of action by increasing the vulnerability of deployed forces. Finally, the proliferation of WMD among Middle East terrorist groups could threaten the U.S. homeland. The September 11 attacks demonstrate the global reach of certain groups and their willingness to stage large-scale offensives against the United States. (See pages 253–298.)

THE UNITED STATES MUST BALANCE OPPOSING INTERESTS IN FORMING MIDDLE EAST POLICY

Given the range of potential crises that could emerge in the Middle East, the United States must carefully consider which policies are likely to produce the best outcome. A critical issue is whether the United States should promote political stability or whether it should encourage democratic reform. Experience in the former Soviet Union and elsewhere suggests that states undergoing the transition to democracy are more likely to become involved in conflicts with their neighbors. Moreover, democratization in the Middle East could open the door to nationalist or fundamentalist groups that are op-

posed to U.S. interests. In the past, when faced with a choice between preserving the stability of a nondemocratic ally and fostering
democratic change, the United States has sided with the incumbent
regime. However, surveys show that this policy has fueled anti-
American sentiment among populations throughout the region. In
the future, the United States will need to make a greater effort to explain its policies to ordinary citizens in the Middle East. It will also
need to weigh the prospects for democratic change with the potential for instability and the loss of key Middle East allies. (See pages
299–315.)

ACKNOWLEDGMENTS

The editors wish to thank the chapter authors for their patience through several rounds of revisions. Theodore Karasik and Marc Lynch thoroughly reviewed the manuscript, greatly improving its quality. Jerrold Green, Edward Harshberger, and C. R. Neu provided useful feedback at all stages of the project, and Risha Henneman and Miriam Schafer provided invaluable administrative assistance.

The editors particularly wish to thank the three authors outside of RAND who participated in this project: Jon Alterman, Director of the Middle East Program at the Center for Strategic and International Studies, Washington, D.C.; Risa Brooks, Assistant Professor of Political Science at Northwestern University, Evanston, Illinois; and Alan Richards, Professor of Economics and Environmental Studies at the University of California, Santa Cruz.

Chapter One

INTRODUCTION

Nora Bensahel and Daniel L. Byman

The security environment in the Middle East has become increasingly complicated during the past decade. Up to and including the 1991 Gulf War, the regional environment was largely shaped by fears of interstate aggression, either by superpower intervention or by regional states against each other. Fears of interstate aggression certainly remain today, but they are manifesting themselves in new ways. The Arab-Israeli conflict has been a persistent source of tension for decades, for example, but it has taken on new dimensions in the aftermath of the failed Oslo process and the recent explosion of violence that shows no signs of abating. These traditional issues have been joined by several more recent problems that defy easy solutions. Weapons of mass destruction (WMD) continue to spread throughout the region, despite international nonproliferation efforts. Terrorists recruited and trained in the Middle East are now carrying out attacks far beyond their own borders, creating strong global interests in countering the sources of this phenomenon.

Many of these security issues are profoundly affected by the many domestic changes occurring in the Middle East. A new generation of leaders is taking power, their skills untested. Social change is transforming the roles of women and the traditional hierarchy in the region. Oil revenues are lower than they were in the 1970s, causing economic problems that range from reduced budgets to rapidly escalating debt. Structural economic problems remain profound, while demands on the state are increasing throughout the region as a result of rising expectations and population growth. New information technologies are providing ordinary citizens with a wider range of viewpoints than they have ever had before, while in a few states, attempts at political reform are increasing their ability to express their views and influence the decisionmaking process.

This report seeks to identify the trends that are likely to shape regional security and their implications for the United States. Each chapter addresses a different substantive area, ranging from political and economic trends to energy policy and weapons proliferation, in an effort to assess each area's long-term impact on regional security. This chapter sets the stage for these issues by identifying U.S. national interests in the region and the potential threats to those interests.

U.S. INTERESTS IN THE MIDDLE EAST

The United States has many vital and enduring interests in the Middle East.[1] Six important U.S. interests include countering terrorism, countering WMD proliferation, maintaining stable oil supplies and prices, ensuring the stability of friendly regimes, ensuring Israel's security, and promoting democracy and human rights.

Countering Terrorism

After the devastating September 11, 2001, attacks on the World Trade Center and the Pentagon, the suppression of terrorism rose to the fore of U.S. concerns in the Middle East. Al Qaeda and other radical Islamist groups draw heavily on the Arab and Muslim world for recruits and funding. In addition, much of their violence and propaganda is directed at destabilizing Middle Eastern regimes that are friendly to the United States. Thus, the United States must confront risks on a governmental level, helping its regional partners secure themselves against terrorist-generated instability, and at a popular level to ensure that nationals in Saudi Arabia, Egypt, Yemen, or other states in the region do not join terrorist groups or provide them with financial or other assistance.

---

[1]What constitutes "the Middle East" is a matter of disagreement. This volume focuses primarily on Iran, Iraq, the Arab states of the Persian Gulf, Egypt, Jordan, and Syria. Other important states, such as Libya and Turkey, are also addressed in several chapters.

In addition to such transnational groups as al Qaeda, state-sponsored terrorism has long been a problem in the Middle East. Iran for many years supported radicals throughout the region in an attempt to spread its Islamic revolution. In addition, Iran has been connected to terror attacks against U.S. forces in Lebanon and was implicated in the 1996 Khobar Towers bombing in Saudi Arabia, which killed 19 Americans. Over time, Tehran's ardor has waned, but it still supports anti-Israeli groups such as the Lebanese Hezbollah and the Palestine Islamic Jihad. Libya and Syria have also provided limited support to radicals, helping them sustain their organizations.

Countering WMD Proliferation

The United States has a strong interest in preventing, or at least managing, the spread of nuclear, biological, and chemical weapons. WMD in the Middle East pose a threat to U.S. partners in the Gulf, to Israel, and to U.S. forces. Adversaries employing WMD might offset the vast superiority of U.S. conventional forces by enabling foes to inflict significant casualties on U.S. forces. As a result, they also threaten to undermine confidence in the U.S. security guarantee.

In the Middle East, the use of WMD is not a hypothetical threat. The Iran-Iraq war witnessed the repeated use of chemical weapons by Iraq and their occasional use by Iran. The 2003 war against Iraq was largely justified as an effort to prevent Saddam Hussein from further developing WMD programs. Iran is pursuing nuclear and biological weapons. Syria and Libya possess vast stocks of chemical weapons, which are used as a strategic deterrent against Israel and, more generally, to compensate for the weaknesses of their conventional forces.

Maintaining Stable Oil Supplies and Prices

The Persian Gulf is a particularly critical region for the United States given its importance to the world oil market. States in the Gulf will remain leading oil exporters in the next decade, although the degree of their dominance will depend heavily on the price of oil. Saudi Arabia alone contains a quarter of the world's total proven reserves;

Iraq has the second largest reserves in the world, possessing more than 10 percent of the world's total; and Iran, the United Arab Emirates (UAE), and Kuwait contain about 9 percent each.[2] By the end of the decade, Iraq's sustainable production capacity could easily double, and perhaps triple, with sufficient foreign investment.

Ensuring the Stability of Friendly Regimes

In addition to its long-standing ties to Israel, the United States has developed close relations with several states in the region. After the 1991 Gulf War, the United States augmented, or at times forged, security ties to Saudi Arabia, Kuwait, the UAE, Bahrain, Qatar, and Oman.[3] Although these states' possession of, or proximity to, large oil reserves was the initial reason for U.S. efforts to build ties, these relations have taken on a life of their own. The United States also has tried to cultivate Jordan, Egypt, and Morocco as moderate Arab voices that are willing to cooperate with the United States on counterterrorism and support the U.S. agenda on a range of issues.

Ensuring Israel's Security

Israel is a democratic, pro-Western country in a turbulent region. Its armed forces and intelligence services are highly competent, increasing the country's value in fighting terrorism and, more generally, in responding to military threats in the region. Many Americans also strongly back Israel, making its security an important political issue for any administration. Continued violence in Israel and Palestinian areas has contributed to anti-U.S. sentiment throughout the region and made it more difficult for friendly Arab and Muslim governments

---

[2] BP Amoco Statistical Review of World Energy 2001, available at http://www.bpamoco.com/centres/energy/index.asp, accessed March 28, 2002.

[3] Many of these relationships became close before the end of the Cold War. The United States established a defense cooperation agreement with Oman in 1980. Well before that, the United States had an unwritten "handshake agreement" with Saudi Arabia, with U.S. forces committed to defending the Kingdom's security. See William B. Quandt, *Saudi Arabia in the 1980s: Foreign Policy, Security, and Oil*, Washington, D.C.: Brookings, 1981; Joseph A. Kechichian, *Oman and the World*, Santa Monica, Calif.: RAND, MR-680-RC, 1995, pp. 139–158; and Nadav Safran, *Saudi Arabia: The Ceaseless Quest for Security*, Ithaca, N.Y.: Cornell University Press, 1998.

to cooperate openly with Washington on a host of issues.[4] This problem has gotten significantly worse since the outbreak of violence in late 2000. The Bush administration has put forth a road map toward a permanent two-state solution and is working with Russia, the European Union, and the United Nations to persuade the parties to adhere to its provisions; yet the violence continues. The United States has an interest in reducing the level of violence in the short to medium term and helping to find a sustainable long-term solution to the Arab-Israeli conflict.

Promoting Democracy and Human Rights

The United States has a broad, worldwide interest in democracy and human rights that has implications for U.S. actions in the Middle East. However, this interest is honored more in the breach than in reality because Israel is the only democratic state in the region. Saudi Arabia, for example, has no free press or free elections, and Saudi women face a variety of restrictions on their travel, employment, and daily lives. Even Egypt, which has had a parliament for decades, has bans on organized political activity and on free speech, and has other basic impediments to democracy. These restrictions elicit at most mild criticism from Washington. As Jon Alterman notes, "American officials have tended to accede to official requests to downplay calls for democratization and to shun extensive contacts with those working against the ruling governments."[5] As a result, even liberal Middle Easterners question U.S. support for democracy. As Murphy and Gause contend, "There is a pervasive sense in the Middle East that the United States does not support democracy in the region, but rather supports what is in its strategic interest and calls it democratic."[6]

---

[4]For an overview of the links between the Arab-Israeli dispute and other U.S. security interests, see Zalmay M. Khalilzad, David A. Shlapak, and Daniel L. Byman, *The Implications of the Possible End of the Arab-Israeli Conflict for Gulf Security*, Santa Monica, Calif.: RAND, MR-822-AF, 1997.

[5]Jon Alterman, "The Gulf States and the American Umbrella," *Middle East Review of International Affairs*, Vol. 4, No. 4, December 2000, electronic version.

[6]Richard W. Murphy and F. Gregory Gause III, "Democracy and U.S. Policy in the Middle East," *Middle East Policy*, Vol. 5, No. 1, January 1997, p. 59.

In the wake of September 11, the U.S. public may be less tolerant of government support for authoritarian states in the region. For example, a survey conducted in November 2001 found that 57 percent of those polled stated that it was "very important" for the United States to press for more democracy in Saudi Arabia, an enormous increase over the 10 percent who responded similarly in a June 1999 poll.[7] To the extent that these trends continue, the United States may have to increase its support for political reform in the region.[8]

Concerns over democratization and human rights often limit U.S. actions and could affect the type of support it would provide in a crisis. For example, if unrest in a Gulf state led to mass demonstrations and the government responded by killing large numbers of unarmed protesters, the United States would have to reconsider arms sales to that country and might otherwise limit ties at least temporarily. Even if unrest arose that threatened the flow of oil or the stability of a friendly regime, the United States would be not very likely to use its own forces to directly assist a regime that used torture, arbitrary arrests, and other forms of repression that would be widely condemned in the United States and the West in general. Furthermore, the U.S. public may grow more cautious about cooperating with autocratic Middle Eastern regimes in the wake of September 11, particularly those that are not seen as cooperating in the war on terrorism, further limiting the U.S. scope of action. Thus, although human rights and democratization are not interests that the United States actively seeks to advance or protect in the Middle East, they are broad concerns that may inhibit U.S. attempts to defend its other interests.

---

[7]The November 2001 poll was conducted by Princeton Survey Research Associates, posted on Lexis-Nexis December 7, 2001, question ID: USPSRNEW.111001, R08B. The June 1999 poll was conducted by Potomac Associates and Opinion Dynamics, posted on Lexis-Nexis December 7, 1999, question ID: USPOTM.99ASIA, R23H.

[8]There is some indication that this trend may be waning. A January 2002 poll found that only 42 percent said that it was "very important" to press for more democracy in Saudi Arabia, and in September 2002, the number was down to 38 percent. Nevertheless, this still remains far above the responses from June 1999. For the 2002 poll data, see results from the Pew Research Center for People and the Press, Year-After 9/11 Poll, available at http://people-press.org/reports/print.php3?PageID=639.

POTENTIAL THREATS TO U.S. INTERESTS

In recent decades, several different types of threats have emerged to the U.S. interests described above. Examples of these threats are presented in Table 1.1.

The greatest danger to regional security in the past was outright aggression by a hostile state. Israel fought wars with its neighbors in 1948, 1956, 1967, 1973, and 1982. In addition, for much of this period it regularly skirmished with Egyptian and Syrian troops as well as Palestinian guerrillas. In the 1970s, Iran and Iraq engaged in a proxy war over the Shatt al-Arab waterway and then fought a brutal eight-year war with each other in the 1980s, which led to disruptions in the flow of oil and destabilized the region. In 1971, Iran occupied several islands claimed by the UAE. Iraq invaded Kuwait in 1990 and was

Table 1.1

Past Challenges to U.S. Interests in the Middle East

External Aggression	External Subversion or Terrorism	Internal Unrest
Arab-Israeli wars (1948, 1956, 1967, 1973, and 1982)	Arab support for radical Palestinian groups	Radical seizure of the Grand Mosque in Mecca (1979)
Iranian and Iraqi attacks on Gulf tankers during the Iran-Iraq war (1987–1988)	Iranian support for Shi'a radicals in Lebanon, the Gulf, and elsewhere (ongoing, particularly active in the 1980s)	Shi'a riots in Bahrain, Kuwait, and the Eastern Province of Saudi Arabia (1979–1981)
Iraqi invasion of Kuwait (1990)	Iranian support for 1981 coup attempt in Bahrain	The intifada (1987–1990)
Iraqi threats to Kuwait (1994)	Iranian-affiliated radicals' attempts to assassinate the emir of Kuwait (1985) and terrorist attacks in Kuwait city (1983)	Radical attacks on U.S. forces in Saudi Arabia (1995)
Iranian and Iraqi WMD programs (ongoing)		Shi'a unrest in Bahrain (1994–1996)
Iranian seizure of Gulf islands claimed by the UAE (1971 and 1992)	Iranian-backed unrest at the hajj	The "al Aqsa intifada" (2000–present)
	Iranian support for Hamas and the Palestine Islamic Jihad	Al Qaeda–related terrorist attacks on U.S. forces, government personnel, and civilians (1992–present)

only expelled by the U.S.-led coalition's massive military effort. For more than a decade afterward, Iraq repeatedly announced its view that Kuwait was an integral part of Iraq, built up troops near the Kuwait border, and made numerous threats against Kuwait, Saudi Arabia, and other regional states.[9]

Aggressive regimes have also attempted to subvert pro-Western countries. When outright invasion failed to defeat Israel, several Arab governments at times provided limited support to Palestinian radicals seeking to undermine Israel. After the Iranian revolution in 1979, Iranian leaders regularly called for the overthrow of Gulf rulers. During the anti-regime demonstrations in Bahrain from 1994 to 1996, Iran tried to take advantage of the unrest by training and supporting Shi'a radicals.

Internal instability also poses a threat to U.S. interests. Palestinian groups have long used terrorism to weaken Israel. In 1987, Palestinians in the West Bank and Gaza began a series of riots and demonstrations against Israeli occupation, the first intifada. Violence continued sporadically in the 1990s, surged after the collapse of peace talks in 2000, and remains intense. In 1979, Saudi and other Arab religious extremists seized the Grand Mosque in Mecca, holding off Saudi security forces for two weeks. Angered by long-standing discrimination and inspired by the Iranian revolution, Shi'a in Bahrain, Kuwait, and Saudi Arabia rioted against their governments in the early 1980s. In 1995, Islamists destroyed the Office of Program Management/Saudi Arabian National Guard office in Riyadh killing seven, including five Americans.[10] It also appears that Saudi, Egyptian, Yemen, and Algerian nationals are a major component of al Qaeda, and many Gulf state citizens provide financial support to a range of anti-U.S. Islamist causes. In general, many states in the Middle East face economic problems and demographic pressures and have few institutions for incorporating public sentiment into

---

[9]For a review, see Daniel L. Byman and Matthew C. Waxman, *Confronting Iraq: U.S. Policy and the Use of Force Since the Gulf War*, Santa Monica, Calif.: RAND, MR-1146-OSD, 2000.

[10]Responsibility for the 1996 attack on the U.S. military's Khobar Towers facility in Saudi Arabia, which killed 19 Americans, remains unclear.

decisionmaking, a combination that suggests that the potential for unrest remains acute.[11]

A CHANGING REGION

Broad strategic, social, and political trends are reshaping the Middle East. These changes will pose new challenges and offer new opportunities for the United States.

For most of the 1990s, Middle East politics, and particularly decisions on security, remained the preserve of elites. Although no regime's-decisionmaking was completely immune from public opinion, in general the public had little input into foreign policy decisionmaking and leaders could mostly cloak their actions. Increases in popular input into decisionmaking and the explosion of new and freer media are expanding the range of viewpoints that are considered while policy is being formulated. True democracy remains far away, but the scope and scale of debate have increased and regimes are less free to pursue unpopular policies without constraint. Moreover, the composition of the elite itself is changing because of the deaths of aged leaders. Since 1997, new leaders have taken power in Iran, Syria, Jordan, Morocco, Qatar, and Bahrain, raising the possibility that these countries' policies will change as well.

The United States may also confront other major power rivals in the Middle East in the coming years. Throughout the Cold War, the United States and the Soviet Union competed fiercely for influence, arming their proxies and backing their causes. In the 1990s, however, Russia, China, and the major European powers limited their involvement, largely confining themselves to commercial transactions, including arms sales. During the coming years, the possible emergence of China as a world power and perhaps renewed competition with Russia may lead to greater extraregional meddling. It is also possible that the campaign against terrorism will unite the major powers and that they will subordinate their other objectives to this shared interest. Much will depend on the extent to which the United

---

[11]For a review, see Daniel L. Byman and Jerrold D. Green, *Political Violence and Stability in the States of the Northern Persian Gulf,* Santa Monica, Calif.: RAND, MR-1021-OSD, 1999.

States is able to form a durable international consensus on the scope of the counterterror campaign.

Military challenges in the region may also shift. Changes in information technology and doctrine are reshaping how the United States fights wars. Middle Eastern states may capitalize on similar shifts to improve their forces, but their military deficiencies will lead to dramatically different applications. They will face an ever-growing technology gap with the United States, which will make it harder for U.S. partners to cooperate with the United States and will increase the incentives for U.S. adversaries to pursue asymmetric strategies. Several regional powers may also seek chemical, biological, and nuclear weapons to offset their conventional weakness with regard to regional rivals and the United States. The future role of the Iraqi military remains undetermined as of this writing, as is the impact of what may become a fairly drawn-out U.S. occupation. Iraq's neighbors may grow increasingly uncomfortable with a U.S. political and military presence along their borders and may change their military posture and security policies accordingly. When addressing these challenges, regional states will give particular importance to the political role of the military, even if it hinders overall military effectiveness.

The region's economies also face many challenges. Corruption, a weak private sector, poor education systems, and other factors will make sustained economic growth difficult to achieve. Decreasing oil prices will make resources more scarce, both for the region's major oil producers and for the poorer states who depend on remittances from expatriate workers.[12] In addition, burgeoning populations will strain even the relatively wealthy oil states of the Persian Gulf. A failure to develop, combined with popular expectations for an improved standard of living, may increase regional instability.

---

[12]See Kiren Aziz Chaudhry, *The Price of Wealth: International Capital Flows and the Political Economy of Late Development*, Ithaca, N.Y.: Cornell University Press, 1997.

THE SHADOWS OF SEPTEMBER 11 AND THE WAR AGAINST IRAQ

The September 11, 2001, terrorist attacks and the 2003 war against Iraq are profoundly affecting the Middle East in general and U.S. policy in the region in particular. Although the ramifications of these events are still being felt, several changes are already evident.

- *A reprioritization of U.S. interests.* Terrorism and WMD proliferation have long been a concern of the U.S. government. However, the scale of the September 11 tragedy has elevated terrorism's relative importance, and the subsequent war with Iraq increased awareness of the dangers posed by WMD proliferation. Other U.S. interests, such as the Arab-Israeli conflict and relations with Saudi Arabia, may be reassessed within this new context.

- *Reduced tolerance for state sponsorship of terrorism.* In the 1980s and 1990s, Iran, Iraq, and other sponsors of terrorism conducted limited strikes without suffering massive retaliation. Such tolerance, however, has now eroded. The toppling of the Taliban in Afghanistan vividly illustrated the U.S. willingness and capacity to overthrow regimes that support anti-U.S. terrorist groups. That point was further emphasized in the spring of 2003, when the Bush administration used Saddam Hussein's possible connections with al Qaeda as one of the justifications for war.

- *A focus on internal stability.* Although all regimes in the Middle East were well aware of the threat that Islamic radicals posed (several regimes had long been fighting Islamic insurgencies and many others monitored and arrested radicals), the attention of the United States was not focused on regional domestic politics. The attacks suggest, however, that the domestic policies of regimes, particularly their willingness to allow citizens to support or join radical causes abroad, directly affect U.S. security.

- *A decline in conventional military threats.* With the toppling of Saddam's regime, the danger of a conventional military conflict has diminished considerably. Although Syria, Iran, and other potential aggressors maintain large forces, in general they do not field modern equipment, are poorly trained, and otherwise pose only a limited threat. In contrast, the region's two greatest military powers, Israel and Turkey, are staunch U.S. allies.

These shifts are only a few of the most important of the many changes that the attacks and the subsequent U.S. response will cause in the region. This report, however, is not intended as a comprehensive assessment of the September 11 terrorist attacks or the war with Iraq.[13] These events are discussed in individual chapters where appropriate, but the themes addressed in this volume remain vital to understanding the region and properly designing policies.

REPORT OBJECTIVES AND STRUCTURE

This report assesses long-term trends in the Middle East region in an attempt to draw implications for U.S. interests in the region. It surveys an array of issues that have shaped the security environment in the past and identifies areas that are likely to change or emerge as important factors in the coming years. Many of these issues have not been traditionally considered security issues, but as this report demonstrates, the internal dynamics of Middle Eastern states have tremendous effects on regional politics.

The structure of this report is thematic, not regional. Although the states of key regions such as the Persian Gulf receive considerable attention, the focus is on broader trends that affect the region (at times excluding Israel) as a whole. The early chapters address factors affecting internal politics of regional states (such as political and economic reform) and gradually broaden to address regional trends that extend beyond the control of individual states (such as the dif-

---

[13]The research for this report began before the September 11 attacks and was completed before the war with Iraq, though all of the chapters have been updated to reflect these important events. RAND, including Project AIR FORCE, has embarked on several extensive studies that discuss the implications of the September 11 attacks and the subsequent struggle against terrorism. See, for example, Lynn Davis, Steve Hosmer, Sara Daly, and Karl Mueller, *The U.S. Counterterrorism Strategy: A Planning Framework to Facilitate Timely Adjustments,* Santa Monica:, Calif.: RAND, DB-426-AF, 2003; David Ochmanek, *Military Operations Against Terrorist Groups Abroad: Implications for the U.S. Air Force,* Santa Monica:, Calif.: RAND, MR-1738-AF, 2003; and Nora Bensahel, *The Counterterror Coalitions: Cooperation with Europe, NATO, and the European Union,* Santa Monica, Calif.: RAND, MR-1746-AF, 2003. Research on Operation Iraqi Freedom is currently under way.

fusion of information technologies and weapons of mass destruction). The report is organized as follows:

- Chapter Two, by Nora Bensahel, reviews the prospects for political liberalization and democratization and surveys how these trends affect states of strategic importance to the United States. Bensahel argues that the United States may have a greater interest in promoting political liberalization than in encouraging democratization throughout the region.

- Chapter Three, by Alan Richards, addresses barriers to economic reform. It examines the leading economic problems facing countries in the Middle East and describes the prognosis for improvement. Richards argues that economic reform programs during the past decade have failed to improve living standards while increasing popular frustration, a combination that will pose continuing governance challenges.

- Chapter Four, by Risa Brooks, explores how various regimes maintain political control of their militaries and discusses contemporary threats to the stability of civil-military relations. Brooks argues that the United States can expect the current pattern of civil-military relations to persist, continuing to undermine military effectiveness, possibly hindering long-term prospects for political and economic reform.

- Chapter Five, by Daniel Byman, examines the implications of regime change in several key states in the Middle East. It identifies the range of plausible regime changes and discusses how government policy might shift, if at all, when new rulers take power.

- Chapter Six, by Ian Lesser, examines how recent changes in the energy market affect regional security and assesses future trends. Lesser argues that the increasing globalization of the oil market has improved energy security but that changing patterns of trade and particularly internal instability will continue to threaten that security in the coming decade.

- Chapter Seven, by Jon Alterman, examines how new information technologies, including the Internet and satellite television, are reshaping the region's politics. Alterman argues that although the most advanced technologies have had little effect on the region, such older ones as photocopiers and fax machines are transforming politics.

- Chapter Eight, by Ian Lesser, examines the role of weapons of mass destruction. Lesser argues that the pursuit of chemical, biological, and nuclear weapons, along with ballistic missiles and other delivery means, changes the region's strategic space, increasing the risk of conflict beyond states' borders and posing additional challenges to the United States.

- Chapter Nine draws together these findings and discusses their implications for regional security and U.S. interests.

In all these chapters, the authors try not only to examine past trends but also to explore future developments. They also try to identify key uncertainties that could alter their findings or that have significant implications for the United States.

Chapter Two

POLITICAL REFORM IN THE MIDDLE EAST

Nora Bensahel

The Middle East has been largely left out of global trends toward de-mocratization.[1] Authoritarianism seems alive and well, as monarchs and ruling families remain firmly in charge throughout the region. Even Egypt, which is nominally democratic, is governed by a single party that restricts political competition and imposes strict limits on the freedoms of speech and association. However, some currents of reform are percolating throughout the region, in ways that are signif-icant even if they are not highly visible. Some states have increased political participation by granting legislatures jurisdiction over se-lected issue areas and allowing citizens to choose their representa-tives through free elections. Other states have eased restrictions on the freedoms of speech and association, allowing people to articulate their interests and opinions more effectively. Although these reform measures have not challenged the ruling regimes' monopoly on power, they do constitute a significant trend.

Political reform is a general term that includes two separate but re-lated processes. *Democratization* involves the expansion of formal structures of citizen participation. Elections are the most important component of democratization, because they allow citizens to exer-

---

[1]Israel and Turkey are obvious exceptions to this generalization, but they possess sev-eral unique features that make them regional outliers. To ensure comparability across cases, this study focuses specifically on the Arab states and Iran. For more on global trends in democratization, see Samuel P. Huntington, *The Third Wave: Democratiza-tion in the Late Twentieth Century*, Norman, Okla.: The University of Oklahoma Press, 1991.

cise control over public policy and to hold leaders accountable for their decisions.[2] Democratization also includes issues related to citizenship, since it determines who may participate in elections. Early definitions of democracy included only the procedural aspects described above.[3] Yet later scholars pointed out that this definition was insufficient: Free elections meant very little if citizens were not allowed to exchange information freely or to organize into interest groups. According to current definitions, democratic states must not only hold free and fair elections but must also guarantee such civil liberties such as freedom of speech, assembly, and association.[4] *Liberalization* is therefore a second aspect of political reform, focusing on the expansion of these civil and political rights.

Democratization and liberalization often occur simultaneously, but they are two distinct processes that do not necessarily enhance each other. As O'Donnell and Schmitter write, progress in one area may come at the expense of the other:

> Authoritarian rulers may tolerate or even promote liberalization in belief that by opening up certain spaces for individual and group action, they can relieve various pressures and obtain needed information and support *without* altering the structure of authority, that is, without becoming accountable to the citizenry for their

---

[2]Rex Brynen, Bahgat Korany, and Paul Noble, "Introduction: Theoretical Perspectives on Arab Liberalization and Democratization," in Rex Brynen, Bahgat Korany, and Paul Noble (eds.), *Political Liberalization & Democratization in the Arab World: Volume 1, Theoretical Perspectives*, Boulder, Colo.: Lynne Rienner, 1995, p. 3; Bahgat Korany and Paul Noble, "Introduction: Arab Liberalization and Democratization—The Dialectics of the General and the Specific," in Baghat Korany, Rex Brynen, and Paul Noble (eds.), *Political Liberalization & Democratization in the Arab World: Volume 2, Comparative Experiences*, Boulder, Colo.: Lynne Rienner, 1998, p. 1.

[3]In 1942, Joseph Schumpeter offered the first modern definition of democracy: "that institutional arrangement for arriving at political decisions in which individuals acquire the power to decide by means of a competitive struggle for the people's vote." Joseph A. Schumpeter, *Capitalism, Socialism, and Democracy*, 3rd ed., New York: Harper & Brothers, 1950, p. 269.

[4]David Collier and Steven Levitsky, "Democracy with Adjectives: Conceptual Innovation in Comparative Research," *World Politics*, Vol. 49, No. 3, 1997, pp. 430–451; Robert A. Dahl, *Polyarchy*, New Haven, Conn.: Yale University Press, 1971; Terry Lynn Karl, "Dilemmas of Democratization in Latin America," *Comparative Politics*, Vol. 23, No. 1, 1991, pp. 1–21; Philippe C. Schmitter and Terry Lynn Karl, "What Democracy Is . . . and Is Not," *Journal of Democracy*, Vol. 2, No. 3, 1991, pp. 75–88; Huntington, 1991.

actions or submitting their claim to rule to fair and competitive elections. . . . Inversely, once democratization has begun and its prudent advocates fear the excessive expansion of such a process or wish to keep contentious issues off the agenda of collective deliberation, they may well continue old, or even create new, restrictions on the freedoms of particular individuals or groups who are deemed insufficiently prepared or sufficiently dangerous to enjoy full citizenship status.[5]

Liberalization and democratization generally do not occur simultaneously in the Middle East. Regimes responding to pressures for political reform have often chosen a slow and deliberate process of liberalization, while democratization lags far behind.[6] The rest of this chapter is organized into five sections. The first section identifies U.S. interests in Middle Eastern political reform. The second section examines pressures for political reform in the region. The third section assesses regional trends in both democratization and liberalization. The fourth section surveys how these trends are playing out in Egypt, Iran, Jordan, Kuwait, and Saudi Arabia. The fifth section analyzes the effect that these developments will have on U.S. security interests.

U.S. INTERESTS IN MIDDLE EASTERN POLITICAL REFORM

The United States has multiple, and often conflicting, interests at stake in Middle Eastern political reform. The contradictions in these interests often result from differing time horizons. Political reform

---

[5]Guillermo O'Donnell and Philippe C. Schmitter, *Transitions from Authoritarian Rule: Tentative Conclusions About Uncertain Democracies*, Baltimore, Md.: The Johns Hopkins University Press, 1996, p. 9. Emphasis in the original.

[6]There is a large literature on the question of whether Islam is compatible with democracy, which is beyond the scope of this chapter. This chapter examines the ways in which political reform efforts may unfold, not whether democracy is sustainable on a permanent basis throughout the region. For good discussions of this question, see Huntington, 1991, especially pp. 307–311; John L. Esposito and John O. Voll, *Islam and Democracy*, New York: Oxford University Press, 1996; Metin Heper, "Islam and Democracy in Turkey: Toward a Reconciliation?" *Middle East Journal*, Vol. 51, No. 1, 1997, pp. 32–43; Roy P. Mottahedeh and Mamoun Fandy, "The Islamist Movement: The Case for Democratic Inclusion," in Gary G. Sick and Lawrence G. Potter (eds.), *The Persian Gulf at the Millennium*, New York: St. Martin's Press, 1997; Glenn E. Robinson, "Can Islamists Be Democrats? The Case of Jordan," *Middle East Journal*, Vol. 51, No. 3, 1997, pp. 373–387.

would serve U.S. interests well over the long term, but in the short term, it has two potentially negative effects: It may increase regional instability, and it could make regimes much more sensitive about cooperation with the United States, particularly in the security realm.

The United States has strong long-term interests in seeing political reform progress through the Middle East. From a normative perspective, democracy and free expression are fundamental American values that should be encouraged throughout the world. The 2000 National Security Strategy defines U.S. core values as "political and economic freedom, respect for human rights, and the rule of law," and identifies promoting democracy abroad as one of the three key goals of U.S. foreign policy.[7] This normative perspective is complemented by a more pragmatic security perspective, which views political reform as essential to long-term regional peace and stability. Democratic states are less likely to face significant internal challenges because popular interests can be expressed and factored into decisionmaking processes. Moderate policies are more likely because representative polities have a dense network of cross-cutting interests that may constrain extremist positions.[8] Perhaps most important to the United States, political science research has shown that democratic states are highly unlikely to go to war with each other.[9] The United States therefore has important long-term interests in promoting political reform in the Middle East, not only because that conforms with important U.S. values, but because it may promote regional stability.

From a shorter-term perspective U.S. interests may look quite different. First of all, the democratic peace argument does not necessarily apply to states undergoing a transition to democracy. In fact, one well-regarded study concluded, "democratizing states are more likely

---

[7]*A National Security Strategy for a Global Age*, Washington, D.C.: The White House, December 2000, pp. 1–4.

[8]This idea dates back as far as *Federalist Paper No. 10*, which argued that expanding the sphere of democracy would guard against the excesses of factionalism. The importance of cross-cutting cleavages was incorporated into the political science literature on democracy in the 1960s. See Seymour Martin Lipset, *Political Man*, Garden City, N.Y.: Doubleday, 1960.

[9]For a good overview of the large literature on this subject, see Michael E. Brown, Sean Lynn-Jones, and Steven E. Miller (eds.), *Debating the Democratic Peace*, Cambridge, Mass.: MIT Press, 1996.

to fight wars than are mature democracies or stable autocracies."[10] This means that Middle Eastern political reform could ironically reduce regional stability in the short run, even if it is essential to regional stability in the long run. Second, political reform could increase internal instability. By allowing an increased range of political viewpoints to be expressed, political reform could lead to serious struggles for influence over policy. Opposition to the ruling regime could be expressed from all parts of the political spectrum, from those who favor authoritarian Arab nationalist or Islamist policies to those who favor increased political liberalization. Struggles among these various positions might be peaceful, but they might also cause increased repression and coercion as ruling regimes attempt to maintain their power in the face of mounting opposition. Third, anti-American sentiment is common throughout the Middle East. Security cooperation with the United States is particularly unpopular, because it demonstrates that current regimes cannot provide security for their own people without depending on external powers. As citizens gain the right to express their opinions more effectively, regimes may become more hostile toward U.S. policy and could be forced to reduce their security cooperation with the United States. Such an outcome would considerably complicate U.S. military planning and operations throughout the region.

U.S. interests in Middle Eastern political reform therefore differ considerably, depending on whether a short-term or long-term perspective is taken and depending on the country in question. The conundrum facing U.S. policymakers is that political reform is essential for long-term regional stability but may increase regional instability and anti-American sentiment in the short run. Ironically, *failing* to adopt any political reform measures could be just as destabilizing as adopting them, since it requires continued rule by coercion. If regimes do not address the dynamics that generate pressures for political reform, regimes run the risk that popular frustrations will spill over into popular opposition and internal unrest.

---

[10]Edward D. Mansfield and Jack Snyder, "Democratization and the Danger of War," *International Security*, Vol. 20, No. 1, 1995, p. 6.

PRESSURES FOR POLITICAL REFORM IN THE MIDDLE EAST

Most Middle Eastern states suffer from a range of economic and social problems, which can generate pressures for political reform by increasing popular dissatisfaction with regime performance. These problems can be grouped into three interrelated categories: economic challenges, demographic trends, and accountability and corruption.

Economic Challenges

Almost all of the Middle Eastern economies depend on oil. Saudi Arabia and the Gulf states depend on receiving revenues from producing oil and selling it on the world market. States without large indigenous reserves, for example, Egypt and Yemen, depend on remittances sent home from expatriate workers who have sought employment in the oil-producing states. Skyrocketing oil prices during the 1970s transformed both types into rentier states, which depend on externally generated rents instead of producing wealth themselves.[11]

The rentier model involves an implicit tradeoff between material well-being and political quiescence. The state does not need to be responsive to its citizens as long as it maintains independent sources of revenue. Political opposition becomes naturally muted as long as the benefits continue to flow, and the state may develop coercive structures to silence opposition altogether. As Kiren Chaudhry explains, "the exceptionally long-term truncation of political rights in most Arab countries has rested, to a large extent, on social acquiescence bought through market protection—through the distribution

---

[11]The oil-producing states created extensive welfare states in order to distribute this wealth to the general population, providing health care, education, and guarantees of employment to their citizens. States that depended on labor remittances could not develop similar distributive structures, since remittances were passed directly to individuals without passing through the state. Nevertheless, the indirect transfer of oil wealth caused these states to dismantle much of their regulatory and taxation structures, making them similarly dependent on externally generated rents. For more on the effects of oil revenues and labor remittances, see Chaudhry, 1997.

of economic entitlements."[12] To the extent that the rentier model continues to be undermined by decreasing oil prices and declining GDP and growth rates, popular discontent and dissatisfaction may grow.

Recent trends indicate that the rentier model is becoming increasingly strained. Oil prices declined dramatically in the 1980s, and even though prices have increased in recent years, they still remain far below the levels set during the 1970s.[13] These lower prices mean that many Middle Eastern states have not had enough income to maintain the standards of living that their populations had come to expect during the boom years. These reduced oil revenues have directly affected living standards in many regional countries. In Saudi Arabia, real GDP per capita rates fell from $13,133 in 1979 to $6,531 in 1998; in the United Arab Emirates, rates fell from $27,750 to $16,323; and in Bahrain, rates fell from $12,859 to $9,688.[14]

Demographic Trends

These economic challenges are likely to be exacerbated by the rapid population growth being experienced by most of the states in the region. As Table 2.1 indicates, many Middle Eastern states are experiencing high levels of population growth. This trend is particularly true in the Gulf states, where annual growth rates are often more than 3 percent annually. Iran has adopted proactive measures to re-

---

[12]See Chaudhry, 1997, p. 295.

[13]For example, Saudi Arabia earned more than $223 billion in oil export revenues in 1980, but forecasts for 2003 revenue reached only $53.8 billion. The statistics for other countries are not quite as bad, but still reflect significant decreases, from $40.1 billion to $11.8 billion in Kuwait, $11.4 billion to $7.1 billion in Qatar, and $40.3 billion to $17.7 billion in the United Arab Emirates. All figures are in constant 2000 dollars. United States Department of Energy, Energy Information Administration, *OPEC Revenues Fact Sheet*, at http://www.eia.doe.gov/emeu/cabs/opecrev.html, accessed June 2003.

[14]These declines are also caused by increased population growth, discussed in the next section. All figures are in constant 1985 dollars. Data taken from Penn World Tables 5.6, available at http://datacentre.chass.utoronto.ca:5680/pwt/index.html, accessed June 2003.

Table 2.1

Population Growth Rates and Percentage of Population Under Age 14

Country	Annual Population Growth Rate (Percent)	Percentage of Population Under Age 14
Bahrain	1.62	29.2
Egypt	1.66	33.9
Iran	0.77	31.6
Iraq	2.82	41.1
Jordan	2.89	36.6
Kuwait	3.33[a]	28.3
Lebanon	1.36	27.3
Libya	2.41	35
Morocco	1.68	33.8
Oman	3.41	41.9
Qatar	3.02	25.2
Saudi Arabia	3.27	42.4
Syria	2.5	39.3
Tunisia	1.12	27.8
United Arab Emirates	1.58	27.7
Yemen	3.4	47
Regional average	2.30	34.3
World average	1.23	29.2

SOURCE: Central Intelligence Agency, *World Factbook 2002.*
[a]Includes return of Gulf crisis expatriates.

verse this trend, but Iran will continue to face economic pressure from its growing young population. Table 2.1 also demonstrates that large percentages of Middle Eastern populations are under age 14, and population growth will become an even more serious problem when this generation enters reproductive age. Even if this generation chooses to have fewer children than its parents' generation did, the sheer number of people having children may continue to drive up population numbers.

Such rapid population growth has the potential to cause increased popular frustration in at least two ways.[15] First, population growth requires commensurate economic growth to maintain current standards of living. If economic growth rates do not keep pace, as they have failed to do throughout the Middle East, individual standards of

---

[15]This section draws heavily on Byman and Green, 1999, pp. 12–14.

living will decline. Second, the large youth population increases demand for education, health care, and other social services. Rapidly expanding these services can be problematic even when economic resources are plentiful, and the current economic conditions may prevent the state from meeting the increased demand for these services. Furthermore, most young people expect higher standards of living than previous generations and may become quite frustrated when economic conditions prevent them from meeting these standards. This trend is particularly salient in the Gulf states, where living standards skyrocketed during the 1970s, and citizens now expect benefits and services that earlier generations did not have at all. To the extent that these expectations are not met, pressures for political reform may grow, particularly among large youth populations, who are more likely to engage in radical causes and opposition movements than their elders.

Accountability and Corruption

One of the most common complaints about regional governments is the lack of accountability of regime elites, which creates widespread opportunities for corruption. Since decisionmaking authority is concentrated at the highest levels of the regime, among people who are born into royal families instead of chosen by merit, citizens have few mechanisms through which they can hold their leaders responsible. Ordinary citizens may not know the precise extent to which the royal family diverts oil revenues for its own use, but they can easily observe conspicuous consumption habits. At a time when Gulf citizens are experiencing reduced personal income, unemployment, and declining services, royal spending often serves as a focal point for complaints about the lack of regime accountability.[16]

Elsewhere in the region, corruption is a part of everyday life. The high degree of state involvement in the economy provides ample opportunities for corruption, ranging from nepotism to outright bribes paid to civil servants. Few states have attempted to solve this problem, because it has become so embedded in everyday economic

---

[16]Byman and Green, 1999, pp. 15–22.

life.[17]   Pervasive corruption is a constant reminder of the lack of regime accountability. Corruption may also enhance frustrations with the economic trends described above, because it makes basic citizen services more difficult and more expensive to obtain.

Possible Regime Responses

Each of these three categories has the potential to generate pressures for political reform, and the trends in each category may become mutually reinforcing. Lackluster economic performance produces popular frustrations with regime leadership. Population growth exacerbates these economic problems, making it harder for regimes to maintain current standards of living, let alone increase those standards. Widespread corruption breeds even more frustrations, as citizens see their personal standards of living declining while royal families spend money ostentatiously, or as they use their limited income for bribes and other payments to secure basic state services. None of these frustrations can be expressed through participatory governance structures, and that may itself breed further frustrations with the governance system. These frustrations become more likely to generate demands for political reform that allows citizens to have at least some say in the decisionmaking process.

Regimes can respond to these demands in one of two ways: They can increase popular participation to defuse growing discontent, or they can resort to increased coercion. Many Middle Eastern states have chosen a strategy that combines elements of both options, adopting limited political reform measures while cracking down on opposition that goes beyond the regime's limits. This strategy has largely succeeded to date for, as will be argued below, the regimes have maintained control over both the form and pace of political reform. Yet it is not clear whether this strategy will be sustainable over the long term.

---

[17]Morocco is one exception to this generalization. See Guilain Denoeux, "The Politics of Morocco's 'Fight Against Corruption,'" *Middle East Policy*, Vol. 7, No. 2, 2000, pp. 165–189.

REGIONAL TRENDS

This section examines some of the political reform measures that Middle Eastern regimes have adopted in response to the challenges identified above. It examines two key elements of democratization, legislatures and consultative councils, and then examines several issues related to liberalization, including political parties, civic organizations, freedoms of speech and the press, and the rule of law. Most of these measures are designed to offset popular dissatisfaction at a general level, but a few, such as judicial reform, tackle some of the specific problems identified above.

Democratization: Legislatures

Bahrain, Egypt, Iran, Jordan, Kuwait, Lebanon, Morocco, and Yemen all have legislatures.[18]   Qatar may be next on the list, as the new constitution approved in April 2003 provides for a legislature where two-thirds of the representatives will be popularly elected.[19]   Legislatures can be an important component of democratization in these states, because they have "become the focal point of Arab efforts to expand and institutionalize political participation."[20]   They are often the only elected bodies of government. Even when legislative elections are not entirely free, with restrictions on eligible candidates and parties, they still provide one of the few opportunities for citizens to express their preferences.

According to recent theoretical work, legislatures contribute to democratization in at least five ways. First, they increase the expression of political demands and improve the quality of public policy debates

---

[18]Bahrain's parliament is the newest of the bunch, having held elections and its opening session in 2002. See Howard Schneider, "Bahrain's New King Sets Date for Vote," *Washington Post*, February 15, 2002; "Bahrain: First Parliament Session in Three Decades," *New York Times*, December 14, 2002.

[19]The powers of the Qatari legislature would remain somewhat circumscribed, since the emir would have to approve legislation for it to go into effect. The constitution, which was approved by almost 97 percent of the vote in that referendum, also includes provisions for the freedoms of speech, assembly, and religion, among others. "Qatar: Vote on Constitution," *New York Times*, April 29, 2003; Paul Martin, "Qataris Vote for Greater Freedom," *Washington Times*, April 20, 2003.

[20]Abdo Baaklini, Guilain Denoeux, and Robert Springborg, *Legislative Politics in the Arab World*, Boulder, Colo.: Lynne Rienner, 1999, p. 5.

by encouraging political dialogue. Citizens thus have an outlet through which they can express frustration or satisfaction with regime policies. Second, legislatures process and satisfy political demands by passing legislation, approving the budget, and providing constituency services. Third, they legitimize government decisions, which increases public support of those policies and facilitates implementation. Fourth, they provide some degree of executive accountability, especially by requiring government officials to provide written and oral testimony. Fifth, they are a forum for conflict resolution, demonstrating that even deep divisions can be addressed through discussion instead of violence.[21]

Middle Eastern legislatures perform all of these functions to some extent, but the scope of their activities generally remains restricted by the regimes in power. Regimes primarily view legislatures as a tool that can increase their own legitimacy, not as genuine arenas of contestation. Regime leaders generally care about maintaining power, not achieving democracy, and they may calculate that even limited increases in participation will strengthen their survival prospects in the long term.[22] They therefore grant legislatures enough power to generate the legitimization effects described above, but stop short of granting enough authority for those legislatures to become autonomous and competing centers of power.

Middle Eastern legislatures operate under significant constraints. Their jurisdiction is often limited to issue areas approved by the regime, which reduces their ability to influence policy and keeps them subordinate to the executive branch. They also suffer from numerous resource and informational constraints that make it hard for them to work effectively even in areas that do fall under their jurisdiction. Middle Eastern legislatures do vary in their ability to influence policy, with Iran near the high end of the spectrum and Egypt near the low end, but they all face some sort of restrictions.[23]

Several of the legislatures with high degrees of centrality and capacity are found in monarchical states. Monarchs in Jordan and Morocco,

---

[21]Baaklini et al., 1999, pp. 47–61.

[22]Baaklini et al., 1999, pp. 30–31.

[23]Baaklini et al., 1999, pp. 63–75.

and to a lesser extent in Kuwait, have increased the powers of the legislature while distancing themselves from the day-to-day operations of the government. The king is then positioned to become an independent arbiter between the government and the parliament, enhancing his reputation as being above normal politics.[24] This risky strategy requires carefully managing the democratization process from above to ensure monarchical control. Yet it seems to have been rather successful in Jordan and Morocco to date, where legislatures have grown increasingly assertive without any apparent reductions in monarchical legitimacy or authority.[25]

Democratization: Consultative Councils

Bahrain, Oman, Qatar, Saudi Arabia, and the United Arab Emirates have established consultative councils as a way to increase representation without holding elections.[26] In principle, these councils allow increased popular input into the policymaking process. However, their power remains fairly circumscribed in most states. They generally serve in an advisory capacity, without any institutional checks on the executive, and are appointed directly by regime leaders. Membership has become increasingly diverse in recent years, as rulers reach out to business leaders, academics, and other key constituencies, but it remains limited to elites who probably will not challenge government policies.[27]

Consultative councils perform an important cooptive function, which may make them an attractive strategy of democratization for rulers concerned about their power base.[28] As council membership expands, an increasing number of groups have at least nominal input

---

[24]Baaklini et al., 1999, p. 155.

[25]Baaklini et al., 1999, pp. 111–132 on Morocco and pp. 133–168 on Jordan.

[26]Oman does hold elections to its consultative council but only to nominate candidates. The sultan then chooses which of the nominees may sit on the council. Abdullah Juma al-Haj, "The Politics of Participation in the Gulf Cooperation Council States: The Omani Consultative Council," *Middle East Journal*, Vol. 50, No. 4, 1996, pp. 559–571.

[27]For an analysis of the composition of Saudi Arabia's consultative council, see R. Hrair Dekmejian, "Saudi Arabia's Consultative Council," *Middle East Journal*, Vol. 52, No. 2, 1998, pp. 204–218.

[28]Dekmejian, 1998, p. 217.

into the decisionmaking process. These groups can no longer claim to truly oppose the government, since they now have some stake in the political system. Rulers often do try to reach consensus with the councils on important policy decisions,[29] but they are free to disregard council advice whenever they deem necessary. Consultative councils therefore enable rulers to increase popular representation without relinquishing any significant decisionmaking power.

Liberalization: Political Parties

Tolerance of political parties varies across the Middle East. Parties remain illegal in many states, including most of the Persian Gulf states, but are legal in Egypt, Jordan, Morocco, Tunisia, and Yemen. Yet even where they are legal, political parties often face notable restrictions. Some states limit the types of groups that can form political parties. Egypt has some of the strongest restrictions in the region, including a ban on all religious-based parties that is designed to keep Islamic groups from gaining representation.[30] Jordan does not explicitly restrict any groups from forming political parties, but it does require all parties to be officially licensed by the state.[31] Middle Eastern political parties also suffer from a lack of resources, both during electoral campaigns and after they gain legislative representation.[32] They generally lack the organizational structure and political expertise that is necessary to formulate coherent political agendas. This problem is even worse for opposition parties, which cannot use state patronage networks to build support for their proposals.[33]

---

[29]Freedom House identifies the emir of Qatar as a leader who often strives to reach consensus with the consultative council. *Freedom in the World 1999–2000,* New York: Freedom House, 2000, p. 397.

[30]*Freedom in the World 1999–2000,* p. 175.

[31]The only group that is consistently denied permission to form a political party is an Islamist group that challenges the legitimacy of the Jordanian state. Laurie Brand, "'In the Beginning Was the State . . .': The Quest for Civil Society in Jordan," in A. R. Norton (ed.), *Civil Society in the Middle East, Volume 1,* Leiden, Netherlands: E. J. Brill, 1995, pp. 162–163.

[32]Morocco is an exception to this generalization: Political parties play an important role in the Moroccan legislature, and they receive significant resources to support their work. Baaklini et al., 1999, pp. 117–121.

[33]Baaklini et al., 1999, pp. 47–49.

Despite these restrictions, the number of political parties is often quite high. According to one study, in 1995 there were 46 political parties in Algeria, 43 in Yemen, 23 in Jordan, 19 in Morocco, 13 in Egypt, and 11 in Tunisia.[34] However, a large number of political parties does not necessarily mean that a wide range of political viewpoints are being represented, for at least two reasons. First, not all parties are opposition groups. Party leaders are sometimes co-opted by the regime, in order to give the appearance of plurality while ensuring that regime policies are not fundamentally challenged.[35] Second, not all of these parties actually win elections. During Yemen's 1993 legislative elections, for example, only seven out of the 43 parties won seats at all, and three of those gained more than 80 percent of the seats.[36] Political parties in the Middle East do not always represent a wide spectrum of political beliefs: Legal restrictions, a lack of resources, regime cooptation, and electoral outcomes all combine to narrow the range of views that they represent.

Liberalization: Civic Organizations

Civic organizations can play a critical role in sustaining democracy. Civil society is generally defined as "associations, clubs, guilds, syndicates, federations, unions, parties and groups [that] come together to provide a buffer between state and citizen."[37] These organizations allow citizens to gather, share information, and organize to represent their interests on their own, outside of state auspices. A vibrant network of civic organizations can act as a check against the excesses of the state, while allowing for greater participation in the democratic

---

[34]Saad Eddin Ibrahim, "Civil Society and Prospects of Democratization in the Arab World," in A. R. Norton (ed.), *Civil Society in the Middle East, Volume 1*, Leiden, Netherlands: E. J. Brill, 1995, pp. 40–41.

[35]Morocco has pursued this strategy to a large extent. See Daniel L. Byman, "Explaining Ethnic Peace in Morocco," *Harvard Middle Eastern and Islamic Review*, Vol. 4, Nos. 1–2, 1997–1998, especially pp. 15–17 and 22; Baghat Korany, "Monarchical Islam with a Democratic Veneer: Morocco," in Baghat Korany, Rex Brynen, and Paul Noble (eds.), *Political Liberalization & Democratization in the Arab World: Volume 2, Comparative Experiences*, Boulder, Colo.: Lynne Rienner, 1998, pp. 174–175.

[36]Ibrahim, 1995, p. 41.

[37]Augustus Richard Norton, "Introduction," in A. R. Norton (ed.), *Civil Society in the Middle East, Volume 1*, Leiden, Netherlands: E. J. Brill, 1995, p. 7.

process.[38]   Civic organizations are also important for states undergoing a transition to democracy.[39]   As three prominent scholars of democratic transitions argue, "As a strong and autonomous associational life may buttress or foster democracy, so the absence of a vigorous sector of voluntary associations and interest groups, or the control of such organizations by a corporatist state, may reinforce authoritarian rule and obstruct the development of democracy."[40]

Civic organizations often fill the void created when political parties are illegal or not fully representative. They have become forums for political activity, such as debating political issues, developing policy alternatives, and pressuring decisionmakers.[41]   Private organizations have grown during the past few decades. The number of Arab civic organizations increased from 20,000 in the mid-1960s to about 70,000 in the late 1980s.[42]   However, these numbers alone may be misleading. Many of these organizations are too small to be significant. In Egypt, for example, there are more than 20,000 nongovern-

---

[38]One study argues that both theoretical work and empirical evidence "argue strongly for the importance to stable democracy of a pluralistic, autonomous, vigorously organized civil society that can balance and limit state power while providing additional channels for the articulation and practice of democratic interests. A rich associational life can supplement the role of political parties in stimulating political participation, increasing citizens' efficacy, recruiting and training political leaders, and enhancing commitment to the democratic system." Larry Diamond, Juan J. Linz, and Seymour Martin Lipset, "Introduction: Comparing Experiences with Democracy," in Larry Diamond, J. J. Linz ,and Seymour Martin Lipset (eds.), *Politics in Developing Countries*, Boulder, Colo.: Lynne Rienner, 1990, p. 21.

[39]Several scholars have noted that the existence of civil society is an important, but insufficient, condition for the successful transition for democracy. Augustus Richard Norton, "Introduction," in A. R. Norton (ed.), *Civil Society in the Middle East, Volume 2*, Leiden, Netherlands: E. J. Brill, 1996, p. 6; Philippe C. Schmitter, "Civil Society East and West," in L. Diamond, M. F. Plattner, Y.-h. Chu, and H.-m. Tien (eds.), *Consolidating the Third Wave Democracies: Themes and Perspectives*, Baltimore, Md.: The Johns Hopkins University Press, 1997, p. 242.

[40]Diamond, Linz, and Lipset, 1990, p. 23.

[41]Examples of such active organizations include the University Graduates Society in Kuwait, the Jassrah Cultural Club in Qatar, and the Association of Social Professions in the United Arab Emirates. Ibrahim, 1995, p. 42.

[42]More recent data are difficult to obtain, but the trends that explain this increase did continue through the 1990s as well. Ibrahim argues that four factors contributed to this growth in the number of civic organizations: increasingly unmet needs of individuals and communities, a larger educated population, greater individual financial resources, and more inventiveness on ways to circumvent the state. See Ibrahim, 1995, pp. 39–40.

mental organizations (NGOs), but perhaps only about 40 percent of them are active and effective.[43] Furthermore, these organizations do not represent all segments of society. Peasants and the urban poor are often not represented through any of these organizations, which means that their interests and concerns remain outside the limited scope of political debate.[44]

Professional associations are active and important types of civic organizations in the Middle East. They bring together doctors, lawyers, engineers, and other professionals to set standards, provide services, sponsor professional development activities, and create a sense of community among their members. These organizations often take on a quasi-political role, enabling their members to debate ideas and articulate their interests in countries where few opportunities for such activities exist.[45] Some of these associations elect their leadership, making them one of the most democratic elements of society.[46]

Professional associations and civic organizations tend to be organized along corporatist, not pluralist, principles. They are either associated with or created by the state, rather than being voluntary, grassroots organizations that remain independent of the state.[47] The state controls which organizations may exist, by requiring them to

---

[43]Ibrahim, 1995, p. 41.

[44]Mustapha Kamel al-Sayyid, "The Concept of Civil Society and the Arab World," in Rex Brynen, Baghat Korany, and Paul Noble (eds.), *Political Liberalization & Democratization in the Arab World: Volume 1, Theoretical Perspectives*, Boulder, Colo.: Lynne Rienner, 1995, p. 140.

[45]Brand, 1995, pp. 165–167; F. Gregory Gause III, *Oil Monarchies, Domestic and Security Challenges in the Arab Gulf States*, New York: Council on Foreign Relations Press, 1994, p. 87; Neil Hicks and Ghanim al-Najjar, "The Utility of Tradition: Civil Society in Kuwait," in A. R. Norton (ed.), *Civil Society in the Middle East, Volume 1*, Leiden, Netherlands: E. J. Brill, 1995, p. 195; Ibrahim, 1995, p. 41.

[46]Brand, 1995, p. 167; Sara Roy, "Civil Society in the Gaza Strip: Obstacles to Social Reconstruction," in A. R. Norton (ed.), *Civil Society in the Middle East, Volume 2*, Leiden, Netherlands: E. J. Brill, 1996, p. 235.

[47]Corporatism is defined as "a system of interest representation in which the constituent units are organized into a limited number of singular, compulsory, noncompetitive, hierarchically ordered and functionally differentiated categories, recognized or licensed (if not created) by the state and granted a deliberate representational monopoly within their respective categories in exchange for observing certain controls on their selection of leaders and articulation of demands and supports." For more on corporatism and pluralism, see Philippe C. Schmitter, "Still the Century of Corporatism?" *Review of Politics*, Vol. 36, No. 1, 1974, pp. 85–131. Quote from pp. 93–94.

obtain and renew official licenses, and often provides financial subsidies to groups that support regime policies. The state often preemptively forms official groups to deal with contentious issue areas, since it can then deny permission for other groups to form around these issues by claiming that they are already being addressed.[48] While corporatism generally narrows the range of articulated interests and groups, it is difficult for the state to dismiss or disband organizations that it officially sanctions.[49] The state may find it hard to ignore their views, particularly if the groups can demonstrate that their membership is united on a specific issue, and it may be more difficult to clamp down on officially sponsored organizations that manage to stake out independent positions.

Liberalization: Freedom of the Press

Press freedoms remain heavily restricted throughout the region. Iraq, Libya, Saudi Arabia, and Syria have no independent media to speak of, and press freedoms remain limited even in states that nominally allow them to exist. Regimes tend to own or heavily subsidize broadcast stations and printing presses, which makes it difficult for independent publications to emerge. Press laws often restrict the topics that broadcasters can address, such as criticism of the regime or discussions of foreign and security policies. Even in states where official censorship does not exist, including Kuwait, Qatar, and the United Arab Emirates, journalists often censor themselves so they cannot be accused of violating press restrictions.[50] Human Rights Watch reports that in the year 2000, journalists were harassed or jailed in Egypt, Iran, Morocco, Tunisia, Yemen, and areas under control of the Palestinian Authority.[51]

---

[48]This can be a risky strategy, since the official group may develop its own interests over time. Yet from a regime perspective, this strategy is probably less risky than allowing independent groups to articulate their own interests and preferences. Jill Crystal, "Negotiating with the State: Political Dialogue in the Arabian Gulf," in P. Salem (ed.), *Conflict Resolution in the Arab World: Selected Essays*, Beirut: American University of Beirut, 1997, p. 265.

[49]Ibrahim, 1995, p. 41.

[50]Freedom House, 2000, pp. 279–280, 397–398, and 506.

[51]*World Report 2001*, New York: Human Rights Watch, 2000, p. 352. See also individual country reports in Freedom House.

However, new technologies are reducing the ability of regimes to control or restrict the information available in their countries. As Chapter Seven argues, the widespread availability of satellite television has allowed independent information to flow more freely throughout the region, without regard for national borders.[52]

Liberalization: The Judiciary and the Rule of Law

All Middle Eastern states have some type of judicial system, but none of these courts can be considered to be truly independent.[53] Rulers retain the power to appoint and reappoint judges, and often informally influence their decisions as well. Few states provide for the right to appeal decisions, and even where that right does exist, appeals are made directly to the heads of state rather than to superior courts. Many states have multiple judicial systems, with regular courts that have jurisdiction over civil cases and special courts that try criminal or military cases. Most of the Gulf states also have a separate Islamic legal system, with different courts and codes of law.[54] In principle, such courts have separate areas of jurisdiction, but in practice they often overlap. Regime leaders sometimes transfer cases from one court system to another, in an effort to secure more favorable rulings.[55]

Rulers have a strong interest in maintaining at least the trappings of an independent legal system because it is a valuable source of regime legitimacy.[56] Such systems allow rulers to claim that they tolerate

---

[52]See also Jon B. Alterman, *New Media, New Politics? From Satellite Television to the Internet in the Arab World*, Washington, D.C.: The Washington Institute for Near East Policy, 1998.

[53]For more detail, see Nathan J. Brown, *The Rule of Law in the Arab World*, Cambridge, Mass.: Cambridge University Press, 1997; and individual country reports in Freedom House.

[54]Frank E. Vogel, "Islamic Governance in the Gulf: A Framework for Analysis, Comparison and Prediction," in Gary G. Sick and Lawrence G. Potter (eds.), *The Persian Gulf at the Millenium*, New York: St. Martin's Press, 1997, p. 276. Iran also has a separate court system for crimes committed by clerics, which contains no right of appeal and falls under the direct control of the supreme leader. Wilfried Buchta, *Who Rules Iran?* Washington, D.C.: The Washington Institute for Near East Policy and the Konrad Adenauer Stiftung, 2000, pp. 97–98.

[55]This tactic is particularly common in Egypt. See Brown, 1997, pp. 114–116.

[56]Brown, 1997, pp. 121–128, 218–220, and 243.

some checks on their power, a theme that appeals to both domestic and international audiences. Rulers seeking such legitimacy therefore have significant incentives to minimize overt interference in judicial decisions and to promote judicial independence in select, noncontroversial issue areas. In Egypt, for example, the regular court system makes fairly independent decisions in divorce and housing cases.[57] Even when the legal and judicial systems are not entirely independent of the regime, they can provide important opportunities for enterprising citizens to seek redress for their grievances.[58]

Table 2.2 summarizes the preceding discussion by noting the potential benefits and limitations of each element of democratization and liberalization.

SURVEY OF KEY STATES

The trends discussed in the previous section are broad generalizations that indicate the breadth of political reform issues and activities throughout the Middle East. This section focuses specifically on political reform efforts during the past decade in Egypt, Iran, Jordan, Kuwait, and Saudi Arabia. These states are strategically important to the United States, and some of their experiences with political reform may serve as a model, either positive or negative, for other states in the region.

---

[57]Brown, 1997, p. 195.
[57]Brown, 1997, pp. 189 and 236–238.

Table 2.2

Benefits and Limits of Political Reform in the Middle East

Component	Potential Benefits	Limitations
Legislatures	Check executive authority Articulate popular preferences Provide outlet for popular frustration with the regime	Restricted areas of jurisdiction Limited resources and expertise

Consultative Councils	Allow some popular input into
	  the decision process
	Represent previously excluded
	  groups
		No formal decisionmaking
		  authority
		Members appointed by the ruler,
		  not elected
		Cooption of potential opposition

Political Parties	Express a variety of political
	  viewpoints
	Field diverse candidates for
	  office
		Illegal in many Middle Eastern
		  states
		Lack resources to promote
		  coherent political agendas
		Parties often co-opted by regime

Civic Organizations	Citizens organize to represent
	  their own interests
	Important check on state power
	Provide forums for political
	  activity where parties are
	  illegal or heavily restricted
		Corporatist structures require
		  close ties to the state
		Often coopted or controlled by
		  the regime
		Some segments of society remain
		  unrepresented

Freedom of the Press	Helps increase regime
	  accountability
	Allows citizens to exchange
	  opinions and debate political
	  issues
		Restrictive press laws
		Formal and informal censorship

Judiciary and the Rule of Law	Check on executive power
	Due process protects civil and
	  human rights
	Enhances regime legitimacy
		Judges appointed directly by
		  ruler
		No independent appeals process
		Separate Islamic and civil codes
		Special court systems

Egypt

The Egyptian political reform process has advanced more in principle than in practice.[59] Democratization has progressed in that leg-

---

[59]For an overview of Egyptian political reform efforts from the 1960s to the 1990s, see
Baghat Korany, "Restricted Democratization from Above: Egypt," in Baghat Korany,

islative elections are held every four or five years, but these elections are characterized by government intervention in the electoral process and widespread fraud and irregularities.[60] Fourteen political parties officially exist, but few of them are politically significant. Opposition groups have won an increasing number of legislative seats in recent years, but none of these parties, either alone or in combination, can challenge the dominant position of the governing National Democratic Party (NDP).[61]

Liberalization has also proven to be a mixed bag. Civic organizations have grown in number during the past couple of decades, but their freedom and autonomy has been shrinking. Associational groups must register with the state, and the government has the legal authority to limit their activities and public meetings.[62] The state also informally penetrates these organizations. For example, more than 60,000 people who work in the Ministry of Social Affairs also belong to civil society organizations.[63] Press freedoms have improved in some ways, especially after a repressive press law was struck down in 1996, but the media still depends on the state for access to resources

---

Rex Brynen, and Paul Noble (eds.), *Political Liberalization & Democratization in the Arab World: Volume 2, Comparative Experiences*, Boulder, Colo.: Lynne Rienner, 1998, especially pp. 46–54.

[60]Baaklini et al., 1999, pp. 233–234; Freedom House, p. 175; Korany, "Restricted Democratization from Above: Egypt," 1998, p. 51; Amy B. Hawthorne, "Egyptian Elections: Rumblings of Change, but NDP Dominance Maintained," *Policywatch* 506, Washington, D.C.: The Washington Institute for Near East Policy, 2000.

[61]The NDP captured 388 of the 444 seats contested during the 2000 legislative elections, less of a majority than the 417 seats it held after the 1995 elections, but still more than enough to pass legislation on its own and to ensure the reelection of the president in 2005. Mustapha K. al-Sayyid, "A Civil Society in Egypt?" in A. R. Norton (ed.), *Civil Society in the Middle East, Volume 1*, Leiden, Netherlands: E. J. Brill, 1995, pp. 275–276; Hawthorne, 2000; Andrew Hammond, "Egypt Gains Another Political Party, Which Looks More Like the Government Than the Opposition," *The Washington Report on Middle East Affairs*, Vol. 19, No. 4, 2000, pp. 35–74; Andrew Hammond, "Though Nominal Winner, Egypt's Ruling NDP Party Embarrassed in Parliamentary Elections," *The Washington Report on Middle East Affairs*, Vol. 20, No. 1, 2001, p. 31.

[62]al-Sayyid, "A Civil Society in Egypt?" 1995, pp. 282–284 and 290.

[63]As noted above in the discussion on corporatism, state penetration may reduce the autonomy of these groups, but close ties to the state can also improve their ability to navigate the government bureaucracy as well as reduce their chances of being disbanded. Korany, "Restricted Democratization from Above: Egypt," 1998, p. 61. It is not clear whether such penetration is part of a deliberate government strategy, or whether many civil servants happen to belong to many civil organizations.

and permits to operate. Even though the number of media outlets has increased in recent years, heavy state involvement and official press restrictions limit the range of viewpoints that are expressed.[64]

The judiciary is somewhat independent of the state and has acted as a check on regime power in certain important cases.[65] Yet questions remain about its adherence to international standards of due process. The government has increasingly transferred jurisdiction of sensitive cases to security and military courts, over which it exerts more control.[66] In a recent high-profile case, the Supreme Security Court sentenced Saad Eddin Ibrahim, a sociology professor and well-known democracy advocate, to seven years in jail on charges of defaming the state. The three-judge panel announced its decision after only 90 minutes of deliberation, leading many to believe that the verdict was politically motivated.[67] After 14 months in prison, the highest Egyptian appeals court released him from prison and ordered a retrial, in a challenge to Egypt's emergency laws.[68] All of these different dimensions indicate that the liberalization process remains in flux. Many freedoms are permitted in theory but restricted in practice, while others are denied altogether; and there are often reversals along the way.

---

[64]The government appoints the editors-in-chief of the three major daily newspapers and has a monopoly on the printing and distributing of newspapers. Mamoun Fandy and Dana Hearn, "Egypt: Human Rights and Governance," in P. J. Magnarella (ed.), *Middle East and North Africa: Governance, Democratization, Human Rights*, Aldershot, UK: Ashgate, 1999, pp. 113–121; Freedom House, 2000, p. 176; Farhad Kazemi and Augustus Richard Norton, "Hardliners and Softliners in the Middle East: Problems of Governance and the Prospects for Liberalization in Authoritarian Political Systems," in H. Handelman and M. Tessler (eds.), *Democracy and Its Limits: Lessons from Asia, Latin America, and the Middle East*, Notre Dame, Ind.: University of Notre Dame Press, 1999, pp. 84–85.

[65]Brown, 1997, p. 128; Kazemi and Norton, 1999, pp. 83–84.

[66]Brown, 1997, pp. 114–115; *World Report 2001*, pp. 372–373.

[67]Neil MacFarquhar, "Egypt Sentences Sociologist to 7 Years in Quick Verdict," *New York Times*, May 22, 2001; Howard Schneider, "Court Hands Scholar Jail Term for Defaming State; Pro-Democracy Think Tank Broken Up," *Washington Post*, May 22, 2001.

[68]Neil MacFarquhar, "Egyptian Court Frees Rights Advocate and Orders Retrial," *New York Times*, December 4, 2002.

Overall, however, political reform in Egypt appears to be moving backward, not forward.[69] Reform has been a top-down process, with the regime pursuing reforms that serve its own interests while failing to adopt any measures that would reduce its firm grasp on power. This was particularly true in the early 1990s, as the Islamic movement gained increasing support throughout Egypt. The Muslim Brotherhood is one of the oldest and most experienced Islamic groups in Egypt, and has built a significant base of political support despite the fact that it is not allowed to form a political party.[70] Its popularity comes not only from its religious message, but because it provides tangible benefits and services to its members that the state does not provide. This high degree of popularity makes it the only credible opposition to the governing regime. One study concludes that if free and fair legislative elections were held, the Muslim Brotherhood would probably win more votes than any other party, including the NDP.[71] As long as the government fears that it could lose elections, it is unlikely to promote any form of democratization.

The government has also cracked down on political and civil rights throughout the country, and continuing declarations of a state of emergency allow the government to arrest suspects at will and detain them for prolonged periods of time without explanation.[72] The government claims that such measures are needed to contain Islamic radical movements, but this threat was largely contained by the mid-1990s. The persistence of these restrictions and crackdowns indicates that the regime seeks to inhibit expressions of peaceful opposition as well.[73]

If current conditions continue, the Egyptian government seems unlikely to restart the political reform process. The popularity of the Islamist opposition poses a grave challenge to the regime's hold on

---

[69]Eberhard Kienle, "More Than a Response to Islamism: The Political Deliberalization of Egypt in the 1990s," *Middle East Journal*, Vol. 52, No. 2, 1998, pp. 219–235.

[70]The Muslim Brotherhood built this base of support by getting its candidates elected to the boards of key syndicates and professional associations, giving the group indirect political influence. Ibrahim, 1995, p. 42.

[71]Baaklini et al., 1999, p. 235.

[72]A state of emergency has been declared almost continuously since 1967. *World Report 2001*, pp. 372–373.

[73]Baaklini et al., 1999, p. 235; Fandy and Hearn, 1999, p. 107.

power, and it is unlikely to adopt power-sharing measures voluntarily. Not only do Egypt's political leaders want to retain their positions, but the military and security forces that provide essential support for the regime also have a strong interest in maintaining the status quo. However, if the political situation changes significantly (if a major economic crisis were to erupt, for example, or if popular frustrations with regime restrictions intensify) the government may be forced to consider political reform as a way to restore some of its eroding legitimacy. The current political system lacks structures that are responsive to public opinion and that can mediate between regime and popular preferences.[74] The Egyptian government may therefore find itself in a precarious position if popular opposition intensifies.

Iran

Iran's political system is extremely complex. Both democratic and authoritarian principles coexist uneasily in the constitution of the Islamic Republic.[75] Iran is technically a theocracy, but clerical and secular authorities share power in a way that guarantees constant competition. In the executive branch, power is split between the clerical supreme leader and the secular president. As the title suggests, the supreme leader is supposed to be the highest governing authority, setting guidelines for foreign and domestic policy and overseeing the media, judiciary, armed forces, and security services. The president has more limited powers, with responsibility for economic and daily affairs. However, the president is directly elected, which increases his legitimacy and ability to influence the supreme leader. This division creates tension and friction between the two officeholders, since neither has enough power to impose his preferences on the other.[76]

Legislative power is similarly divided between the secular parliament and the clerical Council of Guardians. Parliamentarians are chosen through elections, and their responsibilities include drafting

---

[74]Jon B. Alterman, "Egypt: Stable, but for How Long?" *The Washington Quarterly*, Vol. 23, No. 4, 2000, p. 115.

[75]Elaine Sciolino, *Persian Mirrors*, New York: The Free Press, 2000, pp. 72–73.

[76]Buchta, 2000, pp. 2–5 and 22–57.

legislation, ratifying international treaties, and examining and approving the state budget.[77] The Council of Guardians consists of 12 jurists—half appointed by the president, half appointed by the supreme leader—who determine whether laws passed by the parliament conform to Islamic law. This gives them an effective veto over all legislation, a power that they have frequently used in the past. The Council of Guardians also has some judicial functions, since any interpretation of the constitution reached by three-quarters of its members carries the same weight as the constitution itself.[78] This complicated and decentralized governmental structure creates a constant struggle for power, which often impedes effective decisionmaking.

Iran is one of the most democratized states in the region, since both the president and the parliament come up for reelection every four years. These elections are not entirely free: Aspiring candidates for both the presidency and the parliament must be approved by the Council of Guardians, ostensibly to ensure their theological qualifications.[79] However, the outcomes of these elections are not preordained, and often are extremely consequential. In 1997, the Council of Guardians approved four candidates for president, all affiliated with the regime. The council clearly expected that Ali Akbat Nateq-Nuri would win the election, since he was supported by Supreme Leader Khamenei. Yet it also allowed three other candidates to participate, calculating that it would liven up the campaign without posing a significant threat to Nateq-Nuri. This turned out to be a gross miscalculation. Mohammad Khatami had developed a strong following before the candidates were announced, and his popularity continued to grow despite verbal attacks in the conservative press, physical attacks on his campaign headquarters, and rumors that the

---

[77]For more on the history and functioning of the parliament, see Bahman Baktiari, *Parliamentary Politics in Revolutionary Iran*, Gainesville, Fla.: University Press of Florida, 1996.

[78]Buchta, 2000, pp. 2–5 and 58–64.

[79]This vetting process seems to be much more restrictive for presidential candidates. In 1997, the Council of Guardians accepted only four of the 238 candidates for the presidency, while in 2000, the council rejected only about 10 percent of the parliamentary candidates. Buchta, 2000, p. 31; Sciolino, 2000, p. 296. For more on its role in the electoral process, see A. William Samii, "Iran's Guardians Council as an Obstacle to Democracy," *Middle East Journal*, Vol. 55, No. 4, Autumn 2001, pp. 643–662.

military forces would not allow him to win the election. Khatami belonged to the same small ruling circle as the rest of the presidential candidates, but his campaign attracted many dissatisfied voters by stressing culture and democracy while Nateq-Nuri campaigned on a platform of preserving the status quo. When the elections were held on May 23, Khatami won more than 70 percent of the total vote, defeating Nateq-Nuri by wide margins in 24 out of the 26 electoral districts.[80]

Khatami's election demonstrated wide dissatisfaction with the ruling establishment and a strong popular desire for increased political liberalization. However, Iran's clerical authorities did not support a significant reform program. As David Menashri succinctly explains, "The elections gave Khatami a mandate for change, but not the full authority to carry out his preferred policies, nor sufficient power to do so."[81] As a result, the liberalization process has been highly contested, moving forward when the reformers are stronger than the conservatives and moving backward when the situation is reversed. Khatami's conservative opponents had successfully regrouped by the spring of 1998 and successfully removed several of his important allies from power.[82] Yet the reformers won overwhelming victories in both the 1999 local elections and the 2000 parliamentary elections, signaling strong public support for continued reform and giving Khatami's supporters a large majority in parliament.[83]

Despite these electoral victories, the conservatives and reformers continue to struggle over the boundaries of acceptable political liberalization. This dynamic is most evident in the battles over press freedoms. After Khatami's election in 1997, several new reformist newspapers started publishing detailed information about govern-

---

[80]Buchta, 2000, pp. 27–38.

[81]David Menashri, "Whither Iranian Politics? The Khatami Factor," in P. Clawson, M. Eisenstadt, E. Kanovsky, and D. Menashri, *Iran Under Khatami*, Washington, D.C.: The Washington Institute for Near East Policy, 1998, p. 43.

[82]Two of Khatami's most important allies were Gholam-Hosein Karbaschi and Abdollah Nuri, the mayor of Tehran and the interior minister respectively. Both men were tried and convicted on a variety of charges. These trials were watched closely by people throughout the country, and sparked a great deal of public debate. Buchta, 2000, pp. 139–143; Sciolino, 2000, pp. 302–310.

[83]Buchta, 2000, pp. 178–182; Sciolino, 2000, pp. 294–298 and 310.

ment activities as well as critical commentaries about government policies. The hard-line judiciary has repeatedly ordered many of these newspapers to be closed, only to have the editors start publishing them again under a different name. The conservatives in parliament pushed through a more restrictive press law in July 1999, and the judiciary has shut down dozens of newspapers and imprisoned many journalists since then.[84]   The new reformist parliament drafted a bill during the summer of 2000 that would reverse some of the press law's most restrictive provisions, but they dropped it from their agenda after facing extreme pressure from the supreme leader.[85]   Pressure from the supreme leader in December 2000 also seems to have forced the resignation of the liberal culture minister, who had promoted increased press and artistic freedoms.[86] The conservatives seem to have the upper hand at the moment, but journalists continue to test the limits of acceptability by publishing controversial articles and establishing new newspapers after their old newspapers were shut down. The struggle over the boundaries of the reformist press continues, and illustrates how the decentralized power structure creates opportunities for people to challenge the system.

Similar dynamics affect the liberalization process in other issue areas. Iran has a vibrant and active network of civil society organizations, with a long historical tradition. The conservatives have limited the scope of their activities and restricted the ones that they find most offensive, but they have not been able to completely coopt these organizations.[87] Opposition to the concept of an Islamic state is generally not tolerated, but several semi-opposition groups exist which challenge specific policies while accepting the basic legitimacy of the current regime. Such opposition takes a range of forms, from organized student groups that promote cautious domestic reform and openings to the West, to clerics who believe that the state's polit-

---

[84]Buchta, 2000, pp. 143–145 and 187–189; Sciolino, 2000, pp. 249–260.

[85]Parliamentary leaders chose not to challenge the supreme leader on this issue, because they anticipated that the Council of Guardians would veto the bill in any case. *World Report 2001*, pp. 378–380.

[86]"Iran's Liberal Culture Minister Is Out, Dealing Blow to Reform," *New York Times*, December 15, 2000.

[87]Kazemi and Norton, 1999.

ical structure must be reformed.[88] As with press freedoms, the boundaries of acceptable behavior for civil society organizations and opposition groups is constantly shifting, as Iran's many power centers compete for influence.

As Table 2.3 indicates, the overall trend line for liberalization has been positive since Khatami became president in 1997, but notable reversals have also occurred. Khatami won reelection in June 2001 with more than 76 percent of the vote, but it is not clear that the conservative opposition will support a reform program more in his second term than it did in his first term.[89]

Table 2.3

Iranian Political Reform Trends Since 1997

Positive Developments	Negative Developments
Wider range of candidates approved to seek office	Many candidates still rejected by Council of Guardians (especially those outside ruling circle)
Reformers win 1997, 1999, and 2000 elections	Conservative opponents and judiciary block many reform measures
Press freedoms expanded toward start of Khatami's term	Press freedoms curtailed toward end of Khatami's term
Wider tolerance of civic organizations	Serious restrictions remain on collective and individual freedoms of expression

Jordan

Jordanian political reform has advanced significantly in recent years, making Jordan one of the most democratized and liberalized states

---

[88]A substantial number of clerics believe that the state's political structure needs to be reformed, but they disagree about the type of reforms that should be adopted. Some believe that the clergy should withdraw from politics altogether, while others believe that the clergy should retain control of social and religious issues. Many clerics believe that Khamenei is not qualified to be the supreme leader, since he has not achieved the rank of grand ayatollah. Buchta, 2000, pp. 52–55 and 79–101.

[89]Neil MacFarquhar with Nazila Fathi, "Iran's President Wins a New Mandate to Promote Reform," *New York Times*, June 9, 2001; "Make Haste Slowly," *The Economist*, June 16, 2001.

in the region. Democratization started in 1989, when parliamentary elections were held for the first time in over 20 years.[90] More than 600 candidates competed for 80 seats, in one of the freest and fairest elections in Jordan's history. The newly elected parliament represented a variety of viewpoints: Islamic candidates captured a plurality of the seats, but leftist, nationalist, and conservative candidates also won notable victories.[91] It soon became an active forum for political commentary and debate, and passed some of the liberalization measures discussed below.[92] In 1990, the king appointed a commission to draft a new National Charter, which included representatives from every significant political group in the country. Officially adopted in June 1991, the charter combined continued monarchical rule with limited democratic principles. It not only reaffirmed the legitimacy of the monarchy but it also emphasized the importance of the rule of law and called for strengthening a democratic process based on political pluralism. Such principles were a noteworthy step forward for a country that had been ruled by martial law for more than two decades and represented a consensus among the major political actors about the general framework for political reform.[93]

Several liberalization measures were also adopted. Jordan adopted a new law on political parties in 1992, making them legal for the first time since 1957. The law contained several controversial restrictions, such as forbidding parties to have political ties to non-Jordanian organizations and preventing members of the military and security services from forming parties. Yet these restrictions did not seriously impede party formation, as 20 parties registered for the 1993 parliamentary elections.[94] Jordan also adopted a new press law in 1992, which prevented the state from being able to shut down a publica-

---

[90]The reform process started in April 1989, after austerity measures triggered riots in the southern part of the country. For more on this, see Rex Brynen, "The Politics of Monarchical Liberalism: Jordan," in Baghat Korany, Rex Brynen, and Paul Noble (eds.), *Political Liberalization & Democratization in the Arab World: Volume 2, Comparative Experiences*, Boulder, Colo.: Lynne Rienner, 1998, pp. 80–83; Marc Lynch, *State Interests and Public Spheres*, New York: Columbia University Press, 1999, pp. 106–107.

[91]Brynen, 1998, pp. 71 and 75.

[92]Lynch, 1999, p. 116.

[93]Brand, 1995, p. 149; Brynen, 1998, pp. 78–79.

[94]Brand, 1995, pp. 160–163; Brynen, 1998, p. 85.

tion without explanation. Perhaps most important, personal freedoms were expanded. Jordanians now enjoy much greater freedoms of expression and assembly than they did before 1989, which has led to an increasingly vibrant civic life.[95]

These initial political reform measures proceeded quite rapidly, but the process has slowed significantly since then. Parliamentary elections were held in 1993 and again in 1997, but they revealed some of the limits of the reform process. Most of the new political parties failed to institutionalize their base of support, relying on charisma of individual leaders rather than on well-articulated platforms, and fewer than half of the candidates elected in 1993 were affiliated with a party. Many parties boycotted the 1997 elections to protest government policy, including a lack of support for political reform. Turnout for that election was also fairly low, indicating some popular dissatisfaction with the reform process.[96] Elections were supposed to be held in 2001, but King Abdullah delayed those elections, reportedly out of concerns that government opponents would be able to exploit the regional situation. In May 2003, after the conclusion of U.S. combat operations in Iraq, he rescheduled those elections, though they have not taken place as of this writing.[97] Liberalization has also gone through several ups and downs. The 1997 press law amendments, for example, placed further limits on free expression, but many of the original press law's most restrictive provisions were lifted in 1999.[98]

Even though political reform has advanced greatly since 1989, the process remains completely managed from above. Political reform has been primarily an instrumental strategy for the monarchy, enabling it to strengthen its own legitimacy by improving personal freedoms and creating political mechanisms for people to express their discontent. Yet genuine power sharing is not on the agenda. The king remains indisputedly in charge of the political system—a position clearly acknowledged in the National Charter—and can dis-

---

[95]Brand, 1995, pp. 176–178 and 184.

[96]Brynen, 1998, pp. 76 and 85.

[97]Alan Sipress, "Jordan Breathes Sigh of Relief After Iraq War," *Washington Post*, May 6, 2003.

[98]Brynen, 1998, p. 84; *Freedom in the World 1999–2000*, p. 263.

regard the popularly elected parliament as he sees fit. Until now, the king has generally chosen to stay out of the daily political fray, intervening mostly in cases when he can present himself as guarding citizens against the excesses of the state.[99] This political strategy makes sense when there is increasing sentiment against the monarchy, as there was in 1989 and afterward, but it may make less sense if political circumstances change. Civil society organizations remain weak and do not yet have the capacity to effectively pressure the regime from below.[100] The future of the political reform process in Jordan therefore depends on the monarchy's continued calculation that its own interests are being served.

Kuwait

The Iraqi occupation of Kuwait in 1990 and 1991 served as an important catalyst for political reform.[101] The emir restored the National Assembly soon after the occupation ended, with elections held in 1992, 1996, and 1999. These elections have been largely free and fair, making Kuwait the only Gulf state that has achieved significant democratization. Candidates engage in intense public debates during the campaign period,[102] and high turnover of seats means that voters are able to effectively express dissatisfaction with their elected representatives.[103]

Democratization remains limited in at least two important dimensions. First and foremost, only male Kuwaiti citizens over the age of

---

[99]Brand, 1995, pp. 180–181.

[100]Brand, 1995, p. 151.

[101]For more on the linkages between the occupation and political reform efforts, see Baaklini, Denoeux, and Springborg, 1999, pp. 178–188; Jill Crystal and al-Shayeji, "The Pro-Democratic Agenda in Kuwait: Structures and Context," in Baghat Korany, Rex Brynen, and Paul Noble (eds.), *Political Liberalization & Democratization in the Arab World: Volume 2, Comparative Experiences*, Boulder, Colo.: Lynne Rienner, 1998, pp. 105–106; Hicks and al-Najjar, 1995, pp. 200–202; Mary Ann Tétreault, *Stories of Democracy*, New York: Columbia University Press, 2000.

[102]Baaklini, Denoeux, and Springborg, 1999, pp. 188 and 196; Tétreault, *Stories of Democracy*, 2000, pp. 101–123 and 170–172.

[103]In both the 1996 and 1999 elections, only about half of the incumbents won re-election. Ghanim Alnajjar, "The Challenges Facing Kuwaiti Democracy," *Middle East Journal*, Vol. 54, No. 2, 2002, pp. 242–258; Tétreault, *Stories of Democracy*, pp. 173–176.

21 are entitled to vote. That group represents approximately 10 percent of Kuwait's native population.[104] The emir granted the franchise to women by decree in 1999, but the National Assembly rejected this measure when it came back into session later that year, and it is unlikely to revisit this issue any time soon.[105] Second, political parties remain illegal. Informal political groups support specific candidates, but they are not allowed to develop the institutional base that would help them promote their policy agendas.[106]

Liberalization is also fairly advanced, especially regarding civil society. More than 200 formal organizations exist in Kuwait, but informal organizations are the core of civil society.[107] One particularly important feature of Kuwaiti society is the *diwaniyya*, which are weekly gatherings of male friends and family, usually in each other's homes, to discuss issues of the day. The Law on Associations does not govern their activities, so they have served as a forum for political debate for many years and play an important role in electoral campaigns.[108] The press also enjoys substantial freedoms and relative independence from the government.[109] Yet there are limits to liberalization, particularly affecting associational life. Since all formal associations must receive licenses, the state effectively controls the types of groups that exist. Many unlicensed groups emerged immediately after the Gulf War, including many that focused on human rights issues, but in 1993 all unlicensed groups were dissolved by the

---

[104]Kuwaiti citizenship standards are quite strict, requiring people to demonstrate that they or their forebears resided continuously in Kuwait between 1920 and 1960. In 1992, only 82,000 out of Kuwait's 800,000 residents were eligible to vote. These numbers exclude the approximately 1.2 million foreign nationals who live in Kuwait. Hicks and al-Najjar, 1995, p. 190.

[105]Alnajjar, 2002, pp. 245 and 248; Mary Ann Tétreault, "Women's Rights in Kuwait: Bringing in the Last Bedouins?" *Current History*, Vol. 99, No. 633, 2000, pp. 27–32. Kuwaiti courts have also refused to hear cases that address women's rights to vote and run for office. "Kuwait: Women's Rights Case Rejected," *New York Times*, January 17, 2001.

[106]Alnajjar, 2002, pp. 247–248; Crystal and al-Shayeji, 1998, pp. 115 and 121; Tétreault, *Stories of Democracy*, pp. 114–117.

[107]Ibrahim, 1995, p. 43.

[108]Candidates generally cannot win election without meeting with the major *diwaniyya* in their districts. Alnajjar, 2002, p. 257; Ibrahim, 1995, p. 199.

[109]Alnajjar, 2002, p. 255.

state.[110] Public gatherings also require state approval, and the state limits interest representation by coopting existing groups and allowing only one union to form for each profession or industry.[111]

Even with the many limits, Kuwait remains one of the most democratized and liberalized states in the Middle East. According to Freedom House's annual ranking, no country in the region currently scores higher on political rights, and only Jordan scores slightly higher on civil liberties.[112] Of course, when judged by global rather than regional standards, Kuwait is far from being considered a free society. The democratically elected National Assembly has become a central part of Kuwait's political culture, but it has not changed the fundamental distribution of power.[113] The ruling family remains firmly in charge, and the emir possesses the power to shut down the assembly at any time. The greater political and civil freedoms may make it more costly for him to do so, since people may express their dissatisfaction more openly, but it nevertheless remains his decision.

Saudi Arabia

Saudi Arabia is one of the least democratized and liberalized states in the region by objective standards, though some of the steps it has taken are quite notable given its history. The regime faced considerable domestic pressure to adopt some political reform measures in the wake of the Gulf War, because its legitimacy had been seriously weakened by its reliance on foreign troops to ensure Saudi security. In 1991 and 1992, prominent Saudi citizens sent petitions to the king, demanding reform of the political system and strengthening the Is-

---

[110]Jill Crystal, "Civil Society in the Arabian Gulf," in A. R. Norton (ed.), *Civil Society in the Middle East, Volume 2*, Leiden, Netherlands: E. J. Brill, 1996, p. 280; Tétreault, *Stories of Democracy*, 2000, p. 200.

[111]*Freedom in the World*, 2000, p. 280.

[112]On a seven-point scale, where one is the most free and seven is the least free, both Jordan and Kuwait received a score of four for political rights. Jordan received a four for civil liberties, while Kuwait, Egypt, Lebanon, and the United Arab Emirates received a five. Almost all other states in the region received scores of six or seven on both of these dimensions. Freedom in the World, 2000.

[113]Crystal and al-Shayeji, 1998, p. 123.

lamic basis of society.[114] In March 1992, the regime adopted two important measures that were designed to alleviate some of these concerns. First, King Fahd issued the Basic Law, which defines the structure and function of the government for the first time. Its provisions largely reaffirm the status quo, such as recognizing the legitimacy of the monarchy and asserting the supremacy of Islamic law. It does acknowledge some of the broader political rights demanded in the petitions, but it does not contain any mechanism for implementing those rights.[115] Second, the king officially established a Consultative Council, which formalized the traditional Saudi system of informal consultation. The council's functions include reviewing and evaluating foreign and domestic policies, as well as suggesting new decrees.[116]

Neither of these measures constituted genuine political reform. The Basic Law appears to be some form of a Saudi constitution, but it has no legal standing. It is considered to be an expression of the king's will and is therefore subject to change at any time.[117] The Consultative Council also cannot be considered a move toward democratization, because its members are directly appointed by the king, its meetings are closed, and it is limited to a purely advisory role. In recent years, the ruling family has increased the council's diversity by appointing more people from the private sector and academia, but these elites do not represent the vast majority of the Saudi population. The council therefore serves more of a cooptive than a representational function, since it gives Saudi elites an increased stake in the decisionmaking process.[118]

------

[114]A secular petition was also submitted in December 1990, but its impact was small. For details on the contents of these petitions, see Madawi al-Rasheed, "God, the King, and the Nation: Political Rhetoric in Saudi Arabia in the 1990s," *Middle East Journal*, Vol. 50, No. 3, 1996, pp. 362–363; R. Hrair Dekmejian, "The Rise of Political Islam in Saudi Arabia," *Middle East Journal*, Vol. 48, No. 4, 1994, pp. 630–635; Mamoun Fandy, *Saudi Arabia and the Politics of Dissent*, New York: St. Martin's Press, 1999, pp. 50–60.

[115]al-Rasheed, 1996, pp. 363–364; Vogel, 1997, pp. 278–280.

[116]King Fahd did not appoint the members of the first Consultative Council until August 1993. David E. Long, *The Kingdom of Saudi Arabia*, Gainesville, Fla.: University Press of Florida, 1997, pp. 50–52.

[117]Vogel, 1997, p. 280.

[118]Dekmejian, 1998; Fandy, 1999, pp. 39–41.

Saudi Arabia did not adopt any significant liberalization measures after the end of the Gulf War. It received Freedom House's lowest possible ratings on measures of both political rights and civil liberties, one of only four states in the Middle East to receive that score.[119] Freedom of expression is severely limited by laws that prohibit criticism of the government, the ruling family, and Islam. Formal dissent and opposition are not tolerated, and all media outlets are either owned or closely controlled by the regime. Public demonstrations are not allowed, and all professional groups and associations cannot exist without permission from the government. Islamic law is enforced not only by the state-dominated judiciary, but also by a separate religious police.[120]

Starting in January 2003, Crown Prince Abdullah has made numerous statements about the need for political reform efforts in the Kingdom and in other Arab countries. At that time, over 100 prominent Saudis signed a petition that called for democracy and an end to corruption. Instead of sending the signers to jail, as King Fahd had done when a similar petition was submitted in 1992, Abdullah met with some of them at his palace.[121] The tone of the meeting was reportedly conciliatory, though soon after the meeting, Saudi authorities shut down a web site that allowed people to express their support for the petition.[122] Later in January, he put forth an initiative to promote political reform of Arab regimes. Abdullah planned to put the initiative on the agenda of the March 2003 Arab League summit but changed his mind at the last minute.[123]

---

[119]The other three states are Iraq, Libya, and Syria. *Freedom in the World.*

[120]*Freedom in the World*, pp. 422–424; *World Report 2001*, pp. 402–406; Rolin G. Mainuddin, "Democratization, Liberalization, and Human Rights: Challenges Facing the Gulf Cooperation Council," in P. J. Magnarella (ed.), *Middle East and North Africa: Governance, Democratization, Human Rights*, Aldershot, UK: Ashgate, 1999, pp. 136–137.

[121]Catherine Taylor, "Saudi Arabia's Quiet Voices of Reform Start to Speak Up," *Christian Science Monitor*, January 15, 2003; Robert Collier, "Saudis Take Small Step Towards Political Reform; Conservative Monarchy Opens Ears for Criticism," *San Francisco Chronicle*, January 28, 2003; Kim Murphy, "Saudis Take the Slow Road," *Los Angeles Times*, April 9, 2003.

[122]Michael Dobbs, "Reform with an Islamic Slant," *Washington Post*, March 9, 2003.

[123]There was some speculation that Abdullah changed his mind because President Bush publicly called for increased democratization three days before the summit began, and Abdullah did not want the initiative to be seen as a response to U.S. pressure.

Saudi officials have claimed the beginning of a gradual process of democratization, where Saudis would start electing representatives to provincial assemblies and build toward election of a national assembly over a six-year period.[124] The regime has also taken a few actions that signal a possible move toward increased liberalization as well. Abdullah allowed a delegation from Human Rights Watch to visit Saudi Arabia in January 2003, the first time a major international rights group had been granted such access, and later granted permission for a private human rights group to be chartered in the Kingdom.[125] On the legal front, in late March 2003, Saudi officials unexpectedly released Said Zuhar from prison, a prominent Saudi Islamist who had been jailed eight years earlier for criticizing the government, though no explanation was given for his release.[126] Abdullah also reportedly favors judicial reform and may be considering creating new commercial courts that would not be based on the sharia.[127]

Some Saudi officials have publicly (though mostly anonymously) acknowledged the need for reform, particularly in response to the increased domestic and foreign pressures on the Kingdom since September 11. One senior prince noted, "The fact is, reform is imperative and not a choice, and so is participatory government."[128] Yet there is by no means a consensus within the Saudi royal family, with prominent ministers expressing their opposition to Abdullah's plans.[129] Although it is extremely difficult to discern popular sentiment in Saudi Arabia, some press reports have noted that calls for reform are coming from both the liberal and conservative elements of the Saudi political spectrum. The liberals support moves toward

---

James Drummond and Roula Khalaf, "Unity Hides Hope Saddam Will Leave and Spare Area a War," *Financial Times* (London), March 3, 2003.

[124]Patrick E. Tyler, "Saudis Plan to End U.S. Presence," *New York Times*, February 9, 2003.

[125]Collier, 2003; Murphy, 2003; Brian Whitaker, "Saudi King Agrees to Human Rights Panel," *The Guardian* (London), May 8, 2003.

[126]Carol Morello, "Saudis Free Prominent Critic After 8 Years," *Washington Post*, March 26, 2003.

[127]Murphy, 2003.

[128]Tyler, 2003.

[129]Such opponents include Prince Nayef bin Abdul Aziz, the minister of the interior, and Prince Sultan bin Abdul Aziz, the minister of defense. Tyler, 2003.

an elected parliament, increased women's rights, and a more stable and predictable legal and economic order, while the primarily Islamic conservatives want to end corruption, the imprisonment of religious leaders, and ties to the United States.[130] These groups are united in little besides a general desire for reform, however, and the regime is unlikely to adopt reforms that satisfy both of them.

As of this writing, it is difficult to know whether these measures are indeed first steps on the path to genuine reform. Yet the pressures for reform, both from inside and outside the Kingdom, seem likely to continue and perhaps even increase. Any Saudi reform plans will be uneven at best, as the regime tries to satisfy the demands of domestic liberals, domestic conservatives, and the international community. Whether the regime can placate these various constituencies while maintaining power remains to be seen.

IMPACT ON U.S. SECURITY INTERESTS

Political reform in the Middle East has the potential to affect U.S. security interests in two important ways: It could increase instability, and it could make regimes more sensitive about their ties to the United States. Each of these is examined in turn.

Effect on Regional Stability

Political reform could potentially increase regional instability. Democratization increases citizen participation, which means that new interests must be factored into the decisionmaking process. Since many of these interests have not been previously represented in the political arena, they are likely to challenge the status quo and demand that benefits be spread across a wider range of the population. Liberalization may also challenge the status quo, because it allows more political interests to be effectively represented. Whether those interests are represented by such institutions as political parties and civic organizations, or more informally through freer speech in public and in the press, they will become a part of the decisionmaking process as well. These new interests will not always dominate the

---

[130]Murphy, 2003.

political debate, of course, and they may often lose out to more entrenched interests. But political reform measures make new voices an integral part of the political process, and they may change that process simply by being included. They also make it impossible for the government to remain silent on certain issues, as noted in Chapter Seven. Since the ruling regimes no longer control information flows, political reform measures may enable citizens to pressure regimes to stake out public positions on issues, and to hold regimes accountable for those publicly stated policies.

Middle Eastern regimes seem likely to weather the instability caused by political reform, at least in the short run. As the country studies indicate, regimes generally maintain fairly tight control over both the scope and pace of reforms. These regimes are not promoting political reform out of any inherent desire to increase political participation; instead, political reform is an instrumental strategy, designed to increase regime legitimacy of current regimes without jeopardizing their hold on power. Regimes often agree to adopt political reforms in exchange for explicit acknowledgments of the ruling family's legitimacy, as happened in Jordan and Kuwait. They also adopt measures that satisfy key constituents, without expanding the reform process much further.

Often, regimes find that liberalization is a more suitable reform strategy than democratization. Democratization is inherently more risky, because it is harder to control people's preferences once they are a part of the decisionmaking process. Liberalization, by contrast, can proceed more slowly while well-defined boundaries remain in place. Furthermore, key regime supporters often prefer liberalization to democratization, because they tend to occupy privileged positions in society, particularly the state bureaucrats who are a key constituency in most Middle Eastern countries. They fear that democratization will generate demands for a more equitable distribution of state resources, which would inevitably reduce their standard of living. Liberalization is far more attractive to them, since it allows them to speak their minds more freely and to gather more openly in both formal and informal groups. Thus regimes have a double interest in promoting liberalization instead of democratization: It enables them to retain control of the decision process while still satisfying demands of key constituents.

Slow political reform is likely to promote the U.S. interest of continued regional stability. It is likely to be more predictable than rapid reform, because regime leaders retain more control over the process and thus can keep radical forces in check. However, even a strategy of slow political reform cannot completely remove the risks that reform poses to the ruling regime. Political reform is not self-limiting in nature: Small moves toward reform tend to generate demands for more reform, as the eastern European states and the Soviet Union discovered during the late 1980s. Whether that reform spins out of control will largely depend on how regimes respond to early demands for increased reform. A response based on coercion will probably dampen future demands for more reform measures, while a response based on negotiation and compromise is more likely to embolden opposition groups and encourage them to make further demands.

Until now, Middle Eastern regimes have successfully managed to contain the pressures for political reform through the strategy of cooption and coercion described above. However, this strategy is not foolproof. If popular frustrations increase significantly, the costs of coercion will rise correspondingly. Any coercive response by the ruling regime may also fuel the determination of the opposition groups to continue resisting the regime. Furthermore, as of this writing, the impact of the U.S. war in Iraq, and subsequent occupation on regional political dynamics, remains unclear. To the extent that Iraq develops real liberal and democratic institutions, it may serve as a model to other countries in the region. Many members of the Bush administration certainly hoped that a regime change in Iraq would have this effect, and some leaders and citizens in the Middle East are expressing that view as well.[131] But it remains to be seen whether this will be the case, and whether existing regimes will be able to contain increased popular pressures for reform or if the process will spin out of control.

---

[131]See, for example, Carol Morello and Emily Wax, "Hussein's Fall Bolsters Middle East Reformers," *Washington Post*, April 13, 2003; David Lamb, "Arab Leaders May See Iraq as a Wakeup Call," *Los Angeles Times*, April 30, 2003; David R. Sands, "Qatar Says Iraq Will Be Democracy Test Case," *Washington Times*, May 10, 2003.

Sensitivity to U.S. Ties

Many states in the Middle East maintain good relations with the United States, ranging from diplomatic support for U.S. policies to allowing U.S. military forces to be stationed on their territory. Yet many of these states prefer to keep those policies as far out of the public view as possible, since anti-American sentiment runs strong throughout the region. We do not know how deep or widespread this sentiment is, because reliable public opinion data on this subject remain very limited. In Saudi Arabia, where such data are virtually nonexistent, anti-American sentiment could be much deeper and more widespread than we currently think. We do know, however, that regimes remain extremely concerned about appearing too close to the United States and often go to great lengths to keep cooperation as invisible as possible.

If anti-American sentiment is as widespread as regimes currently fear, or if it increases in the wake of the U.S. campaign against terrorism in Afghanistan and beyond, political reform could have a very adverse effect on regional cooperation with the United States. Both democratization and liberalization enable people to express their preferences more easily, and if those preferences really are for reduced cooperation with the United States, regimes will have an increasingly difficult time justifying their current policies. This could lead to pressure for less open cooperation, especially regarding U.S. military forces stationed in the region. Regimes may become even more reluctant to reach formal security agreements with the United States, because domestic audiences see such agreements as proof that the regimes are incapable of providing security without external assistance. Increased sensitivity to ties with the United States could also spill over into decreased support for other U.S. regional initiatives, such as the peace process, anti-proliferation measures, and counterterrorism.

CONCLUSION

The United States has contradictory interests in Middle Eastern political reform. It has a normative interest in seeing democracy and civic freedoms spread around the world, since these are fundamental American values. In the Middle East, however, such developments could potentially undermine the U.S. interest in regional stability and continued security cooperation. Whether this potential comes to pass depends largely on the ways in which regional regimes choose to pursue political reform. Slow political reform is more likely to serve U.S. short-term interests than rapid reform, because the forces that oppose security cooperation with the United States are more likely to be contained. As time horizons shift to the longer term, the United States has an interest in ensuring that the reform process continue steadily on, so that citizens enjoy greater political participation and can hold their regimes accountable for their behavior. If such reform does not progress, increased popular frustrations could increase instability by spilling over into conflict or even overthrowing their current regimes. Such outcomes, while not extremely likely, would seriously damage the U.S. interest in regional stability.

Chapter Three

ECONOMIC REFORM IN THE MIDDLE EAST: THE CHALLENGE TO GOVERNANCE

Alan Richards

Many students of the world economy portray Middle Eastern[1] countries as "global losers," lagging seriously behind other major world regions.[2] Looking ahead, the economic challenges facing the region are certainly severe, while the policy response appears limited. A comparison of the region's performance either with that elsewhere in the world or with the severity of the challenges facing the region leaves little room for optimism. Economic stagnation undermines regime legitimacy and even, in some cases, the capacity to govern. The problem is particularly serious because stagnant economies cannot provide adequate jobs for the rising tide of young job seekers. The mixture of regime incapacity, rising unemployment and poverty, and very young populations is politically highly volatile.

At the same time, important changes in economic and social policy have been made in the last five to ten years. Such changes, particularly when combined with a possible "silver lining" in demographic developments, offer a more hopeful perspective. Further, from the perspective of local ruling elites, these problems may be "disastrous,

---

[1]"Middle Eastern" here means Iran and the Arab countries; the focus among Arab countries will be on Egypt and the Asian Arab countries, although some reference will also be made to North African countries.

[2]See Thomas Friedman, *The Lexus and the Olive Tree*, New York: Farrar, Straus, Giroux; 1999; Gary Hufbauer, *China, the United States and the Global Economy: Trends and Prospects in the Global Economy*, Washington, D.C.: Institute for International Economics, November 1999.

but not serious." Many of the economic problems facing Middle Eastern countries have been serious for at least a decade. In no case has the problem, however severe, posed a fundamental threat to the stability of the regime (with the arguable exception of Algeria). Although the lives of many young people in the region are significantly impoverished by their inability to obtain a job that meets their expectations, the political consequences have so far been contained by the "muddling through" approach of most governments to economic policy change.

The durability of this seeming stability is doubtful. In particular, the mounting pressures outlined below may well have a cumulative effect. Economic policies have changed—but the changes have not raised living standards much. One may be also highly skeptical concerning the sustainability of such limited growth as it has occurred. Evidence from such sources as the World Bank strongly suggests that problems of environmental degradation in the region are sufficiently severe that recent increases in per capita income—desultory as they are—may be entirely illusory. When ecological constraints (especially those of water supplies) are included, the challenges facing the region during the medium term appear more daunting still.

Just because regional elites have maintained their power so far does not mean that they will be able to continue to do so in the medium run. The easy (typically, budgetary and macroeconomic) changes have typically already been implemented, yet unemployment and stagnant living standards persist. Many (e.g., the World Bank) advocate deeper changes in response. These may or may not produce the desired results; however, such changes do pose a greater challenge to existing habits of governance: Greater reliance on the rule of law typically threatens the levers of state power; reduced reliance on public-sector employment usually implies greater negotiation with significant private agents, etc. It is unsurprising that such changes are more strongly resisted, and it is far from clear that they can be implemented without profound political change.

During the past 20 years, there has been some consensus on what economic policies ought to be adopted to improve economic management and thereby to restore growth of incomes and job creation. This view holds that only a private-sector led, export-oriented economic development strategy has a chance of coping with the development challenges facing the region. This consensus is best articulated by the World Bank and IMF,[3] but it has many other adherents, particularly in the U.S. government and in American academia and think tanks. Key elements of this "Washington Consensus" include government budgetary balance, low inflation, market determined prices, and reduced reliance on direct, quantitative government regulation.

No one has formulated a more persuasive policy mix than the Washington Consensus for the Middle Eastern context. However, two important caveats deserve emphasis. First, there are reasons to fear that, although the Washington Consensus may be the best available strategy, it too may fail, especially for the very poor nations and the relatively rich states of the Gulf Cooperation Council (GCC.) The best strategy may just not be good enough, given the magnitude of the challenges and some specific features of regional political economies. Second, the strategy also faces formidable obstacles in other countries of the region where the strategy might more plausibly work.

It may be argued, of course, that economic failure will not automatically translate into political disaster. There is no consensus on how deeply these economic challenges threaten existing regimes. Although mounting economic difficulties pose grave challenges to governance for all regimes, as discussed in Chapter Two, there is much uncertainty about how well various regional governments can manage these challenges. At one extreme, these challenges may undermine not only governance, but also governability. In some countries, particularly the poorest ones, the challenges may overwhelm any governmental structure, leading to the collapse of order, as in Afghanistan or Somalia. However, even very deep economic problems may not bring down regimes that can continue to funnel enough patronage to key supporters and to repress dissidents. There is no simple correlation between economic stagnation and governability.

---

[3]See World Bank, *Claiming the Future: Choosing Prosperity in the Middle East and North Africa*, Washington, D.C.: The World Bank, 1995; International Monetary Fund, *Building on Progress: Reform and Growth in the Middle East and North Africa*, Washington, D.C.: International Monetary Fund, 1996.

Regional governments and elites have so far shown a marked preference for a gradual, even dilatory pace of reform. The reasons for this vary from case to case, but are typically a combination of two factors. First, regimes fear—with some reason—that the social dislocations that full-scale economic reform would entail run a high risk of being politically destabilizing. Second, powerful vested interests either block reforms or ensure that the specific kind of reform yields disproportionate benefits to them, at the expense of other social groups. The result has been a very mixed picture, in which regimes have embraced some, and often many, economic reforms (especially in macroeconomic policy), yet they have postponed or evaded more complex reforms, such as privatization, reform of regulatory rules, and development of the rule of law. Whether because of the inherent difficulties facing any economic policy, or thanks to the unevenness of reform, the results have been disappointing. Although in some countries economic performance in the mid- to late-1990s was considerably better than that of the previous ten years, in no country has growth as yet been fast enough to lower unemployment and to raise real wages and living standards.

From a U.S. political perspective, the performance of the past decade may offer the worst of both worlds. Regimes are widely perceived as kowtowing to Washington and "embracing Western dictates." This makes them vulnerable to Islamist criticism, which, of course, transcends economic policy matters. However, failure of the reforms to deliver reduced unemployment and rising living standards makes World Bank appeals to "press on" with reform increasingly less persuasive to many people in the region.

The rest of this chapter has three parts. The first reviews the basic economic challenges facing the region. These challenges threaten governance and political stability in two ways: directly, since some challenges lead citizens to challenge governments (e.g., the youth unemployment problem) and indirectly through states' responses to the economic challenges (e.g., budgetary austerity). Second, the chapter briefly reviews the reform performance of selected key countries: Egypt, Jordan, Iran, Saudi Arabia, and Syria. Third, the chapter summarizes the implications of the interaction of economic challenges and policy responses for governability and political stability.

THE KEY ECONOMIC CHALLENGES FACING THE REGION

The key challenges facing Middle Eastern economies in the medium term include: restoring economic growth, restraining population expansion, providing jobs, alleviating poverty, coping with urbanization, saving water and halting environmental destruction, obtaining food, and attracting money for investment. Each is discussed in turn.

Restoring Economic Growth

The recent experience with economic growth has been dismal. During the past 20 years, Organization for Economic Cooperation and Development (OECD) countries have seen their per capita incomes rise by some 1.4 percent per year. East Asia (excluding Japan) has, of course, grown much faster, at 5.8 percent per year, a rate that doubled per capita incomes in 12-1/2 years. Even Latin America, with its notorious "lost decade" of the debt-ridden 1980s, saw per capita incomes rise at just under 1 percent per year during the past two decades. By contrast, per capita incomes in the Arab states today are little different from what they were in 1980; some analysts would argue that per capita growth has actually been negative, which is clearly the case for some countries, notably the Kingdom of Saudi Arabia.[4] Real wages and labor productivity today are about the same as in 1970. This performance is the worst of any other major region of the world except for the countries of the former Soviet Union. Even sub-Saharan Africa has done better.

Both geography and history have conspired to undermine growth. The region has been cursed by a geographical inheritance of little water, much oil, and a highly strategic location. Despite the enormous sums of foreign exchange that oil revenues have supplied, oil has been a very mixed blessing. Most analysts concur that oil revenues weakened the competitiveness of non-oil traded goods and reduced pressures toward more accountable governance. Oil rents encouraged governments to deepen and extend already existing

---

[4]Hufbauer, 1999; World Bank, *World Development Report 2000*, New York and Oxford: Oxford University Press, 2000.

state-centered, inward-looking, import-substituting policies.[5] Oil also contributed to a continuation of baleful 19th century legacies of strategic location, which, arguably, distracted elites from the task of economic development by forcing them to concentrate on national defense questions, and to continue traditions of dictatorial, arbitrary governance.

Oil price booms laid a weak foundation, and oil price collapse wreaked further damage. The decline of real international oil prices in the early to mid-1980s sharply shifted the terms of trade against the region. As World Bank analysts put it, "Oil prices and output go together." Oil prices were as important for such non-oil countries as Yemen and Sudan as for oil exporters—through the mechanism of labor remittances, the entire region shared in the massive transference of oil rents that characterized the period of 1973 to 1982. (The elasticity of remittances with respect to oil prices is about 0.6.)

From a political perspective, poor growth performance matters only if measured growth (say, GDP or GNP) is a reasonably accurate measure of families' incomes and welfare. Although the overall impression of both "oil boom" and "oil bust" is valid, there are reasons for skepticism about both the speed of the boom and the depth of the bust. There was less growth, and certainly less sustainable development, during the boom than the national accounting data suggest.

This is simply because of the key role of oil, a depletable natural resource, whose rents accrue directly to the government. From a long-term, development perspective, much of the measured "growth" of the oil boom years was not a sustainable income flow, but included receipts from the drawing down of an exhaustible resource. As El Sarafy demonstrates, correcting for this feature can have a substantial impact on adjusted GDP—by 5 percent for Egypt and Tunisia, for example, and over 13 percent for Oman.[6] The boom years also over-

---

[5]Rent is used throughout this chapter in the orthodox economic sense: the difference between market price and the opportunity cost of production. For a further discussion in the Middle Eastern context, see Alan Richards and John Waterbury, *A Political Economy of the Middle East,* Boulder, Colo., and London: Westview Press, 2nd ed., 1996, p. 17.

[6]Salah El Sarafy, "The Proper Calculation of Income from Depletable Natural Resources," in Y. J. Ahmad (ed.), *Environmental Accounting for Sustainable Development,* Washington, D.C.: World Bank, 1993.

state the development of these economies since the boom was, of course, based not on changes in quantities but on shifts in prices: Unlike the East Asian case, incomes in the Middle East grew for the reasons that were fundamentally exogenous to the difficult process of structural transformation. This matters, because the entrenched habits of rent collection provide poor preparation for today's hyper-competitive international economy.

It is instructive to compare the stars of economic development, the East Asians, with Middle Eastern and North African (MENA) countries. The World Bank undertook the methodologically standard comparison of growth of the two regions from 1960 to 1985.[7] They did this through a residual calculation, in which incomes per capita are a function of investment and education. Since these variables explain only 45 percent of the difference in East Asian and MENA growth, the authors asserted that "55% of the differences in growth are due to productivity differences." Such a conclusion is far too sanguine. For the Middle East, much of the change in the value of output was simply the result of price changes and not the fruit of *any* (efficient or inefficient) process of investment. Such considerations suggest that the gap between East Asian and MENA countries was even larger than the 55 percent calculated by the World Bank.

Although one might logically argue that, if national income data overstate the growth of regional economies during the oil boom, then these same data should understate the extent of the decline of the economies during the past 15 years. However, particularly from a political perspective, there is an asymmetry here. First, oil export quantities have fallen little, if at all—there has been little change in the depletion of the depletable resource. Second, the informal economy, which by definition is not measured, is surely not only large today, but larger than it was in the past. As the measured economy shrinks or stagnates, many have shifted their activities to unmeasured activities.

From a political perspective, what matters is the consumption level of households, whether relative to others or to the recent past. Consumption levels have fallen in many cases, and are under consider-

---

[7]World Bank, *Claiming the Future*, 1995.

able strain everywhere, but the informal economy and household networks have probably protected household incomes more than national accounting data would suggest. The "windshield survey" technique suggests that incomes have fallen less than national data suggest.

What really counts politically are *perceptions*,[8] and here there is little doubt that regional perceptions are of stagnation and declining income standards. Certainly most indigenous observers of the region, local residents, economists, pundits, and the like concur that times are hard. There is a widespread perception that the oil boom years presented opportunities, and that these opportunities are now gone. Often, such observers are not slow to blame national governments for these perceived failures.

In summary, regional (and national) growth performances have been, at a minimum, unimpressive during the past 15 years. The dominant impact of oil rents has confused the situation to some extent, but there is little doubt that the region has performed poorly, and that many people are no better off, and many people are worse off, than they were 15 years ago. Governments helped to create this situation: Understanding the current crisis in the region requires recognizing that the oil boom, coming historically on the heels of post-independence import substituting industrialization strategies, spawned the same vested interests, fostered the same mind-sets, and underwrote the very social contracts that today block policy adaptation. Oil price declines created pressure to reform, but so far, governments have been unable to overcome the baleful legacies of recent history.

Restraining Population Expansion

The two key demographic facts of the region are that the rate of population growth remains high, and that fertility rates have been falling rapidly during the past decade. The population of the Middle East and North Africa is now growing at about 2.7 percent per year.

---

[8]"Men in general are as much affected by what a thing appears to be as by what it is, indeed they are frequently influenced more by appearances than by reality." Niccolo Machiavelli, *Discourses on Livy*, I.25.

At this rate, the population will double in about 26 years. This is the fastest rate of growth in the world, exceeding even that of sub-Saharan Africa. However, population growth rates have fallen quite sharply in the past ten years, from 3.2 percent in the mid-1980s to 2.7 percent in the mid-1990s. Sharp fertility declines caused this change; there are reasons to expect further falls.

This generalization hides substantial variation across countries and regions. Although population growth rates and total fertility rates have fallen markedly in Egypt, Iran, and Tunisia, they have remained stubbornly high in Gaza and Yemen. Indeed the total fertility rates in Gaza (7.5) and Yemen (7.4) are among the highest in the world. The Gazan rate is also very high in relation to per capita income.

Even countries whose fertility rates are falling rapidly will continue to experience population growth, both because fertility remains well above replacement levels and because past population growth ensures that there are many women who will soon enter their child-bearing years (so-called "demographic momentum"). The population of the region may reach roughly 600 million by 2025, some six times more people than in the 1950s. Such growth poses numerous economic challenges, ranging from food and water to jobs and housing.

Rapid past population growth combined with sharp falls in fertility have two major implications. First, most Middle Easterners are young. In Iran, for example, half of the population is less than 15 years old. By 2025, the number of people aged 0–14 years will roughly double. Second, as Williamson and Yousef have argued, the rapid fall in fertility may lead to a rapid decrease in the "dependency ratio" (the number of people under 15 and over 65 to the working-age population).[9] When this has happened elsewhere, as in East Asia in the 1970s and 1980s, dramatic increases in national savings rates ensued. For Williamson and Yousef, the demographic change caused the savings change (this is the natural result of their life-cycle savings model). They are quick to note, however, that whether such savings find their way into productive and job-creating investment depends on many other factors.

---

[9]Jeffrey G. Williamson and Tareq Yousef, "Demographic Transitions and Economic Performance in MENA," unpublished paper, Harvard University, 1999.

Providing Jobs

These savings will need to be channeled into job-creating investment, if unemployment and/or falling wages and rising poverty are
to be averted. For at least the past decade, the supply of labor has
outrun the demand for workers every year. Past high fertility levels,
combined with rising female participation rates (from very low levels) have created the most rapidly growing labor forces in the entire
world (3.4 percent per year, 1990–1998).[10] In some countries, the
situation is even more serious, including Algeria (4.9 percent), Syria
(4.8 percent), and Yemen (5.6 percent).[11] Although the rate of
growth attributable to past population growth will decelerate in
some countries (e.g., Tunisia) during the next ten to 15 years, the
decline in fertility is, as always, accompanied (largely caused by)
rising female education—which also simultaneously leads women to
seek to enter the labor market. It is highly unlikely that the growth of
the supply of labor will decelerate within the medium term.

At the same time, the demand for labor has grown sluggishly. Simple
economics tells us that, given such a mismatch between the growth
of demand and supply, either the wage will fall, unemployment will
rise, or (most likely) some combination of both will occur, with the
precise mix varying with specific labor market structures. Government policies have not only reduced the rate of growth of the demand for labor, but have also fostered inflexible labor markets.
Decades of government job guarantees for graduates have induced
students to seek any degree, regardless of its utility in the production,
since a degree, by itself, has long been a guarantee of a government
job. Governments cannot now provide the necessary jobs, but statist
policies impede private-sector job creation. Meanwhile, the educational system has produced large numbers of young people with
enough education to be unwilling to work at manual labor jobs, but
insufficient skills to be productive in today's world economy.

Despite data difficulties, several generalizations may be made. Current levels of unemployment are high, as Table 3.1 demonstrates,

---

[10]World Bank, *World Development Report 2000.*

[11]By way of comparison, the labor supply has grown at 0.8 percent in the United
States and 0.4 percent in the European Union.

Table 3.1

Unemployment in the Middle East: A Compendium of Estimates

Country	Unemployment Rate	Remarks
Algeria	30 percent	Data from 1999.
Egypt	12 percent	Data from 2000. Some estimates are as high as 20 percent.
Iran	20 to 25 percent	Data from 2001.
Jordan	15 percent	Official rate. 1999 CIA estimated 25 to 30 percent.
Lebanon	18 percent	Data from 1998.
Libya	29 percent	Data from 2000.
Morocco	15 to 22 percent	Data from 2000.
Saudi Arabia	14 to 18 percent	Rates are higher among graduates.
Syria	12 to 15 percent	Data from 1999.
Tunisia	16 percent	Data from 1999.
Yemen	35 percent	Data from 1999.

SOURCES: Saudi Arabia, U.S. Embassy, Riyadh, and *New York Times,* 8/26/01; Iran, Eric Rouleau, *Le Monde Diplomatique,* www.en.monde-diplomatique.fr/2001/06/05iran; all others: MEDEA Institute (European Institute for Research on Mediterranean and Euro-Arab Co-operation), and CIA *World Fact Book,* 2001.

and the problem will probably get worse in the near to medium run. Unemployment primarily affects young, semi-educated, urban people, whose anger fuels political unrest. Unemployed youth provide fertile fishing ground for Islamist radicals throughout the region. The problem posed to governance is severe.

The remedy to the long-term problem has worsened and in many cases will continue to worsen the problem in the short term. Demand for labor has grown sluggishly both because output growth has lagged, and also because of specific policy biases against labor-intensive, job-creating growth. Not only do the statist, inward-looking policies sketched above retard growth, but they also raise the capital-intensity—and reduce the job-creating effect—of whatever growth does occur. But changing these policies requires laying off workers in state-owned enterprises and the bureaucracy, a move that frightens many leaders.

The employment problem is the most politically volatile economic issue facing the region during the medium term. Unemployment encourages relatively educated, young, urban residents to support radical Islamist political movements. There are, of course, *many* complex cultural forces behind these movements; no "economic determinism" is implied here. The Ayatollah Khomeini is reported to have said that "the revolution is about Islam, not the price of melons." Much deeper issues of identity and legitimacy are at stake. For example, we should remember that although unemployed, frustrated young men throughout the region can turn to Islamism, they can also turn to drugs and crime, to apathy, indifference, muddling through, dogged hard work, or any number of other, personal "coping" strategies. The decision to join a revolutionary movement is a deeply personal, idiosyncratic one. Socioeconomic contexts are important for understanding these movements, but they hardly provide a full explanation for them. Nevertheless, huge numbers of discontented young men (and women) are a major threat to internal stability throughout the region.

Alleviating Poverty

There is a large and growing debate about the extent and severity of poverty in the region. Since the definition of both is inherently subjective, such debate is hardly surprising. With the exception of a few countries, the debate rages in the absence of good data. This analysis offers the following generalizations on the state of poverty in the region.[12]

- Only Jordan, Morocco, and Tunisia have estimates of poverty based on detailed household surveys. The available data suggest that poverty in Jordan rose sharply from 1987 to 1991, improved until the mid-1990s, and may have increased since then. Poverty declined in both Morocco and Tunisia in the late 1980s. There is some evidence that poverty increased in Morocco during the 1990s, when the economy was hammered by repeated droughts. Such a performance is particularly discouraging, because

------

[12]The information in this section is based on Ragui Assaad, Alan Richards, Charles Schmitz, and Michael Watts, "Human Security of the New Millennium: Poverty and Sustainable Livelihoods in the Arab Region—Elements for a Poverty Alleviation Strategy," New York: United Nations Development Program, 1997.

Morocco implemented more far-reaching economic reforms, and did so earlier, than most other countries in the region.

- Some data for the first half of the 1990s exist for Egypt, Algeria, and Yemen, although the studies are less comprehensive and rigorous. All three cases have had a clear increase in poverty but there is sharp disagreement over the magnitude of the increase.

- Poverty is clearly a growing problem in some countries (Iraq, Somalia, Sudan) where there is very poor or nonexistent documentation.

- Very little is known reliably about poverty in Libya, Syria, and Lebanon.

The World Bank presents the most optimistic perspective on regional poverty.[13] This study asserts that, when compared with other regions of the developing world, MENA has "relatively limited" poverty. The number of poor persons (defined as those with yearly incomes less than Purchasing Power Parity [PPP] $365 per year) was 5 percent, and the depth and severity of poverty were low.

One can easily object to this rosy picture. In the first place, the Bank's "absolute poverty line" is simply too low to be meaningful for most countries of the region, particularly from a political perspective. Poverty is, inescapably, a relative concept, especially if we are concerned with politics and policy. "Poverty lines" are the modern equivalent of "subsistence" in classical political economy, and, then and now, subsistence has a relative, social element. The report's poverty line ($370 PPP per person) is far below average $PPP per capita incomes for most countries: The ratio of per capita GNP to the poverty line, both in PPP dollars, is unreasonably high when compared with a similar calculation for the United States, where GNP per capita is about 6.5 times greater than the poverty line. Corresponding MENA figures are 9.9 for Egypt, 11.4 for Jordan, 8.8 for Morocco, and 13.8 for Tunisia.[14]

---

[13]See Willem van Eeghen, "Poverty in the Middle East and North Africa," World Bank, unpublished, 1995.

[14]In 1992, the poverty line in the United States for a family of four was $14,335. The endpoints of the 95 percent confidence interval around the Bank's point estimate for poverty in MENA are 13 and 51: No estimate of the poor as a percentage of the

From a political perspective, what counts is the relative social definition of poverty. Poverty is always and inevitably partly relative: Poor
people in Egypt, Jordan, or Algeria (and those who sympathize with
their plight) do not compare themselves to the poor in Bangladesh or
Madagascar; they feel "poor" relative to their fellow Egyptians, Jordanians, or Algerians. It is the higher estimates of poverty that are
more politically relevant.

Other reports and studies confirm this rather less sanguine picture.
The Mashreq Report estimates the rate of poverty for the region to be
33 percent, and argues that poverty is growing in the region.[15] Ali
uses a relative poverty line and finds the incidence of poverty to be
some 1.5 to 1.9 times higher than the World Bank's estimate,
depending on the country.[16]

What are the political consequences of poverty? Poverty provides a
fertile recruiting ground for opponents of regimes (and therefore
poses a challenge to governance) in at least two ways. First, some
poor people, particularly younger ones with some (often limited) education, join violent opposition movements. The basic profile for
today's violent militant is a young person with some education, who
may also have recently moved to the city. Such young people are often unemployed or have jobs below their expectations. In North
Africa, they are colorfully known as the "*hetistes*."[17] Some evidence
from Egyptian arrest records suggests that many of those arrested for
violent activities against the regime come from the shantytowns surrounding large cities—that is, from some of the poorest urban areas
of the country.

---

population between 13 and 51 percent can be ruled out. Sheldon H. Danziger and
Daniel H. Weinberg, "The Historical Record: Trends in Family Income, Inequality,
and Poverty," in Sheldon H. Danziger, Gary D. Sandefur, and Daniel H. Weinberg
(eds.), *Confronting Poverty: Prescriptions for Change*, Cambridge, Mass.: Harvard
University Press, 1994, pp. 18–50.

[15]"Poverty in the Mashreq Region," United Nations Development Program, unpublished report, 1995.

[16]Ali Abdel Gadir Ali, "The Behavior of Poverty in the Arab Region," in *Preventing and
Eradicating Poverty*, New York: United Nations Development Program, 1996, pp. 61–
80.

[17]A Maghrebi word that blends the Arabic *heta* (wall) with the French suffix *iste:* "one
who leans against the wall."

The spread of violent opposition in Upper Egypt is also plausibly related to poverty. The *Sa'id* (Middle and Upper Egypt) is the poorest region in the country. Moreover, there, as elsewhere in the country, poverty has been rising during the past ten years. The poverty situation deteriorated during the past decade, thanks to the collapse of unskilled wages. These had risen over 350 percent in real terms from 1973 to 1985, largely thanks to emigration for work in the Gulf states (public job creation also played a role). With the collapse of the regional oil in the war-related migration to Iraq, and in the ability of the public sector to create jobs, wages for unskilled workers fell by over 50 percent. As Sa'idis increasingly move to cities, they "export" the problem of Islamism to more visible locations, such as the major cities of Egypt.

As the profile of the militants suggests, poverty breeds opposition in a second, indirect way. Most people find the presence of widespread poverty and human degradation offensive. We are thinking, reasoning beings: We look around us, and then draw our own conclusions. The presence of widespread poverty delegitimizes regimes in the eyes of those who spend a lot of time thinking about what they see, such as intellectuals, journalists, and students.

Throughout history, most revolutionaries have not come from poor families. Revolutionaries, whether of the Leninist or Islamist variety, can usually "pronounce their haitches" (are from privileged backgrounds), as George Orwell famously remarked in the 1930s. However, they did find the appalling poverty of their societies to be morally outrageous and took action accordingly. The widespread perception of a regional regime's failure to provide adequate standards of living contributes to the often noted "crisis of legitimacy" in the region.

Even relatively "invisible" poverty, such as that in rural areas, has important political implications. In some cases, small towns and rural areas do provide recruits and support for militants. However, regimes are typically more concerned with urban opposition. But rural poverty exacerbates the problems of cities. Rural poverty, of course, fosters rural to urban migration. As rural poverty is "exported" to the cities, not only do the number of potential militants rise, but also the difficulties of regimes in dealing with urban problems mount. Rapidly growing numbers of poor urban dwellers multiply the demands on urban administrations. In an age of increasingly scarce governmental resources, meeting these demands becomes increasingly difficult. Such government failure further delegitimizes governments in the eyes of both the poor urbanites themselves plus intellectuals and students. Rural poverty does not stay "politically invisible" for long.

The Jungle of Cities

The number of urban dwellers is growing much more rapidly than populations as a whole. The number of urban Middle Easterners has increased by about 100 million in the past 35 years. Roughly half of the population of the region now lives in cities. The number of urban dwellers is expected to rise from its current level of over 135 million to over 350 million by 2025. From 1985 to 1990, the most rapid growth was in secondary cities—6 percent—compared with a growth rate of 3.8 percent for the 19 largest cities with populations of more than 1 million in 1990. This trend has continued during the 1990s. Public services and utilities are already overwhelmed. In Jordan and Morocco, for example, one-third of the urban population lacks adequate sewerage services. Urban water supplies are often erratic. Governments attempt to provide urban services through heavy subsidies. These strain government budgets and thwart the necessary investments to extend and improve services.

The rapid urbanization of the region challenges governance in at least three ways. First, the rapid growth of cities strains infrastructure—and government budgets. Governments' perceived inability to cope with mundane problems like housing, sewerage, potable water supply, and garbage collection further weakens already strained regime legitimacy. Second, the process of migration from rural to urban areas is always disorienting for many migrants. Whether in Ayachuco or Asyut, the mix of rural-urban migration with discontented provincial intellectuals has proved highly toxic to existing governments. The disoriented recently arrived rural migrants to cities provide fertile fishing grounds for Islamic militants, particularly when the (allegedly) decadent mores of the cities shock the sensibilities of the newcomers. The problems are also made more acute by the difficulties that migrants sometimes find in obtaining work (e.g., in the Maghreb). Third, urban discontent is clearly more politically volatile and dangerous to regimes than is rural. Rapid urbanization strains budgets, legitimacy, and governance, while swelling the ranks of regime opponents.

The magnitude of the problem dwarfs available resources to cope. Managing these problems adequately will be expensive. The World Bank estimates that solving the problem of municipal solid waste collection for the region as a whole will require $4–6 billion of investment over a ten-year period, while solutions to water distribution and air pollution will be still more expensive.[18] Governments are unlikely to be able to afford to provide services at below cost to urbanites if coverage is to be extended and health hazards are to be reduced.

The problem is both cause and effect of governance difficulties. At least in part, the problems stem from the weak tax base of most urban entities. Few cities have much independent tax authority, thanks to the fiscal centralization in most countries in the region. At the same time, macroeconomic austerity has deprived many municipalities of the funds needed to cope with urban problems. The problems of urbanization are fundamentally caused, of course, by rapid urban population growth; they are significantly exacerbated, however, by governments' lack of revenues. Coping with urbanization is another force pressing governments to reform their policies.

Governments are very widely perceived as having defaulted on their responsibilities to their citizens. This situation provides radical opponents of existing regimes with excellent opportunities. Islamists, in particular, have been nimble in filling the niche vacated by fiscally retrenching governments. Islamists have created schools, clinics, day-care centers, and dozens of other NGO-style activities, to substitute for penurious and incompetent local government. The contrast of the incompetence of the Egyptian bureaucracy and the dedication of Islamist NGOs in caring for victims of the Cairo earthquake neatly illustrates the point. Islamic charities can draw on a vast reservoir of private wealth, particularly in the Gulf states.

---

[18]World Bank, *Middle East and North Africa Environmental Strategy: Towards Sustainable Development*, Washington, D.C.: The World Bank, 1995.

Saving Water

Coping with increasingly scarce water constitutes an inescapable challenge to government policy. Five facts about the water situation seem particularly relevant.

First, water is becoming increasingly scarce. Renewable water resources per capita have fallen from 3,500 m^3 in 1960 to 1,500 m^3 in 1990 to 1,250 m^3 today. The World Bank projects that there will be only 650 m^3 per person by 2025 (compared with a worldwide average of 4,780 m^3 per person in that year). Water use in ten countries and Gaza already exceeds 100 percent of renewable supplies.

Second, water quantity problems are exacerbated by water quality problems. These become increasingly serious as nations seek to solve the "water quantity" problem through reuse of water. Technologies exist to do this safely, but they require considerable funds and careful management. Neither is abundant.

Third, from an economic perspective, the burden of adjustment to increasingly scarce water must fall on the agricultural sector, because the economic value of water is much lower in farming than for domestic or industrial use. Politically, however, such a shift is very difficult; past government programs to redistribute land, reclaim land, and increase domestic agricultural production to plug the food gap have created powerful interest groups that will oppose reallocation of scarce supplies away from their farms. And given the already serious pressures on urban infrastructure, no government wishes for a rapid acceleration of rural-urban migration—which is what large-scale water transfers from farms to cities could imply.

Fourth, government water management systems suffer not only from lack of funds, but also from managerial cultures that were geared to a situation of relatively abundant water.

Fifth, most water resources in the region are rivers and aquifers that cross international frontiers. There is a sharp clash between economic/engineering logic, which would favor managing a river basin as a unit, and political considerations, marked by fear and distrust of one's neighbors.

Some analysts fear that military conflict over water may erupt in the not-too-distant future. Although there are many reasons to doubt this, heightened tension over water is likely. For example, successful management of the water problem will require greater regional cooperation. If states are willing to risk this, then the engineering and economic obstacles are not large. However, many (probably most) states appear reluctant to take such economically rational steps. Domestically, the usual economic remedy for coping with water scarcity, greater reliance on markets, is very difficult to implement. Water markets are likely, at best, to play a relatively minor role in most countries. There are many solid economic reasons why this is so.[19] The political difficulties are even more severe, particularly when governments consider eliminating existing subsidies to farmers or trying to regulate overdraught of groundwater.

Obtaining Food

The Middle East is the least food-self-sufficient region in the world. During the 1980s, demand growth decelerated (thanks to declining incomes) and supply response accelerated. Regional agricultures used more land, more water, more fertilizer, more machines, and more labor—all just to keep up with population growth. In the 1990s the story was similar: The FAO reports that food production per capita in 1999 was some 4 percent above that of 1990. As usual, there is wide country variance. Although Egypt's food production per capita rose some 20 percent from 1990 to 1999, Jordan and Saudi Arabia experienced a fall (of 22 percent and 41 percent, respectively).[20] There is also evidence of diminishing returns in agriculture. The rate of growth of agricultural value added slowed from 5.5 percent in the 1980s, to 1.7 percent in 1990–1997.[21]

---

[19]Alan Richards and Nirvikar Singh, "No Easy Exit: Property Rights, Markets, and Negotiations over Water," *Water Resources Development*, Vol. 17, No. 3, 2001; David Seckler, David Molden, and Randolph Barker, "Water Scarcity in the Twenty-First Century," *International Journal of Water Resources Development*, March 1999.

[20]Food and Agriculture Organization, *The State of Food and Agriculture, 2001*, Rome: Food and Agriculture Organization, 2001.

[21]World Bank, *World Development Report 2000*.

Unless there is a remarkable acceleration in the pace of technological change in farming, the water constraint dooms attempts at food self-sufficiency. The "food gap," or the difference between consumption and domestic production, is projected to increase at roughly 3 percent annually during the coming decade. The region is already importing "virtual water" (water embodied in imported food) roughly equal to the annual flow of the Nile.

In short, increasingly the region must export to eat. This, however, poses deep dilemmas for policymakers. First, most analysts believe that the new world trading rules of the Uruguay Round and World Trade Organization (WTO) will raise (slightly) world cereal prices. It will be more, not less, difficult to feed populations through imports should these projections become realities. Second, relying on food imports means that countries are increasingly dependent on the wider health of the global economy, something that they are nearly powerless to affect. Third, sustainable increases in food imports require sustainable increases in other exports, which is precisely what economic reform is intended to achieve. The necessity to pay for imported food—ideally with job-creating, labor-intensive exports—constitutes a key argument for the urgency of economic reform.

Attracting Money for Investment

None of the above problems can be successfully managed without much higher levels of investment. Consider the employment problem. The total number of new jobs that the region will require by 2010 is roughly 47 million. The investments required to employ those workers are estimated by the World Bank at about $31 billion in Iran, $30 billion in Morocco, $25 billion in Algeria, $14 billion in Egypt, and $12 billion in Tunisia.[22] Growth rates must reach levels of 7 to 10 percent to employ new job seekers and to reduce the numbers of the unemployed. The challenge is huge.

Governments cannot provide such money; it can only come from private local citizens, and, to a lesser extent, from foreigners. So far, however, governments of the region have failed to attract the neces-

---

[22]Nemat Shafik, personal communication, August 1995.

sary funds. The low level of (and even more, the inefficiency of) investment, in turn, exacerbates governance problems via economic stagnation, rising unemployment and poverty, deteriorating cities, and increasingly scarce water.

A few facts should suffice to make the point. First, very large sums of money are held "offshore" by citizens of Middle Eastern countries. Second, the region has captured a nugatory amount of the total worldwide flows of direct foreign investment. Apart from oil companies, most foreign investors shun the region. At the same time, the efficiency of national investment has been declining.

In addition, several MENA countries now face a "debt crisis," the fruit of years of living beyond their means. Interest payments on debt as a percentage of GDP now rival those in chronically indebted sub-Saharan Africa and are similar to those that plagued Latin America in the 1980s. Consider one critical debt ratio, the present value of debt as a percentage of exports. As a rule of thumb, any country with a ratio over 200 percent is said to suffer from debt overhang: a level of indebtedness that deters private investors from risking their capital. Investors fear that the large size of the public debt will force the government to raise taxes, either directly or indirectly, through the inflation tax.[23] In either case, a prospective investor will lose. Servicing an external debt requires an internal transfer (from private to public sectors) and an external one (from the indebted country's government to the foreign creditors). Domestic debts require an internal transfer. These transfers must come from local sources, creating fear among potential investors. On this criterion, Algeria (284 percent), Jordan (228 percent), and Syria (419 percent) have important debt overhang difficulties, Morocco (183 percent) and Turkey (167 percent) remain troubled, while the problem in Yemen (over 1,000 percent) and the Sudan is entirely unmanageable.[24]

Work habits, high efficiency wages, and archaic infrastructures are some of the factors inhibiting investment and therefore growth. However, there is an emerging consensus that, in the Middle East as

---

[23]The large majority of external debt in Middle Eastern countries is public debt.

[24]Data are for 1998. Data for Sudan—whose membership in the World Bank has been suspended—are not available. World Bank, *World Development Report 2000*.

elsewhere, investment is impeded by defective governance. Key factors here include:

- Public sectors dominate the nonfarm economy. Their demands often crowd out private investors.

- Taxation is high and arbitrarily administered. Larger firm size is discouraged.

- Regulations are complex and opaque, and become breeding grounds for governmental corruption.

- Legal systems are weak and/or overloaded, offering little practical redress.

The challenges facing regimes of the region are daunting. So far, the main policy prescription for coping with such problems is a shift toward a more private-sector driven, open, and market-oriented economy. Such policies, it is hoped, will generate jobs while simultaneously producing exports to buy the food to take pressure off of increasingly scarce water supplies. We turn now to a more detailed examination of the economic challenges and policy responses in Egypt, Jordan, Iran, Saudi Arabia, and Syria.

EGYPT

Egypt illustrates the reform challenges faced throughout the region. Egyptian economic reform began in 1991. During the past decade, some progress was made toward converting a grotesquely overregulated, unbalanced socialist economy into a more modern economy with a greater role for the private sector. Growth rebounded during the 1990s, averaging 4.9 percent per year from 1991 to 2001. However, significant problems remain. Stabilization has been fairly successful, while structural adjustment has been weaker. There are signs that reform's pace has slackened recently.

Most important, reforms to date have failed either to reduce unemployment substantially or to halt the decline in real wages. At best, reforms have prevented unemployment from rising. The transition to growth led by labor-intensive exports has not happened. Growth in the 1990s was mainly driven by domestic demand rather than by trade expansion; in 1999, merchandise exports were only 3 percent of

GDP in 1999, and, worse still, exports today are less labor-intensive than they were a decade ago.[25] Living standards have, at best, shown very modest improvement.

At the same time, accusations of corruption in the privatization process abound, and many observers speak of the rise of "crony capitalism," similar to Suharto's Indonesia. Privatization seems to have resembled the Russian case, with a few insiders reaping most gains. Newly wealthy Egyptians are flaunting their wealth in a conspicuous consumption binge that offends the poor and provides ready propaganda for radical Islamists.[26] The government is widely perceived as a geriatocracy, devoid of new ideas, while budgetary stringency has led the state to withdraw from some welfare functions (e.g., disaster relief, medical care, education), leaving a vacuum increasingly filled by Islamists. The medium-term political implications are disquieting.

The Background of Reform[27]

On the eve of the 1991 Gulf War, the Egyptian economy was in shambles. Growth turned negative in the late 1980s; by 1990 the country had amassed international debts of nearly $50 billion; its debt/GNP ratio of roughly 150 percent was arguably the highest in the world at the time. Real wages of unskilled workers had plummeted by 40 percent in four years, while civil servants earned only about half of their 1973 salaries. The level of open unemployment had doubled during the decade. The quality of government health, transportation, and educational services had dropped from already dismal levels, which was, and is, exploited by Islamist extremists.

At the core of Egypt's macroeconomic crisis were three macroimbalances: the gaps between domestic savings and investment, imports and exports, and government revenues and spending. The collapse

---

[25]World Bank, *Egypt: Social and Structural Review*, Social and Economic Development Group, Middle East and North Africa Region, Report No. 22397-EGT, June 20, 2001.

[26]David Hirst, "Egypt Stands on Feet of Clay," *Le Monde Diplomatique*, October 1999.

[27]This section draws on Alan Richards, "The Political Economy of Dilatory Reform: Egypt in the 1980s," *World Development*, Vol. 19, No. 12, December 1991.

of oil revenues and mounting losses of public-sector companies undermined public savings, while private savings were deterred by negative real interest rates on Egyptian pound deposits and by great uncertainty by private wealth holders as to the future direction and credibility of economic policy. Investment flowed into infrastructure, rather than into traded goods production; investment was increasingly inefficient and capital-intensive, creating few jobs.

Like so many other middle-income countries, Egypt plugged the twin gaps by borrowing from abroad, largely from foreign governments. Egypt's foreign debt climbed from about $2 billion in 1970 to some $21 billion in 1980 to just under $50 billion in early 1990. This latter figure was roughly 150 percent of GNP; in 1990 debt service payments consumed over 25 percent of exports. The average government deficit for FY 1982–1990 was 21.2 percent of GDP. Revenue fell with oil receipts, while spending was inelastic downward for the usual political reasons: blockages by vested interest groups who would lose sinecures and economic rents, and fears of popular wrath over subsidy cuts. Some 80 percent of government spending consisted of subsidies, public-sector salaries, interest on the public debt, and the military. The last two were sacrosanct, forcing all adjustment on the spending side onto the first two.

As new foreign lending dried up in the latter half of the 1980s, the deficit was increasingly financed by monetary expansion. Inflation accordingly rose to roughly 25 percent, with the usual baleful results: further distortion of price signals, sharply negative real interest rates that exacerbated the savings-investment gap, and (thanks to fixed nominal rates) a steadily increasing overvaluation of the exchange rate. Such underpricing of increasingly scarce foreign exchange discouraged the production of traded goods and favored imports over exports; in short, it greatly exacerbated the trade gap.

Microeconomic distortions reinforced macroimbalances. Egyptian price distortions of the 1970s and 1980s were internationally notorious. The divergences between private and social rates of return in industry were little short of astonishing. In the second half of the 1980s, price reforms began to be implemented in agriculture, but cotton remains underpriced even today. Prices in Egypt have borne little relation to social scarcities.

Price distortions interacted synergistically with the regulatory environment to create a producer's nightmare. Consider the increase in capital intensity. On the one hand, the relative price of labor to capital rose as labor emigration pushed up wages, while accelerating inflation and financial regulations created strongly negative real interest rates. Supervisory personnel, who are so crucial to successful labor-intensive production techniques, were particularly scarce during the migration boom. Because laws made it almost impossible to fire workers, labor costs became overhead. Regulations were, and remain, voluminous, ubiquitous, opaque, and arbitrarily enforced.

The Gulf War created an entirely new situation. Indeed, it provided a strategic opportunity that the Egyptian government swiftly seized. The government adopted a reasonably conventional stabilization and structural adjustment package, endorsed by the IMF, in exchange for massive debt relief. Such a bargain was attractive both economically and politically. Economically, the reduction of up to $20 billion of debt cut yearly interest payments by $2 billion for the next ten years. Politically, the deal was easier to sell domestically, since the government could plausibly argue that its creditors were shouldering part of the burden of past mistakes. By "front-loading" the reforms, international donors hoped to change the payoffs facing the government: if they failed to reform, they would not enjoy subsequent tranches of debt relief.

The Promise of Reform

In May 1991 agreements with the Fund and the Bank were signed. The program contained six components:

1. The stabilization program contained the usual *macroeconomic measures*. In particular, the program mandated banking reform, which made the Egyptian pound a convertible currency, created new financial instruments (in effect, "Treasury bills" issued by the Central Bank), and raised nominal interest rates. Macroeconomic targets that were monitored were net foreign assets, net domestic assets (government + state-owned enterprises + private sector) and public-sector borrowing (government + state-owned enterprises).

2. The Structural Adjustment Loan (SAL) provided for a *privatization program* covering sale of government assets and setting up legal and institutional mechanisms for a better management of the public share in corporations. The Central Bank's regulatory functions were also to be strengthened.

3. *Price liberalization* measures included raising the farm-gate price of cotton in steps to be equal to the world price in 1995, except for a small export tax on extra-long staple cotton, in which market Egypt has some market power. Cotton marketing and trade were to be liberalized; subsidies on fertilizers and pesticides, halved in FY 1991, were to be completely liberalized by FY 1993. Energy prices were to rise to international levels by 1995, rail tariffs were to be raised, and price guidelines for intercity bus transport were to be removed.

4. *Trade liberalization* was to be achieved by cutting import bans and licensing requirements, eliminating import deposits, lowering tariffs to between 10 percent and 80 percent, and reducing the variability of tariffs. Export restrictions were to be reduced and then eliminated, and the drawback system was to be extended to indirect exports.

5. *Investment licensing* was to be abolished by December 1993. Trade in fertilizer and cement was to be privatized, and labor laws were to be reformed so that private companies could more easily lay off or fire workers.

6. A *Social Fund*, with a capital of some $600 million largely provided by European donors, was to reinforce the social safety net by providing labor-intensive public works to generate employment, offering loans to small and microenterprises, and retraining public-sector workers.

The Performance

The first component of reform, macroeconomic stabilization, did fairly well for most of the 1990s. The United States forgave the roughly $7 billion of military debt up front. Some 15 percent of the remaining debt was forgiven in May 1991 following the IMF's approval of an 18-month Stand-By Arrangement, which was extended another six months. A further 15 percent was forgiven in September

1993, when the IMF concluded that the first set of reforms had been successfully concluded, and agreement was reached on an Extended Fund Facility. The final tranche, about 20 percent of the original debt, was forgiven in 1996. Egyptian debt is now quite manageable, constituting $31 billion; its present value is estimated at 29 percent of GNP.[28]

Reform of banking laws and a firm government commitment to a fixed nominal exchange rate stimulated an influx of offshore money. International reserves soared, rising from $2.68 billion in 1990 to $11.7 billion in 1993, and peaking at $26.7 billion in 1995. This money is largely short term and highly liquid. However, because Egypt's capital account had not been fully liberalized, the country was spared the worst effects of the Asian financial crisis of 1997. Nevertheless, reserves have fallen, particularly since 1998, declining to $15 billion in 2000.

Fiscal reform was also initially very successful. Government deficits have fallen from more than 20 percent of GDP before the Gulf War to 2.5 percent in 1993–1994. By 2000, deficits had risen to 3.6 percent of GDP. Fiscal discipline has combined with tight monetary policy to cut inflation from more than 25 percent in 1990, to 11.2 percent in 1992–1993, to 6 percent in 1994–1995, and to 3 percent in 2000. Macro-economic performance has been the strongest component of reform.

Until 1998, the government pursued tight fiscal and monetary policies. The balance of payments was stabilized, and the rate of economic growth picked up. However, there are two major problems: The current macroeconomic posture blocks export-led growth, and the sluggishness of microeconomic and structural reforms such as privatization and deregulation impede a more vigorous private-sector response. These problems have combined to retard achieving the ultimate goal, the acceleration of growth, and job creation and real wage increases.

The current macroeconomic posture implies that high interest rates will continue to attract Egyptians' funds abroad. Other things equal, such interest rates reduce investment and growth. Such rates are

---

[28]World Bank, *Egypt: Social and Structural Review*, 2001.

probably less significant as a growth impediment than remaining regulatory problems, but they do need to be addressed. However, so long as the Egyptian government persists in its present policies of exchange rate management, the government cannot reduce interest rates. Here there are significant differences of views between many Egyptian government officials and many foreign observers, including the World Bank.

The Egyptian government acknowledges that inflation has exceeded that of its major trading partners during the past decade. Because the nominal exchange rate has been pegged since the devaluation of February 1991, the real exchange rate has become increasingly overvalued. By 1997, the World Bank estimates the overvaluation to be some 37 percent compared with the February 1991 level, and 40 percent compared with the 1987 level (when foreign exchange controls were partially relaxed). The government argued that Egyptian exports are inelastic with respect to the exchange rate, and that a fixed nominal exchange rate is essential for investor confidence in the entire economic reform package (the so-called "nominal anchor" argument). The government has pegged the credibility of its reform efforts to the nominal exchange rate. While oil exports are, of course, inelastic with respect to the exchange rate, this is much less obviously so for workers' remittances, especially for nontraditional manufactured goods and processed agricultural commodities. The overvalued exchange rate contributes to the relatively sluggish growth performance of the Egyptian economy by weakening such exports—the hoped for "engine of growth" for jobs and incomes.

A common rejoinder from Egyptian government officials and economists is to note that current (low) growth figures are for *measured* growth. Most Egyptian economists stress that much economic activity goes uncounted. They argue that the so-called "informal sector" is booming. It is certainly true that casual observation is not wholly consistent with a gloomy picture of economic stagnation. It is also true that the regulatory morass of Egyptian policy creates large incentives for unreported activity. Deregulation would not only benefit growth by reducing disincentives for investment, but also improve policymakers' understanding of the economy by improving the quality of data. Improved data would help all participants in the current macroeconomic policy debate by increasing the consensus on what is actually happening in the Egyptian economy.

Even if the current growth figures are underestimates, and even if, therefore, the Egyptian economic performance has recently been more robust than existing data suggest, current exchange rate policy is quite risky. The government's current interest rate policy is largely responsible both for the government's ability to maintain an over-valued real exchange rate and also for the existence of large foreign exchange reserves. However, most of the capital inflows have been in short-term government securities. Such a policy is reminiscent of the Mexican situation before the crash of the peso in December 1994, when a political event triggered a run on the peso.[29]

It is reasonable to ask how long the Egyptian government can maintain its present posture. The recent historical experience with such a nominal anchor policy is disquieting. Similar policies have been tried in Chile (1978–1982), Mexico (1994–1995), and Argentina (today). In each case, the nominal anchor was deemed (reasonably) necessary to bolster investor confidence. But in each case, the country was ultimately forced to undertake large, sudden devaluations when the credibility of the overvalued rate finally became unsustainable (often the result of some exogenous "shock to confidence" of a political nature). The resulting recessions were typically very sharp: In Chile, output fell by 14 percent, and over one-quarter of the labor force was unemployed. Mexico's experience was equally grim. There is no obvious reason why Egypt, which is following similar policies, should be spared a similar fate. Unfortunately, as elsewhere, shifting from a "nominal anchor" policy is a bit like dismounting from a tiger—getting off may be as dangerous as staying on.

Most crucially, the short-term liquid savings have yet to be translated into investment in the real economy. Only such investment can generate sustainable employment growth. There is consensus among observers that reforms of the real economy are proceeding sluggishly. In particular, progress on privatization has been slow. Privatization occurred mainly after 1996; about half of some 314 public enterprises have been privatized. However, the regulatory regime remains largely untouched, particularly at the level of implementa-

---

[29]The Egyptian government's situation is somewhat less risky than that of Mexico, because the deposits are not dollar denominated, which placed all of the exchange rate risk on the Mexican government.

tion.[30] The rules of the game are still opaque, and investors maintain a wait and see attitude. The regulatory environment and the slow pace of privatization undermine one of the main goals of exchange rate management.

Since 1998, there are increasingly disturbing signs. First, the macroeconomic achievements seem to be in jeopardy, largely thanks to the government's insistence on maintaining *both* a fixed nominal exchange rate *and* pursuing its growth objectives. Egypt's exchange reserves have fallen, credit expansion has accelerated, government payment arrears have accumulated, and the level of dollarization has increased.[31] Continued high levels of protection discourage production for export. Meanwhile, new job seekers have unemployment rates over 15 percent, and real hourly wages for men in 1998 were only two-thirds those of 1988. Urban poverty has increased from 20.3 percent in 1991 to 22.5 percent in 1995.[32] These are the most conservative estimates available; other sources find considerably higher levels of poverty and show steeper levels of increase. To support the exchange rate and to finance continuing although smaller fiscal deficits, the Egyptian government has borrowed heavily domestically. Debt service now consumes about a quarter of the budget. The analogy with Indonesia in the last days of Suharto is disturbing.

The Political Economy of "Creeping Cronyism"

Egyptian reform was delayed until 1991, moved cautiously since then, and has failed to solve the fundamental problems of the political economy. Three factors best explain this pattern of change: the structure of interest groups; the personality and priorities of the leadership, particularly President Mubarak's; and the presence of substantial international rents.

---

[30]Examples abound of middle- and lower-level officials continuing to enforce old rules, even when these have been officially changed by the Cabinet.

[31]World Bank, *Egypt: Social and Structural Review*, 2001.

[32]Rural poverty decreased considerably from 28.6 to 23.3 percent. From a political perspective, however, the urban rate is much more important. The last national household survey was conducted in the mid-1990s. No further data are available, and estimates vary widely. World Bank, *Egypt*.

The principal losers from economic reform in Egypt were precisely those upon whom the regime had traditionally relied for support, and whose ability to act collectively was institutionalized under Nasser: organized labor and managers in state-owned enterprises, government bureaucrats, and holders of import licenses and other rent seekers. Egyptian reformers faced a powerful phalanx of vested interests that blocked the adoption (and still more, the implementation) of policy change. The government managed to reduce employment in public enterprises slated for privatization from 1.2 million in 1990 to 950,000 in 1996 by offering various early retirement schemes. However, redundancies remain substantial, but the government understandably fears the political consequences of mass layoffs in a labor market that is already failing to absorb the yearly crop of 500,000 new job seekers.

The pattern of reform has also reflected interest group alignments. The top layers of the army and bureaucracy—the power elite created by the Nasser regime—have, in a manner similar to their former Russian allies, responded with alacrity to the new opportunities offered by banking liberalization and privatization. A symbiosis between government regulators and speculative entrepreneurs has developed; insider trading is rampant, particularly in the construction sector, where public land may be sold very cheaply to a friend who then resells it at its market value. As one astute observer put it, "At first sight, it might seem that power has moved from the barracks to the boardroom. More to the point, the army has moved into business."[33]

One can overemphasize the strength of interest groups in Egypt, however. Take the potential losers from reform: These face "free-rider" problems in opposing reform and, given the highly centralized political system in Egypt, would probably fall to a determined effort by the president.[34] Similarly, determined action from the top could

---

[33]Quoted in Hirst, 1999.

[34]John Waterbury, *Exposed to Innumerable Delusions: Public Enterprise and State Power in Egypt, India, Mexico and Turkey*, Cambridge, UK: Cambridge University Press, 1993.

do much to contain corruption. The president, however, chooses to move as slowly as possible, and his two sons, Ala'a and Gamal, are major players in the "business-bureaucrat" symbiosis.

Leadership always matters for reform, but, arguably, in Egypt it matters even more. The Egyptian political system is extremely centralized, with most key decisions made by the president and his closest advisors. The men close to Mubarak are very much men of the old order: There has been very little turnover in the Cabinet, and hardly any in key portfolios. Mubarak, a military man, has surrounded himself with engineers—not a set of backgrounds conducive to wholehearted embrace of market-friendly reform. Mubarak is no "technopol," or economist-turned-politician, like Turgut Ozal. His experience at the Sadat assassination is said to reinforce his caution. He is in his seventies and has not appointed a successor. His caution is legendary, his compatriots aged, and his regime sclerotic.

Economic rent provides the third prop of dilatory reform. Through the 1970s, oil rents, whether directly in the form of oil export revenues or indirectly as workers' remittances from the Gulf and Iraq, permitted the Egyptian government to pursue business as usual. The collapse of oil rents in the early- to mid-1980s greatly increased the pressure for reform. Although there were important changes (particularly of the government budget), a consistent reform program was not even formulated until mid-1986, not implemented until May 1987, and abandoned in November 1987. Throughout the 1980s, the government procrastinated as problems mounted, long after oil rents had dwindled.

Currently, higher oil prices permit somewhat greater rent from this source. However, the key rent is strategic. Ever since Sadat's turn to the United States in the late 1970s, the regime has successfully and skillfully exploited its unique position as the largest Arab nation, and the first (and until 1994, the only) Arab state to have signed a peace treaty with Israel to extract concessions from the United States, the European Union, and through these, international agencies such as the IMF and the World Bank. The Mubarak government skillfully utilized "strategic rent" to delay reforms for half a decade after the oil price collapse of mid-1986.

But even strategic rent had its limits. On the eve of the Gulf War, pressure for change was mounting. The IMF, badly burned in 1987, was taking a harder line, while the U.S. connection was endangered by Egypt's coming dangerously close to violating the Brooke Amendment. After failing to meet the targets of the May 1987 stand-by agreement with the fund by November 1987, several years of complicated negotiations ensued. The Egyptian government used its strategic importance to extract favors from the United States, and to induce the United States to lobby the IMF to exercise great restraint in dealing with Egypt. While this dance was performed, the problems mounted. The patience of all parties was running out, as Egyptian policymakers appeared to take an ever-shorter perspective on the problem.

But then, of course, Saddam Hussein dramatically restored Egypt's strategic rent. Mubarak's support of the Gulf War coalition was partly repaid with exceptionally generous debt-forgiveness terms. Throughout the 1990s, the pace of reform has been frequently questioned and the regime repeatedly prodded by the United States, the World Bank, and the IMF. But, at the end of the day, Egyptian caution always prevailed: Strategic rent enabled—and enables—the government to move at its own slow, opaque, and unaccountable pace.

Although Egyptian reform is often held up as an example of progress (particularly by the World Bank), reality is rather different. The combination of interest-group structures, strategic rents, and the personality of the president has yielded patchwork reform, which has failed to accomplish its central goal of launching the economy on a path of employment-generating growth, led by manufactured exports. The largest Arab economy is failing to provide the necessary jobs for young men, which delegitimizes the regime in the eyes of its increasingly restless youth.

JORDAN

Like Egypt, Jordan illustrates how a country's configuration of interest groups can hinder the reform process. Much more than Egypt, Jordan shows how external events can undermine even a determined reform effort. Jordan has repeatedly overcome internal divisions, embraced reform, and enjoyed modest success, only to be derailed by regional developments entirely beyond the Kingdom's control. Jordan is a small country with an inherently weak domestic economic base. Its population is small (5 million), it has no oil, and it is surrounded by neighbors that are either richer and/or militarily stronger. Until ten years ago, the country relied heavily upon external grants and loans, transportation services to the Gulf, and the export of skilled labor. The 1991 Gulf War temporarily demolished all three sources of foreign exchange.

During the first half of the 1990s, growth was surprisingly strong, fueled by the repatriated capital of Jordanians expelled from the Gulf and sound macroeconomic management. From 1992 to 1995, the country enjoyed a boom, with GDP growth of 9 percent. However, the faltering peace process, the decline in oil prices, and reduced demand from Asian economies after 1997 dragged growth down to 1.5 percent from 1996–1999. This led to the adoption of a new round of economic reform, in which Jordan joined the WTO and offered plans to accelerate privatization. It seems highly likely that the aftermath of the terrorist attack on the United States on September 11, 2001, and the subsequent wars in Afghanistan and Iraq will once again illustrate the vulnerability of the Kingdom's economy to negative external shocks.

Elements of Jordan's vulnerability include its possession of few natural resources and a rapidly growing population. These structural features of the economy interacted with policy decisions to create additional difficulties:

- A relatively large public sector
- A small private sector with a small but growing industrial component
- Chronic trade imbalances (currently averaging about $2 billion annually)
- A heavy foreign debt burden (currently about $8 billion, with a net present value of 110 percent of GDP).

To make matters worse, Jordan suffers from increasingly acute, chronic water shortages. This problem appears to be one of both supply and pricing. The largest consumer of water is agriculture

(70 percent in 1990), while household consumption accounted for 24 percent of consumption. Jordan has only 198 cubic meters per capita (1998), and with a population growth rate exceeding 3 percent per year, pressure on water supplies is becoming increasingly acute. (As a rule of thumb, less than 500 cubic meters per capita indicates severe water stress). Existing groundwater resources are being radically overutilized; withdrawals are estimated at some 180 percent of recharge.[35] A system of water pricing that heavily subsidizes water use by wealthy, influential, and (often) Palestinian farmers in the Jordan Valley has exacerbated shortages elsewhere in the Kingdom.

The continuation of the Arab-Israeli conflict stymied regional arrangements for joint use of shared rivers such as the Jordan and the Yarmuk. Many observers hoped that the 1994 treaty with Israel would help to alleviate these problems. Water-sharing arrangements in the Jordan and Yarmuk rivers, combined with sharing of groundwater, were intended to increase Jordan's short-run water resources by 100 million cubic meters. It was also hoped that technology transfer and regional cooperation would increase resources still further over the long term.

None of these benefits has yet materialized. The combination of severe drought in the late 1990s and increasingly difficult Jordanian-Israeli relations as the Israeli-Palestinian peace talks stalled, and then collapsed, have undermined, but have not eliminated, regional cooperation. Although Israel reconsidered its initial 1999 decision not to give Jordan the 50 million cubic meters that Jordan believed it had been promised by the treaty, the incident dramatized the difficulties of cooperation in the current regional political environment. Despite various clauses in the treaty calling for joint water infrastructure projects, none has begun. Water problems remain a central worry for the regime, with no simple solution in sight.

Jordan is not a mineral-rich country. Although the country has substantial deposits of phosphates and potash, these products are subject to greater price fluctuations than industrial exports. Unlike its neighbors, Jordan is not a major oil producer. Modest quantities of crude oil were discovered in 1983, but Amoco and Hunt oil withdrew

---

[35]Christian Chesnot, "Drought in the Middle East," *Le Monde Diplomatique*, February 2000.

from prospecting in the country in 1989. Oil imports have continued to be a major drain on the economy and on foreign currency.

Jordan's principal resource is its people. The government has made substantial investments in human capital formation. Health conditions in the country are among the best in the region; government figures place Jordan's primary (over 95 percent) and secondary (65 percent) enrollment rates at among the highest in the Arab world.[36] Adult literacy today is one of the highest in the region: about 94 percent for men and 80 percent for women. Over the past ten years school enrollment rates have grown by nearly 4 percent a year.

Unfortunately, population growth threatens to undermine these achievements. Jordan's population was estimated at 3,453,000 in 1990, prior to the influx of 200,000 to 300,000 expatriates who returned from Kuwait in the wake of the Iraqi invasion. The strategy of exporting human capital temporarily collapsed. The current 3 percent birth rate represents a decline from 3.6 percent a decade ago. The average number of children per mother (total fertility rate) has declined from 7.4 in 1976 to 5.2 in 1992 to 4.5 percent in 2000. The population in 2000 was over 5 million. Most alarmingly, the labor force is projected to grow by nearly 5 percent per year over the next ten years.

Quality problems in the educational system raise expectations without providing truly competitive skills in international comparative perspective. The problem appears to be especially acute at the university level, where a combination of rising enrollments and declining expenditures has seriously jeopardized educational quality. The result is increasing pressure on government educational budgets, high unemployment among graduates, and mounting frustration. This situation poses a serious challenge to political stability and is a problem in all countries of the region.

The Jordanian labor market combines high levels of unemployment with labor imports. Unemployment among the unskilled is concentrated among elderly illiterates. This is presumably because of the premium unskilled labor markets place on physical strength. The

---

[36]See http://www.kinghussein.gov.jo/resources3.html.

other, more politically relevant dimension of unemployment is that of graduates, at least one-fourth of whom do not have a job. Unemployment rates in Jordan are a monotonically rising function of education.

Jordan has also been a labor importer. Foreign laborers, largely from Egypt and South Asia, fill jobs in the construction, agricultural, and domestic help sectors that Jordanians have traditionally eschewed for cultural and low wage level reasons. Despite graduate unemployment, family support allows graduates to avoid the social stigma of less-skilled labor.

Jordan would have faced unemployment problems much earlier had the country not been able to rely in the 1970s upon the out-migration of some one-third of its labor force, largely to the Arab oil states of the Gulf region. In 1987 some 325,000 Jordanians were working abroad, while the domestic workforce stood at 550,000. At that point, unemployment was officially reported to be 10 percent, although the official statistics probably represent underreporting. Although the Gulf War temporarily closed employment in the oil states, today perhaps 300,000 Jordanians are again working outside of the country.

One possible medium- to long-term solution to the employment problem is the expansion of light industry and services. At present, Jordan's manufacturing sector tends to be organized in small-scale operations with small workforces. The regulatory and financial regimes impede business expansion. The industrial sector contributed 25 percent of GDP in 1998, up from 11.6 percent in 1985. Together with mining it accounted for 11.4 percent of the workforce in 1998.

The Jordanian economy is overwhelmingly a service economy, which accounts for two-thirds of GDP. Any sensible strategy for development must include services development. Some potential areas include Arabic language computer software and tourism. High hopes were placed on the possible positive impacts of the peace agreement with Israel. Although tourism boomed briefly, it collapsed in the wake of the renewed violence in Israel and Palestine since September 2000.

Jordan has long suffered from chronic trade imbalances. The 1988 devaluations of the Jordanian dinar cut the trade deficit somewhat.

The gap between imports and exports was $1.7 billion in 1988, $1 billion in 1989, $1.5 billion in 1990, and $1.4 billion in 1991. Despite further reform after the Gulf War, the trade gap rose to $2.4 billion in 1993, and stood at $2 billion in 2000. In the late 1990s, the gap between imports and exports was nearly 20 percent of GDP. Part of the trade imbalance derived from an excessive consumerism and consumption of foreign goods, many of them luxury items. However, the trade deficit is largely structural, deriving from the small manufacturing base, the paucity of natural resources, and the large net food-importing requirement.

The consequence of prolonged trade imbalances was the accumulation of international indebtedness. From 1984 to 1988, the proportion of public and publicly guaranteed foreign debt to GNP rose from 59.3 to 95.1 percent. The debt service ratio increased from 13.8 to 29.8 percent during the same period. The repayment burden eventually became unsustainable and the IMF was called in the spring of 1989. Jordanian debt before the peace treaty with Israel was at least $7 billion; Jordanian officials assert that the total debt was closer to $8.8 billion.[37] Debt has at least stabilized since 1994; the most recent estimates place the debt at $8.4 billion. The "debt overhang" remained over 250 percent throughout the decade (260 percent in 1991; 228 percent in 2000), which discourages private investors.

Jordan has long relied on foreign aid for investment in both military hardware and infrastructure. In the 1980s, lower liquidity levels among Gulf oil states led to a significant drop in aid to Jordan. Still, in 1989, Official Development Assistance (ODA) was some 6.3 percent of GNP, the highest in the region. While the Gulf states did promise assistance in the wake of the 1989 economic riots, transfers ceased upon Jordan's refusal to support the anti-Iraq coalition in the 1991 Gulf War. Such aid has not been resumed: In 1998, ODA was only 5.7 percent of GNP. Unlike Mubarak, King Hussein was unable to translate friendship with the West and signing a peace treaty with Israel into large-scale debt reduction. However, the U.S. Senate's passage of the U.S.-Jordan Free Trade Agreement following the ter-

---

[37]Remarks by Dr. Jawad Al-Anani, Minister of State for Prime Ministerial Affairs, at The Washington Institute for Near East Policy, Washington, D.C., July 28, 1994.

rorist attacks of September 11, 2001, shows that the Kingdom can still garner some important strategic rents.

Economic Reform in Jordan

Policymakers recognized the need for economic reform by the mid-1980s, but real progress did not begin until the economic crisis of 1988–1989. The original agreement reached between the government and the IMF called for a reduction of the budget deficit, a reform of the tax system, a tighter credit policy, a more prudent debt management and borrowing policy, a decrease in the rate of inflation, an improvement in the current account to a balanced position in 1993, and the building up of foreign currency reserves to cover three months' worth of imports.

The government was clearly committed to meeting the conditions of the agreement with the IMF. Despite extensive parliamentarian railing against the agreement, at no point did any member of parliament (MP) or group of MPs come forward with an alternative plan. When it came time to pass the 1990 budget, there was no attempt by parliament to advocate increased spending as a way out of such problems as unemployment. In effect, the parliament endorsed the IMF package. The case illustrates the point that, in a crisis, the old guard is often disorganized, without a program, and unable to resist determined leadership.[38]

Despite the government's good faith in its implementation of IMF conditionality, the Gulf crisis destroyed the original timetable of reforms. Thousands of refugees flooded into Jordan. The Kingdom's political position on the crisis further exacerbated the situation, since coalition states were disinclined to alleviate Jordan's refugee problem. The embargo against Iraq deeply hurt Jordan's commercial, industrial, and overland transport sectors. The blockade of the port of Aqaba led shippers to avoid using it even for other purposes. Jordan also lost its Kuwaiti and Saudi markets as well as Gulf state aid because of the Kingdom's failure to join the anti-Iraq coalition. The regional instability also cut into Jordan's increasingly important

---

[38]Waterbury, 1993.

tourist trade. Assessments of the economic impact of the crisis on Jordan range from $1.7 to $5 billion.

The Gulf crisis also caused the budget deficit to exceed projections in 1991 by JD 121.7 million, reaching JD 216.7 million. As a result of these economic dislocations, Jordan put a moratorium on the payment of its rescheduled debts, a situation about which the IMF was reportedly very understanding. An IMF team arrived in Jordan in mid-September 1991 to prepare a new letter of intent, and a new agreement was announced in October 1991. Jordan largely fulfilled the terms of this obligation and achieved the promising results in the early 1990s noted above.

Jordan's Memorandum of Understanding with the IMF of July 4, 2000, lays out the intent for the next phase of economic reform, adopted as a response to the deceleration of growth in the late 1990s. The program emphasizes privatization, tariff reduction, and other policy changes necessary to meet WTO membership requirements (Jordan joined the WTO in January 2000). Although there are domestic difficulties with implementing some aspects of these reforms, the key difficulty, as is so often in Jordan's history, is the negative impact of exogenous events: The stagnation and then collapse of Israeli-Palestinian peace talks, the Al Aqsa intifada, and the threat of regional war after September 2001 and the 2003 war in Iraq have all undermined confidence and deterred foreign investment.

Crafting Credible Reforms

In comparative regional perspective, Jordan has been quite successful in adopting economic reform policies. The three keys to this success are good leadership, support by a critical constituency of businessmen, and extensive "use of others," such as the IMF and World Bank.

Barriers to reform include significant internal and external political risks. The external problems have already been discussed. Domestically, the main problem has not been the oft-cited one of fear of social unrest in the wake of subsidy cuts. The government did, of course, face riots in Ma'an and elsewhere in the late 1980s as it took the first reform steps, but such disturbances did not greatly slow the pace of reform.

Much more important, privatization faces a critical political difficulty. Downsizing the state implies that the regime's core constituency, "Trans-Jordanians" (non-Palestinians), will disproportionately lose: The Trans-Jordanians are overrepresented among
state functionaries, and Palestinians dominate the private sector.
Members of the key tribes—e.g., the Majali, Bani Hassan, Bani Sakhr,
Bani Hameideh, and the Adwan—are threatened not only by possible
down-sizing of the government, but also by the (presumed) competition from Israeli and, especially, West Bank entrepreneurs in the
wake of the peace agreement. Former prime minister Abdul Raouf al
Rawabdeh stressed this point in his opposition to privatization.[39]
His replacement may or may not lead to an acceleration of
privatization, which may or may not be politically destabilizing.

Leadership, as usual, matters greatly. Until the death of King
Hussein in February 1999, implementing reform provided yet another example of Hussein's legendary political agility. Jordan is a
small, militarily weak country in a rough neighborhood, with a foreign policy that dominates domestic policy. Indeed, in Jordan, foreign policy *is also* domestic policy. Unfortunately, if you use one
instrument to aim at two targets, you are likely to miss both. The
principal political barrier to sustainable growth in Jordan is regional
instability. A weakness of King Hussein's leadership from an
economic point of view was the "churning" of top personnel; there is
low continuity at the relevant Cabinet positions, or at the prime
minister's level. In contrast with Morocco, a stable change-team
seems absent from the Jordanian scene. This practice has continued
under Abdullah, who replaced his first appointed prime minister,
Rawabdeh, with Ali Abu al-Ragheb in June 2000.

The regime is strongly supported by the upper tier of merchants, in-
dustrialists, agribusinessmen, and wealthy farmers—the Jordanian
bourgeoisie. These "king's men," drawn from both Palestinian and
Trans-Jordanian communities, have strong ties to the regime, and to
some extent have submerged their ethnic identity into a sense of
being Jordanians. Their views must be considered by top decisionmakers; they are critical allies of the king on issues ranging from the

---

[39]"Jordan's Predicaments," *Strategic Comments*, International Institute of Strategic
Studies, Vol. 7, No. 7, 2001.

Islamists to the peace process. Any policy that threatens their interests would be difficult to sustain.

In addition to regional fears, at least three problems impede improving the climate for private business. First is debt overhang. Obtaining debt relief may be a necessary condition for the success of the new strategy. Although the govenment has lobbied strenuously for this, so far it had not had great success. Instead, part of the U.S. payoff for Jordan's signing the 1994 treaty was the drafting of a Free Trade Agreement with Jordan. Second, private-sector activity in Jordan has historically often relied on state contracts. The symbiosis of state and private business is extensive, unsurprisingly, given the small size of the country and its elite. The business elite also usually hold multiple assets and diversified asset portfolios. They are usually not unambiguous winners or losers from reform. Their support of reform typically comes from their (often intense) loyalty to the king, who has protected them for decades, and a general preference for markets rather than controls.

The combination of the need to placate this key constituency, plus the fact that many key businessmen benefit as rent seekers from current arrangements, explains the sluggish reform of the regulatory regime in Jordan. Despite the presence of free zones and industrial estates, Jordan has attracted very little foreign direct investment, while Jordanians hold over $6 billion offshore.

King Abdullah has done reasonably well managing the treacherous foreign and domestic politics of the Kingdom. But maintaining the fragile balance between East Bankers and Palestinians, Islamists and regime supporters, in such an unstable and lethal regional environment is inherently deeply problematic. That Jordan has done as well as it has, despite repeated negative external shocks, is a testament to the skill of its leadership and to the soundness of its policy mix. But the fact remains that youth unemployment, and its discontents, has not been substantially reduced after ten years of reform efforts: Unemployment stands at 25 to 30 percent, and 30 percent of the population lives below the national poverty line. Jordan shows the limits of even strong reform efforts in the face of the "youth bulge" and the unstable regional political environment.

IRAN

Iran has a state-centered, stagflationary economy. Per capita incomes declined precipitously during the 1980s, more gradually from 1993 to 1997. Only during the past half decade has the rate of economic growth exceeded that of the population. The economy is plagued by widespread unemployment, chronic budgetary deficits and inflation, declining living standards, and widespread poverty.

Iranian economic decline was particularly marked during the 1980s. Income per capita in 1992 was estimated to be some 38 percent below what it was at the time of the 1979 revolution. Two factors explain this miserable performance. First, the growth of output sharply decelerated, thanks to declining oil prices, the stress of the war with Iraq, and economic mismanagement. Second, the rate of population growth rose: The rate increased from 2.9 percent between 1966–1967 and 1976–1977 to 3.9 percent between 1976–1977 and 1986–1987. The total fertility rate soared to 6.2. Consequently, population grew from about 40 million in 1980 to perhaps 55 million in 1990.

Although economic growth failed to revive during the late 1980s and early 1990s, the rate of population growth plunged. Indeed, the fall in fertility in Iran may have been the fastest such decrease ever recorded.[40] Today the total fertility rate (TFR) in Iran is approximately at replacement level (2.0).[41] The population growth rate has plummeted from 3.3 percent (1980–1990), to 1.6 percent (1990–1999), to an estimated 0.72 percent in 2001.[42]

Three important consequences of this demographic picture are, first, the large majority of Iranians are young: 50 percent are younger than 18, and roughly two-thirds are younger than 30. Second, a labor force bulge of young people born in the 1980s have begun entering the labor market. Third, thanks to the rapid deceleration of population growth in the 1990s, labor force additions will not remain as

---

[40]Rodolfo A. Bulatao and Gail Richardson, "Fertility and Family Planning in Iran," Middle East and North Africa Discussion Paper Series, No. 13, Washington, D.C.: The World Bank, November 1994.

[41]Central Intelligence Agency, *The World Factbook 2001*, Washington, D.C.: U.S. Government Printing Office, 2001.

[42]Central Inteligence Agency, 2001.

high for as long as they will elsewhere in the region (although increasing female labor force participation could change this). However, today between 720,000 and 850,000 new workers enter the labor force every year.

Employment creation has not come close to keeping pace. Unemployment rose from 10 percent in the early 1980s to 25 percent today.[43] Over two-thirds of all new jobs created since the revolution have been in the public sector. More than 80 percent of all college graduates in the country work for the state. Iran displays all the usual regional symptoms of high and rising unemployment of semi-educated young people. Some analysts believe that over half of the Iranian population lives in poverty.[44] A GDP growth rate of 6.7 percent per year is necessary to provide jobs to new labor-force entrants—that is, just to keep the already high level of unemployment from rising. The economy has not yet remotely approached such an achievement.

These failures need to be weighed against the apparent increase in consumption per capita of various foodstuffs in urban areas, the apparent narrowing of rural-urban income gaps, increases in enrollment ratios, increases in male (and especially female) literacy, the decline in fertility, and reductions in infant and child mortality. The only way to explain the combination of falling incomes per capita and increasing consumption of food is to posit an increase in the equality of income distribution, in which a higher share went to people with a higher marginal propensity to consume food. Consumption of food, water, and energy is very generously subsidized, consuming some 15 to 20 percent of GDP.[45] A plausible characterization of Iran under the mullahs is "shared poverty."

As Amouzegar and others point out, however, other evidence contradicts the picture of rising equality.[46] Perhaps the consumption

---

[43]As usual, estimates of unemployment vary widely, from 14 to 25 percent.

[44]Central Intelligence Agency, 2001.

[45]Jahangit Amouzegar, "Khatami and the Iranian Economy at Midterm," *Middle East Journal*, Vol. 53, No. 4, Autumn 1999.

[46]Jahangit Amouzegar, *Iran's Economy Under the Islamic Republic*, London and New York: I. B. Tauris, 1993; Eliyahu Kanofsky, *The Middle East Economies: The Impact of*

figures have been doctored for political purposes, or perhaps national income accounts are faulty because as much as 40 percent of Iranian national income is produced in the underground economy.[47] During the past decade, income gaps have been widened, for three reasons: the emergence of crony capitalism, thanks to the half-hearted and ill-conceived "reforms" under Rafsanjani; a vast, hugely expensive subsidy system (some 15 to 20 percent of GDP), 87 percent of which accrues to the (relatively richer) cities; and a system of multiple exchange rates, which offers great scope for corruption.[48]

Both the revolution itself and the Iran-Iraq war greatly stimulated the centralization of economic decisionmaking and led to the creation of statist, command-economy-style allocation mechanisms. The government implemented price controls, rationing of consumer goods, a deliberately overvalued exchange rate, strict quantitative regulation of imports, and tight controls over banking. The government also constructed the familiar regulatory maze for private investors, who needed to obtain numerous permits. Nationalization was written into the Constitution, as were far-reaching subsidy and welfare measures.

Some 580 companies were nationalized in the wake of the revolution. These were all medium- to large-scale enterprises. Like most developing countries, Iran displays marked industrial dualism, in which a large number of very small firms coexist with a much smaller number of medium- and large-scale enterprises. This division also coincides with a "private-public" split. All large industries, and the large majority of medium-scale enterprises, are run by the public institutions, particularly the *bonyad*, or "foundations," which were set up during the revolution. These entities own some 20 percent of the country's assets, contribute 10 percent of GDP, and are strongholds of the most conservative elements of the clergy.[49] The largest of these, *Bonyad Mostazafan* (Foundation of the Oppressed), owns some 400 companies distributed in most industries and tolerates no

---

Domestic and International Politics, Begin-Sadat Center for Strategic Studies, Bar-Ilan University, Israel, 1998.

[47]Amouzegar, 1999.

[48]Amouzegar, 1999.

[49]Biijan Khajehpour, "Domestic Political Reforms and Private Sector Activity in Iran," *Social Research,* Summer 2000.

competition. This entirely unaccountable institution owns perhaps 25 percent of the non-oil economy. The public industrial sector suffers from mismanagement and overstaffing; it incurred losses in fiscal 1997 and 1998 of some $15.6 billion.[50]

Unsurprisingly, performance has been poor. Manufacturing output stagnated during the 1980s (actually declining at a rate of 0.1 percent per year). Some industries fared far worse than this: Automobile production in 1992 was only 15 percent of the pre-1979 level. Growth revived during the 1989–1992 period, when the manufacturing sector grew at double-digit rates. However, much of this growth was capital intensive and absorbed less than 10 percent of the new entrants to the labor force during this period. More recently, industrial growth has improved somewhat and is estimated at 4.4 percent.[51] The policy mix (labor laws, overvalued exchange rates, subsidized credit) increases industrial capital intensity and reduces the employment elasticity of growth.

This poor performance is due to the revolution itself and to the usual problems of statist, inward-oriented policies. The revolution and ensuing war may be blamed for political interference (particularly by the *komitehs*), labor strikes, exodus of managerial skills, and electrical power shortages. Inward-oriented policies such as tariffs and a grossly overvalued exchange rate insulated firms from competition, permitting inefficiency to flourish and creating a vested interest in the continuation of these policies. It is easy to understand why one of the cornerstones of both Rafsanjani's and Khatami's reform policies has been privatization. As we shall see, however, progress here has been minimal, despite a decade of rhetoric.

Agriculture performed rather better. Agricultural output increased by 54 percent from 1980 to 1990. Growth in the early 1990s was also strong, reaching 4.9 percent between 1991 and 1995.[52] However, most of this growth was the result of expansion in acreage, not increases in yields. Fertilizer consumption rose by one-third, and the number of tractors roughly tripled. Such a pattern of technological

---

[50]Amouzegar, 1999.

[51]Central Intelligence Agency, *The World Factbook 2001*.

[52]Food and Agriculture Organization, 2001.

change is roughly compatible with increases in land areas dominating increases in crop yields as sources of growth.

In recent years, Iranian agriculture and rural society have been devastated by the worst drought in a generation. More than half of the population has been affected, and rural to urban migration has accelerated. The southeast of the country (Sistan-Baluchistan) has been the hardest hit, but all 28 provinces have felt the effects of drought. The government estimates that 12.4 million acres of farmland have been ruined. In 1999 agricultural output fell by 6 percent. The drought's impact on both rural and urban areas has been exacerbated by serious mismanagement of water resources. Drinking water is rationed in more than 30 cities, while no one, either in farms or cities, has any incentive to use water efficiently. Reform of water resources management poses yet another pressing challenge to Iranian policymakers.

Agricultural growth before the drought was partly due to the Pahlevi inheritance, especially in large multipurpose dams and primary irrigation channels, and partly due to the government's own policies. The government offered very generous subsidies to cereal producers: Wheat producers received subsidies equal to 80 percent of the cost of production and the government purchased 85 percent of the crop.

These policies had the goals of pumping oil money into rural areas and achieving food self-sufficiency. The first seems to have succeeded. Although larger farmers received the lion's share of the benefits (as in the United States), smaller farmers also benefited. The second goal was not attained, however. Demand outstripped domestic supply, and imports continued to supply about 25 percent of consumption.

Such self-sufficiency drives always entail the usual negative consequences of the distortions in relative prices. The creation of a government monopoly in grain trading reduced efficiency. Very heavily subsidized cereal prices encouraged the plowing up of marginal land formerly used for livestock grazing. This not only reduced livestock productivity but also contributed to soil erosion, which, in turn, has accelerated the silting up of reservoirs and undermined some traditional farming systems for managing rangelands. The policy mix also encouraged overpumping of groundwater, damaging aquifers. The folly of neglecting agriculture under the Pahlevis has been replaced by unsustainable subsidization and relative price distortion under the mullahs. Meanwhile, the decline in public agricultural investment to one-third of its earlier level has created substantial backlogs for rehabilitation and maintenance of existing structures.

Part of the reason why the regime failed to achieve self-sufficiency was the gross mismanagement of the exchange rate. The exchange rate affects the relative price of every single good and service in the economy. The government's management of the rial was very poor until quite recently. Until 1989–1990, the exchange regime was tightly controlled and very complex, with some 12 different exchange rates. Although reform in 1991 simplified the system to three rates and reduced controls, in 1993 the free market price of foreign exchange was 20 times higher than the official rate (in 1982 it was twice as high). This gap has since been reduced as the Central Bank closely watched the illegal curb rate and tried to adjust its policy accordingly, particularly during 1999–2000. One of the rates was abolished, and the gap last year between the Tehran Stock Exchange (TSE) rate and the market rate fell from 40 percent to 2 percent.[53] This favorable development was entirely due to the effect of increased oil prices on the budget; structural weaknesses have remained largely untouched.

In general, the Islamists in Iran increased the centralization of the economy, redistributed income toward the poor and the rural areas, instituted unsustainable welfare and agricultural policies, and mismanaged the macroeconomy. Above all, they have failed to meet the challenge of job creation. Private investment has not been enticed into job-creating production of labor-intensive goods and services. Private economic agents continue to view the regime's commitment to a market economy with considerable, and well-justified, skepticism. Today, after over a decade of lip service to reform, the economy remains stagnant.

Several interlinked forces account for the stasis of Iranian economic policy. The Islamic Republic of Iran has always rested on a coalition of groups with disparate economic interests. The coalition included

---

[53]International Monetary Fund, 1996.

populist, unemployed or underemployed youth and students, urban *lumpens*, conservative *bazaaris*, *mullahs*, and segments of the professional middle class. At the time of the revolution, the opposition to the Shah seems to have been as widespread as Polish opposition to Communist rule. Like Solidarity, the initial coalition led by Khomeini was a very large tent indeed. Over time, it seems to have narrowed, but the regime still rests on an uneasy alliance of two very different sets of interests: populist lower and lower-middle classes, and prosperous mullahs and those with whom they do business.

More specifically, Amouzegar discerns two main groups of political actors: radicals, a grouping of "economically dependent radical *mullahs* (of mainly poor, provincial origin) and . . . left-wing elements infiltrating the high ranks of the bureaucracy"; and conservatives, with "strong financial and blood ties to the *bazaar* (who) have tended to represent the interests of landlords and the urban bourgeoisie," on the other.[54] Amouzegar also discerns the pragmatists, which arose after Khomeini's death, who "also have close affiliations with the wealthy, but . . . have mainly *managed* and handled national wealth rather than *owned* it."[55] This last group is the core of support for "reform mongering."

The interests of each of the regime's two core supporters are institutionalized in the system of subsidies and welfare (for the popular classes) and in the *bonyad* (for the richer mullahs), often joined by wealthy bazaaris, who enjoy monopoly power as holders of quotas and licenses. These two interlinked, powerful groups are classic "rent seekers," who obstruct change.

Change has also been impeded by the structure of political institutions. Article 44 of the Iranian constitution reads, "The economy of the Islamic Republic of Iran is to consist of three sectors: state, cooperative and private, and is to be based on systematic and sound planning. The state sector is to include all large-scale and mother (sic) industries . . ."[56] The weakness of both the president and the Majlis further impedes reform. In essence, any act of the Majlis or

---

[54]Amouzegar, 1993, p. 32.

[55]Amouzegar, 1993, p. 32.

[56]Khajehpour, 2000.

decree of the president can be overturned by the supreme leader, Ayatollah Khamenei.   Further, the *bonyad* are explicitly excluded from the purview of the Majlis. Finally, the composition of the Majlis has impeded change. Consider this recent incident:

> the Guardian Council, which vets parliamentary legislation, rejected most privatizations under Khatami's five-year development plan as unconstitutional.   Earlier, parliament had blocked key market-oriented elements in the plan on the grounds that the poor would suffer. Among the setbacks to the planned privatizations were votes to maintain government control on banks and insurance companies, allowing limited room for private activities in these sectors. The new moves also undermine government efforts to end the state's monopoly on airlines, the railways and other transport systems as well as telecommunications, water and power.[57]

Khatami has not provided strong leadership on economic reform. This is partly because of his background and interests (he knows essentially nothing about economics), and partly because his main political program is social and political. Khatami seeks, above all, to strengthen Iranian civil society, to improve its relations with the outside world, to liberalize the political system, and to expand the scope of personal choice for ordinary Iranians. Given the strength of the vested interests, which oppose this program, and his weak hand, thanks to the constitutional power of the supreme leader, he has not focused strongly on economic policy. Further, his coalition for a freer and stronger Iranian civil society includes many who hold traditional socialist views on the economy.

Two final considerations may be noted. First, Khatemi's program for enhanced rule of law is an essential prerequisite to a reform program that would produce a sustainable growth in living standards. Privatization of the *bonyad* in the current institutional environment would almost certainly simply change the specific form of crony capitalism, rather than stimulate any real gains in productivity. Unaccountable and corrupt private monopolies would simply replace the current unaccountable and corrupt monopolies of the semi-public *bonyad*. Second, the pressure to reform the economy is becoming steadily stronger (although the increase in oil prices since 1999 has bought

---

[57]Reuters, March 6, 2000.

some time). The regime is acutely aware that the disaffection of the young continues to grow.

The configuration of interests, the institutional structure, and the nature of leadership suggest that reform will continue to be desultory. One consolation for American policymakers is that, by contrast with all of the other countries analyzed here, such failures will certainly not benefit religious fanatics. Indeed, the failures will probably simply increase the already palpable contempt with which the mullahs are held by large numbers of youth.[58]

SAUDI ARABIA

The Kingdom of Saudi Arabia faces many of the same problems as other countries of the region. It has a large, bloated bureaucracy and public sector, a very high rate of population growth and a consequently young population, a high rate of youth unemployment, serious water shortages, and periodic budgetary difficulties. It has also embraced various aspects of economic reform, such as macroeconomic austerity, subsidy cuts, and privatization plans. As a classic "mono-crop" exporter, the Kingdom also seeks to diversify its economy. In all of this, the Kingdom is very similar to many other developing countries.

At the same time, of course, Saudi Arabia is radically different from the other states considered here. Any state is unique, but, to paraphrase George Orwell, some states are more unique than others. Two factors place the Kingdom in a "category of one": the oil economy and the structures of governance. The Kingdom has roughly one-fourth of the oil reserves on the planet. Not only is its production capacity of roughly 10.5 million barrels a day one of the highest in the world, but also it can vary its production from 10 to 3 million barrels a day. This high but variable production capacity gives Saudi Arabia great influence within the Organization of Petroleum Exporting Countries (OPEC) and in the world oil market. Given the highly inelastic demand function for oil in the short run, the Kingdom enjoys some market power over short-run oil prices. Saudi Arabia

---

[58]Eric Rouleau, "Iran's 'Referendum for Democracy,'" *Le Monde Diplomatique,* June 2001.

therefore has some ability to change the government's revenues—in the short run. Oil exports dominate the economy, accounting for 90 to 95 percent of Saudi export earnings, 75 percent of the budget, and about 35 to 40 percent of GDP.[59]

Several consequences follow from these simple facts of oil. The Kingdom's revenues depend upon the fortunes of the oil market, and although the government enjoys a degree of market power over these prices, such market power is limited by both demand and supply side forces. On the demand side, the Saudis learned to their cost the consequences of overshooting what for them would be a desirable oil price in the early 1980s, when high prices stimulated considerable conservation measures. The demand for oil is a derived demand; final demand is therefore mediated by technology. (For any final demand for, say, transportation miles, the resulting demand for oil depends on the energy-efficiency of, say, automobiles.) High prices also induce technological change on the supply side, particularly in exploration and extraction. Saudi oil market power, although real, is limited.

Long-run trends on both the demand and the supply sides imply a steady deterioration of both Saudi market power and the reliability of oil revenues for the Kingdom over the long run. Very large gains in automobile engine efficiency by using fuel cells and other technologies are no longer pipe dreams. Hybrid cars are already on the market and get 48–60 miles per gallon. Many analysts expect that much greater advances will be seen within the decade. Similar savings from efficiency are expected in other areas. One need not agree with all of former oil minister Shaykh Ahmad Zaki Yamani's forecast to understand why the Kingdom of Saudi Arabia is concerned to diversify its economy.[60]

---

[59]United States Embassy in Riyadh, "Saudi Arabia: 2001 Economic Trends," May 2000.

[60]"On the supply side it is easy to find oil and produce it. And on the demand side there are so many new technologies. The hybrid engines will cut gasoline consumption by something like 30 percent. . . . Thirty years from now, there is no problem with oil. Oil will be left in the ground. The Stone Age came to an end not because we had a lack of stones, and the Oil Age will come to an end not because we have a lack of oil." CBS News, June 25, 2000, available at http://cbsnews.com/now/story/0percent2C1597percent2C209367-412percent2C00.shtml.

Accomplishing such diversification is, of course, very difficult. It is impeded by the structure of the labor force, by work habits, and by the structures of governance. The forms of governance are the second feature setting the Kingdom apart from all other states. Although there are different perspectives on the Kingdom's political economy, one persuasive "optic" is that of Islamic familialism.[61] The Kingdom is governed by the House of Saud, which has an estimated 6,000 to 10,000 princes.[62] The royal family is allied by marriage to virtually every significant familial (sometimes called "tribal") grouping in the country. The resulting webs of relations are complex and often opaque to outsiders. Fandy persuasively argues that such linkages imply that the royal family is both inside of the state and outside of it, located in the middle of a (familial-based) civil society. The dense network of personal and marriage ties are important for patronage and support, as well as for other, more symbolic modes of mutual influence.

Crucially, all of this is tied together by loyalty to Wahhabi Islam. Although, of course, the oil-rich Eastern Province contains significant numbers of Shi'a, one of the fundamental structures of rule of the Kingdom is the alliance of the House of Saud with "*ulama*" of the Wahhabi school of Hanbali jurisprudence. The enormous prestige afforded by the Saudi role as "Protector of the Two Holy Places" (Mecca and Medina) is both used and defended by the ruling elite; it also forms the basis of challenges from opposition elements. The regime will go to great lengths to protect its reputation as an Islamic state. Any policy decision must be defensible in Wahhabi Islamic terms.

A second useful view of the Saudi political economy is provided by the "rentier state" perspective.[63] Oil revenues are largely economic

---

[61]This concept is developed in detail and used persuasively to analyze opposition movements in the Kingdom by Mamoun Fandy, *Saudi Arabia and the Politics of Dissent,* 1999.

[62]Daryl Champion, "The Kingdom of Saudi Arabia: Elements of Instability Within Stability," *Middle East Review of International Affairs Journal,* Vol. 3, No. 4, December 1999.

[63]See Chaudhry, *The Price of Wealth,* 1997; Rayed Khalid Krimly, "The Political Economy of Rentier States: A Case Study of Saudi Arabia in the Oil Era: 1950–1990," Ph.D. dissertation, Department of Political Science, George Washington University, 1993.

rent, and the production process is both state-owned and highly capital-intensive. Consequently, state revenues are largely independent of local people, whether as producers or taxpayers. Such rents free the state from some (but certainly not all) of the domestic pressures that confront less geologically fortunate states. The presence of rents thus allows the state to deflect pressures for more accountable governance. The logic continues that when rents decline, the state faces greater pressure to reform.

The Development of a State-Centered Political Economy

With some 65 percent of GDP in the hands of the state, the Saudi government dominates the formal economy. State economic prominence was an important consequence of the oil boom of the 1970s and early 1980s. The civil service grew from 13,000 in 1962 to 232,000 in 1981, to which we should add another 81,000 part-time or nonclassified employees.[64] Saudi Arabia established a giant public-enterprise sector, with more than 40 corporations in housing, storage, agriculture, and the Saudi Basic Industries Corporation (SABIC). In the plan period 1976 to 1980 alone, Saudi Arabia disbursed $290 billion, which went into infrastructure, port development, and new industrial cities at Jubail and Yanbu. The 1980–1985 development plan, although less spectacularly funded, was designed to put Saudi Arabia on an industrial footing. Then–oil minister Yamani prophesied that Saudi Arabia would soon rank alongside Argentina, Brazil, and South Korea as a semi-industrialized country. The airline, the telecommunications system, and many other infrastructures are all managed and owned by the public sector.

The government also implemented sweeping welfare policies. As usual, these were designed to bolster regime legitimacy and to distribute the oil wealth among the various, complicated familial networks. Also as usual, such subsidies induced serious distortions in the economy and created grave difficulties for future development. Consider farm subsidies. Saudi Arabia paid farmers from five to six times the international price of wheat during the early 1980s, while simultaneously subsidizing inputs; the effective rate of protection

---

[64]Nazih Ayyoubi, "Arab Bureaucracies: Expanding Size, Changing Roles," Department of Politics, University of Exeter, England, unpublished manuscript, 1985.

(the combined impact of protected output prices and subsidized inputs) may have reached 1,500 percent in the late 1980s.[65] Saudi government loans to farmers rose from under $5 million in 1971 to over $1 billion in 1983; from 1980 to 1985 the Saudi government spent some $20 billion on agriculture, mostly in the form of subsidies.[66] The results were spectacular for the key food-security crop: At an estimated cost of $2.12 billion in subsidies, the Kingdom became the world's sixth largest wheat exporter. Production rose by more than 700 percent from 1971 to 1983, entirely replacing imports and actually creating a small export surplus.

Critically, nearly 90 percent (13.3 of 15.3 cubic kilometers) of agricultural water was deep aquifer fossil water. At the 1990 rate of abstraction, usable reserves were estimated to last for a maximum of 25 to 30 years. Fortunately, budgetary concerns greatly reduced these subsidies during the fiscal crunch of the early 1990s. From 1992 to 1995 subsidies to wheat producers fell more than half ($850 million, down from $1.87 billion in 1993). However, with more than 45,000 private and nearly 5,000 multiuse public wells, farmers seem to have simply shifted away from wheat into fruits and vegetables. Although the efficiency of water use has increased as a consequence, groundwater depletion, stimulated by "food security" fears, continues.[67]

Pressures for Reform

Pressures for reform first emerged in the late 1980s and have continued to be strong. A rapidly growing population, a stagnant economy, and burgeoning public deficits have generated the impetus for policy change. At the peak of oil prices in the early 1980s, the population of the Kingdom was slightly over 10 million. Today it stands at nearly 23 million and will rise to at least 30 million by the end of this decade. In 1986 per capita GNP stood at some $16,500. Today it is about $6,000. The sluggish growth of the economy, far below the rate of population growth (3.4 percent from 1990 to 1999), has also been

---

[65]Peter W. Wilson and Douglas F. Graham, *Saudi Arabia: The Coming Storm*, New York: M. E. Sharpe & Co., 1994.

[66]*Economist*, April 6, 1985, pp. 80–83.

[67]"AQUASTAT: Saudi Arabia," Food and Agriculture Organization, 1997, at http://www.fao.org/waicent/faoinfo/agricult/agl/aglw/aquastat/sauarab.htm.

quite incapable of providing jobs for the rapidly growing numbers of Saudi youth. Some 100,000 young Saudis enter the labor market each year. Only half of them find jobs in either the public or private sectors.[68] Unemployment is high, as shown earlier in Table 3.1. This problem will remain pressing for decades. Due to cultural norms and to the difficulty of women finding employment outside of the home (Saudi women constitute only 6 percent of the national labor force), the average Saudi woman will have between six and seven children during her lifetime (TFR = 6.4). Over 50 percent of the population is under 18. The labor force will therefore continue to grow rapidly in the coming decades. Providing jobs for these young people is an urgent spur to economic policy change.

During the oil boom, the government had provided most of the jobs. However, this has long since ceased to be possible, and for several years there has been a ban on new civil service jobs. Since 75 percent of government revenue comes from oil sales, the low prices of the past 15 years have tightly constrained government action. The government first began running deficits in 1984; two years later, they had reached 20 percent of GDP, a clearly unsustainable level. Austerity has since reduced deficits to more macroeconomically manageable levels, but deficits persist (See Table 3.2). Such deficits, in the face of the rising "youth bulge," constitute another pressing goad

Table 3.2

Budgetary Deficit as a Percentage of GDP

Year	Percentage of GDP
1996	−3.7
1997	−2.9
1998	−9.5
1999	−6.5
2000	+7.5
2001	0.0 (estimate)

SOURCE: U.S. Embassy, Riyadh, http:// usembassy.state.gov/riyadh/wwwhet01.html

---

[68]United States Embassy in Riyadh, "Saudi Arabia: 2001 Economic Trends."

for economic reform. It is widely understood throughout the Kingdom that only a thriving, rapidly growing private sector can provide the necessary jobs. The government hopes that policy changes will facilitate such a process.

The budgetary deficit has led to the accumulation of substantial government indebtedness. At the end of 1999, public-sector debt exceeded 120 percent of GDP, central government debt was some 115 percent of GDP, and parastatal losses were about 5 percent of GDP.[69] Such debt is mainly financed by two large pension funds, funds that now have much cash, thanks to the low number of retirees relative to workers. However, growing interest payments on the debt are crowding out other expenditures. In common with most governments, austerity has hit capital budgets far harder than recurrent expenditures. In consequence, the construction industry has been depressed for years, and the aging infrastructure is not being updated and replaced.

The government officially denies the existence of unemployment. The government argues that since there are some 5 million foreign workers in the Kingdom, and since Saudis could allegedly fill those places, unemployment does not exist. At best, this is a semantic quibble; more likely, it is simply wrong. Many, perhaps most, of the jobs now occupied by foreigners would not or could not be filled by Saudis, at least not yet. At the low end of the job market, and as in advanced industrial countries, throughout the Gulf foreign workers do the hard, difficult, and dirty jobs that nationals disdain. Saudis are no more likely to sweep streets in Riyadh and Jeddah than native-born Californians are to do so in San Francisco or Los Angeles. This is highly unlikely to change. It is not necessary to posit a "mudir syndrome," although such a phenomenon may well exist.[70] It is simply that, as Piore persuasively argued, jobs provide not only a wage and salary, but also an identity and a social status.[71] At the

---

[69]The government also has a foreign debt of some $26.3 billion; however, this is only about 33 percent of exports. Unlike some of the other countries reviewed in this chapter, the Kingdom has no "debt overhang" problem.

[70]The phrase comes from Champion. *Mudir* means "director" in Arabic; the idea is that Saudis want to be managers, brokers, or bosses, not workers.

[71]Michael J. Piore, *Birds of Passage: Migrant Labor and Industrial Societies*, Cambridge and New York: Cambridge University Press, 1979.

higher end of the market, many Saudis continue to lack sufficient skills to replace foreigners. This is now changing, but the process of transition will not be swift.

The difficulties here may be seen in the performance of the Saudi government's "Saudi-ization" of the workforce. The government has promulgated decrees enjoining private businesses to increase the percentage of Saudis on their payroll by 5 percent per year. This target has not been met, and employers have resisted. Both foreign and local employers say they cannot find Saudis with suitable training. Privately, they also complain that few Saudis have the kind of work ethic that they wish to see in their employees. There is evidence that the pressure of unemployment has, over time, been a force for change. Saudis are now found as receptionists, as kitchen staff, and hotel staff. But as one employer said, "Immigrants cost less, do as they are told, arrive on time and are prepared to work six days a week."[72] Social mores and habits may change, but they do so slowly. Such mores, then, constitute one barrier to successful reform.

Further Obstacles to the Reform Process

Apart from fairly successful programs of macroeconomic stabilization, Saudi reform efforts to date have concentrated on opening local capital markets to foreign participation, revising laws affecting foreign investment, privatization, and Saudi accession to the WTO. Each faces a variety of difficulties and obstacles. Since banking is widely considered the strongest element of the private sector, the first and second components of reform may have some promise. However, the government has promulgated new rules permitting foreign ownership of mutual funds, which has improved banks' profitability. The government has yet to follow up such changes with permission for foreigners to invest in the Saudi stock exchange. The Saudi market, with a capitalization of some $60 billion, is the largest in the region, but only 76 firms are traded, and the ratio of capitalization to GDP is lower than in some neighboring countries (such as Egypt). Although "Washington Consensus" advocates claim that

---

[72]Alain Gresh, "The World Invades Saudi Arabia," *Le Monde Diplomatique*, April 2000.

further liberalization of the stock market will boost growth,[73] there is little reason to suppose that Saudi firms will discontinue their German style of finance, getting most of their capital from reinvested profits and from banks to which they may be closely linked by familial ties.

In common with other countries of the region, there has been much rhetoric about privatization. As elsewhere, the gap between talk and action is wide. Large state monopolies, including ARAMCO, SABIC, STC, and SEC, dominate the economy. The American embassy reports that the privatization effort to date "has been largely limited to allowing private firms to take on certain service functions . . . which complement the work of still dominant state agencies."[74] But so far, "there has not been a single sale of existing assets, with a transfer of management control, in any state corporation." The Kingdom recently explored the idea of privatizing some shares of the Saudi Telephone Company. After much talk, and various missions, the government shelved the plan.

The government has been equally slow to change the rules governing foreign private investment or to alter the rules of business behavior more generally. The usual maze of controls prevails, and the private sector is heavily dependent on the state for access, information, and capital. Estimates of the amount of offshore funds held by Saudis range from $300 billion[75] to $600–$700 billion.[76] Some of these funds are no doubt held abroad as part of a perfectly sensible diversification and risk-diffusion investment strategy by very wealthy agents. But some of it stays abroad because of the lack of profitable investment opportunities at home.

There may be sound political reasons why the government resists the urging of American and World Bank/IMF economists on privatization and deregulation. Fundamentally, such changes, unless carried out very carefully and gradually, could easily be politically destabiliz-

---

[73]See United States Embassy in Riyadh, "Saudi Arabia: 2001 Economic Trends."

[74]United States Embassy in Riyadh, "Saudi Arabia: 2001 Economic Trends."

[75]Jean François Seznec, "The Perils of Privatization in the Gulf," Lecture at Center for Contemporary Arab Studies, Georgetown University, Washington, D.C., March 19, 2001. See http://www.ccasonline.org/publicaffairs/Seznec3192001.htm.

[76]United States Embassy in Riyadh, "Saudi Arabia: 2001 Economic Trends."

ing. There are echoes of each of the earlier case studies here. As in Egypt, the government does not want to launch any sudden changes that might add to existing unemployment. As in Jordan, the government has used the state sector as a political balancing mechanism. Some, including Seznec, argue that King Fahd deliberately split the government between the royal family, which controls the ministries of interior and defense, and the nonroyal civil service, which controls the ministries of finance and petroleum. Such a move, he argues, helps to restrict the power of the princes, whose behavior is often perceived to be un-Islamic, greedy, and, therefore, destabilizing. In this view, the civil service sees itself as defending nonroyal Saudis. Open privatization would permit the many hugely wealthy princes to reenter areas where they now have relatively little influence. In short, privatization could easily lead to a kind of "crony capitalism," in this case, led by wealthy princes. Given the undercurrent of Islamist opposition to the regime, it may be unsurprising that the government moves very slowly in this arena. And as in Iran, an entrenched phalanx of vested interests blocks reform. Serious reform not only would weaken the civil service, it would also require substantially reducing the vast subsidies and perquisites extended to the princes.

Finally, Saudi accession to the WTO carries peril as well as promise. Embracing globalization is, to say the least, politically tricky, given the political structure of Islamic familialism. The fundamental difficulty is simple: The rules of the WTO clash with the Wahhabi interpretation of *shari'ah* at many points. In Saudi Arabia, as elsewhere, regime opponents warn of a "cultural invasion." WTO accession is likely to strain the House of Saud-Wahhabi "ulama" alliance. American trade negotiators too often provide handy propaganda for local Islamists. Demanding that Saudi Arabia open cinemas, for example, is a classic case of U.S. domestic lobbies pushing their own interests to the detriment of U.S. national security. The U.S. embassy asserts that accession to the WTO will "result in an open, transparent, and rules-based trade regime." It is far more likely that Saudi Arabia will continue to move very slowly and gradually, walking the razor's edge between economic stagnation and culturally and politically destabilizing reform. The House of Saud has done this with great skill for several generations. Whether it can continue to do so in the face of unprecedented pressures such as the youth bulge and globalization, remains to be seen.

SYRIA

Syria suffers from many of the same economic difficulties as other states in the region. It has a burgeoning population, a very rapidly growing labor force, and a large external debt. The sprawling, Soviet-style, state-dominated economy fails to provide jobs and to attract investment. Exports are dominated by oil, whose price also affects the country through its impact on neighboring countries, which both employ Syrian expatriate workers and contribute substantial foreign aid to Syria. The country's agriculture remains heavily dependent upon highly variable rainfall, which subjects the economy and society to periodic violent negative shocks by drought. Syria is plagued by the usual environmental problems: unsustainable extraction of groundwater, pollution of aquifers and rivers, increasingly severe urban water shortages, and desertification. In many ways, Syria's problems are typical of those of most countries in the region.

Syria's claim to uniqueness is that it may have done the least to reform its economy of all the countries considered here. Syrian reforms have never involved any significant involvement from either the IMF or the World Bank. Syrian reforms have been almost entirely homegrown; although this could easily be a positive feature, in practice Syrian reforms have been marginal at best. The explanations for the absence of reform are far from unique, however. The strength of entrenched interests and the regime's power base have both combined with the presence of substantial rents to retard the pace of reform. Syria provides a classic case of dilatory reform.

Like many other countries in the region, the pressures for more substantial change remain strong, and may be gathering force. Although strong vested interests remain unchallenged, rents, particularly oil rents, have proved weaker during the late 1990s than in the first half of the decade. Some additional pressure for reform may therefore be expected, in much the same pattern as occurred during the late 1980s (see below). If oil prices remain steady, and if, as expected, they decline over the next decade, then Syria, whose reserves of oil are already dwindling, may face more serious pressure to reform.

Predicting oil prices is, of course, an extremely tricky business. This is much less true for predicting future job needs for the Syrian economy. Some 200,000 young Syrians enter the labor force every year. The labor force is growing by 4 percent per year, fully five times faster than the labor force of the United States, and ten times faster than the labor force of the EU. This growth will not decelerate for at least a decade. It is estimated that the country will need $4 billion of investment to provide enough jobs over the coming decade; in 1999, however, the country received only $47 million in foreign investment.[77]

Some of the strength of the economy may be traced to the country's relatively strong agricultural sector, which accounts for 29 percent of the GDP and employs 40 percent of the labor force. The sector contributes 14 percent of exports, and provides inputs for the country's principal non-oil manufactures (textiles, tobacco, food processing, leather, and beverages). Such industries provide perhaps 50 percent of total manufacturing employment. From 1986 to 1996, agricultural output increased by 30 percent, a very respectable performance, given that 80 percent of cropland is nonirrigated. Although the sector has been subjected to some of the same controls as the rest of the economy, farmers were never squeezed to the same extent in Syria as they were, for example, in prereform Egypt. Part of the explanation for the better treatment of the farm sector is that the base of support of the Baathist regime lies in part with rural notables, particularly in minority areas, but also among the Sunni majority.[78]

The Syrian leadership has shown considerable skill in using both economic and strategic rents to protect the fundamental structures of its economic rule. Syria's principal export is petroleum (65 percent of total value in 1998). The country has been able to attract substantial remittance flows from its workers abroad and has managed to entice the return of some Syrian capital held abroad. Thanks

---

[77]Bank of Beirut and the Arab Countries, *Economic Report*, 3rd Quarter, Beirut: BBAC, 2000.

[78]Raymond Hinnebusch, *Peasant and Bureaucracy in Bàthist Syria: The Political Economy of Rural Development*, Boulder, Colo., and London: Westview Press, 1989.

to its skillful manipulation of regional politics, the country has managed to attract substantial foreign assistance from the Gulf states. Syria's participation in the Gulf War coalition was rewarded throughout the 1990s by the Gulf states. Finally, Syria's de facto occupation of Lebanon has provided additional rents.

Riding the Roller Coaster of Rents

Syrian economic policy has closely mirrored the trends in external rents. During the 1970s, when oil prices were high, the state greatly expanded its role, as Hafez al-Assad used state direction of the economy as one of several ways to consolidate his control of the country. As the inefficiencies and deficiencies of an inward-looking, state-directed economy became apparent, the regime did little until, by the late 1980s, external rents could no longer paper over these structural weaknesses. The government made many pronouncements, and promulgated a few reforms, which were largely aimed at generating non-oil exports. The partial success of these reforms, and the upsurge in strategic rents thanks to Syria's participation in the Gulf War coalition, permitted the regime to avoid deeper, structural reforms throughout the 1990s.

During the oil boom years of the 1970s, Syria under Hafez al-Assad became a classic Arab socialist economy. Between 1970 and 1982, employment in Syria's public-sector enterprises rose from 57,000 to 119,000, or, in the latter year, to half the entire industrial workforce. In just two years the public-sector wage bill doubled, going from 3.5 percent to 6 percent of GDP. In 1979, Syria's total workforce was about 2.1 million, of which about a third were engaged in agriculture. Combined public-sector and civil-service employment probably totaled 350,000. There may have been 230,000 Syrians in uniform and, although there is some overlap with the preceding categories, perhaps 200,000 members of the Ba'ath party.[79] Some 220,000 workers, in both the public and private sectors, were unionized and under Ba'athi supervision. Although the Syrian state's control of the economy was never as systematic as that of the Soviet Union, there were

---

[79]Alisdair Drysdale, "The Asad Regime and Its Troubles," *MERIP Reports*, No. 110, November–December 1982, pp. 3–11.

many parallels, from planning to the dominance of state-owned enterprise, to the ubiquitous secret police.

Such state dominance came at the expense of economic efficiency. The strategic sectors became used to their privileges and to low levels of performance. The state has hesitated to alienate those sectors by asking more of them or paying them less. This was particularly true for the military: In 1981, Syrian defense outlays were 13 percent of GNP, placing it among only ten nations worldwide to spend more than 10 percent of GNP on defense. Inflation and a growing external debt, which grew tenfold between 1970 and 1983 to $2.3 billion, plagued the economy, especially after the Syrian intervention in Lebanon in 1976.

In a manner typical of state-dominated, import-substituting developing countries, Syria was increasingly unable to generate sufficient exports or to maintain adequate levels of investment. Like Egypt, it suffered from the "twin gaps" of rising deficits of both its foreign accounts and government budget. From 1980 to 1988 the current account was in persistent deficit and Syrian involvement in the Lebanese civil war strained the government's budget. The economy grew at 2.4 percent during the decade, well below the rate of population growth.

In this environment, the government promulgated some home-grown reform measures. It is notable that the government did this with essentially no participation from the IMF and the World Bank. Syria has accepted Bank and Fund missions, and has utilized their reports as an input into the policy process, but Syria has never entered into any formal policy dialogue with these institutions. Syria services just enough of its debt to the World Bank to avoid being declared insolvent, but otherwise largely ignores the Bank. Nor has it ever taken out any substantial standby loans from the IMF. International agencies and Western governments have had essentially no leverage over the Syrian state's economic policies.[80]   This is, of course, in marked contrast to Egypt and Jordan.

---

[80]Volker Perthes, *The Political Economy of Syria Under Asad*, London: I. B. Tauris, 1995.

Three factors have permitted Syria to follow such a course. First, the government is sufficiently ruthless and efficient internally that dissent caused by economic hardship has little impact. Few Syrians have forgotten the events in Hama in 1982, when government troops killed an estimated 10,000 citizens to suppress an Islamist uprising. Second, the government has used its strategic position and its foreign policy decisions to acquire alternative sources of finance from Arab sources, and until 1985, from the Soviet Union and the German Democratic Republic. Third, Syria increased its oil exports from the mid-1980s until the present. All of these factors permitted the regime to avoid international loans and the accompanying pressure to embrace the Washington Consensus.

From its inception, the Assad government cultivated wealthy, urban, largely Sunni mercantile interests. Even in the early and middle 1970s, measures such as the creation of several "free zones," liberalization of import restrictions, and encouraging private companies to act as intermediaries between foreign firms and state-owned enterprises helped to consolidate the "Alawite soldier–Sunni merchant" alliance. The government further strengthened this alliance as the regime sought to alleviate the serious foreign exchange crisis, which was created by the current account deficits of the 1980s. In 1983 the government allowed private manufacturers to keep 50 percent of their hard currency earnings from exports for their own imports; in 1987, the percentage was raised to 75 percent, and the classes of goods covered was broadened. The leading scholar of this process, Volker Perthes, notes how these reforms worked primarily by reducing the incentives for smuggling. Draconian legislation against currency smuggling (very lucrative, given the wide gap between market and official rates) merely concentrated operations in the hands of a few, very well connected actors with close ties to the regime.[81] Further liberalizations of currency dealings continued into the 1990s, and the government has consistently tried to move official exchange rates closer to market rates. The differences between "Arab Socialism" and "Mafya-Kapitalism," Russian-style, have blurred considerably in Syria.

---

[81]Perthes, 1995.

The government also sought to improve the trade balance by introducing qualitatively similar piecemeal reforms in the vital agricultural sector. Beginning in the mid-1980s, the government permitted the entry of private agents into agricultural marketing of all except a few strategic goods (cotton, wheat, and sugar-beets). Private exporters of farm goods received favorable exchange rates, and ceilings on farm size were rescinded. Such measures contributed to the very strong performance of Syrian agriculture during the 1980s, when the country also enjoyed good weather.

The results were encouraging. The private-sector share of non-oil imports rose from 25 percent in the mid-1980s to over 63 percent in 1994; private non-oil exports rose from 46 to 78 percent.[82] Homegrown reforms were aimed at the trade balance and helped to reverse the deterioration of the 1980s. Such policy changes simultaneously strengthened the soldier-merchant alliance.

The Limits of Reform

The limits of reform may be seen most clearly with changes in investment rules and regulations. Investment Law No. 10 was promulgated in 1991 to attract investment by both Syrians and foreigners. Under this law, which covered investments of over 10 million LS ($240,000), investors could propose projects in any economic sector. Approved projects are given a seven-year tax holiday, are largely exempt from customs duties and import restrictions, and are granted generous profit and foreign exchange repatriation. The government hoped that such a law would entice sorely needed investment.

It has not happened. As of 1997, exactly one foreign firm (Nestle) has invested in the manufacturing sector.[83] Private Syrians, meanwhile, are estimated to hold more than $25 billion overseas. The government has not seemed unduly concerned, perhaps because rents returned during the 1990s. First, the government collected a handsome dividend for nimbly joining the Gulf War coalition. Unofficial

---

[82]Paul Rivlin, *Economic Policy and Performance in the Arab World,* Boulder, Colo., and London: Lynne Rienner, 2001.

[83]"Syria Now," *Middle East Economic Digest,* May 16, 1997, pp. 14–18.

estimates of the resulting aid are some \$4–5 billion.[84] Second, oil production rose strongly as exploration brought new sources of oil on line. Output increased from 160,000 barrels per day in 1985 to 610,000 bpd ten years later. For the past seven years, oil has amounted to nearly two-thirds of Syrian exports. The strengthening of oil prices during the past several years has provided further rents. Third, the Syrian economy has reaped considerable "protection rents" from its de facto occupation of Lebanon. One million Syrians, perhaps one-seventh of the labor force, work in Lebanon, and they send home between \$1 and \$2 billion a year. Lebanese businessmen make substantial payments to the Syrian army, Syrian businessmen find many profitable opportunities in Lebanon, and Lebanon provides many consumer goods that ease the life of many a Syrian. Finally, although there is little reliable information, it is widely believed that some prominent Syrians profit from the narcotics business, based in the Beka'a valley in Lebanon.

Syria, like Iran and Saudi Arabia, has implemented few of the Washington Consensus prescriptions. There has been liberalization of the trade sector and improved macroeconomic management, but very little relaxation of government control. Notions of a "level playing field" and "accountable governance" are quite ludicrous in the Syrian context. Syria remains a closely controlled dictatorship, with the levers of power firmly in the hands of the Alawite officer corps. This classic "neo-Mamluk" regime enjoys the support of a substantial segment of the Sunni merchant elite and of peasant notables, as well as the core support of the Alawite minority and military officer corps.[85] Such support, combined with rents, has permitted the regime to fend off any pressures for deeper reforms.

Further reforms may emerge under Bashar Asad. As before, the driver will probably be any downturn in rents. There are some reasons to expect such a change. As elsewhere, oil prices will be crucial. If they decline, the government will once again be under considerable pressure. Whatever happens to oil prices, Syrian oil reserves are small, and production is expected to decline by the middle of the

---

[84]Kanofsky, 1998.

[85]Richard Bulliet, "Twenty Years of Islamic Politics," *Middle East Journal*, Vol. 53, No. 2, Spring 1999.

decade. Population and the labor force will continue to grow. The pressure on the regime is likely to increase. But it is much too early to rule out a continuation of business as usual in Syria. The regime's power base is strong, its ruthlessness unmatched. Syria has found ways in the past to collect strategic rents and thereby avoid reform. It may find ways to continue to do so.

IMPLICATIONS

There is both good and bad news for governments in the basic picture presented above. On the positive side, the same economic development strategy that would successfully manage the growth/ poverty/employment problem—increased reliance on private-sector-led export growth—would simultaneously provide adequate food security at the national level. Countries that can plausibly reform their macroeconomies by balancing budgets, maintaining realistic exchange rates, dismantling excessive regulations, and promoting exports have at least a fighting chance of coping with these varied socioeconomic challenges.

From a U.S. policy perspective, the downsides are equally evident. It may be useful to present a "taxonomy of difficulties" facing those who would embrace the Washington Consensus by dividing the countries of the region into three groups: the "newly industrializing countries" with a relatively advanced level of industrial development, such as Algeria, Egypt, Jordan, Morocco, Syria, and Tunisia; the low-income countries, such as Afghanistan, Mauritania, Sudan, and Yemen; and the "oil-rich" states of the GCC.

Relatively Advanced Countries

Washington Consensus policies presumably have the best chance of working in such advanced countries as Egypt, Jordan, Syria, and Iran, where the potential for labor-intensive exports would be greatest. However, the needed policy shifts may themselves be destabilizing, not only because the necessary changes involve austerity, but also because special interests that are major props of regime support and that occupy important subsidized positions within the bureaucracy face important challenges. Examples of the latter range from East Bank Jordanians to Egyptian workers in state-owned enterprises. It is simply not obvious that one can create the kind of economic institutions (such as the rule of law and a level playing field for investors) that most economists believe are necessary for sustained growth, while preserving the core support of the regimes. To say the least, regimes are most unlikely to weaken their political base; they have not done this, and it seems politically naïve to expect them to do so. The chances that conventional economic reform will raise incomes, employment, and foreign exchange seem modest.

Over the longer haul, the needed changes are also likely to be destabilizing in another way: Attracting the necessary volume of investment in the region will almost certainly require greater governmental accountability and more transparent rules of the economic game. This is not to say that democracy is needed for growth; it is merely to suggest that regimes will probably not attract the necessary private capital from their own citizens or from foreigners if they persist in their arbitrary, authoritarian practices. Whether regimes are willing to take such risks is, to say the least, doubtful.

From an investment perspective, the precise form of government is much less important than the presence of predictability and accountability. In the short term or medium term, autocracy can, in theory, provide such public goods. Whether this is possible over the longer run seems quite dubious. Experiences in Indonesia and Korea strongly suggest that when "crony capitalism" (based on opaque, unaccountable deals between private investors and government officials) falters, successfully reviving investment requires institutional reforms that enhance accountability and predictability. Such reforms have occurred in Korea but not in Indonesia. Korea's dramatic recovery from the Asian financial crisis of 1997, and Indonesia's continued floundering, are, at least in part, plausibly related to the marked differences in responses each made to crisis. So far, the record in the Middle East with enhancing accountability and predictability has been weak.

Finally, the chances of Washington Consensus policies actually succeeding are reduced because these countries suffer from significant weaknesses in international export markets compared with major competitor countries from Eastern Europe and South and Southeast Asia. In particular, they lack adequate infrastructure and skilled labor, particularly the "sergeants of industry" (e.g., foremen) necessary for modern industrial production. Despite the falls in wage levels and standards of living, efficiency wages (wages deflated by labor productivity) remain high relative to their international competitors. Oil rents have deeply infected wage levels, and labor productivity remains constrained by institutional, infrastructural, and human capital difficulties.

Low-Income Countries

The situation in such low-income countries as Yemen is far more dire, and so are the chances of Washington Consensus policies succeeding. For example, exports are highly unlikely to provide adequate food security or sufficient numbers of jobs (what, exactly, would Yemen export that was not agriculturally based, other than its own people?). At the same time, domestic productive capacity has been and is being damaged by population growth and property rights issues (e.g., for groundwater); natural resource degradation may have gone so far as to be very difficult to reverse. Depleted aquifers, denuded hillsides, and overgrazed steppes are poor foundations for *any* growth strategy. Further, thanks to past population growth, the labor force is growing so rapidly that provision of sufficient jobs through the "private-sector-led export model" is simply not credible: Infrastructure is far too poor, and the labor force is overwhelmingly illiterate.

The grim facts are that, at best, economic development in such countries is mainly a holding action, designed to prevent further deterioration and the consequent complete breakdown of order. The danger is that of breakdown into the anarchy of a Somalia or Afghanistan, and the concomitant risks of the development of terrorist safe havens. Socially, economically, and politically, the situation is very grim.

Oil-Rich Countries

Such reforms as have been implemented in the oil-rich countries of the GCC have been largely driven by fiscal problems. The relief that the last several years have afforded seems unlikely to last: The "rent ceiling," given by alternative energy production costs, is perhaps about $25 per barrel. Even at this maximum (and unlikely) price, revenue will be short.

The imperatives of spending have (at least) three proximate causes. First, the GCC states (except for Bahrain) continue to spend large sums on military hardware. Many locals, particularly in Saudi Arabia, question the utility of such spending. Nevertheless, spending remains high, which is quite understandable in view of the profound regional political tensions. Second, the GCC states have local populations that are thoroughly dependent upon, and expect to receive, a wide variety of consumer subsidies. Governments' ability to meet their side of the social contract is increasingly in doubt. Some cuts have been made, but the threat to (already often well-eroded) regime legitimacy such changes threaten forces governments to move very carefully and slowly here. Finally, and most important, the large majority of nationals are employed by the state—as many as 80 percent in Kuwait, for example. Consequently, shortfalls in government revenue translate quickly into difficulties with employment creation. It has proved very difficult to change people's expectations. Repeated attempts to force private firms to hire more locals have foundered on the greater energy and lower reservation wage of expatriate labor at lower skill levels, while the difficulties with educational systems sketched above make it difficult to replace highly skilled expatriates with local workers. Since the labor force is growing at one of the highest rates in the world, it is not plausible to imagine that the public sector can greatly reduce its wage bill. In summary, since revenues will be squeezed, and costs are inflexible downward, fiscal problems are likely to persist. Washington Consensus policies are largely irrelevant here.

The need for job creation is particularly acute, given the weakness of a demographic transition in the GCC states: Mortality rates have fallen sharply, but fertility rates have fallen only very moderately and remain very high by international standards. High rates of population growth 15 to 20 years ago translate into very rapidly growing labor supplies today. For fiscal reasons, the government cannot provide the new jobs required to absorb this labor. But neither can the private sector currently take up the slack in employment creation, because the sector is too small and too dependent on state largesse.

Finally, the countries of the Gulf have limited comparative advantages in non-oil goods or services. Wage rates, seriously inflated by past oil rents and current consumer subsidies, are far too high to compete in low-wage activities, but skills are too low to compete in more sophisticated activities. This problem has been noted earlier for Iran and Egypt, but it is far more serious for the GCC countries.

CONCLUSION

In short, the countries of the Middle East face grave economic challenges in the coming decade(s). We know of only one plausible management strategy—private-sector-led, export-oriented growth. However, the success of this *faut de mieux* strategy in most countries of the region is quite doubtful. Consequently, mounting economic problems will continue to pose challenges to governance. But so long as regimes continue to have access to enough money for internal and external security, and have support from at least some fairly united subsection of the population, they may continue to survive. However, as the example of the Soviet Union shows, when a regime lacks the support of most of its people, contingent events and mistakes by the top leadership can lead to rapid disintegration and regime change.

Chapter Four

CIVIL-MILITARY RELATIONS IN THE MIDDLE EAST
Risa Brooks

Military establishments are among the most—if not the most—important domestic constituencies in the states of the Middle East. Despite periodic experiments with political and economic liberalization, the region's Arab states in particular remain solidly nondemocratic.[1] Political leaders rely ultimately on coercive power to maintain their positions and depend upon their armed forces to defend against challengers and opponents. For this reason, military organizations are constituencies no authoritarian leader can afford to ignore. In fact, political leaders have proven quite successful in managing relations with their armed forces. Throughout the Middle East, leaders have attained and retained political control over their militaries, even as they continue to depend on their officers' loyalty to maintain office. Analyzing the bases of this political control provides crucial insight into the internal logic of the region's authoritarian regimes. Civil-military relations are essential for evaluating the past and future stability of the key U.S. adversaries and allies in the region.

Assessing civil-military relations is also significant for regional relations and broader U.S. security interests. Civil-military relations often compromise their military effectiveness and consequently the capacity of allies and adversaries in the region to project conventional military power. Military establishments play a dual role in the authoritarian regimes of the Middle East. They act as defenders of state and sovereignty against external adversaries. Yet they also de-

---

[1] For details of these patterns of liberalization, see Chapter Two of this volume.

fend the regime from internal opponents and challengers. This dual mandate creates particular pressures for leaders. They must ensure the support and quiescence of military leaders, which as final guarantors of the regime are imbued with substantial political influence, while arming themselves against external threats in the region. In fact, the dual mandate of these militaries contains an inherent contradiction: Maintaining political control often compromises the potential effectiveness of military forces in conventional war. Rarely have authoritarian leaders proved capable of securing both their regimes and their states, a fact underscored by the pervasive ineffectiveness of their armed forces in the region's many wars.

Since the 1970s the region has apparently been stable in leadership and civil-military relations. This chapter explores the sources of this stability, analyzing the strategies and tactics that leaders use to maintain political control of their military establishments. Next, the chapter examines how those strategies and tactics contribute to weaknesses in military organization and leadership. These sections focus on civil-military relations in the nondemocratic states of the region: those states that maintain dual-mandate militaries. Many examples are drawn from pivotal states in the region, including Syria, Egypt, Jordan, and Iran, although the focus is on general patterns that could be applied in different ways to the authoritarian regimes across the region (and potentially beyond). The final section examines potential challenges to the current state of civil-military relations, including succession struggles, regional tensions, and the infiltration of armed forces by Islamist groups. The chapter concludes with policy implications and recommendations for the United States.

FROM COUPS TO STABILITY

In the post-independence era, the defining feature of politics in the Middle East, especially its Arab countries, was the proliferation of military takeovers of government.[2] Many Arab states experienced at least one, if not multiple, serious attempts at a coup d'état in the decades after World War II. From 1961 to 1969, for example, at least

---

[2]Eliezer Be'eri, "The Waning of the Military in Coup Politics," *Middle Eastern Studies*, Vol. 18, No. 3, January 1982, p. 69.

27 successful coups and serious attempts at military takeovers were recorded in nine Arab countries.[3] Even more striking, the era of the coup d'état gave way to a remarkable stability in leadership.[4] King Hussein, until his death in 1999, ruled Jordan for more than four decades, since 1953. Hafez al-Assad ran Syria for nearly 30 years, dying in the presidency in June 2000. Saddam Hussein ruled Iraq for almost 25 years. Hosni Mubarak has run Egypt nearly as long, since 1981. Syria and Jordan have even successfully managed peaceful transitions in recent years, thus far avoiding violent or tumultuous power struggles and coup d'états.

This leadership stability is all the more notable given the ongoing centrality of the military in these authoritarian regimes. Military establishments continue to play a central role in politics, despite the eclipse of overt demonstrations of their influence through the coup d'état. The military's central position stems from its role as the primary repository of force, and therefore the ultimate guarantor of regime security. Most regimes maintain security services that specialize in monitoring and policing potential opponents to the regime. Many times these are highly trained and efficient entities, yet they also often compete with other powerful bureaucratic constituencies for resources, and at times lose out in the process. In Egypt, for example, the 300,000 strong Central Protection Force (CPF), which is housed in the Interior Ministry, has traditionally been considered a second-rate force, staffed by conscripts that failed to meet the criteria for acceptance in the conventional armed forces. Yet even where these entities are well-trained and efficient in safeguarding against popular opposition, conventional military forces remain the ultimate guarantors of the regime.

Indeed, regular military forces are used to guard against the police and security services. When some 20,000 of the CPF rioted over low pay in 1986, the Egyptian army deployed three divisions, nearly a quarter of its regular army, to suppress the rebellion. In Syria, Rifaat al-Assad's stand against the regime in 1984 was countered by Special

---

[3]Be'eri, 1982. Also see Ekkart Zimmerman, "Toward a Causal Model of Military Coups d' État," *Armed Forces and Society*, Vol. 5, No. 3, Spring 1979.

[4]This is also a commonly noted feature of Arab politics. For example, see Hamza Hendawi, "Hussein's Long Years in Power Not So Unusual in Arab Politics," *The Associated Press*, February 9, 1999.

Forces and other loyal military units; at the time Rifaat was in charge of the mainline force for regime security. Similarly, riots in the Jordanian towns of Kerak in 1996 and Ma'an in 1998 required military intervention to calm the situation. Conventional militaries are the essential force of last resort. As one analyst put it, "without the active participation or at least the expressive approval of commanders of the military, no Arab government can hold on to the reins of power."[5]

THE INGREDIENTS OF POLITICAL CONTROL

Maintaining political control over the military requires depriving military leaders of both the means and motive to challenge the regime. Leaders resort to a variety of inducements and safeguards to influence the costs and benefits of conspiring against the regime. Many are specific tactics employed in the management of the military organization, while others are influenced by external events and forces, which leaders are less capable of actively manipulating.

Social Support

One of the basic hedges against military intervention is maintaining a social base of support for the regime outside the military establishment. Economic interests, religious minorities, civil bureaucracies, party apparatuses, and popular or mass groups can be significant elements in the social infrastructure of Arab regimes. In effect, civilian support balances the power of the military. For example, one of Hafez al-Assad's advantages in the consolidation of power in the early 1970s was that unlike many of the short-lived regimes that preceded his, he undertook economic measures that helped win support from the Damascene capitalists, providing an initial social base for his rule.[6] Bashar al-Assad's capacity to maintain social support, or at least acquiescence, for his leadership is also a crucial hedge against opposition from within the Syrian elite, including the military, and

---

[5]Be'eri, 1982, p. 80.

[6]Moshe Ma'oz, *Syria Under Hafiz al-Assad: New Domestic and Foreign Policies*, Jerusalem Policy Papers, 15, Jerusalem: Hebrew University of Jerusalem, 1975, p. 10.

may explain his (very) tentative steps toward liberalization.[7] In fact, although seldom sufficient, one of the principal motivations for military intervention in political rule is social and economic crisis, and a concomitant loss of social support for the regime.

When dissatisfaction with a regime results in overt opposition, the consequences for civil-military relations can be even more destabilizing. Opposition invites repression, which increases the public profile of military leaders, and reinforces a leader's dependence on them for his position; consequently it tips the political-military balance of power in the military's favor. Hence, in the aftermath of the suppression of the 1986 CPF riots in Egypt, the political stature of Minister of War Field Marshal Abdel al-Halim Abu Ghazala (the top military officer in Egypt) increased substantially.[8]

Overt demonstrations against a regime can destabilize civil-military relations in another way. As discussed below, they test the loyalties of the military, especially junior officers and rank and file who are called upon to fire on their social equals, with whom they may identify heavily. Although leaders may call on military forces to repress public opposition, doing so is not without risks and costs.

Stacking the Deck

A second common technique of political control is to form alliances with a minority group, thereby creating vested interests in the perpetuation of the regime. Especially if they are implicated in the repressive activities of the regime or are objects of resentment for their privileged status, minority groups have self-interested reasons for protecting the status quo. Hence they make fairly safe allies. During the period of Baathist rule in Iraq, the minority Sunni tribes, many from towns and villages in Iraq's center, occupied key posts in the

---

[7]See Neil MacFarquhar, "Syria Reaches Turning Point But Which Way Will It Turn," *New York Times,* March 12, 2001; "Bashar Assad First Six Months: Reform in a Dangerous Environment," *Mideast Mirror,* January 26, 2001. Bashar came into office and attempted liberalization in a variety of political and economic areas. Although reforms continue, they do so at a snail's pace, with significant backtracking, as Bashar has run up against opposition from the old-guard.

[8]Robert Springborg, *Mubarak's Egypt: Fragmentation of the Political Order,* Boulder, Colo.: Westview Press, 1989, pp. 101–103.

regime. Sectarian bias is also apparent in Syria, where many important positions, including top positions in the military, are held by
members of the Alawi community, the religious sect from which the
al-Assad clan originates.[9] In Jordan, Bedouin families from the east
bank of the Jordan river are the bedrock of the regime;[10] their ongoing support for the Hashemite lineage is vital. Sons from these
prominent families occupy high positions in the military and civilian
bureaucracy. Indeed, the monarchy has tried to ensure that almost
every Bedouin family has at least one member in the military.[11]

Servicing the Military Constituency

Leaders also want to create vested interests within the military itself.
This entails looking after the corporate "requirements" of the military organization and private interests of its top officers. Corporate
prerogatives come in a variety of forms, from freedom from external
oversight of budgetary matters, to commitment to invest in high-
technology weapons systems, to the maintenance of large military
budgets.

Political leaders look after the private interests of their military officials in a variety of ways. Among them is turning a blind eye to corruption in the armed forces. In the Syrian military, for example, officers deployed to Lebanon benefit from the administration of smuggling networks and related black-market activities, much like Egypt's
officers profited from smuggling activities during the Yemeni civil

---

[9]For an excellent account of how Assad has drawn on the Alawi community in Syria,
and tribal relationships in key appointments in the military, see Asher Susser, "The
`Alawis, Lords of Syria," in Ofra Bengio and Gabriel Ben-Dor (eds.), *Minorities and the
State in the Arab World*, Boulder, Colo.: Lynne Rienner, 1999, especially p. 136.
Another dimension of the strategy has been to rely disproportionately on *rural* Sunnis,
as opposed to the urban Sunni majority.

[10]These are referred to as either Trans-Jordanians, East Bankers, or simply Jordanians
when discussed in context of the country's Palestinian majority, refugees from previous Arab-Israeli wars.

[11]Interviews with U.S. officials by Nora Bensahel and Daniel Byman conducted in
May 2000 in Amman, Jordan. On the position of East Bankers in the Jordanian military
see Asher Susser, "The Palestinians in Jordan: Demographic Majority, Political Minority," in Ofra Bengio and Gabriel Ben-Dor (eds.), *Minorities and the State in the Arab
World*, Boulder, Colo.: Lynne Rienner, 1999.

war (1962–1967).[12] The Egyptian military's involvement in commercial activities, substantial since the late 1970s, also create opportunities for private benefit for the officers running these unmonitored agricultural, industrial, and service enterprises. Finally, senior officers often get benefits unavailable to their subordinates, including better pay, health care, subsidized transportation, housing, and relief from customs duties on luxury items.

Internal Security Agencies

The proliferation of internal security entities is a commonly noted feature of Arab states. These entities take a variety of forms, including stand-alone agencies and specialized units or departments of the conventional armed forces. Appointments to leadership positions are highly selective. In Syria and Iraq, for example, relatives and members of tribes allied with the regime frequently head these entities. Also notable is their sheer number.[13] Most regimes have multiple, if not dozens, of security and intelligence entities, with often vaguely differentiated mandates. Intense bureaucratic rivalries among them are encouraged, consistent with dynamics sometimes referred to as "counterbalancing." These entities fulfill a number of crucial roles for regime security, including:

Monitoring. The entities track civilian society and report on potential sources of opposition. They also monitor each other's activities. In fact, the proliferation of these entities and fierce competition encouraged among them is an extremely effective safeguard against the growth of opposition movements from within the security edifice itself. The entities have a strong incentive to report on each other, in-

---

[12]The military chiefs that benefit from these activities have been a major obstacle to reform and reducing corruption in Syria. See Raymond Hinnebusch, *Authoritarian Power and State Formation in Ba'athist Syria*, Boulder: Colo.: Westview Press, 1990, p. 159; Neil Quilliam, *Syria and the New World Order*, Reading, UK: Garnet Publishing, 1999, pp. 83–84. Also see the discussion of Syria in Chapter Two.

[13]For example, on Iraq's security entities see Sean Boyne, "Inside Iraq's Security Network: Part One," *Jane's Intelligence Review*, July 1991, pp. 312–314; Andrew Rathmell, "Iraqi Intelligence and Security Services," *International Defense Review*, Vol. 24, No. 5, May 1991, p. 393. On Syria see Carl Anthony Wege, "Assad's Legions: The Syrian Intelligence Services," *Intelligence and Counterintelligence*, Vol. 4, No. 1, Spring 1990; Middle East Watch, *Syria Unmasked: The Suppression of Human Rights by the Asad Regime*, New Haven, Conn.: Yale University Press for Middle East Watch, 1991.

creasing the odds that information will be forced to the top. The large number also acts as a barrier to collusion, increasing the collective action problems to organizing effective action against the political leadership.

Balancing. The entities provide a counterweight to the conventional armed forces. In addition to performing security functions, these entities are often extremely powerful in the politics of the regime. They represent alternative political constituencies that a leader may use to balance the influence and authority of conventional military bureaucracies and their leaders.

Defense. These entities are regularly called on to quell social disturbances. They are also called to defend the regime in the event of a coup d'état. Hence they are the mainline forces that act in defense of the regime.

The proliferation of internal security entities is one of the most pervasive features of authoritarian government in the Middle East. The resources, tools and methods of these entities make them highly effective at rooting out opposition and preventing coups. They increase the technical barriers to plotting in secrecy. The competitive nature of their relationships creates political obstacles to building a sizable and cohesive opposition movement from within the regime.

Dual Militaries

Beyond creating independent agencies or carving off specific units from the conventional forces for internal security, in some cases states have developed full-blown dual militaries to counter their regular armed forces.[14] For example, during the 1980s and 1990s, the Iraqi Republican Guard evolved from a small regime security force into a sizable ground force. The Guard's six divisions (three armored, one mechanized, two infantry) were approximately one-third the size of the conventional army, and they enjoyed a dispropor-

---

[14]On parallel militaries see James T. Quinlivan, "Coup-proofing: Its Practice and Consequences in the Middle East," *International Security*, Vol. 24, No. 2, Fall 1999, pp. 141–148.

tionate share of quality equipment and skilled manpower.[15] Saudi Arabia also has a dual military force, the National Guard. Today the National Guard is nearly equivalent in size (three mechanized infantry brigades, five infantry brigades) to the regular army (three armored brigades, five mechanized brigades, one airborne brigade).[16] Similarly, Iran's Islamic Revolutionary Guard Corps (IRGC) was created to defend the revolution against reactionary forces, including the regular armed forces. Since its early days as a paramilitary force, the IRGC has grown into a military force that rivals the regular armed forces in size and strength.

These dual militaries have several distinctive features. First, they tend to have a distinct command structure. In Iraq, the Republican Guard answered directly to the Presidential Palace and was supervised by Saddam's son Qusay.[17] In Iran, the IRGC and the regular army's commands are only nominally integrated at the highest levels.[18] In Saudi Arabia, the Army and the Guard are under the control of different princes, with Prince Abdullah himself retaining the position of commander of the National Guard. Second, these dual militaries tend to be staffed by those groups and individuals political leaders consider most loyal and vested in the regime. Tribal affiliations are heavily emphasized in top appointments in Iraq and Saudi Arabia; the Saudi National Guard is commonly referred to as a "tribal force," staffed by clans loyal to the Saud family.[19] Third, they are deployed in patterns conducive to regime security. Thus within the Saudi National Guard, tribal forces are grouped into distinct regions and deployed to cover every critical urban and populated area in the

---

[15]Figures appear in the International Institute for Strategic Studies (IISS), *The Military Balance 2000–2001*, Oxford:, UK Oxford University Press, 2000, pp. 140–141. On the growth of the Republican Guard see Andrew Cockburn and Patrick Cockburn, *Out of the Ashes: The Resurrection of Saddam Hussein*, New York: HarperCollins, 1999, p. 146.

[16]*IISS 2000*, pp. 152–153.

[17]Anthony H. Cordesman, *Iraq and the War of Sanctions*, Westport, Conn.: Praeger Publishers, 1999, pp. 152–153.

[18]For a review, see Daniel Byman, Shahram Chubin, Anoushiravan Ehteshami, and Jerrold Green, *Iran's Security Policy in the Post-Revolutionary Era*, Santa Monica, Calif.: RAND, MR–1320–OSD, 2001.

[19]On Saddam Hussein's efforts to "tribalize" the Republican Guard in recent years see Cordesman, *Iraq and the War of Sanctions*, p. 79.

country; hence they act as a barrier to the seizure of major population centers and facilities in the event of a coup.[20] In Iraq, Republican Guard Units were deployed in and around Baghdad, at garrisons near strategic access points to the city.[21]

Size

The inflated size of many militaries in the region may also bolster political control. Egypt and Syria both maintain a substantially larger force than they can train or support effectively.[22] Yet there are advantages to maintaining a large military, since compartmentalized and competitive subunits create political obstacles to building a cohesive anti-regime coalition. It also creates technical barriers to plotting a coup, which involves recruiting—in complete secrecy—a network of pivotal units with the access and mobility to detain the political leader and to seize control of all key communication systems and strategic points in the capital. Zisser notes, for example, that the "Syrian army's size and complexity . . . has made it almost impossible, or at least very complicated, to employ force in changing the face of the regime . . ."[23]

Institutional Tactics

Leaders use a variety of institutional measures designed to preclude opposition from the armed forces that could challenge their position. These management techniques help ensure that personnel whose political loyalty is secure occupy sensitive positions in the armed forces, especially those affording access to units likely to be pivotal in a coup d'état. Further, these techniques facilitate monitoring and provide information about the activities of the armed forces and its personnel.

---

[20]Anthony Cordesman, *Saudi Arabia*, Boulder, Colo.: Westview Press, 1997, p. 139.

[21]Cordesman, *Iraq and the War of Sanctions*, p. 71.

[22]Anthony Cordesman, *Perilous Prospects: The Peace Process and the Arab-Israeli Military Balance*, Boulder, Colo.: Westview Press, 1996, p. 17.

[23]Eyal Zisser, "The Renewed Struggle for Power in Syria," in Moshe Ma'oz, Joseph Ginat, and Onn Winckler (eds.), *Modern Syria*, Brighton, UK: Sussex Academic Press, 1999, p. 49.

Among the most common of these institutional techniques is the elevation of partisan affiliations relative to merit in appointment and officer promotion criteria and processes. Leaders seek to advance individuals whose loyalty to the regime is relatively assured, at times at the expense of promoting officers of independent spirit, charisma, and military talent. Posting rotations similarly may be governed by political expediency. In these dual-mandate militaries officers are often either rotated out of pivotal positions to prevent them from building factions, or entrenched when their loyalty is assured. Political leaders sometimes engage in mass dismissals, or purges, especially when large sections of the officer corps are suspect in the eyes of the political leadership. Regimes also incorporate safeguards in chains of command, to facilitate the monitoring of military activity. Officers outside the formal chain of command, but with direct ties to the political leadership, may maintain informal command or oversight responsibilities, especially for sensitive tactical units. Sometimes, these evolve into full-blown dual, or shadow, command structures that overlap or compete with formal hierarchies. Consequently, formal command and control processes often tell only part of the story of how authority is actually exercised within these dual-mandate militaries.

These institutional tactics have a variety of incarnations, but they have a common logic: They safeguard against the emergence of powerful factions in a position to take action against the regime. The sheer dearth of successful coups since the 1970s in such countries as Egypt, Iraq, and Syria testifies to the efficacy of these institutional tactics, as well as the utility of the broader repertoire of techniques for managing relations with the military discussed above. Those few coup plots in these regimes significant enough to be reported in the press have been snuffed out long before tanks are ever deployed in the capital.

Leader Incentives

Analyzing the strategies and tactics leaders use to maintain political control of their militaries provides insight into the internal logic of these regimes. They highlight a variety of imperatives that leaders face in maintaining power. First, leaders are likely to be wary of unpopular foreign and domestic policies or regional tensions that threaten to inflame domestic populaces and opposition movements. Regular citizens are not in and of themselves a direct threat to their positions in office. Rather the danger comes in undermining the social base that balances military influence in the regime. Mass opposition, especially when it manifests in open demonstrations and defiance of political authority, also tests the loyalties of military personnel, who may themselves be disenchanted with the regime's policies. In a telling discussion of the Iranian revolution, for example, Hashim recounts how it was the failure of the officer corps to mobilize against the dissident clerical movement and reluctance to take up arms against ordinary citizens that paved the way for the revolution's success.[24]

Second, leaders must maintain access to resources to satisfy the private and corporate interests of their officers and military organizations. This creates pressures on leaders to maintain policies to protect these prerogatives. For Bashar al-Assad, the substantial rents military (and civilian) personnel extract from the occupation of Lebanon might complicate any future Syrian withdrawal from Lebanese territory.[25] For similar reasons, the purchase of sophisticated, high-prestige weapons systems has an undeniable political appeal for leaders, even when expenditure on less glamorous equipment would better serve military needs. Third, the imperatives of political control suggest that a range of bureaucratic decisions, from how large a military to maintain to how much to spend on it, will be governed by political expediency, at times at the expense of bureaucratic efficiency and reform. Reforms that challenge military prerogatives and the organizational structures of political control face steep obstacles. Real change in these areas will require more than just improved management, or even a serious commitment to reform by politicians, but arguably a complete transformation in these regimes and the authoritarian politics that underlay them.

---

[24]Ahmed S. Hashim, "Civil-Military Relations in the Islamic Republic of Iran," in Joseph Kechichian (ed.), *Iran, Iraq, and the Arab Gulf States*, New York: Palgrave, 2000, pp. 36–37.

[25]For a discussion of the importance of these rents to the political economy of the Syrian regime see Chapter Three. For a commentary on the potential for a redeployment in the future see comments by Bashar in "Bashar Assad: No Change in Syria's Peace Terms, and Its 'Doors Are Open' to Saddam and Arafat," *Mideast Mirror*, February 9, 2001.

POLITICAL CONTROL AND MILITARY EFFECTIVENESS

Civil-military relations affect regime stability, but also affect states' military effectiveness. The strategies and tactics used to maintain political control of the military, especially the institutional tactics, have come at significant cost in military capabilities. They undermine these states' capacities to translate their often significant strengths in men and equipment into actual fighting power.[26] Dual-mandate militaries therefore pose critical dilemmas for leaders: Mechanisms of political control often contradict principles of efficient and professional military organization.[27] These tradeoffs are especially apparent in three critical areas: command and control, leadership, and intelligence and strategic assessment.

Command and Control

As noted above, political control is often assured through command and control procedures. Among Arab forces, and in authoritarian militaries more broadly, there is a tendency to heavily centralize de-

---

[26]This is Millet and Murray's definition of military effectiveness. See Allan R. Millett, Williamson Murray, and Kenneth H. Watman, "The Effectiveness of Military Organizations," in Allan R. Millett and Williamson Murray (eds.), *Military Effectiveness: Volume 1: The First World War,* Boston: Allen & Unwin, 1988, pp. 1–30. It provides a useful framework for some of the organizational dynamics that compromise the capacity to use resources efficiently and promote standards of behavior and processes conducive to an effective fighting force. Sociologists, in contrast, often equate military effectiveness with small unit behavior and unit cohesion. Operations Research emphasizes firepower and numbers, often in large-n models of battlefield outcomes. Political scientists have also explored the question of effectiveness, arguing that such factors as culture, regime type, norms, and social structure influence effectiveness. See Kenneth M. Pollack, *The Influence of Arab Culture on Arab Military Effectiveness,* Ph.D. dissertation, Massachusetts Institute of Technology, 1996; Daniel Reiter and Allan C. Stam III, "Democracy and Battlefield Military Success," *Journal of Conflict Resolution,* Vol. 42, No. 3, June 1998, pp. 259–277; Theo Farrell, "Transnational Norms and Military Development: Constructing Ireland's Professional Army," *European Journal of International Relations,* Vol. 7, No. 1, March 2001, pp. 63–102; Stephen Peter Rosen, *Societies and Military Power,* Ithaca, N.Y.: Cornell University Press, 1996.

[27]Similar observations have gained increasing notoriety in recent years. See for example Mark Heller, "Iraq's Army: Military Weakness, Political Utility," in Amatzia Baram and Barry Rubin (eds.), *Iraq's Road to War,* New York: St Martin's Press, 1996; Risa Brooks, *Political-Military Relations and the Stability of Arab Regimes,* International Institute for Strategic Studies, Adelphi Paper 324, Oxford University Press, December 1998; Quinlivan, 1999; Barry Rubin, "The Military in Contemporary Middle East Politics," MERIA, Vol. 5, No. 1, March 2001.

cisionmaking authority. This guarantees that the political leadership and its most trusted leaders retain maximum authority over their subordinates' activities. While there are sound political reasons for this, a failure to decentralize operations can impede the fluidity, clarity, and responsiveness of command and control procedures. Iraqi operations in the first phases of the Iran-Iraq war offer a quintessential, if perhaps extreme, example of this dynamic. Saddam Hussein retained a stranglehold over command, personally directing Iraqi operations in many cases, despite his own lack of real military experience. In general in dual-mandate militaries, officers in the field are given very narrow latitude and must regularly confer with commanders in the rear. Accordingly, the centralization of command often coincides with the attenuation of the organization's hierarchy. As one Western military officer posted in the region once described the Egyptian command, its structure is like "a tower with a pyramid on top."[28]

In addition to centralizing command authority, shadow commands, similar to the methods of party control used in communist systems, reduce military effectiveness. Thus, during the early phases of the Iran-Iraq war, Baathist party cadres kept careful watch over the activities of the military;[29] and party officials continued to "micromanage" military affairs.[30] In Syria, Alawi deputies are assigned to units under the command of Sunni officers[31] and retain direct links with command headquarters. In Iran, placing personal representatives of the country's supreme religious leader in major military commands facilitates clerical oversight of the armed forces.[32]

These and related command and control practices compromise military effectiveness in three ways. First, they affect the ability of these organizations to exploit opportunities that arise on the battlefield in a timely fashion, because of the delay in receiving authorization and instruction from command headquarters. For example, on the sec-

---

[28]Personal communication, Western military officer, Cairo, June 1998.

[29]Charles Tripp, *History of Iraq*, Cambridge: Cambridge University Press, 2000, p. 237.

[30]Cordesman, *Iraq and the War of Sanctions*, p. 113.

[31]Hinnebusch, 1980, p. 160.

[32]See Michael Eisenstadt, "The Armed Forces of the Islamic Republic," *MERIA*, Vol. 5, No. 1, March 2001.

ond day of the 1982 war in Lebanon, Hafez al-Assad sent his deputy chief of staff for Operations, General Ali Aslan, from Damascus to Lebanon to evaluate the military situation, rather than relying on local commanders. Eisenstadt concludes that Assad therefore "wasted precious time and forfeited any possibility of responding in a timely matter to the rapidly unfolding events there."[33] More specifically, these militaries will be at a systematic disadvantage in maneuver warfare.[34] Maneuver depends on speed, initiative, and the decentralization of command authority. Armies lacking these attributes will be hard pressed to execute such actions.

Second, these command and control procedures affect interservice and intraservice coordination. Shadow commands, competition, centralization, and compartmentalization lead services and their subcomponents to be run as competitive fiefs, undermining organizational coordination. Effective joint commands across services, which integrate air, ground, and sea resources, will be difficult to realize in any effective or meaningful sense. For example, in both Jordan and Saudi Arabia, the armed services, despite U.S. prodding, do not talk regularly to each other.[35] Within services, the coordination of different combat arms is difficult to implement. Such structural barriers to cooperation were starkly evident in weaknesses in Egyptian air defenses on the eve of the June 1967 Arab-Israeli war, when a long-standing feud between the air force and the artillery over command and control procedures for antiaircraft guns and missiles remained unresolved.[36] In the 1991 Gulf War, Iraqi forces showed poor capacity for employing artillery fire in support of their defensive operations.[37]

---

[33]Michael Eisenstadt, *Arming for Peace? Syria's Elusive Quest for Strategic Parity*, Washington Institute Policy Paper 31, Washington, D.C.: Washington Institute for Near East Policy, 1992, p. 58.

[34]Allan C. Stam, III, *Win, Lose, or Draw: Domestic Politics and the Crucible of War*, Ann Arbor: University of Michigan Press, 1996.

[35]Interviews with U.S. officials by Nora Bensahel and Daniel Byman in Amman, Jordan, and Riyadh, Saudi Arabia, May 2000.

[36]Mohamed Abdel Ghani al-Gamasi, *The October War: Memoirs of Field Marshal el-Gamasy of Egypt*, Cairo: The American University in Cairo Press, 1993, p. 60.

[37]Stephen Biddle, "Victory Misunderstood: What the Gulf War Tells Us About the Future of Conflict," *International Security*, Vol. 21, No. 2, Fall 1996, pp. 159–160.

These handicaps in command are likely to worsen, not improve, with new developments in the practice of war. Many analysts agree that modern warfare involves increasing reliance on combined arms within services, as well as the integration of air, sea, and land based systems across them, all coordinated with integrated networks and doctrine. Sophisticated weapons systems also require a substantial logistical and support infrastructure in the field and hence require complex, but efficient command, control, and communications procedures.[38] In sum, services operating with compartmentalized systems will have a difficult time assimilating the systems that support high-technology combat and, consequently, adapting to new practices in warfare.

Finally, these command and control practices may adversely affect the initiative and independence of action of tactical units on the battlefield. Tactical unit commanders are forced to rely heavily on superiors in the rear and are not encouraged to act independently. Moreover, these settings tend to reward deference to authority. Saddam Hussein, for example, publicly punished officers when they became outspoken.[39] One can easily imagine how such behavior can breed negative incentive structures that suppress initiative. Where that system rewards deference, the ethos of an organization reflects those values over time. Over time such practices contribute to an organizational culture that discourages independent action.

Leadership

The effort to guarantee the military's loyalty has vital consequences for the skill and merit of senior officers, especially those occupying key positions. Although a leader may be both a loyal officer and a talented commander, there are good reasons to expect this to be the exception, not the rule. If an individual lacks charisma—an essential ingredient to building a loyal faction of supporters—he is less likely to pose a potential threat. Western officers reported in 1998 that after

---

[38]Gene I. Rochin and Chris C. Demchak, *Lessons of the Gulf War: Ascendant Technology and Declining Capability*, Policy Papers in International Affairs, No. 39, University of California, Berkeley, Berkeley: Institute for International Studies, 1991, pp. 23–24.

[39]See Anthony H. Cordesman and Abraham R. Wagner, *The Lessons of Modern War, Volume 2: The Iran-Iraq War*, Boulder, Colo.: Westview Press, 1990, pp. 58–59.

sidelining the charismatic Abu Ghazala in 1989, Mubarak appointed colorless, and therefore nonthreatening, individuals to top positions in the military hierarchy.[40] Leaders lacking in skill, and hence primarily dependent on political sponsorship for promotion, also may be more likely to see their fortunes tied to the regime. They may thus prove more compliant and responsive to political directives. Although politically safe, uncharismatic sycophants lack the capacity to motivate and inspire their subordinates, undermining morale and unit cohesion and ultimately tactical effectiveness.

In addition to carefully regulating appointments, the use of rotation schedules to safeguard against military opposition can undermine military effectiveness. Leaders may be cycled through rapidly, and removed exactly when they are forming the very bonds that make a tactical unit cohere on the battlefield. Alternatively regimes may entrench their military leaders for years, if not decades, in positions to prevent them from widening their support base. This can lead to the decay of their military skills and competency to command forces in the event of war. The entrenchment of military leaders was common under Syria's Hafez al-Assad. Bashar appears thus far to be continuing the practice.

It is difficult to overestimate the significance of strong leadership and the corollary negative effects of weak leadership on military effectiveness. Perhaps the effects are most vivid in the quality of commanders in war. So egregious was the promotion of political lackeys in Egypt in the 1967 war that Israel had singled out a string of incompetent division and brigade commanders, including the political alliances responsible for their promotion to those positions.[41] Similarly, sycophants occupied top command positions in the Iraqi army during the early phases of the Iran-Iraq war (1980–1988), including the 1980 attack on Iran, to the substantial detriment of its operations.[42] Politicized appointments and divide and rule strategies can also compromise intra- and interservice cooperation by weakening the ethos of cooperation and personal bonds among leaders. Where

---

[40]Interview, Western military officer, Cairo, June 1998.

[41]Trevor N. Dupuy, *Elusive Victory: The Arab Israeli Wars, 1947–1974*, New York: Harper and Row Publishers, 1978.

[42]Heller, 1996; Cordesman and Wagner, 1990, pp. 58–59.

those personnel and training policies compromise merit and fail to place the highest value on attention to duty and (external) mission, those professional and personal relationships inevitably suffer.

Intelligence and Information

To survive, authoritarian regimes must keep opposition in check. Neutralizing opposition requires good information about the activities of groups and individuals, potentially or manifestly, at odds with the regime or its policies. Leaders in authoritarian regimes make substantial investments in monitoring social and political activity. As noted above, the proliferation of intelligence and security entities is common.

These entities have adverse implications for external intelligence functions, on the strategic, operational, and tactical levels. Substantial resources that might otherwise be dedicated to monitoring and assessing the capabilities of foreign militaries are absorbed by internal regime functions. For example, air force intelligence, an influential entity in Hafez al-Assad's Syria, plays a key role in civilian monitoring. During the 1960s, Egypt's external intelligence operations were so poor that the high command lacked vital information about the range of Israeli Mirages before the 1967 war and was unprepared for the latter's cratering bombs, which rendered Egypt's runways useless.[43] Second, politicized command structures complicate the exchange of intelligence and information within the military establishment. Compartmentalized and centralized command procedures complicate the horizontal effective exchange of information. At best, this slows the spread of vital information; at worst, operational and tactical commanders lack necessary information or receive false data. In addition, services and their internal intelligence functions, fiercely protective of their domains, may prove unwilling to share information when they view each other as competitors for influence and resources.

An additional by-product of political control can prove especially damaging to strategic intelligence—big picture assessments of an en-

---

[43]The range of the Israeli Mirages had been underestimated. See al-Gamasi, 1993, p. 60.

emy's capabilities, options, and intentions. The problem lies in the disincentives military leaders often have to supply information that will harm their political standing—information that contradicts the political leaders' conclusions, assessments, and preferences. Bad news and contradictory views thus tend to be underreported. Even where a political leader tolerates bad news and is not especially inclined to punish the messenger, the dynamics of appointment processes work against good reporting: A leader appoints politically likeminded officers to important positions because he believes these men will be more willing to follow his plans. But critical views and alternative perspectives may not be represented in the decisionmaking process.

Sycophancy has enormous downsides in strategic decisionmaking. During the Iran-Iraq war, local commanders feared to pass bad news up the command chain, creating a "situation in which Saddam Hussein's strategic decisions and way of handling the war were not seriously criticized by the military leadership who dared not challenge his authority."[44] In particular, the decision to launch the war in 1980, premised on a striking miscalculation of the Iranian reaction to the offensive, was taken in a context in which sycophants were reluctant to question Saddam Hussein's strategic calculus.[45] The Iraqi president himself later admitted that he had misjudged the Iranian reaction.[46]

POTENTIAL OFFSETS TO POLITICIZATION

The adverse effects of strategies and tactics of political control on military efficiency and organization are substantial. Several factors, however, can alleviate some of these pathologies and allow the state to make better use of its resources.

---

[44]Efraim Karsh, *The Iran-Iraq War: A Military Analysis*, Adelphi Paper 220, International Institute for International Studies, Oxford: Oxford University Press, 1987, p. 43.

[45]Geoff Simons, *Iraq: From Sumer to Saddam*, London: Macmillan Press, 1994, p. 277.

[46]Tripp, *A History of Iraq*, p. 233.

Centralized Command Structures

Centralized command structures have some advantages. They can facilitate comprehensive top-down reform. Good leadership goes a long way in centralized organizations: Change at the apex of leadership has enormous ramifications for activities below. The possibilities of top-down reform are especially pronounced in set piece operations, where planners can foresee and control the unfolding of events. This is key to how Egypt orchestrated its dramatic showing in the crossing of the Suez Canal, which preceded the October 1973 war. Everything from operational plans to tactics and training was highly scripted and practiced, under the leadership of Egypt's skilled high command.

Even with good leaders, however, highly centralized systems continue to have a difficult time coping with unanticipated developments. This point is again underscored by Egypt's performance in the 1973 October war. The war's turning point, the Israeli breech of Egypt's defensive line and crossover to the west bank of the Suez Canal, was facilitated by a failure in the lower echelons of Egypt's command structure. Officers in the canal zone failed to adequately assess, comprehend, and relay information about the breakthrough to the high command. The delay in Egypt's response time, and the failure to fortify the area or prepare for an immediate counteroffensive, provided a crucial window of opportunity to Israeli forces.

Technology

The adoption of new technologies can mitigate some weaknesses in military activity.[47] New technologies may offset the intrinsic disadvantages of centralized command structures for operational tempo and responsiveness. Technical innovations in software and hardware allow greater real-time battlefield management, through the electronic gathering and analysis of information. These technologies reduce feedback time, allowing for quicker action-reaction-counter-

---

[47]An excellent analysis of how civil-military relations affect the incorporation of new technologies appears in Stephen Biddle and Robert Zirkle, "Technology, Civil-Military Relations, and Warfare in the Developing World," *Journal of Strategic Studies*, Vol. 19, No. 2, June 1996, pp. 171–212.

action chains, and may therefore facilitate more effective command from the rear. The acquisition of these systems could prove an advantage to centralized militaries, where command is concentrated at the top for political reasons.

Advanced command and control systems are not a panacea. The effective use of such technologies still depends on human factors. These systems multiply the extant strengths and weaknesses of operational commanders. Centralized commands give good leaders substantial leverage over battlefield events. They also allow an incompetent leader to do substantial harm. These systems place a premium on skilled leadership. In principle, they help synthesize and process information to ease the strain on human faculties; yet in practice, they also require greater technical sophistication and the capacity to interact continuously with a variety of technical and human systems.

The consequences of other technologies for dual-mandate militaries are less sanguine. For example, the proliferation of precision weapons will probably do little to enhance, and may harm, their military effectiveness, by magnifying the effects of their organizational inefficiencies. The targeting and control systems for precision weapons, whether based on laser guiding or global positioning, are sophisticated and require better training than for "dumb bombs." Mediocre leadership and the absence of a culture of critical analysis and rigorous training may stymie the incorporation and utilization of these systems where they are acquired. In addition, the effective use of these precise weapons may depend on utilizing fire from different platforms and coordinating the actions of different combat arms and service branches; hence, they require expertise in combined arms and jointness, which are problematic in dual-mandate militaries. Many of these countries cannot achieve the maximum capabilities of the advanced platforms they *already* possess, because of a lack of leadership, skilled personnel, maintenance, and effective intra- and interservice coordination. In this light, their prospects for realizing the full benefits of new and even more sophisticated technologies are low.

In general, high-technology weapons systems may have little marginal utility precisely because their acquisition is not motivated fully by a desire to address gaps and overcome weaknesses in capabilities. This is especially true with regard to such high-prestige, glamour systems as the 16 F-16 fighter aircraft purchased by Jordan from the United States.[48] Perhaps, more gains to effectiveness could have been achieved for the resource-deprived Jordanian military from investment in "nuts and bolts," from boots for soldiers to spare parts for its aircraft. This is all the more true when one considers the substantial and ongoing burden maintaining the fighter aircraft places on Jordan's limited military budget. Yet, military leaders' corporate interests, including their desire to enhance their organization's status and resources, often push them toward high-prestige systems. Servicing the military requires sating these desires. In this sense the purchase of the F-16s by King Hussein (himself a pilot) served a political as much as a military purpose.

Specialization and the Internal/External Division of Labor

The development of security entities charged with the daily administration of regime security can allow conventional military forces to focus on their external roles and functions to some degree, alleviating some of the negative effects of daily involvement in internal affairs. For example, the use of Egypt's Central Protection Forces as the frontline force in the battle against Islamic militancy may have allowed the Egyptian military to maintain its "professional" ethos and external orientation. Hafez al-Assad appears to have sought to impose a division of labor in his armed forces soon after formally coming to power in 1970. He pursued a "dual policy in seeking to reconcile political control with military professionalism," by emphasizing political loyalties in senior appointments to units charged with regime defense and emphasizing professional competence and discipline in the larger army.[49] Despite leaders' efforts to minimize the organizational pathologies of dual-mandate militaries through functional specialization, there are inherent limits to these strategies. The danger is that a military that identifies too much with its external

---

[48]Jordan has also received Challenger-One tanks from Britain (renamed "Al-Hussein" tanks). After Abdullah acceded to the throne in February 1999, Britain promised to supply Jordan with 288 tanks. See "Britain Makes New Delivery of Tanks to Jordan," *Agence France Presse*, September 1, 2001. The United States also supplies a large amount of military aid to Jordan. For 2003, the Bush administration is seeking to increase military aid to $198 million, from $75 million in 2002. This is in addition to economic aid.

[49]Hinnebusch, 1990, p. 159.

roles may be unwilling to use force internally. In Egypt, for example, when the military agreed to suppress conscripts, it did so reluctantly, protective of its post-1973 "professional" identity.[50]

A professionalized officer corps may prove more willing to act independently. In Iraq in 1982, the military command and its Baathist counterparts, frustrated by Hussein's ill-fated strategic and operational decisions, worked out a cease-fire proposal to submit to Iran abandoning all territorial claims by the president and returning the situation to the prewar status quo, all without the participation of Saddam Hussein.[51] Despite Hussein's efforts to exploit kinship loyalties in appointments, officers of his Republican Guard and their regular army counterparts again challenged Saddam Hussein's strategic and operational control over the war in the summer of 1986, after serious losses to the Iranians, including that of the al-Faw peninsula. Subsequently, military leaders were granted greater latitude in running the war, and reforms were undertaken within the Republican Guard.[52]

In theory, specialization of intelligence functions and separation of civilian and military intelligence may also be possible, but in practice, the logic of political control works against a clear division of labor. Intelligence and security entities necessarily will have overlapping mandates and blurred domains of responsibility, to induce competition and comprehensive reporting on each other. Unmonitored entities, extricated from this intelligence infrastructure, invite secret activities and plotting. The imperatives of regime security thus complicate the effort to carve off agencies dedicated solely to foreign adversaries.

International Factors

International events may also alter the civil-military equation. The military itself may press for greater professionalization when faced with the prospect of war. Some of this dynamic was evident in the attitudes of Egypt's military chiefs in preparation for the October

---

[50]Brooks, 1998, pp. 39–40.

[51]The Iranian leadership rejected the proposal. Tripp, *A History of Iraq*, p. 236.

[52]Tripp, *A History of Iraq*, pp. 241–242.

1973 war when many of them clearly recognized the pitfalls of politicization.[53] In addition, political leaders themselves may be most prone to relax controls on appointments and command in the course of war, when losing to an adversary becomes in itself a potential threat to a leader's tenure in office. Hence, in the final phases of the Iran-Iraq war, after devastating early losses to the Iranians, Saddam Hussein allowed professionals greater influence over planning and command.[54] Nevertheless, as noted above, he did so under pressure from his military command, and only after serious losses to the Iranians.

The Unconventional Alternative

Finally, the biggest way these states may offset their conventional weakness is with the procurement of weapons of mass destruction (WMD), including biological, chemical, and nuclear weapons, and the delivery systems that support them. This is especially true for the use of these weapons at the strategic level. These weapons heighten the regional and international bargaining power of those who possess them: A state's inability to mount a successful air or ground campaign may be irrelevant if its leader can credibly threaten to deploy missiles armed with WMD warheads against an adversary's cities. The development of missile technology and WMD for strategic use has other advantages. As Ian Lesser notes in Chapter Eight, these weapons are conducive to centralized command and control. Hence they not only serve security/strategic interests but are consistent with civil-military imperatives.

The utility of these weapons for tactical use (as a war-fighting device) is slightly more complicated. On the positive side, they may allow

---

[53]al-Gamasi, Chief of Operations in the October 1973 war, details many of these attitudes. See al-Gamasi, 1993.

[54]Saddam delegated control over military operations following Iran's capture of the former oil terminal of al-Faw in early 1986. He also allowed regular army units of proven skill and competence to be integrated into the Republican Guard. Even so, he created a new presidential security unit; some analysts also trace the genesis of the Special Republican Guard to these reforms (others to the early 1990s after the Kuwait war). On the command changes and reforms see Cordesman and Wagner, 1991, pp. 52–63; and "Iraq's Army: The Lessons from the War with Iran," *The Economist*, January 12, 1991, p. 36. On the changes in the security infrastructure see Rathmell, 1991, and Boyne, 1991.

these militaries not only to transcend but actually to compensate for conventional weaknesses, if these weapons are integrated into tactical doctrine and operations. Iraq's ultimate successes against Iran in the Iran-Iraq War were due in part to the introduction of chemical weapons in the final phases of the conflict. Lesser notes how these weapons could be used to disrupt the mobilization of enemy forces, or for other purposes. On the negative side, the deployment of these weapons for use by tactical units poses some political risks. It requires the decentralization of authority to local commanders, which these regimes are apt to be wary of, especially with weapons with such destructive capacity. Moreover, despite their strategic utility, WMD would be of only limited utility in protecting the regime against an actual attack or in ensuring regime security. The use of chemical or biological weapons for use in defending the capital against a coup attempt or mass demonstration would probably devastate the regime's home base. In the event of an actual attack by external forces, these weapons would be of limited military utility in defending borders and the capital, especially in the absence of competent commanders and units to deploy them and integrate them into defensive operations. In short, WMD may compensate for some tactical weaknesses and provide bargaining leverage in strategic relations, but they do not substitute for an effective conventional military capability.

POTENTIAL CHALLENGES TO CIVIL-MILITARY RELATIONS

Chief among the factors that threaten to disrupt the present equilibrium in political-military relations is leadership succession. As discussed in Chapter Five, the Arab Middle East is in a state of transition from aged leaders to a newer generation. Notable cases of recent transitions include Qatar (June 1995), Jordan (February 1999), Morocco (July 1999), and Syria (June 2000).

Many of these successions appear to have proceeded quite smoothly, at least in their early phases. In Jordan, a critical U.S. ally in the region, King Abdullah has effectively stepped into his father's shoes and assumed leadership of the country. Since his accession to the throne there has been continuity in the country's domestic and foreign policies, although high unemployment and poverty continue to challenge this resource-dependent "buffer" state. Of the recent transitions, Syria has the greatest potential risk for civil-military tensions. For the moment, Bashar al-Assad's position appears secure. Since coming to power, Bashar has taken tentative steps toward liberalizing Syria's economy and allowing greater freedom of speech and association.[55] The leader appears to have found a comfortable middle ground in steering the country between hard-core reformers and pro–status quo forces; the security chiefs and old guard elite have settled upon him as an unthreatening compromise candidate.[56]

In part, Bashar's position in Syria has been made more secure by his father's use of the levers of political control to prepare the ground for his son. In the months and years leading up to the succession, important members of the old guard and potential obstacles to the younger Assad's consolidation of power were removed from key positions, in many cases after years if not decades of occupying them.[57] For three decades Hafez al-Assad also maintained control

---

[55]In the first year after his accession, the regime appeared to be pursuing reform with a deliberate agenda. After running up against obstacles among the Baathist old guard and elite, the regime was forced to slow its hand. However, Bashar has not altogether abandoned his reformist push. In the cabinet reshuffle in December 2002, he appointed technocrats and former members of international organizations to top economic posts. On the old guard's resistance see "Lessons from Syria's Experiment with Democracy," *Mideast Mirror*, July 5, 2001, and "Syria's Assad Sees Little Cause for Optimism," *Mideast Mirror*, July 1, 2002.

[56]Volker Perthes, "The Political Economy of the Syrian Succession," *Survival*, Vol. 43, No. 1, Spring 2001, p. 148. Recent reports reveal little evidence of contention over his rule from within the ruling elite, although the Damascus regime is extremely careful about guarding information about internal affairs and behind-the-scenes intrigue. Bashar's reformist agenda did ruffle more than a few feathers among the old guard and it is unsurprising that he has slowed the pace and comprehensiveness of political and economic change.

[57]Among the significant casualties were Ali Haydar, long-serving commander of the Special Forces; Adnan Makluf, chief of the country's Presidential Guard; and Ali Duba, formally deputy, but *de facto* chief of Military Intelligence, who was dismissed only months before Assad's death, after it was all but expected that the president would extend Duba's tenure, then aged 70, beyond the usual retirement age of 67 for generals. Many analysts attribute changes in the Syrian command structure in the mid- and latter 1990s to Assad's efforts to prepare the ground for his son's succession. In many cases, these individuals had occupied positions for decades, and were retired (ostensibly because of their age) or shifted to new positions out of concern that the older generation would be reticent to accept Bashar's leadership unconditionally, and to pave the way for a younger group of officers dependent on the patronage of the younger man for their positions. See Susan Sachs, "Leaders of Syria Building Support for Son of Assad," *New York Times*, June 12, 2000; Zisser, 1991. Specifically, on Ali Haydar see Brooks, 1998, p. 58; on Makluf see Zisser, 1991, p. 41; and on Duba see

over his security and intelligence chiefs with a system of divide and rule; competition was encouraged among rival fiefs as a way of preventing any single group from becoming too powerful. Consequently, the basic ingredients for a factionalized power struggle within the military and security elite are in place. The quality of decisionmaking has also changed from unquestioned hierarchy under Hafez al-Assad to a more collective style of leadership.[58] Intraregime disputes could yet devolve into a power struggle should the consensus around Bashar's leadership erode. In the first years of his rule, Bashar was not tested by a severe political or regional crisis. However, future tensions in the region, including those caused by the presence of U.S. forces in Iraq and the Palestinian-Israeli conflict, could catalyze such a power struggle.[59] Syria faces many potentially daunting challenges, both domestically and regionally. Among these are unchecked population growth and the need for new jobs, longstanding dependence on oil-related income, dire need for foreign investment, and potentially declining standards of living and increasing poverty. Moreover, relations with Lebanon or between Lebanon and Israel could yet prove problematic for Syria.[60] As Perthes puts it, should Syria face any external or internal disturbances, the security and military chiefs might "decide that Bashar al-Assad was not, after all, the right man for the job."[61]

Critical countries such as Saudi Arabia, Libya, and Egypt have yet to face the transition in leadership.[62] In all three countries aging leaders occupy top positions; while sons and relatives are sometimes

---

"Exit of Syria's Military Intelligence Chief Leaves Assad's Son-in-Law as De Facto Boss," *Mideast Mirror,* Vol. 14, No. 30, February 14, 2000. Also notable is the decision to pursue Hikmet Shehabi, retired Chief of Staff, on corruption charges, which effectively put him on the regime's "hit list," in June 2000; Shehabi was forced to flee the country days after Hafez al-Assad's death. See "Are Khaddam, Hariri and Jumblatt on Damascus's Corruption Hit List," *Mideast Mirror,* Vol. 14, No. 108, June 8, 2000; "Former Syrian Chief of Staff Is Next on Anti-Corruption Hit-List," *Mideast Mirror,* Vol. 14, No. 106, June 6, 2000.

[58]Perthes, 2001, p. 147.

[59]MacFarquhar, "Syria Reaches Turning Point," 2001.

[60]On these potential economic and regional disturbances see Perthes, 1991, pp. 144–145, 151–152.

[61]Perthes, "The Political Economy of the Syrian Succession," p. 149.

[62]On succession in the region see "Like Father, Like Son," *The Economist* (U.S. edition), June 2, 2001.

singled out as possible successors, their capacity to consolidate power, especially in places like Egypt, is uncertain.[63] Elite power struggles threaten to involve the military as a direct participant and to promote splits within it, as contenders court sections of the officer corps to bolster their bid for power. In Egypt, for example, rumors abound about Mubarak's intention to groom his son as a possible successor, although in April 2001 the president openly denied he favored his son in an interview with the *Washington Post.*[64] Analysts also predict that Mubarak will choose a vice president, after 20 years of leaving the position vacant. This would be an important step because the position of vice president is considered a major stepping-stone to the presidency. In addition to focusing on Mubarak's son, some observers point to individuals in the military and security services as likely candidates.[65] There is certainly a precedent (both Sadat and Mubarak were former military officers) and, more important,

---

[63]In Iraq, Qusay, Saddam's son, was often singled out as his chosen successor; Saddam had been increasing his responsibilities and expanding his role in the regime, to the apparent consternation of his elder son, Uday. See "Major Personnel Changes Expected in Baghdad," *Mideast Mirror*, Vol. 11, No. 130, July 8, 1997; "Paper Controlled by Uday Notes 'Absurd' Report on Qusay's Powers," Babil', Baghdad in Arabic, August 5, 1999, p. 3, reported in *BBC Monitoring Middle East—Political, BBC Worldwide Monitoring*, August 7, 1999; "Saddam's Second Son Gets Succession Boost," *Ha'aretz*, May 20, 2001.

Egypt, of course, has experienced two previous transitions from Nasser to Sadat in 1970 and from Sadat to Mubarak (upon the former's assassination in 1981). But these events were more traumatic than is sometimes remembered. On the succession question in Egypt see Brooks, 1998, pp. 60–64. On Libya see Thomas Olstead, "A New Generation of Leaders Will Shake Up the Mideast," *U.S. News and World Report*, February 22, 1999.

As noted in Chapter Five, considerable uncertainty remains, even where succession is likely to be a family affair, as in Saudi Arabia. See Jerrold Green, *Leadership Succession in the Arab World: A Policy-Makers Guide*, Center for Policy Options, Los Angeles, Calif.: University of Judaism, Summer 2000. For an earlier analysis of the Saudi case see Joseph Kechichian, *Political Dynamics and Security in the Arabian Peninsula Through the 1990s*, Santa Monica, Calif.: RAND, MR-167-AF/A, 1993, pp. 50–52.

For an overview of succession issues in these countries, and more broadly in the region, see Chapter Five.

[64]See E. S. McKee, "Still Waters on the Nile," *The Jerusalem Report*, November 8, 1999. Also see the discussion in Mary Ann Weaver "Egypt on Trial," *New York Times*, June 17, 2001. Mubarak's denials came in an interview with Lally Weymouth, a *Washington Post* reporter, reported in "Mubarak: 'Jerusalem Can Stop Everything,'" *The Jerusalem Post*, April 3, 2001. Also see "Egypt: Talking About a Vice President," *Mideast Mirror*, September 5, 2001.

[65]"Egypt: Talking About a Vice President," 2001.

an undeniable political logic to choosing someone with a military background: In Egypt, as elsewhere in the region, a secure hold on the military's allegiance is essential to maintaining control over the succession and preventing elite conflicts from splintering into overt power struggles.

A second potentially destabilizing force stems from the variety of tensions and conflicts among the states in the region. The link between regional instability and civil-military relations is indirect but is potentially critical for the internal stability of key Arab allies. Among the critical issues is the unresolved Israeli-Palestinian conflict, which since the fall of 2000 has worsened considerably. Poor Palestinian-Israeli relations increase popular alienation in Muslim capitals, especially in Saudi Arabia, Jordan, and Egypt, which are U.S. allies, and in the latter cases maintain unpopular peace treaties with Israel. These regimes are forced to resort to increased repression, which on a regular basis involves their security and intelligence services. However, the prospect of military involvement in the repression of widespread demonstrations is of real concern. In addition to destabilizing the regime's political-military balance of power, such a potentiality might test the loyalties of junior officers and soldiers forced to fire on family, friends, and communities with which they identify.[66] If military support for these regimes is jeopardized, they become more vulnerable to opposition elements from within the regime, and beyond.

The U.S. war on terrorism and the reconstruction of Iraq also are potential sources of instability within Arab states. To the extent U.S. activities increase resentment toward status quo regimes and provoke anti-American demonstrations, these activities potentially undermine key allies' civil-military relations. Such regimes as Jordan have been forced to clamp down on social opposition and demon-

---

[66]The dangers of testing these loyalties were evident in the Syrian regime's widespread campaigns of repression of Islamic activism in the late 1970s and early 1980s. In at least two documented incidents units ordered into action in Sunni cities split along sectarian lines; the discipline of the Sunni units collapsed in the face of orders to take action. See Hinnebusch, 1990, pp. 163–164.

strators opposed to U.S. policy in the region.[67] This pits the security services and the conventional armed forces that back them against mainstream opinion. Thus far, pivotal U.S. allies such as Egypt and Jordan have successfully contained social opposition. But it is difficult if not impossible to anticipate when these domestic tensions could shift the political-military balance of power. Security forces and military leaders could act against demonstrators, or perhaps more likely, there could be behind-the-scenes pressure to relax pro-U.S. positions and appease popular opinion. These are potentially important considerations for how the United States crafts policy in the region. In short, controversies over the prosecution of the war on terrorism, U.S. policy toward the reconstruction of Iraq, and the stalemate in Palestinian-Israeli peace could have ramifications far beyond their immediate domains.

A final threat to stability in civil-military relations comes from factionalism and religious fundamentalism in the armed forces. There is very little reliable information available in the public arena that would indicate the extent of fundamentalist penetration of the armed forces in these regimes. These issues are nonetheless vital to assessing civil-military relations for two reasons. Factionalism can be a precursor to military intervention in politics. A faction that commands a substantial following in the armed forces is a prerequisite to building an effective coup coalition. Coups are born from secret cells in the armed forces and depend largely on cultivating a core group of supporters and then expanding its horizontal and vertical linkages in the armed forces. Although it is difficult to plot in secrecy, the potential remains that a disaffected unit might, without notice, succeed in removing a leader in a key Arab capital, such as Syria or Egypt. Factionalism in the armed forces is all the more worrisome when militant fundamentalist sentiment is high within the officer corps. The latter can provide the ideological glue for a disaffected group, and the motivation to move against a regime, despite

---

[67]During the 2003 Iraq war, for example, there were large demonstrations. In that case, the security services largely kept them under control. Nevertheless, fear was expressed by Arab leaders and outsiders that these demonstrations could get out of hand and destabilize these regimes. See Andrew Gumbel, "The Iraq Conflict: Arab Governments Struggle to Control Protests Against Us," *The Independent*, March 26, 2003; Neil MacFarquhar, "Arab Protesters Focus Ire on U.S.," *New York Times*, April 6, 2002; "Jordan's Street Moves Again," *Mideast Mirror*, July 26, 2002.

the substantial personal risks involved to the conspirators. Fundamentalist "infiltration" remains a stated objective of militant groups battling the Egyptian regime since the 1990s.[68] The fact that the regime has now largely broken the militant organizations does not fully alleviate the concern that they may succeed in courting sections of the officer corps.

IMPLICATIONS FOR THE UNITED STATES

The above picture of civil-military relations in the Middle East has three sets of implications for the United States. A first set relates to the continuity of civil-military relations, and overall stability, of the region's authoritarian regimes. In the absence of some major disruptive event—possibly in the form of a succession struggle, widespread regional and domestic turmoil related to the Palestinian-Israeli conflict, the reconstruction of Iraq, or the infiltration of Islamist groups into the officer corps—the United States can bank on continuity in civil-military relations in most of the region's regimes. For better or worse, the status quo is likely to persist.

The United States can reinforce the present equilibrium in civil-military relations in several ways. Continuing military aid to allies in the region effectively channels resources to political leaders in these regimes. Foreign Military Financing (FMF) granted to Egypt and Jordan by the United States, aside from any military utility, supports leaders' abilities to satisfy corporate interests, and therefore bolsters stability in civil-military relations. Similarly, military-to-military contacts and joint training undergird diplomatic cooperation by creating vested interests and formal and informal relationships with foreign military organizations and their leaders. Access to high-technology weapons systems, spare parts, and the prestige of exercising with the U.S. military can shape military preferences in ways favorable to American policy.

Although efficacious, policies that support the present configuration of civil-military relations and authoritarian politics have a potential downside. Bolstering political control in the short term probably

---

[68]Samia Nakhoul, "Egyptian Militants Aim to Infiltrate Armed Forces," *Reuters*, August 23, 1993.

undercuts the potential for long-term political and economic reform in U.S. allies. The penetration of societies by vast security and intelligence bureaucracies stunts the growth of civil society by making it risky to engage in political discourse in public, and often in private. Bolstering the military bureaucracy with resources and prerogatives perpetuates a constituency that is a major obstacle to serious economic or political restructuring. The private and corporate benefits that military organizations and their leaders enjoy as a result of corruption within the private and public sectors only magnify these challenges. These considerations may seem trivial in light of the risks to immediate policy objectives in Iraq and the war on terrorism if the United States presses its allies for major changes in internal politics. They nonetheless present a major dilemma for those trying to secure the region and protect U.S. interests in the longer term. As Chapter Two highlights, supporting the status quo within U.S. Arab allies may compromise the potential for democracy and peace in the region.

An additional set of implications relates to the conventional military capabilities of states with dual-mandate militaries. The authoritarian states of the Middle East are likely to exhibit predictable strengths and weaknesses on the battlefield. In particular, they will exhibit rigidities in command and control. Political leaders and their military chiefs in dual-mandate militaries should be reluctant to delegate to frontline commanders. Command will tend to be concentrated in the rear, with potentially adverse effects on operational tempo and responsiveness. The quality of leadership should vary widely, as the imperatives of political control sometimes conflict with advancing talented and skilled officers. In addition, these militaries will perform better with, and may prefer, heavily scripted operational plans over fast-paced, decentralized, and fluid operations. They should face barriers in assimilating complex technologies, especially those that require integrated command and control procedures. Moreover, patterns of deployments, and the units assigned to external defense, will tend to reflect the requirements of regime security. The best-equipped and trained units, paradoxically, may be those least likely to be committed in battle against a foreign military.

These strengths and weaknesses represent a mixed blessing for the United States. Adversaries' capacities to effectively employ their often significant material resources on the battlefield are limited. But,

as a result of the imperatives of political control, the potential benefits of coalition warfare and military cooperation with U.S. allies are
also constrained. In fact, the weaknesses of these dual-mandate
militaries in leadership, command and control, interservice coordination and maneuver may mean that coalition warfare often has
more political utility than military benefit.

The analysis also has implications for the success of the U.S. war on
terrorism. Many of the United States' authoritarian allies have mutual interests in neutralizing religiously inspired opposition movements active in the region, because radical groups that oppose the
United States also often oppose rule by the region's secular, repressive regimes. In addition, the proliferation of security and intelligence agencies in these regimes means that they have an indigenous
capability to pursue radical movements. Strong central authorities,
with efficient monitoring and repressive apparatuses, benefit the
United States in prosecuting the war on terrorism. Yet the political
power of the armed forces and security services also poses some
risks. If radical elements succeed in winning the sympathy of key
factions of the armed forces, these countries' support for U.S. policy
could be jeopardized. Political leaders will have to appease their officers or potentially risk their positions in office.

Regional tensions such as those stemming from the Palestinian-
Israeli conflict and U.S. administration of Iraq are also potentially
destabilizing to civil-military relations. Opposition within local
populations in the Middle East to the policies of their government,
the United States, or other states may force these regimes to rely
more heavily on repressive policies. On a regular basis, security services police demonstrators and activists and root out opposition.
But in the event security services prove incapable of managing a
mass outpouring of opposition, military authorities could be called
upon. This, in turn, could indirectly destabilize the delicate balance
of power between civil and military authorities, and in the worst
case, prompt the military to refuse to act in defense of these regimes.
Instability in governing regimes and a breakdown in central authority would pose even graver risks to the United States in its effort to
apprehend and dismantle terrorist networks, promote stability in
Iraq, and advance peace between Palestinians and Israelis.

A final set of implications relates to the U.S. effort to promote democracy in Iraq in the aftermath of the spring 2003 war. Building a military that is professionalized and committed to democratic values is essential to the long-term success of the democratic reform project in Iraq. Yet the recent history of the Iraqi military will pose significant obstacles to U.S. and allied efforts to promote change in civil-military relations. Even if the Iraqi military is restructured and retrained, the legacy of organizational norms that favor partisanship over merit in appointments, encourage extremely centralized and hierarchical systems of command, and permit broad repression and corruption within the chain of command will probably persist for some time. Supplanting them with merit-based standards of conduct and more militarily efficient organizational structures will require considerable skill and patience. Even more challenging will be advancing an ethos within the officer corps that reflects a commitment to democratic institutions and ways of life. In sum, it will take time and dedication by U.S. authorities if the conventions of democratic professionalism are ever to become embedded in a rebuilt Iraqi military. Those U.S. officials charged with overseeing the development of a new military must become well acquainted with the structures of political control to which this dual mandate was long accustomed. Only with a clear understanding of the past can strategies for successful reform be developed and implemented.

Chapter Five

THE IMPLICATIONS OF LEADERSHIP CHANGE IN THE ARAB WORLD

Daniel L. Byman

The politics of the Middle East may be more dependent on the ambitions and whims of individual leaders than in any other region of the world. Middle Eastern leaders are often unconstrained by domestic political institutions or popular sentiment: Their ambitions and preferences, as well as their weaknesses and foibles, can make the difference between war and peace, revolution and stability. Leadership change in the Middle East, however, is infrequent and seldom routinized. The region often seems frozen in time, with certain leaders—Muammar Qadhafi of Libya, Yasir Arafat in the Palestinian Authority, and Hosni Mubarak of Egypt, among others—ruling for decades. As Glenn Robinson remarks, "If anything, the contemporary Arab world has been marked by too much political stability at the top, not too little."[1]

Table 5.1 suggests that a thaw is occurring. Although many Arab leaders came to power in the 1970s or 1980s, the last several years have seen remarkable change. In 1997, President Khatami won the Iranian election, campaigning to reform the revolutionary system. In 1999, new leaders came to power in Algeria, Bahrain, Jordan, and Morocco, and in 2000 one of the most enduring leaders in the world, Syria's Hafez al-Assad, passed away.

---

[1] Glenn E. Robinson, "Palestine After Arafat," *The Washington Quarterly*, Vol. 23, No. 4, Autumn 2000, p. 77.

Table 5.1

Heads of State of Selected Middle Eastern Countries

Country	Head of State	Year Born	Year Came to Power (formal ascension)
Algeria	President Abdelaziz Bouteflika	1937	1999
Bahrain	Amir Hamad bin Isa Al Khalifa	1949	1999
Egypt	President Mohammad Hosni Mubarak	1928	1981
Iran	President Mohammad Khatami	1943	1997
Jordan	King Abdullah II	1962	1999
Kuwait	Amir Jabir al-Ahmad al-Jabir al-Sabah	1926	1977
Libya	Col Muammar Abu Minyar al-Qadhafi	1942	1969
Morocco	King Muhammad VI	1963	1999
Oman	Sultan Qaboos bin Said Al-Said	1940	1970
Palestinian National Authority	President Yasser Arafat	1929	1968
Qatar	Amir Hamad bin Khalifa Al-Thani	1950	1995
Saudi Arabia	King Fahd bin Abd al-Aziz Al-Saud	1923	1982
Syria	President Bashar al-Assad	1966	2000
United Arab Emirates	President Zayid bin Sultan Al-Nuhayyan	1918	1971

SOURCE: *Chiefs of State and Cabinet Members of Foreign Governments.* Central Intelligence Agency, http://www.cia.gov/cia/publications/chiefs/index.html (accessed on April 3, 2001). When this report went to press, the leadership of Iraq had not yet been selected.

This chapter first examines how to conceptualize the issue of regime change.[2] It then assesses the implications of regime change in Saudi Arabia, Syria, and Egypt. These countries were chosen because of their importance in the region and to the United States. Syria represents a regime hostile to U.S. interests in a key region of the Middle

---

[2]This chapter examines regime change that occurs for natural causes (through the death of a leader) or through some process of internal political change (through a coup or assassination, for example). It does not examine cases of regime change that occur through external coercive military force, as was the case in Iraq in 2003.

East. Egypt and Saudi Arabia, on the other hand, are perhaps the most important partners Washington has in the region.[3]

For each case, this chapter attempts to discern what policies stem from geopolitical concerns and are thus likely to be shared by most conceivable regimes and which policies are due to particular types of regimes (e.g., Islamist versus a military regime). In addition, it attempts to note the particular strengths and weaknesses of current leaders and their possible heirs to tease out how a change in the individual at the helm may affect government policies. When possible, the relative power of various alternative leaders is assessed to give a sense of the likelihood of various succession alternatives.

New regimes are likely to be cautious as their leaders try to consolidate power. However, new leaders may be particularly hesitant to risk unpopularity by cooperating with U.S. initiatives. Missteps are inevitable. Leaders may also overestimate their military forces' strength, trust unduly in international support, believe they can intimidate their adversaries, or otherwise have misperceptions that might lead to conflict. The potential changes, of course, are not all negative. In Saudi Arabia, Crown Prince Abdullah may be able to dampen anti-regime sentiment and initiate difficult reforms.

It is tempting for the United States to try to intervene in the process of regime change. The United States has few effective instruments for limited intervention, and open pressure often backfires. To hedge against unexpected change, Washington should consider increasing contacts with leaders and factions who are out of power but enjoy considerable support. The United States should also focus more on cultivating public opinion. Given that many countries are vulnerable to sudden change, and almost all may at some point hesitate to provide access to placate domestic opinion, having many options is necessary.[4]

---

[3]Examining leadership change elsewhere in the Middle East would also be valuable. Iran, Libya, and the Palestinian Authority would also be important to examine given the potential for dramatic change in these countries.

[4]At times, a regime's leadership may prove so dangerous that military intervention is required to topple a regime. The U.S.-led campaign against Iraq in 2003 is one example. This chapter, however, focuses on leadership change in ways that exclude direct efforts to topple a regime. Many of the implications are immediately relevant to considerations of whether a regime should or should not be removed.

PARAMETERS OF REGIME CHANGE

Regime change and its implications are difficult for outsiders to predict. Western knowledge of elite politics in the Middle East is often limited. Indeed, even well informed locals are often caught by surprise: Few in Jordan anticipated that King Hussein would alter the long-established successor from his brother Hassan to his son Abdullah in his dying weeks. At times, the surprise is far more dramatic. Iran suffered a revolution in 1979 that caught almost all observers by surprise; other countries regularly suffered coups or unrest that few predicted.

Leaders differ tremendously, even if their countries' social systems and strategic environments hold constant. Leaders are capable of dramatically changing their country's foreign policy orientation, going to war despite unfavorable military circumstances, designing new domestic institutions or weakening old ones, or otherwise shaping—in addition to reacting to—their domestic political structures and international circumstances.[5] Egypt's President Sadat, for example, led Egypt out of the Soviet camp into the American one, conducted a successful surprise attack on Israel, negotiated a peace agreement with Israel, liberalized Egypt's economy, and otherwise transformed Egypt's domestic, regional, and international policies.

Indeed, dramatic rapid regime change is possible in the Middle East, where both demagogues and visionaries have appeared with surprising frequency. During the 1950s and 1960s, Egypt, Iraq, Libya, Syria, and Yemen all experienced military coups. In 1979, a popular revolution ousted the Iranian regime. Algeria's attempt to open up its political process in the early 1990s led to a de facto military coup and a civil war. Even such democratic countries as Turkey and Israel have dramatically changed their policies when new leaders have risen to the fore.

Greater public influence on decisionmaking is also possible, and may even be likely. As discussed in Chapters Two and Seven, liberalization and democratization are proceeding fitfully in the region, while the information revolution is making more citizens aware of events

---

[5]Daniel Byman and Kenneth Pollack, "Let Us Now Praise Great Men: Bringing the Statesman Back In," *International Security*, Vol. 25, No. 1, Spring 2001, pp. 107–146.

and able to react to them quickly. These trends hardly constitute the complete transformation of Arab politics, but they do suggest that popular opinion is a growing force that should be considered by U.S. decisionmakers. To be clear, public opinion will not exercise a direct influence, but it may constrain what leaders do, particularly if they are politically weak.

Categories of Regime Change

Regime change can follow at least three paths. First, and most obviously, it can involve a transition from one leader to another from the same cadre or power base. This would include the transition from father to son in Bahrain, Qatar, Morocco, Jordan, and Syria in the last decade, the shift to another member of the family (e.g., from Saudi Arabia's King Fahd to his half-brother, Crown Prince Abdullah as the king's health has faltered), or a transition to a leader who comes from the same set of elites and interests as the existing leader (e.g., Vice President Mubarak's ascension after the assassination of Egyptian President Sadat in 1981). This transition need not be formal or even peaceful: A coup that replaced one military leader with another (Hafez al-Assad over Salah Jadid) or *coups de famille* (e.g., Oman's Sultan Qaboos' peaceful takeover from his father) would fall into this category as well.

The second category of change involves a shift from one set of elites to another. The range of alternatives is, in theory, vast. Elites can come from a different ethnic group, a different social class, a different region of the country, and so on. In the Middle East, however, religious leaders are usually the most organized set of rival elites. For the most part, Middle Eastern regimes have successfully co-opted or repressed trade unions, intellectuals, professional associations, and merchants. Religious groups are harder to suppress. They typically draw on an existing organization of mosques and community networks. Because religion is integral to the lives of many citizens, few regimes are willing to openly suppress religious practice. Moreover, several Middle Eastern regimes depend on religion for their legitimacy. Thus, it is not surprising that in recent years Islamists have proven a grave challenge to area regimes. Islamists captured the state in Iran and Sudan, while they have at times posed a serious challenge to the regimes of Syria, Egypt, Saudi Arabia, Bahrain, Jordan, Algeria, Libya, and the Palestinian Authority.

A third category of change involves a shift from elite-based rule to a regime that more closely involves the general population. This could occur because a popular revolution installs a regime that depends on large segments of the population or from a move toward democratization, which allows ordinary individuals a greater voice in politics and the selection of leaders. In many circumstances, however, this may not represent a change in the face of the leadership, but rather the interests the leaders represent. Existing leaders may try to cultivate the populace out of a genuine commitment to democracy, to gain support for unpopular changes, or to bolster their power against rival elites.

Each of these categories requires a different level of analysis. The first level is individual: What are the strengths, weaknesses, idiosyncrasies, and objectives of particular individuals? The second level is elite based, focusing on what characterizes a particular family or power base. The third level involves assessing potential rival groups and their agendas. How do these elites differ from the current ruling elites? Do they have different goals, or rely on different social groups for support? The converse to these questions is understanding the sources of stability. What are the geopolitical realities and limits that will inhibit changes?

The following three country studies draw on these different levels of analysis. The analysis of each country examines the different politics of key members of the current elite, the agendas of rival groups, and the sentiments of the populace at large.

LEADERSHIP CHANGE IN SAUDI ARABIA

Succession in Saudi Arabia appears stable. The Al Saud, who have governed the Kingdom since Abd al-Aziz seized power in a daring raid on Riyadh in 1902, have survived Western imperialism, Arab nationalism, Islamic extremism, external aggression, and other threats to their rule in the 20th century. In so doing, they have strengthened their hold on Saudi society and smoothly passed the leadership from one member of the family of Abd al-Aziz to another.[6]

Yet change, even dramatic change, remains possible in Saudi Arabia. Given the lack of formal checks on the monarch's authority, the transition from King Fahd to Crown Prince Abdullah, and the imminent succession after that, has important implications. In addition, the power and autonomy of the Al Saud are not certain: A rival might emerge who better reflects public sentiment or that of rival elites, such as the Kingdom's many Islamists.

This section explores the possible pace of change in Saudi Arabia, examining different succession alternatives and their policy implications. It also tries to identify what will not change. In Saudi Arabia (as in all countries), policy is shaped by geography and the opinions shared by Saudis of all political stripes.

Change Within the Al Saud

King Fahd's final days are near, and his successor, Crown Prince Abdullah, is consolidating power. King Fahd already relinquished day-to-day leadership to his half brother after his stroke in 1996. Abdullah, however, is in his late 70s and is only two years younger than Fahd, raising the prospect that another leader may take his place shortly.[7]

Al Saud Constants. Regardless of which ruling family member takes power, the next king is likely to share certain characteristics and objectives that are common to the family in general. The Al Saud, in general, agree on most issues. As once prince commented, "We

---

[6]Indeed, in many ways the problems the Kingdom encountered with such inept rulers as Saud bin Abd al-Aziz demonstrate the vitality of the Al Saud. In what was in essence a family coup, Saud's powers were curtailed in the early 1960s because of his economic mismanagement and bungled attempts to resist Nasser's threatened pan-Arab revolution; his brother, the highly competent Faysal, was given additional power and eventually made king.

[7]The Kingdom does not have a British-style succession where the monarchy passes from father to son. Succession has passed among the sons of Abd al-Aziz but will soon have to go to the next generation.

never debate direction. We debate its focus, speed, style, emphasis, colors."[8]

Most would-be leaders place the Al Saud's family interests ahead of those of Saudi Arabia in general. Ensuring their continued rule is thus a priority, one that often trumps more standard economic and strategic concerns. As a result, security concerns often reflect efforts to deflect domestic opposition as well as attempts to secure the country's borders.[9] The family was particularly sensitive to Saddam Hussein's repeated challenges to its legitimacy; relations with Iran, in contrast, have improved since 1996, as the regime in Tehran has toned down its rhetorical challenges to the Al Saud.

In style, any leader is likely to be conciliatory and a consensus builder. Although technically a monarchy, the Al Saud exhibit many characteristics of an oligarchy: Leadership is often collective and consensus-based, resulting in steady but slow decisions.[10] Since consolidating power, the Al Saud in general have proven cautious, reacting to rather than shaping events.

The family is ambivalent in its attitude toward the United States. Fahd, Abdullah, and other Saudi leaders recognize the importance of security ties to the United States and appreciate the U.S. role in defending the Kingdom against Iraq. They fear, however, that the U.S. commitment may be transitory. In addition, they recognize that the United States is not popular in the Kingdom and are concerned that a U.S. presence is a rallying cry for oppositionists at home.[11] The Al Saud seek to continue the security relationship with the United States but prefer it to be low profile whenever possible. Current proposals to reduce or eliminate the permanent U.S. military presence in the Kingdom are falling on sympathetic ears.

---

[8]See Susan Sachs, "Saudi Prince Urges Reform, and a Move from Shadow," *New York Times,* December 4, 2000.

[9]F. Gregory Gause III, *Oil Monarchies: Domestic and Security Challenges in the Arab Gulf States,* New York: Council on Foreign Relations, 1994, p. 120.

[10]Nadav Safran, *Saudi Arabia: The Ceaseless Quest for Security,* Ithaca, N.Y.: Cornell University Press, 1988, pp. 451–456.

[11]Gause, 1994, p. 122; Simon Henderson, *After King Fahd: Succession in Saudi Arabia,* Washington, D.C.: The Washington Institute for Near East Policy, 1994, p. 47.

This ambivalence is particularly profound with regard to cooperation on counterterrorism. The Al Saud recognize that Islamic militancy as championed by al Qaeda is a threat, perhaps the greatest threat, to their rule. However, open cooperation with the United States only adds credibility to the Islamist charge that the Al Saud is a puppet of Washington. The Al Saud weathered such criticism during the 2003 war against Iraq, but the family remains concerned that this may undermine its legitimacy.

Succession After Fahd. Although the Al Saud share many objectives, which member of the family leads the country remains a vital question. Abdullah differs from Fahd in several ways, with implications for the regime's domestic and foreign policies. Abdullah is also perceived as more pious and concerned about reducing royal family profligacy than is Fahd. He has strong ties to many of Saudi Arabia's conservative tribal leaders. Although he is not anti-American, he has at times criticized Washington harshly for its pro-Israel stance and is less comfortable with Western values.[12]

If Abdullah successfully consolidates power, and lives long enough to wield it, he may be better able than Fahd or most likely successors to tackle the knotty problem of economic reform. Abdullah recognizes that the Kingdom's economy requires liberalization and his personal probity enables him to ask Saudis to make sacrifices where other leaders would be accused of hypocrisy. He is also more willing to try to cut royal family interference in business.[13] Second, Abdullah will be better able to manage Islamist criticism of the regime. His honesty and piety are respected by Islamists, making the regime under

---

[12]See Sachs, 2000; Henderson, 1994, p. 42. In May 2001, Abdullah turned down an invitation to visit Washington because of U.S. support for Israel in the "Al Aqsa" intifada. Abdullah also appears more willing than Fahd to cut government spending and open Saudi Arabia up economically. To the surprise of many observers, he has pushed for Saudi membership in the World Trade Organization. He has also tried to push aside military leaders, including family members, known for their graft.

[13]"Can Crown Prince Abdullah Lead His Desert Kingdom into the 21st Century?" *Business Week*, May 21, 2001, available at http://www.businessweek.com:/2000/00_30/b3691008.htm, accessed on May 19, 2001; Youssef M. Ibrahim, "The Saudi Who Can Speak Our Language," *Washington Post*, February 24, 2002 (electronic version).

his rule less vulnerable to charges of corruption, perhaps the leading weapon in the Islamists' arsenal of rhetoric.[14]

The picture of succession after Abdullah is not clear. The Al Saud formed a Family Council in 2000 to help ensure consensus on key issues, but this has not led to clarity with regard to who will rule in the future. Ignorance of Saudi politics is lessening but is still profound, particularly with regard to the dynamics of ruling family decision-making. Although the regime appears stable, this perception is founded on few data. Even natives have little insight into leadership issues.[15]

With this caveat in mind, several names are commonly raised when the question of succession is raised. Fahd's brother, Prince Sultan, the minister of Defense and Aviation, is widely considered to be next in line after Abdullah. Other full brothers of King Fahd—Abd al-Rahman, Turki, Nayef, Salman, and Ahmad—are also contenders. Several of the sons of the late King Faysal (Saud, Turki, and Khalid) are respected as administrators and may be considered as candidates as Fahd's brothers age.

Several of these potential leaders, like Abdullah, are experienced administrators (several oversee strategic provinces in the Kingdom) who share the Al Saud's general perspective on the region and the world in general. However, they are not equally skilled. The sons of Faysal are believed to lack a deft political touch, raising the possibility that the regime will not manage dissent well.[16] Sultan, the most likely successor after Abdullah, is viewed by many as among the most grasping of the potential claimants to the throne, a perception that will increase the alienation many Saudis feel toward the ruling family and make belt-tightening more difficult.

---

[14]M. Ehsan Ahrari, "Political Succession in Saudi Arabia: Systemic Stability and Security Implications," *Comparative Strategy,* Vol. 18, No. 1, 1999, p. 25.

[15]Ahrari, 1999, p. 13. On March 1, 1992, King Fahd spelled out the procedures for succession. The throne is to remain in the hands of the children of Abdel Aziz, the founder of Saudi Arabia. The king will choose which among them will take the crown. This goes against tradition, however, where the royal family collectively decides who among them is most worthy. In addition, the king's decree excluded several collateral family branches, making it particularly controversial. Ahrari, 1999, p. 17; Henderson, 1994, p. 21.

[16]Henderson, 1994, pp. 21–28.

Two problems may emerge depending on who takes power and the circumstances of the transition. First, the Al Saud may be less unified than in the past. The lack of a clear contender after Abdullah may lead to dissent within the ruling family. Second, it is possible that a leader may emerge who is a poor administrator or who does not seek to rule, such as King Saud (1953–1964) and King Khaled (1975–1982), respectively. The Kingdom has weathered such problems in the past through collective leadership that included several highly competent individuals, such as the current King Fahd, who bolstered King Khaled. Whether collective leadership would work if similar problems emerged in the future is uncertain.[17]

Although the Al Saud appears firmly entrenched, our limited knowledge of Saudi political dynamics requires an assessment of potential leadership alternatives. Saudi Islamists are probably the most organized and popular source of opposition. They differ dramatically from the Al Saud and they disagree with the United States on such issues as the presence of U.S. forces in the Kingdom and the degree of support to give to Islamic militants. In addition, a leader who better reflects popular preferences could emerge. This latter possibility would usher in a new era for U.S.-Saudi relations, one in which cooperation is more difficult.

Constants in Saudi Society

For most Saudis domestic concerns appear to take priority over foreign affairs. In the 1950s and 1960s, much of the Saudi elite was consumed with the question of the proper attitude toward Arab nationalism, but most Saudis today are focused on issues of corruption, prosperity, and morality. Foreign affairs are often ancillary to these issues, or viewed with these concerns in mind.

Many Saudis oppose close relations with the United States and see the United States as a foe rather than friend. As F. Gregory Gause argues, "Many Saudis . . . continue to think that their country's finest hour was when it defied the United States with the 1973 oil em-

---

[17]Saud almost drove Saudi Arabia into bankruptcy and led to the Al Saud's overthrow. Ahrari, 1999, p. 16.

bargo."[18] Saudis accept many conspiracy theories about U.S. intentions in the region, and even Western-educated liberals believe the United States seeks to protect the Al Saud, not Saudi Arabia.[19] Nor do the Saudi people share the regime's attempt to balance American and Arab concerns on the Palestinian issue. Unauthorized demonstrations against Israel, rare in Saudi Arabia, occurred in response to the outbreak of the "Al Aqsa" intifada.[20] Although many Saudis do not support terrorism against the United States, at least some segments of the Kingdom favor attacks. Many others embrace conspiracy theories about who was responsible, while far more believe that U.S. policy in the Middle East is the ultimate cause of the attacks.

Saudis in general have little love for Iraqis and even less for Iranians. Although the suffering of the Iraqi people under sanctions received attention in opposition circles, this appears in large part as a means of criticizing U.S. policy. The suffering of Iraqis in the 1980s received little sympathy. Many Saudis, particularly Islamists, are also virulently anti-Shi'a, considering them apostates. As a result, they are suspicious of Iran's regime and also of the future of Iraq, which has a Shi'a majority. Islamist Saudis would view a secular Iraq, or one dominated by Iraq's Shi'a, with concern. However, a more democratic Iraq that had an accountable government would also be viewed as a potential model for the Kingdom, increasing pressure on the Al Saud to liberalize.

Saudi Islamists

Saudi Islamists are probably the most organized source of opposition to the regime and, if the Al Saud became paralyzed by infighting or if the Saudi economy became mired in a recession, they might find an opening for increased influence. Through a network of mosques, schools, and religious associations, many supported by the state, Islamists have a means to organize and propagate their message. Perhaps 20 percent of Saudis see themselves as extreme conservatives

---

[18]Gause, 1994, p. 122.

[19]Gause, 1994, p. 141.

[20]See Sachs, "Saudi Prince Urges Reform," 2000.

on matters of religion, with many more sharing many of the objectives of the Islamists.[21]

The Islamists' attitude toward the Al Saud is ambivalent. Leading Islamist critics of the regime believe that Islam is under siege and that the Al Saud have contributed to, rather than fought against, this problem. More mainstream Islamists are troubled by the profligacy of many of the Al Saud, which they see as reflecting an overall degeneration of Saudi morality. Crown Prince Abdullah, however, is respected for his piety and honesty.[22]

The Islamist agenda would represent a departure from Al Saud policy in several ways. The Islamists' primary agenda is internal: They seek to resist Westernization and secularization, and otherwise preserve Saudi Arabia's traditional order. Islamists also oppose the corruption and conspicuous consumption that have characterized much of the Al Saud's rule.[23] Their economic plans appear muddled. They issue vague calls for justice and an end to corruption, but provide few specifics. However, Islamists also have an ambitious foreign agenda. They call for aiding Muslim causes throughout the world and, as an obvious corollary, oppose ties to anti-Islamist Arab regimes, such as Syria, and to the United States for its support for Israel.[24]

In the eyes of many Islamists, the United States is a dual threat. Islamists disagree with many aspects of U.S. foreign policy, which is viewed as hegemonic and hostile to Islam. Islamists also see the United States as a cultural threat: The U.S. military presence, in their view, brings with it Western promiscuity, vice, and threatening social mores. Many Islamists believe that the U.S. troop presence emboldens women and others to challenge traditional roles.[25] A U.S. withdrawal from the Kingdom would reduce some of this criticism, but

---

[21]Mamoun Fandy, *Saudi Arabia and the Politics of Dissent,* New York: St. Martin's Press, 1999, pp. 4 and 33.

[22]Fandy, 1999, pp. 3 and 36.

[23]Fandy, 1999, p. 56.

[24]See Sachs, "Saudi Prince Urges Reform," 2000; Fandy, 1999, p. 59.

[25]Gause, 1994, p. 142; Fandy, 1999, p. 49. For example, the protest of Saudi women drivers during Operation Desert Shield is believed by Islamists to have been encouraged by the U.S. military presence.

more ineffable concerns regarding U.S. culture and supposed hostility to Islam will keep these grievances acute.

Geopolitical Constants

Saudi Arabia is vulnerable. It lacks the population and fighting power to defend itself from the armies of its large neighbors and would be open to aggression or intimidation should the United States withdraw is forces from the region. Any successor regime will also rely on Western technical assistance to increase oil production capacity and streamline the production process. Even if a different leadership comes to power, it will face this security problem and thus may be compelled to look outside the Kingdom for assistance. The toppling of Saddam's regime gives the Kingdom breathing space for years to come, but both Iraq and Iran remain long-term concerns given their large populations and historic aspirations for regional leadership.

Any successor regime is likely to find itself facing dilemmas comparable to those that have plagued the Al Saud. Under the Al Saud's leadership, the Kingdom "was simply too rich and ostensibly influential to be ignored by others, and too weak and cautious to be able to ignore them."[26] Alternative leaderships are likely to share this combination of wealth and weakness. Unlike the Al Saud, however, a new regime may not recognize the problem until the threat is strong and imminent.

Implications

Who rules in Riyadh is a vital question for the United States. Although the most likely alternatives are favorable to U.S. interests, dramatic regime change remains a distinct possibility and, should it occur, Saudi Arabia may go from a leading U.S. ally to a potential foe. The majority of Saudis appear hostile to the United States and to Israel. Although they are not likely to ally with Iran or Iraq, they might curtail cooperation with the United States, particularly the U.S. military. Geopolitics may eventually force them to find an outside power

---

[26]Safran, 1988, p. 449.

to balance Iraq, but it may take years or an immediate crisis for a new regime to fully appreciate its vulnerability.

Domestically, Saudi Arabia may become more conservative, not less. Political liberalization and the growth of civil society are likely to empower Islamists, who are the best organized opposition force and have a message that has strong popular appeal. The regime may also face pressure to avoid contentious economic reforms, particularly if it is not able to rein in the royal family's conspicuous lifestyle.

Even if Saudi Arabia retains a strong relationship to the United States, it may have difficulty acting decisively. Consolidating power will take time, and Abdullah's age makes it likely that the succession question will be an active one for some time to come. As a result, any leader will have to gain a consensus among the Al Saud in general, a process that is at best time consuming and at worse paralyzing.

Even if there is no overt change from the Al Saud to another faction in Saudi society, future leaders may be less willing to sacrifice their popularity at home to preserve a strong relationship with the United States. Although the Al Saud in general recognize the importance of security ties to Washington, a shortsighted leader facing domestic pressure may cut ties or curtail U.S. activities to court the favor of the Islamists.

LEADERSHIP CHANGE IN SYRIA

The regime Bashar al-Assad heads is likely to remain in power, but its grip could become weaker in coming years. Bashar's father, Hafez, ruled Syria with an iron hand for almost 30 years until his death in 2000, transforming the chronically unstable country into a bulwark of stability. This transformation came at a price. The regime relied on brutal repression, economic cronyism, and minority rule to stay in power. It is not clear whether the inexperienced Bashar can inspire the same mix of loyalty from his henchmen and fear among his opponents while successfully reforming the economy, as he has promised to do. Assessing the outlines of regime change in Syria is thus essential if we are to understand the range of possible, if not necessarily likely, scenarios for the country's future.

Bashar Versus Hafez

Definite portraits of Bashar al-Assad and his father Hafez are difficult to draw. Bashar has been on the Syrian stage for less than a decade, while his father was famously known as the "Sphinx of Damascus" because he puzzled observers in Syria and the region as to what his true goals were. Nevertheless, given the concentrated nature of power in Syria's political system, understanding any differences between the two is essential.

Bashar lacked the experience his father had when he took power. After years in the military (and thus, in Syria, in politics), Hafez became a key figure after a military coup in 1966 that led his Alawi community to power. In 1970, he formally took control after ousting his rivals. Unlike his father, Bashar had little background in politics or governing when he took power. His older brother Basil had been groomed for the throne, but he died in an automobile crash in 1994. Bashar, then only 28 and an ophthalmologist living in England, was quickly elevated.[27]

Both leaders appear to share several similarities. Neither lets ideology blind them to the necessities of power politics. Hafez worked with Christians in Lebanon against Arab nationalists, tried to divide the Palestinian camp, aided Iran over Iraq during their eight-year war, and otherwise turned his back on the Baath's Arab nationalist agenda. Shortly after taking power, Bashar made a tentative rapprochement with Iraq and Jordan and otherwise tried to preserve calm abroad while he consolidated power at home.

It is not known if Bashar shares several qualities that helped Hafez stay in power and preserve Syria's influence. Hafez was cautious. After Israel's overwhelming victory in 1967, Hafez became acutely aware of Syria's military limits and tried to avoid a direct confronta-

---

[27]Any pretense that Bashar was being selected according to established rules was quickly dispelled. In the six months before Hafez' death, Bashar went from being a colonel to the commander-in-chief of Syria's military. On the day of his father's death, the constitution was amended, lowering the age for assuming the presidency from 40 to 34, Bashar's age. Rachel Bronson, "Syria: Hanging Together or Hanging Separately," *The Washington Quarterly*, Vol. 23, No. 4, Autumn 2000, p. 97.

tion even as he used terrorism to maintain pressure on Israel.[28]
Hafez was also calm and collected even in the face of military disasters or widespread instability. Finally, Hafez was often ruthless, willing to turn on longtime comrades and slaughter tens of thousands of Syrians to stay in power.[29] As a result, he could advance his agenda, even if it was not popular at home, and otherwise dominate the political debate.

Bashar's inexperience, in contrast, inspires neither fear nor confidence. Friends describe his demeanor as meek and awkward.[30]
Many doubt whether he can rule effectively and, more fundamentally, whether he has the right to rule.[31] As a result, he must move cautiously while consolidating his rule.

So far, Bashar's biggest impact has been in the domestic area. He has not initiated changes that would fundamentally threaten the system or his rule, but minor dissent is tolerated, a dramatic change from his father's draconian policies. Bashar has emphasized economic reform in his speeches. In addition, he has allowed human rights organizations and civil society to reemerge, albeit tentatively.[32]

Bashar has also eased, though not ended, several of Syria's most contentious foreign policy rivalries. Relations with Turkey have im-

---

[28]Martha Neff Kessler, "Syria, Israel and the Middle East Peace Process: Past Success and Final Challenges," *Middle East Policy,* Vol. 7, No. 2, February 2000, p. 70.

[29]Harvey Sicherman, "Hafez al-Assad: The Man Who Waited Too Long," *Peacefacts,* Foreign Policy Research Institution, Vol. 7, No. 1, July 2001, electronic version.

[30]"Bashar's World," *The Economist,* July 17, 2000, electronic edition.

[31]Bronson, 2000; "Syria," p. 95.

[32]Public meetings, long banned, are now tolerated, and several hundred political prisoners have been released. Bashar's regime has allowed petitions calling for change to circulate. He has also tried to increase access to mobile telephones and the Internet, both of which were suspect because of their potential for sedition. Roula Khalaf, "Bashar Steps Out of His Father's Shadow," *Financial Times,* January 16, 2001, p. 15; "Bashar's World"; Alan Makovsky, "Syria Under Bashar al-Asad: The Domestic Scene and the 'Chinese Model' of Reform," *Policywatch* 512, Washington, D.C.: The Washington Institute for Near East Policy, January 17, 2001, electronic version.

proved since he took office.[33]   Bashar also proved more amenable to cooperating with Saddam's Iraq, even in the regime's dying days.[34]

Hafez's attitude toward the Israeli-Palestinian dispute was a mixture of pride, contempt, and opportunism. He thought little of Arafat and the Palestinian movement in general, but he believed that the Palestinian dispute was at the center of regional instability. Thus he sought to control and guide the Palestinian struggle, reducing any radicalism that could shake his regime while trying to direct it to weaken Israel in a manner that served Syria's purposes. But his policies may not be entirely Machiavellian. Some analysts believed that he saw his dignity, and that of Syria, as linked to the manner in which the dispute was resolved, a belief that made him reluctant to make concessions in the peace negotiations.[35]

Bashar initially continued his father's approach on the peace negotiations. Like his father, he has called for "peace of the strong"— meaning, in effect, few Syrian concessions on the Golan Heights. As the second intifada continued, moreover, he allowed (and at times may have encouraged) Arab and Islamic radicals (in Syria and particularly in Lebanon) to attack Israel. He has also used pan-Arab and anti-Israel rhetoric to shore up support among Syrians in general. In addition, he has supported Hezbollah's attacks on Israel as a means of keeping pressure on the Israeli government. Because of his weak domestic position, making any concessions to Israel beyond what his father promised would be difficult. However, Bashar's support for anti-Israel radicals goes beyond domestic politics. He appears committed to at least some degree of support for radical activity.

---

[33]The roots of this rapprochement lie in the Syrian expulsion of the Kurdish Workers Party (PKK) head Abdullah Ocalan in October 1998, a decision made under threat of Turkish military intervention.

[34]Ahmad S. Moussalli, "The Geopolitics of Syrian-Iraqi Relations," *Middle East Policy*, Vol. 7, No. 4, October 2000, pp. 104–105.

[35]Henry Seigman, "Being Hafiz al-Assad: Syria's Chilly but Consistent Peace Strategy," *Foreign Affairs*, May/June 2000, p. 3; Kessler, "Syria, Israel and the Middle East Peace Process," p. 72.

A Shift from Bashar to Other Domestic Actors

Bashar has not made it clear who will succeed him should he die prematurely. The most likely threat is from rivals within the power elite, particularly the Alawi "Barons." A less likely danger, but one that would more profoundly change Syria, would be an Islamist-influenced regime.[36] Whoever takes power would probably have considerable latitude to implement his policies because of the weak state of Syrian institutions.

The Alawi "Barons." In his years in power, Hafez al-Assad created a family and clan-based system with a veneer of ideology.[37] Hafez systematically placed members of his Alawi community in the country's leading security and army posts. These individuals control (though they do not always formally head) military intelligence, the General Intelligence Directorate, Air Force Intelligence, and Political Security, as well as several elite military units that in effect serve as a praetorian guard. These "Barons" could move against Bashar if he proved incompetent or threatened their hold on power.

Should a putsch within the elite occur, it is not likely to result in a dramatic change in Syrian policy, particularly with regard to foreign policy. These "Barons" are focused on ensuring their community's, and of course their own, dominant position more than on any

---

[36]Any ruler would also have to contend with the sentiments of Syria's population, but there is little information on their preferences. Syrians appear reconciled to Israel's existence but in general favor a hard line on any negotiations. In contrast to much of the Syrian leadership, sympathy for the Palestinian cause runs deep. A shared history and close proximity to many refugees have left many Syrians acutely aware of the Palestinians' miseries. Most Syrians appear to see peace as likely, but desirable only if it involves significant Israeli concessions. Most Syrians seek a complete return of the Golan Heights as a condition for peace, and Hafez al-Assad's refusal to make concessions on this issue appeared to have widespread support. Kessler, 2000, pp. 68–81.

[37]There is a nominal Baath ideology. It promotes a secular version of Arab unity, led by a small vanguard, which in turn is led by a supreme leader. That said, Syria (and the other nominally Baath state, Iraq) has used the ideology as a pretext for political domination by an individual, constructing an authoritarian state to this end. Siegman, 2001.

particular policy goal.[38] Like Hafez al-Assad, they will have to avoid highly controversial policies that might stir up popular resentment. However, it is possible that a leader may emerge and consolidate power and, like Hafez, be able to impose his own vision on Syria and its policies.

Syrian Islamists. Islamists in Syria are weak. The Baath regime devastated the Islamist movement after its opposition led to widespread violence and instability in Syria from 1977 to 1982. Arrests, imprisonment, torture, and other forms of repression, including the destruction of the city of Hama, a stronghold of the Muslim Brotherhood involving thousands of civilian deaths, left the movement without an effective leadership or organization inside Syria.[39]

Islamist sentiment remains powerful. Perhaps 70 percent of Syrians are Sunni Muslims, and religious organizations retain a social network throughout Syrian society.[40] Islamists are highly suspicious of the Alawi-led regime. Many Islamists see Alawis as apostates, and they all oppose the vigorous secularism that the Baath party champions. Assad's brutal crackdown on Islamists in the early 1980s led to an enduring hatred among Islamist ranks.[41] Even many less religious Sunnis regard the Alawis as upstarts and seek to restore their community's former dominance. If infighting paralyzed the Alawis, particularly if it led to a split in the military, Islamists might increase their influence.

An Islamist takeover would result in a wholesale transformation of Syrian society. The imposition of Islamic law and more traditional dress codes would replace the secular credo of the Baath. Moreover, Alawis and Sunnis who benefited from the current regime would probably be dispossessed and possibly severely repressed. The Is-

---

[38]Michael Eisenstadt, "Who Rules Syria? Bashar al-Asad and the Alawi 'Barons,'" *Policywatch 472*, Washington, D.C.: The Washington Institute for Near East Policy, June 21, 2000, electronic version. For a thorough overview of the role of ethnic and sectarian factions during the last 35 years, see Nikolaos Van Dam, *The Struggle for Power in Syria: Politics and Society Under Asad and the Ba'th Party*, New York, London: I. B. Tauris, 1996.

[39]Van Dam, 1996, pp. 111–117.

[40]Bronson, 2000, p. 100.

[41]Kessler, 2000, p. 86; Van Dam, 1996, pp. 107–108.

lamists' foreign policy views are not carefully articulated but, like Islamists elsewhere, the Syrian Muslim Brotherhood is highly critical of peace negotiations with Israel.[42]

Geopolitical Constants

Whoever is in power in Damascus must confront several bitter realities of Syria's current political position. Most important, Syria is poor. The economy slowly stagnated under Hafez al-Assad, and Bashar's halfhearted efforts to liberalize have so far done little. Any regime will have few resources to co-opt domestic interest groups or to build up Syria's military strength. Unlike Saudi Arabia, Syria lacks economic influence.

Damascus will be vulnerable to bullying by its stronger neighbors. Syria's conventional military forces are weak, and the gap between it and its neighbors, especially Turkey and Israel, is likely to grow. Military forces are large in size but poorly equipped and not well trained. Many of the elite units are focused on domestic stability, not on protecting Syria against its enemies. In 1998, Ankara forced it to stop support for the Kurdistan Workers Party (PKK) through a direct threat of military force. In addition, Syria cannot risk too much escalation in its confrontation with Israel, as in the end Israel's superior forces would easily defeat those of Syria.

As a result of this conventional weakness, Syria will probably rely heavily on chemical weapons, missile programs, and other asymmetric threats. Missiles allow Syria a means to strike Israel, something its troubled air force and poorly trained and equipped army probably could not accomplish. In addition, missiles allow Syria to deliver chemical weapons, a potential deterrent against Israel's nuclear forces. Damascus will probably retain its ties to terrorist organizations, even if it does not employ them, to preserve a cheap and effective means of striking its opponents.[43]

---

[42]Van Dam, 1996, p. 92.

[43]Monterey Institute of International Studies, Center for Nonproliferation Studies, "Syria's Scuds and Chemical Weapons," available at http://cns.miis.edu/research/wmdme/syrscud.htm, accessed on January 19, 2001.

Implications

Whether Syria's current power elite will support Bashar over the long term remains an open question. Should he stumble they may oust him or reduce his authority, transforming the country from a dictatorship into an oligarchy. Bashar's need to consolidate power will probably make him cautious, particularly on contentious foreign policy issues such as peace negotiations with Israel.

In addition, efforts to reform Syria's backward economy—which is necessary if Syria is to avoid a steady decline in power and influence—may also generate instability. Allowing the free movement of individuals and the exchange of ideas poses a direct challenge to the Baath's domination of political discourse in the country. The Syrian merchant class has traditionally been a Sunni stronghold, and the Baath's economic reforms emphasized state control or industrialization as a means to offset the political power of the merchants.[44] In addition, many within Bashar's Alawi and Sunni power base depend on exclusive access to government contracts and corruption to ensure their advantage. As *The Economist* notes, "If the army cannot use its private road into Lebanon as a tax-free conduit, how will it dodge the 250 percent duty on cars and other luxury imports?"[45]

Instability is even more likely if other Alawi leaders or Islamists take power. As Nikolaos Van Dam notes, "In Syria the principle of collective military leadership has, however, never been practiced successfully for long."[46] Politics could return to the chronic instability of the 1950s and 1960s, when coups were the order of the day. If the Alawis were forced from power, violence and unrest are even more likely as Islamists and other victims of the Baath rule seek their revenge.

The impact of regime change will be far more profound at home than abroad. A shuffle within the Alawi elite would probably result in little change. Although an Islamist-influenced government would be far more hostile to Israel, it too would be bound by Syria's weak economy and crumbling conventional forces. A more hostile regime

---

[44]"Bashar's World."

[45]"Is Syria Really Changing?" *The Economist,* November 18, 2000.

[46]Van Dam, 1996, p. 132.

in Damascus might make cooperation on issues such as counterterrorism more difficult, but given the poor state of U.S.-Syrian relations in general the overall impact will be limited.

LEADERSHIP CHANGE IN EGYPT

Egyptian President Mubarak does not rule with the same degree of control as do the leaders of Saudi Arabia and Syria, but this looser rule is a strength of the Egyptian system, not a weakness: It indicates that the regime is well-entrenched and goes beyond a single individual, family, or communal group. Yet Egypt's regime, like those of other Arab states, relies on a mix of co-optation and coercion to assure its rule. The Egyptian public, particularly elements that oppose the current regime, are ignored or repressed. As the public and opposition have widely different objectives than the current regime in Cairo, regime change could result in a fundamental transformation of Egypt's domestic politics and foreign policy.

Change Within the Egyptian Elite

Egyptian President Mubarak is often considered an unremarkable leader. Mubarak's views appear closer to the norm of Egyptian elites than those of past Egyptian leaders. In many ways he appears to typify the views of Egypt's military and security leadership. He lacks Nasser's charisma or Sadat's dynamism.[47] Mubarak is stolid, conservative, and predictable. Domestic stability is his primary concern. He has avoided grave mistakes in his 20 years in power, but at the same time he has allowed the government to become torpid.[48]

There is no clear succession procedure should Mubarak die, but an immediate successor would probably have a military or security

---

[47]Sadat in particular was a rare leader. As Jerrold Green notes, "Anwar Sadat was not only able to assume power and to retain it, but also to exercise it with, at times, breathtaking boldness, innovation, imagination, and courage." Jerrold D. Green, "Leadership Succession in the Arab World," University of Judaism, The Center for Policy Options, Summer 2000, p. 16.

[48]This composite of Mubarak is taken from the author's interviews of several U.S. government officials, academic analysts, and policy analysts.

background.[49] Mubarak has not appointed a vice president, probably to prevent any rival from building a power base.[50] Since the monarchy was overthrown in 1952, however, all of Egypt's leaders have come from the military. Possible candidates include Omar Suleiman, a veteran of Egypt's security services; the head of the air force, Ahmed Sharif; Armed Forces Chief of Staff Magdi Hatata; and Osama al-Baz, a political advisor to Mubarak.[51] With the exception of Osama al-Baz, these individuals have little experience with foreign policy. This relatively narrow circle of military and security leaders has tried to co-opt other military and government officials as well as leading businessmen while keeping the Egyptian people away from decisionmaking.[52]

Egyptian elites share one overriding objective: to ensure their own grip on power. They enjoy a privileged economic position and believe the current system is a bulwark against religious radicalism. Leaders, however, can have tremendous latitude: Nasser and Sadat demonstrated that Egyptian leaders have considerable leeway on even such core issues as economic reform and relations with Israel. However, security and military elites are sensitive when economic reforms or foreign policy changes might spill over into unrest at home.

Many Egyptian elites recognize the importance of the U.S.-Egyptian relationship. Since the signing of the Camp David treaty in 1979, the United States has provided almost $40 billion in military and economic aid. Some elites believe this assistance helped Egypt turn its stagnating economy around after the Gulf War. In addition, the United States is viewed as a stabilizing force with regard to Israeli-

---

[49]Technically, the speaker of the People's Assembly becomes the president until the Assembly chooses a candidate, who is then subject to a popular referendum. However, that candidate is expected to be determined by Egypt's power brokers and then handed down to the Assembly for ratification.

[50]Egyptians joke that "the most dangerous job in Egypt is to be the second-most powerful person in the country." Jon B. Alterman, "Egypt: Stable, but for How Long?" *The Washington Quarterly*, Vol. 23, No. 4, Autumn 2000, p. 113.

[51]Author's interviews with U.S. academics; Alterman, "Egypt: Stable but for How Long?" p. 114.

[52]Alterman, "Egypt: Stable but for How Long?" p. 113.

Arab tension.[53] Some business elites see peace and ties to the United States as necessary if Egypt is to prosper. That said, many elites have been highly critical of the U.S.-Egyptian relationship, particularly as the Middle East peace negotiations have soured, even though they recognize that it does bring Egypt a range of benefits.[54]

Geopolitical and Societal Constants

Whoever rules Egypt will have to contend with the country's distinct characteristics and geopolitical situation. These include:

- Expectations of leadership. Egyptians have always considered themselves the leading Arab nation, a perception reinforced by its large population and proud history. Both the Egyptian people and elite expect their leaders to take an active role in Arab and regional issues.

- Military weaknesses and strengths. Egypt is militarily strong, on paper. It possesses large quantities of sophisticated equipment.[55] If there is an "Arab" force deployed in the Gulf to assist the states of the Gulf Cooperation Council, Cairo is a logical candidate to lead it. That said, Egypt's military poses little challenge to Israel: Its level of training is poor, it does not use advanced technology well, and it cannot conduct combined arms operations. Should the Egyptian-Israeli relationship sour completely, a conventional military option is not available.

- In general, Egyptians outside the ruling circle do not seek a close relationship with the United States. The Egyptian media, including progovernment organs, are often highly critical of U.S. poli-

---

[53]Yoram Meital, "Domestic Challenges and Egypt's U.S. Policy," *Middle East Review of International Affairs,* Vol. 2, No. 4, November 1998, electronic version.

[54]For example, Abd al-Halim Abu Khazala, a former defense minister, once considered a possible successor to Mubarak, wrote that U.S. ties to Israel damage Egypt's interests. See Meital, 1998.

[55]The United States has sold Egypt modern tanks, artillery pieces, fighter aircraft, and other systems that have augmented Egypt's military. For a review, see David Honig, "A Mighty Arsenal: Egypt's Military Build-Up, 1979–1999," *Policywatch* 447, Washington, D.C.: The Washington Institute for Near East Policy, March 21, 2000.

cies and lambaste the "Jewish lobby" in Washington.[56] U.S. support of Israel is roundly criticized, as Egyptians believe that Washington can deliver concessions from Israel.[57] As the second intifada has continued, this criticism has grown. The United States is generally seen as high-handed and biased against Arabs. The Al Aqsa intifada and the war against Iraq has worsened the perception of the United States. In one poll taken by the Pew Charitable Trust in the last months of 2002, only 6 percent of Egyptians held a favorable opinion of the United States.[58] Thus, while current Egyptian elites appreciate the benefits of ties to Washington, this appreciation is not reinforced by a broader sentiment of good feeling toward the United States.

The Islamist Alternative

Islamists represent the most organized source of opposition to the current order. There are many tendencies within the broad Islamist movement, ranging from the radical *Jama'a al-Islamiyya* to more mainstream organizations such as the Muslim Brotherhood, to the many individual religious leaders who regularly work with the Egyptian government. The groups are often at odds with one another, and even groups with similar objectives have highly different views on how to pursue them.[59]

Islamist movements draw on several grievances to enhance their popularity. Islamist groups have capitalized on feelings of alienation among Egypt's poor, many of whom believe they have little voice and few opportunities. Even many Egyptians who do not endorse the Is-

---

[56]Abdel Monem Said Aly, "Egypt-U.S. Relations and Egyptian Foreign Policy," *Policywatch* 448, Washington, D.C.: The Washington Institute for Near East Policy, March 24, 2000, electronic version.

[57]This view is endorsed by many Egyptian leaders. President Sadat claimed that the United States holds "90 percent of the cards" with regard to Israel's policies. As quoted in Meital, 1998.

[58]http://www.pbs.org/newshour/bb/media/july-dec02/kohut_12-05.html. This figure may be high as it coincided with the debate over the decision to go to war with Iraq, a particularly unpopular decision.

[59]For a comparison, see David Zeidan, "Radical Islam in Egypt: A Comparison of Two Groups," *Middle East Review of International Affairs*, Vol. 3, No. 3, September 1999, electronic version.

lamist ideology are sympathetic to it. Islamists are widely seen as honest, and their message promises dramatic change. In effect, they represent the only voice of opposition to the current order.[60]

Islamist goals are at variance with the policies of the current regime. As with Islamists elsewhere, their primary agenda is domestic: They seek the implementation of the Islamic sharia as Egypt's law. Many Islamist groups are hostile toward Jews and Christians, including Egypt's large Coptic Christian community, which is roughly 6 percent of the population.[61] Many are also suspicious of Sadat's and Mubarak's economic liberalization programs, instead endorsing vague calls for economic justice and a major government role in the economy. In their rhetoric, Islamists seek a return to a policy of confrontation with Israel and are highly critical of close ties to the United States.[62]

For now, Islamists are not likely to topple the current regime. Radical Islamist organizations such as *Jamaa'at al-Jihad* and the *Jama'a al-Islamiyya* engaged in a disorganized paramilitary struggle against the regime from 1990 until 1997, resulting in perhaps 1,300 casualties.[63] In the course of fighting the insurgency, Egyptian security forces arrested thousands of Islamists and penetrated and disrupted revolutionary cells. The regime licensed and controlled previously independent Islamist civil organizations, both radical and mainstream, and purged the armed forces of suspected radicals. Non-Islamist opposition voices, fearing the Islamists' radical message,

---

[60]In addition, many wealthy Muslims, including many outside Egypt, give generously to religious causes, strengthening religious influences. Egyptians working in Saudi Arabia were exposed to a far harsher and more extreme version of Islam. Fawaz Gergez, "The End of the Islamist Insurgency in Egypt? Costs and Prospects," *Middle East Journal*, Vol. 54, No. 4, Fall 2000, p. 600; Alterman, "Egypt: Stable but for How Long?" 2000, pp. 109–110.

[61]Central Intelligence Agency, *CIA Factbook*, "Egypt," available at http://www.odci.gov/cia/publications/factbook/geos/eg.html#People, accessed on April 26, 2001.

[62]Gerges, 2001, pp. 602–603; Zeidan, 1999; Fawaz Gergez, "The Decline of Revolutionary Islam in Algeria and Egypt," *Survival*, Vol. 41, No. 1, Spring 1999, p. 114. In the mid-1990s, the United States established contacts with mainstream Islamists, such as the Muslim Brotherhood, as a hedge should instability sweep Egypt. It discontinued such contacts after heavy pressure from the Egyptian government and a broader belief that contacts legitimated the very forces Washington opposed. Gerges, 2000, p. 606.

[63]Gerges, 2000, p. 592.

backed the government's campaign.[64] The campaign devastated the Islamists: Radical groups were shattered, and mainstream groups such as the Brotherhood found themselves on the margins of the overall debate.[65] The regime continues to arrest and detain suspected radicals, making it difficult for them to recruit and organize.

In addition to repressing the Islamists and their supporters, the regime also tried to co-opt less radical elements during the mid-1990s. The regime promoted the trappings of Islam, increasing religious education and media programming. Mainstream Islamists, such as those at Al-Azhar, the ancient institution of higher learning, were allowed to vehemently criticize secular intellectuals.[66] This co-optation reduced the power of the radicals, but it increased the power of the more mainstream movements.[67] If Egypt's economy stagnates such that the regime finds itself seeking greater popular legitimacy, it may allow Islamists additional influence.

Implications

Leadership change within Egypt's elite may alter the emphasis of Egypt's foreign policy but not its direction. A leader other than Mubarak may be more willing, and more able, to go outside the narrow consensus in the current elite, shaping Egypt's policy rather than simply implementing agreed-upon goals. A shift outside the current power base to an Islamist regime would represent a far more fundamental change, but Islamists too would face limits on their freedom of action because of Egypt's military weakness.

Political liberalization is likely to founder, while economic reform will probably be limited. Even though support for liberalization may be considerable, there is no organized base for it. The current regime has successfully portrayed itself to other elites as the only bulwark

---

[64]Gerges, 2000, pp. 603–604; Alterman, "Egypt: Stable but for How Long?" 2000, pp. 110–112.

[65]Gerges, 2000, pp. 600–601.

[66]Steven Barraclough, "Al-Azhar: Between the Government and the Islamists," *Middle East Journal*, Vol. 52, No. 2, Spring 1998, pp. 239–245.

[67]Gerges, 2000, pp. 593–594; Alterman, "Egypt: Stable but for How Long?" 2000, pp. 108 and 112.

against the Islamists and will not hesitate to play up this concern if challenges to its rule mount. Because the regime relies heavily on business interests, economic changes are likely to avoid a return to the state-dominated policies of the past. That said, reform is also likely to avoid measures that threaten the existing businesses' position, even if this results in reduced competition and productivity.

Egypt's close relationship with the United States rests on thin foundations. Cooperation on counterterrorism is excellent, but this is usually conducted behind the scenes. Because the Egyptian populace and potential opposition figures are not supportive, and because many elites are at best lukewarm about ties to Washington, the regime may be tempted to distance itself from Washington should it find itself in a domestic crisis. This temptation will be acute if Palestinian-Israeli tension is high and the United States is seen as close to Israel. Efforts to liberalize the regime as a means to offset and channel dissent could lead to increased criticism of the U.S.-Egyptian relationship.

The regime's co-optation of mainstream Islamists also has far-reaching foreign policy implications. Many traditional Islamic authorities now have a degree of autonomy from the government that they use to press it on issues of religious importance, particularly social issues.[68] They may use this autonomy to press for changes in Egypt's foreign policy, particularly with regard to the peace negotiations or relations with the United States in high-profile issues.

The "Cold Peace" with Israel could get even colder. Peace for Egypt is necessary for good relations with the United States, and the limited quality of the Egyptian military makes a military confrontation difficult to conceive. However, the regime may become less supportive of concessions by the Palestinians, use more bellicose rhetoric, reduce economic ties, or otherwise distance itself from Israel.

A hardening of positions toward Israel could lead Egypt to renew its quest for weapons of mass destruction. Egypt is believed to have a stockpile of chemical agents and has not signed the Chemical Weapons Convention, though it is not believed to have a significant

---

[68]For a review, see Barraclough, 1998.

biological or nuclear program.[69] Increased tension with Israel, however, could cause Cairo to seek WMD as an offset to Israel's conventional military superiority.

PREPARING FOR REGIME CHANGE

As the above analysis suggests, the most probable scenarios are variations on current themes. Sons will succeed fathers, or members of the same power base will take the helm if a current leader dies or becomes ill. The potential for change, however, is quite large. Leaders are often out of touch with the population as a whole, and opposition voices have little say. As a result, a shift in ruling elites could lead to dramatic changes in a country's policy. Indeed, given the centralization of power in most Arab states, even a shift from one member of an existing power elite to another could have important implications for U.S. policy. Geopolitical realities and social constants will limit change or shape it to some degree, but dramatic shifts in a country's alignment and policies are possible.

This final section summarizes several of the most pressing concerns and dangers that emerge from the above cases. It identifies signposts that would suggest that regime change may occur. It then offers actions to shape the environment to prevent unfavorable regime change and, if this cannot be averted, proposes hedging actions to minimize any dangers.

Potential Risks and Opportunities

Leadership change in the Middle East raises the risks of several dangers. Among the most important, for friends as well as adversaries, are the difficulties inherent to consolidating power. Even if there is no change in a regime's power base, a new leader will still have to establish his supporters in power while minimizing the influence of potential challengers. During this interim period, a leader's ability to make policy will probably be circumscribed. Moreover, new leaders will be focused primarily on domestic politics and may be reluctant

---

[69]Center for Nonproliferation Studies, Monterey Institute of International Studies, "Nuclear, Biological, Chemical, and Missile Capabilities in the Middle East," available at http://cns.miis.edu/research/wmdme/egypt.htm, accessed on January 29, 2001.

to take risks on foreign policy. Given that open ties to the United States are questioned by their populace, new leaders may hesitate to risk unpopularity by cooperating with U.S. initiatives.

More generally, U.S. alliances and positive developments in the peace negotiations rest on a thin foundation. Leaders who are not beholden to public opinion are better able to make concessions to Israel or at least moderate their government's policies. If liberalization occurs in Egypt or Saudi Arabia, to say nothing of an increase in Islamist influence, then anti-U.S. and anti-Israel policies are likely to gain strength.[70]

The inexperience of some leaders also poses risks. Although Crown Prince Abdullah is highly experienced, Bashar al-Assad remains a neophyte. Future leaders of Saudi Arabia after Abdullah, and the successors to Mubarak or Saddam, may be more skilled in domestic politics than in foreign affairs. This may lead simply to missteps and clumsiness, but it also could have far graver consequences. Leaders may overestimate their military forces' strength, trust unduly in international support, believe they can intimidate their adversaries, or otherwise have misperceptions that might lead to conflict.

Democratization is also a mixed proposition. As discussed in Chapter Two, successful liberalization and power sharing raise the prospect for more stable regimes. However, many populaces in the Middle East are hostile to the United States and if they gain a greater voice their regimes are likely to face pressure to reduce ties to Washington. Islamists in particular are often the best-organized and best-prepared to take advantage of a more open political system.

Recommendations

The United States should anticipate potential changes to current assumptions about regime stability and shape and hedge accordingly.

Anticipating Changing Assumptions. Planning for regime change requires recognizing when assumptions about how a regime will behave are vulnerable. Obviously, analysts should continue to follow

---

[70]Green, 2000, p. 6.

the changing fortunes of individual leaders to best determine who may take power should a current leader die or become incapacitated. Anticipating more fundamental shifts is far more difficult. Predicting a coup, revolution, or other forms of rapid and radical regime change is exceptionally difficult. However, certain indicators suggest a country is likely to face regime instability, including:

- The presence of partial democracy. In general, mature democracies and established autocracies are fairly stable. Regimes that are in transition, however, often face unrest and instability and are more likely to go to war. If Egypt, Syria, or other regional states liberalize, they may be vulnerable to sudden changes.[71]

- A crisis among the elite. Many revolutions began after a split in the existing elite. As a result, regimes may find it difficult to re-press or co-opt dissent, providing opportunities for revolutionaries.

- The spread of populism. Even if democracy does not spread, elites may rely more on populism to mobilize support for their rule. For many years, politics in the Middle East was the purview of elites such as military leaders, security officials, wealthy landowners, and businessmen. If leaders appeal more and more to the people for support, popular views, which are often at odds with those of current regimes, will matter more.

Shaping and Hedging. The United States should also consider actions to shape the environment to make any regime change more favorable and, should that not be practical, hedge against unfavorable changes.

Given the importance of regime change, it is tempting for the United States to try to intervene in the process. Unless the United States is willing to intervene decisively as it did in Iraq, it often has little influence over succession in most countries and in general lacks enough

---

[71] *State Failure Task Force Report: Phase II Findings,* Science Applications International Corporation: Washington, D.C.: July 31, 1998, pp. 19–22; Edward D. Mansfield and Jack Snyder, "Democratization and the Danger of War," *International Security,* Vol. 20, No. 1, 1995, pp. 5–38.

information to use what little influence it possesses. Pressure may backfire, leading to the rise of anti-U.S. leaders.[72]

Washington should also consider increasing contacts with leaders who are out of favor and factions that are out of power but enjoy considerable support. Focusing exclusively on the current power set risks being blindsided should dramatic change occur, as it did in Iran. Islamist groups deserve particular attention. Many of these groups are hostile to the United States, but dialogue is possible with some members, and indeed necessary if many of the stereotypes and conspiracy theories are to be dispelled. Establishing contacts with nonregime figures, of course, will anger the regime, a tricky balance to negotiate.

The United States should also focus more on cultivating public opinion. The current U.S. focus on elites will be less fruitful in the coming years. The possibility that publics may play a greater role in decisionmaking than in the past is currently a danger for the United States because of the hostile perceptions many Arab publics hold toward U.S. policy. Washington should attempt a media strategy that explains U.S. positions, going beyond the standard Western outlets and focusing on Arab satellite television stations and newspapers. The United States should also consider increased student and military exchanges to improve familiarity with the United States.

The U.S. military should consider a diverse and redundant basing structure and access arrangements as a hedge against instability or change in one country. Given that many countries are vulnerable to sudden change, and almost all may at some point hesitate to provide access to placate domestic opinion, having many options is necessary. States like Saudi Arabia and Egypt, where domestic and opposition opinion appears firmly against ties to the U.S. military, are of particular concern.

---

[72]Green, 2000, pp. 3–5. Indeed, information is often lacking among Middle Eastern elites. As Jerrold Green notes, "No one was more surprised at the election of President Mohammad Khatami than was Khatami himself" (p. 5).

Chapter Six

ENERGY AND MIDDLE EASTERN SECURITY: NEW DIMENSIONS AND STRATEGIC IMPLICATIONS

Ian O. Lesser

After almost 20 years of limited attention, energy security questions are once again part of the strategic discourse. Instability in world oil prices and concerns over the domestic energy situation in the United States have led to fears of a "third" energy crisis. As a dominant energy producer and exporter, the Middle East, as a region, is at the center of this revived debate, a reality strongly reinforced by the September 2001 terrorist attacks, the debate over U.S.-Saudi relations, and the war in Iraq. Energy is a leading factor in Western strategic perceptions regarding the Middle East, and a factor in the region's view of itself. It is also a key variable in the prosperity and stability of regimes and an unavoidable part of the regional security calculus. The most pressing policy problems confronting the United States and its allies in the Middle East, including terrorism, the stabilization and reconstruction of Iraq, the Arab-Israeli conflict, and containment policies toward Iran and Libya, all have an energy dimension. Energy questions and Middle Eastern affairs are inextricably linked in Western strategic perception. Traditional aspects of this linkage persist, even as conditions within the region and in world energy markets have changed substantially.

To a considerable extent, policymakers and strategists are influenced by the legacy of two previous energy crises in the early 1970s and the early 1980s. These experiences left indelible images of the use of oil for political coercion, and the vulnerability of modern industrial (and post-industrial) economies to disruptions in the energy market.

These images, in turn, draw on a much older tradition of concern about access to strategic resources, a tradition with notable disconti- nuities between perception and reality.[1] Simply put, governments have almost always overstated the problem of resource scarcity and exposure to cutoffs and have consistently equated *dependency* with *vulnerability* in energy and non-energy trade.

Much has changed since 1973 and 1982. Alarmist predictions about the dwindling of hydrocarbon resources have proven unfounded. Significant new reserves have been discovered in the Middle East and elsewhere, and the pace of discovery is accelerating as a result of technological change. The proliferation of transit routes for energy has created new opportunities for interdependence and conflict and has changed the nature of the energy security question from one fo- cused largely on relations between producers and consumers to a more complex equation in which transit states and nonstate actors play a more important role. Post-industrial economies in the devel- oped world are now less reliant on energy inputs. The United States and Europe are importing more oil, but much of it comes from out- side the Middle East, while Asia looms large as a growing importer of energy from the Gulf and the Caspian. For much of Europe, energy security is now as much about gas as it is about oil.

Middle Eastern producers also face a changed environment. The use of oil as a political weapon, and even the ability to maintain cohesion within OPEC, has proven difficult. Regimes in the Gulf and North Africa, accustomed to the petro-dollar prosperity of earlier decades, face the prospect of continued demographic pressure, budget bur- dens, and instability in energy prices—prices that are now lower in real terms than in 1973. Saudi Arabia offers the most prominent but by no means the only example of the potentially destabilizing com- bination of population growth, mounting unemployment and under- employment, and political discontent, all in the context of depressed energy prices. Producers as well as consumers feel vulnerable

---

[1]See Ian O. Lesser, *Resources and Strategy*, New York: St. Martin's Press, 1989; and Ian O. Lesser, *Oil, the Persian Gulf and Grand Strategy: Contemporary Issues in Historical Perspective*, Santa Monica, Calif.: RAND, R-4072-CENTCOM/JS, 1991.

against the background of a new debate about equity in energy prices and an even larger debate about globalization.[2]

The region and the West have seen multiple examples of the resilience of energy infrastructure and markets in the face of physical risks. Despite widespread fears, neither the Iran-Iraq war nor the 1991 Gulf War resulted in serious supply disruptions (nor, for that matter, did the 2003 war in Iraq). Turmoil in Algeria has had no noticeable effect on oil and gas production, or exports to European markets. The end of the Cold War eliminated another leading source of perceived risk—the fear that energy producing regions and energy transport routes would be threatened in a conventional conflict between NATO and the Warsaw pact.

In short, the parameters of the energy security debate have changed substantially, but many of the images from earlier decades remain unchanged. This does not mean they can be ignored. The accretion of historical images regarding energy security continues to play a role in shaping the perceptions and behavior of leaderships in the region, in the West, and elsewhere. Analysts and industry experts may be confident about the essential fungibility of oil supplies in a globalized market, and the ability of the market to compensate for regional supply crises, but strategists and policymakers often seem unconvinced. Oil retains its aura as a strategic commodity, and gas is increasingly seen in this light as well.

Energy issues have internal, regional, and extraregional implications for Middle Eastern security. They can affect the stability of regimes and their national power and potential. Energy resources and transport routes can be the stakes of rivalries, and energy-related revenues can influence the pace and extent of military modernization, and therefore military balances. Not least, energy trade continues to shape the regional interests and policies of extraregional actors—the United States, Europe, Russia, and China, among others—and can affect the prospects for conflict and cooperation among outside powers.

---

[2]See Martha Caldwell Harris, "The Globalization of Energy Markets," in Stephen J. Flanagan, Ellen L. Frost, and Richard L. Kugler (eds.), *Challenges of the Global Century*, Washington, D.C.: National Defense University, 2001.

Today, energy is arguably less central to Western strategy in the Middle East than it was in earlier decades. Moderate prices, demonstrated resilience in energy markets, and the rise of other issues such as terrorism and the proliferation of weapons of mass destruction have contributed to a somewhat reduced role for energy on the Middle Eastern agenda. Access to energy is an important part of the rationale for Western engagement, but it is no longer the dominant rationale.[3] At the same time, more attention is now rightly given to the question of how energy issues interact with other factors, from demographics to arms transfers, to affect regional security.

This chapter explores the changing dimensions of energy geopolitics in the context of Middle Eastern security through 2010. It first surveys key trends in world energy trade and the current debate over their meaning. It then discusses key emerging issues—elements of change—in the energy security and regional security equation. The final section offers conclusions and policy implications.

WORLD ENERGY TRENDS AND THE ENERGY SECURITY DEBATE

Almost from the start of the oil era, the Middle East has been intimately tied to energy security perceptions. The modern focus on oil as a strategic commodity has its origins in the 1911 decision by the British Admiralty to convert its battle fleet from coal to oil. At the time, the United States was still the world's leading oil producer, but the focus of British interest was Mesopotamia, where the Anglo-Persian Oil Company held a concession.[4] The Second World War, in particular, underscored the critical importance of oil not only for military operations but also to fuel war economies.

This reality continued to shape grand strategic thinking through much of the Cold War, waxing and waning in step with assumptions about the likelihood of a protracted conventional conflict between

---

[3]By contrast, in the mid-1970s, Western strategists contemplated the seizure of oil fields in North Africa and the Gulf as a matter of national survival.

[4]The Arabian Peninsula did not emerge as a significant producer until after World War II, and, in fact, America remained the leading supplier of petroleum product to the allied effort in 1914–1918, and again from 1939–1945.

East and West. Cold War strategic concerns about the Middle East focused in part on the potential for proxy wars and escalation, but also on a perceived Soviet threat to oil supplies in Iran and the Arabian Peninsula and the nearby sea-lanes—a threat that could affect the global "correlation of forces" and impede the defense of central Europe.[5] Energy and lines of communication linked Middle Eastern and European security and gave rise to notions of "theater interdependence."

Access to energy supplies in adequate amounts and at reasonable prices has been a leading concern of both developed and developing nations since the first modern oil crisis of the early 1970s. That crisis was precipitated by the 1973 Arab-Israeli war and the Arab oil embargo. It actually began somewhat earlier, at least in industry and government perception, with the progressive nationalization of oil companies and the renegotiation of Western oil concessions in North Africa and the Gulf. The economic disruptions caused by the crisis of the early to mid-1970s reinforced the existing Western perception of oil as a strategic commodity, vital to the prosperity of modern societies.

After two decades of moderate prices, energy is once again part of strategic debates. The rollback of the Iraqi invasion of Kuwait in 1991 was justified, in part, as an act in defense of world access to oil, with the United States as the ultimate guarantor of global energy security.[6] More realistically, the rationale was to keep substantial oil resources out of the hands of an ill-intentioned and aggressive regime. In the years since the Gulf War, interest in energy security has ebbed and flowed, driven by periodic volatility in the oil market, and most recently by concerns about the working of energy markets inside the United States. The problem of electric power supply and demand, while not an energy security issue in the global sense, has nonetheless inspired growing attention to energy matters and has forced a reassessment of national energy policy. Combined with continued

---

[5]The perceived threat to Iran following the Soviet invasion of Afghanistan gave rise to the "Carter doctrine," asserting U.S. determination to defend Gulf oil. The "Brown doctrine" later extended this commitment to embrace non-Soviet threats.

[6]In reality, oil was one among many factors shaping conflict in the Gulf and the rationale for Western intervention. See Lesser, 1991.

turmoil in the Middle East, these considerations have brought energy security back to the foreign and security policy agenda.

The Outlook for Oil Supply and Price

The current debate over energy security divides, roughly, into three schools. The first argues, along the lines of the "limits to growth" school of the 1970s, that world oil reserves are limited relative to global needs, and will be depleted sooner rather than later by ever increasing demand from the developed and the developing world.[7] The leading proponents of the "depletion" school, including geologists Colin Campbell and Jean Laherrere, argue that the world is approaching, or may already have reached, the psychologically important halfway mark in terms of remaining reserves (roughly 900–1,000 billion barrels of production versus perhaps 2,000 billion barrels of total reserves). The result, in this view, will be an eventual supply "crunch" and marked friction over prices. Optimists, such as analysts with the U.S. Geological Survey, suggest this half-depletion point is still decades away, in the worst case. Not surprisingly, most analyses, including those by the International Energy Agency (IEA), assume a position somewhere in between, looking to half depletion between 2015 and 2030.[8] In the more optimistic scenarios, new discoveries and more efficient extraction of current reserves are the key factors arguing for price moderation. In the most dramatic scenarios, the "depletion" school anticipates a world of $100/barrel oil, with all of the economic dislocation this might imply.

The second school envisions trouble ahead, but for more complex reasons. In this view, recent increases in oil prices, albeit from low levels, are indicative of an underlying tightness in world oil markets, with conditions not unlike those of 1973 and 1979: rapid expansion in the global economy, crude production at nearly full capacity worldwide, declining investment in new production, and deliberate limits on OPEC production to sustain higher prices.[9] Under current

---

[7]In general, this is a view that will unfold well beyond the time frame of this report, which only looks as far as 2010.

[8]"Will the Oil Run Out?" *The Economist*, February 10, 2001.

[9]Mamdouh G. Salameh, "A Third Oil Crisis?" *Survival*, Vol. 43, No. 3, Autumn 2001, p. 129.

conditions, elements of this thesis look doubtful, with slower growth in the world economy and the prospect of new energy investments in the Gulf, including Iraq, and elsewhere. It is also a view that accepts relatively pessimistic assumptions regarding reserve depletion. This view is common especially among oil analysts in the Middle East, and implies renewed friction between producers and consumers in the near term, with oil prices in the $50/barrel range a distinct possibility.

A third school sees trouble arising from glut, rather than scarcity. In this view, the increasing efficiency of exploration and production is counterbalancing growing demand (virtually all analysts agree on the significance of new demand in Asia for the global energy picture over the next decades). The exploitation of Caspian oil, Venezuelan tar sands, and other less conventional sources, together with the end of restrictions on new investment in Iraq and the eventual end of such restrictions in Libya and perhaps Iran, will further boost proven reserves and increase capacity. The result could be prolonged periods of cheap oil, helpful for consumers in the West as well as the developing world, but potentially destabilizing across the Middle East and Eurasia. This is an energy security argument that sees security risks arising from conditions within key producing states: growing populations and mounting debt, with energy revenues steady or declining. The resulting unrest could undermine already precarious regimes in the Gulf, North Africa, and even the Caspian. This, in turn, could lead to supply interruptions of a very different sort as internal strife interferes with production and exports.[10] Apart from periods of crisis, this is a world of sustained prices as low as $10/barrrel.

This analysis aims, above all, to characterize the debate and set parameters for expectations through 2010. A consensus view, taking into account demographic and political as well as economic judgments, suggests a world in which "meeting the increase in demand for energy will pose neither a major supply challenge, nor lead to

---

[10]See Amy Myers Jaffe and Robert A. Manning, "The Shocks of a World of Cheap Oil," *Foreign Affairs*, Vol. 79, No. 1, January–February 2000, pp. 16–29.

substantial price increases in real terms."[11] The underlying resource and production factors do not argue for substantial price shocks in an oil market that has long been globalized and with a commodity that is essentially fungible. That said, in the opinion of most analysts, the oil market could still be characterized by price volatility based on disruptive events and speculative behavior, with uncertainties for producers as well as consumers. Many of the world's leading producers, and all of those in the Middle East, are currently producing at or near capacity, increasing the exposure to short-term supply problems (e.g., the limited ability for leading producers such as Saudi Arabia to compensate for a cutoff of Iraqi exports, as seen in 2001). Russia and some West African producers may have a bit more flexibility to increase production under these conditions.

The Aftermath of September 11 and the War in Iraq

The events of September 2001 and uncertainties regarding regional security, including a heightened risk of instability in Saudi Arabia and the uncertain future of postwar Iraq, may increase the prospect for price volatility. Nonetheless, in the aftermath of the terrorist attacks on New York and Washington, oil prices actually fell, driven by assumptions of low to modest economic growth and lower energy demand worldwide.[12] By late November 2001, oil prices had fallen almost $4.00 from preattack levels to $22 per barrel. In the first few months of 2002, prices remained in the $22–$23 range. In the fall of 2002, with shrinking inventories and growing uncertainty about the

---

[11]*Global Trends 2015: A Dialogue About the Future with Nongovernment Experts,* Washington, D.C.: National Intelligence Council, 2001, p. 28. This assessment is in line with others. See, for example, *Energy Security: Evaluating U.S. Vulnerability to Oil Supply Disruptions and Options for Mitigating Their Effects,* Washington, D.C.: General Accounting Office, December 1996; Energy Information Administration, *International Petroleum Monthly Assessments; Strategic Energy Policy: Challenges for the 21st Century,* New York: Council on Foreign Relations, 2001; *International Energy Outlook,* Paris: International Energy Agency, 2000; and CSIS Panel Report, *The Geopolitics of Energy into the 21st Century: Volume 2—The Supply-Demand Outlook 2000–2020,* Washington, D.C.: CSIS, 2000. Moderate assumptions also guide the administration's recently published *National Energy Policy* report. Other sources reflected in this analysis include the *BP Amoco Statistical Review of World Energy 2000* and the 1999 *OPEC Annual Statistical Review.*

[12]See Alex Berenson and Jonathan Fuerbringer, "Oil and Gas Prices Tumble, but Stocks Soar Worldwide," *New York Times,* September 25, 2001, p. 1.

consequences of a looming American intervention in Iraq, prices rose sharply to near $30 per barrel. In May 2003, after the war in Iraq ended, prices hovered between $24 and $26 per barrel. This pattern suggests continued market sensitivity to political and security-driven factors against a background of moderate, even weak, demand-driven pressure on prices.

As the regional aspects of the coalition counterterrorism strategy and the reconstruction of Iraq unfold, the sensitivity of the oil market to both underlying economic trends and instability in oil producing states will be tested. The critical questions in this regard will be the stability of the Saudi regime in the face of regional tensions and the position of Iraq itself. Much remains unclear as of this writing, but the occupation authorities and a subsequent Iraqi government might rapidly take advantage of new investment and a more permissive export regime to boost production. Under this scenario, Iraq might rapidly become the number two oil producer, second only to Saudi Arabia, and a critical factor in world pricing. Against a background of continued weakness in the international economy, prices might fall substantially, which would be a boon for consumers, but potentially destabilizing for such key producers as Saudi Arabia and Iran.

An extended period of international control over Iraqi oil production and exports would place very significant control over production and pricing in the hands of consuming countries in the West and Asia. Major Middle Eastern producers such as Saudi Arabia and Iran (and Russia) would be in an uncomfortable position, one reminiscent of an earlier period of European and American oil concessions in the region. In short, war in Iraq has raised enormous uncertainties regarding prices, supply security, and regional stability, with a wide range of potential outcomes.

Changing Patterns of Dependence

Even with steady growth in proven reserves worldwide, the Middle East will continue to occupy a dominant position in world energy trade. Currently, the Middle East accounts for roughly 70 percent of proven oil reserves. This percentage is actually expected to increase with new exploration, and the overall contribution of Middle Eastern supply to world trade will grow with increases in production capacity. Russia and the Middle East together will also account for roughly three quarters of world gas reserves.[13] Caspian oil and continued development of resources elsewhere, including West Africa and Latin America, will diversify the energy picture but will not reduce the overall importance of the Gulf over the next decade.[14] However, if recent increases in Russian oil production and exports continue, some analysts believe that Russia could eventually displace Saudi Arabia as a leading supplier to the West, even if Gulf production retains a dominant position in world markets.[15]

The Middle Eastern contribution to world energy supply may also increase through political developments. Saudi Arabia has recently loosened its policy regarding foreign participation in energy production and refining, with the aim of attracting new capital for investment in the country's aging production infrastructure. The willingness of European energy companies to invest in Iran and Libya will further exploration and production over the coming years. The reconstruction of Iraq and the gradual reintegration of Iraq into the world economy may bring a significant producer back to the world market.

The Middle East will remain a dominant producer, but import patterns have changed and will continue to change significantly over the next decade. Most analysts expect energy demand in Asia, especially in China and India, to rise substantially, some day replacing North America as the world's leading energy consumer. The rise in Asian energy demand is expected to comprise much of the total increase in world oil demand from some 75 million barrels per day to more than 100 million by 2015. Most of this new Asian demand will be met through imports from the Persian Gulf and, to a lesser extent, Russia and the Caspian. As much as 75 percent of Gulf production may go to Asia by the end of the decade.

---

[13]*Global Trends 2015*, 2001, p. 30.

[14]Caspian oil will make an important but marginal contribution, perhaps on the order of the contribution from the North Sea. It is unlikely to prove "another Gulf." See Richard Sokolsky and Tanya Charlick-Paley, *NATO and Caspian Security: A Mission Too Far?* Santa Monica, Calif.: RAND, MR-1074-AF, 1999.

[15]See Edward L. Morse and James Richard, "The Battle for Energy Dominance," *Foreign Affairs*, Vol. 81, No. 2, March/April 2002, pp. 16–31.

Changes in the pattern of oil trade have been slow to affect Western strategic debates. Many Americans take for granted the notion that U.S. oil imports come largely from the Middle East. But this has not been so in recent decades. Canada and Mexico have loomed larger, and the most recent trend has been toward larger imports from the Western Hemisphere and the Atlantic, including West Africa. In recent years, the United States has imported roughly 10 percent of its oil from the Middle East. The Department of Energy forecasts that by 2020, 64 percent of American oil needs will be met by imports, mostly from the Western Hemisphere.[16] European imports from the Gulf have also been declining in relative terms. By 2015, it is likely that only 10 percent of Gulf oil will flow to Western markets and 75 percent will go to Asia.

Although the United States will be increasingly dependent on an Atlantic rather than a Middle Eastern and Eurasian system of supply, this oil will still be obtained at world market prices. What happens in the Gulf will influence the supply and price of oil elsewhere, but the link will be less direct. Oil is a global commodity, but oil trade still reflects shipping costs, one factor behind the proliferation of new pipeline schemes across Eurasia and the Middle East. Globalization in the oil market contributes substantially to energy security, but it does not altogether remove regional sources of risk. As the link between Gulf oil and Western energy security becomes less obvious and direct, however, the political problem of justifying Gulf defense may become more difficult. A decade ago, when U.S. reliance on Gulf oil was already declining but Europe and Japan remained more dependent on the region, American policymakers already faced the question of "whose oil are we defending?" Looking toward 2010, if viewed in narrow terms, the likely answer will be China and other Asian consumers. It is a prospect that could place a premium on encouraging a cooperative rather than a competitive relationship with Beijing regarding Middle Eastern affairs, building on China's growing stake in stability in and around the Gulf. India, too, is likely to acquire a larger stake in Gulf security based on its own growing imports.

---

[16]Patrick L. Clawson, "Oil Resources: Markets, Politics and Policies" in Richard L. Kugler and Ellen L. Frost (eds.), *The Global Century: Globalization and National Security*, Vol. 2, Washington, D.C.: Institute for National Strategic Studies, 2001, p. 730.

EMERGING ISSUES

Beyond fundamental questions of supply and demand for oil and changing import patterns, some longstanding and some new more specific issues are affecting the role of energy in Middle Eastern security. Taken together, these issues are likely to play a central role in the way the United States and other international actors view energy security matters, as well as the prospects for friction and cooperation.

The Rise of Gas

Until very recently, energy geopolitics was essentially the geopolitics of oil. As a globally traded commodity, oil has dominated the energy security debate. With the important exception of nonproliferation and safeguards, nuclear energy has largely been the province of domestic public policy, where the security issues concern the safety of civil nuclear power (and, perhaps, to a lesser extent, terrorism). Access to oil in adequate amounts and at reasonable prices will remain the key variable in the energy security equation over the next decades, but it will be accompanied by increasing attention to the supply and transport of natural gas. For some consuming states, principally in Western Europe and Asia, gas will figure very prominently in the energy security calculus.

Demand for gas is expanding rapidly worldwide. It is an efficient, cost-effective, and increasingly favored fuel, not least for environmental reasons. World gas trade rose by 12 percent in 2000 alone.[17] Over the next decade, gas usage is likely to increase more rapidly than usage of any other source of energy and could increase by 100 percent by 2015. As with oil, it is assumed that this tremendous growth will be driven by the rapid expansion of demand in Asia (at the moment, gas usage in Asia is very low by Western standards). It is also a resource that appears far from exhaustion: It is estimated that some 95 percent of the world's natural gas remains in the ground.[18]

---

[17]*Gas Daily* (FT Energy), May 3, 2001, p. 1.

[18]*Global Trends 2015*, 2001, p. 28.

Unlike oil, gas is a regional rather than a global commodity. Transportation costs are a critical factor in gas trade, and although natural gas can be shipped in specialized vessels as liquefied natural gas (LNG), the cost is high and the safety concerns at LNG terminals are substantial. Indeed, in the wake of the dramatic terrorist strikes in the United States in September 2001, the risks associated with highly explosive LNG are likely to be taken even more seriously worldwide (LNG terminals already tend to be located well away from populated areas, further increasing transport costs). As a result, pipelines capable of delivering gas to large markets at competitive prices are the key element in the geopolitics of gas. The network of pipelines for gas transport has expanded significantly over the last decade, creating a complex web of supply infrastructure within Europe, as well as infrastructure bringing gas to European markets from Eurasia, North Africa, and elsewhere in the Middle East.

Europe is used to thinking about the security of gas. Starting in the early 1980s, western Europe began to import large amounts of gas from the former Soviet Union through Russian pipelines. In the context of Cold War concerns, the issue of Russian gas became a source of friction in transatlantic relations, with many strategists and policymakers in Washington worried about the security implications of European dependence on gas supplies from the East. Europe, especially Germany, tended to take a less concerned position on the reliability of Russian supplies and saw gas trade as a useful contribution to economic détente. As with the question of oil supply, Europe tended (and still tends) to argue that energy trade is not highly vulnerable to politically inspired interruptions, not least because exporters, dependent on energy revenues, need to sell the product somewhere.

At the same time, Europe began to invest in infrastructure for the transport of gas by pipelines (as well as LNG) across the Mediterranean. The Trans-Mediterranean pipeline linking Tunisia and Sicily brought Algerian and Libyan gas to European markets. The capacity of this pipeline (actually five lines) has been greatly expanded in recent years. Gas trade across the Mediterranean has also benefited from the construction of a new line across the Maghreb, bringing

Algerian gas to Spain via Morocco and the Strait of Gibraltar. In the near term, gas will also arrive in Europe from much further afield, from the Caspian and Central Asia, perhaps via Iran and Turkey. This southeastern route had been the least developed of Europe's avenues of gas supply, but it too is set to expand considerably over the coming decade.[19]

Today, Europe depends on North Africa for roughly 25 percent of its gas needs. For Spain, Italy, Portugal, and France, the dependency is much greater. As an example, Spain relies on Algeria for roughly 70 percent of its supply, Portugal for over 90 percent.[20] Maps of current and planned gas routes across Eurasia and the Middle East portray a supply network of extraordinary complexity and reach.[21] The net effect is a system of gas trade that is truly transregional in scope, with enormous security implications.

The emerging network is not simply a hub-and-spoke arrangement designed to bring gas to European markets. There are also important subregional lines in existence or under construction. The "great game" model of a limited number of major competing routes, and a propensity for friction and conflict, may not apply in the case of gas infrastructure (it may not even apply in the case of oil pipelines, where multiple routes and alternative avenues for energy trade are also becoming the norm). The proliferation of routes within and between regions argues for increasing redundancy and the ability to offset interruptions in supply. Where several states are involved in gas transport, and where valuable pipeline revenues are at stake, there will probably be a shared interest in the stability of these arrangements. Economic interdependence based on gas trade may therefore be a force for stability in both the western and the eastern Mediterranean.

Morocco and Algeria, traditional competitors, share a stake in the security of the trans-Maghreb pipeline. A similar situation exists in the case of Libya and Tunisia. Turkey's growing energy needs (even in

---

[19]Presentation by Giaccomo Luciani, ENI, Rome, 1999.

[20]Estimates compiled by RAND colleagues Nurith Berstein and Richard Sokolsky from OECD and other sources.

[21]See, e.g., *Gas in the CIS and Europe*, London: Petroleum Economist/Ruhrgas, 2000.

light of the country's economic travails) are driving a wide range of gas transport schemes, some involving regional joint ventures. As an example, Greek and Turkish energy concerns hope to build a pipeline across the Adriatic, linking Greece via Italy to North African sources of supply, and opening a route from Algeria and Libya to the large Turkish market, currently supplied mainly by Russia.[22]

Impossible under current circumstances, but potentially important over the next decade, would be the exploitation of offshore gas deposits near Israel and Gaza. Prior to the deterioration in Arab-Israeli relations, plans were under way for the construction of a gas pipeline spanning the eastern Mediterranean, bringing supplies from Egypt (and possibly Qatar) up the coast of the Levant to Israel, Turkey, and southeastern Europe. Constraints in relations with Israel are the leading obstacle to the expansion of Egyptian gas exports, both because Israel is among the lucrative markets for Egyptian gas and because pipelines to consumers in Syria or Lebanon bypassing Israel would be expensive to build.[23] The discovery of new, commercially viable gas and oil deposits in the eastern Mediterranean has also spurred negotiations between Cyprus and Lebanon regarding the demarcation and exploitation of these resources.[24]

Further afield, there has been discussion of a new pipeline to bring Iranian gas to the growing Indian market, either offshore or, if bilateral relations permit, via Pakistan. Ambitious schemes of this sort would serve to extend the system of transport for Middle Eastern gas, not only to Europe, but to South Asia. In sum, the next decade is likely to see a far more complex supply picture for gas, with many more points of interdependence.

The structural dependencies implied by the fixed infrastructure for gas trade may be reduced through the expansion and diversification

---

[22]A Turkish deal with Iran for a 25-year supply of gas has fallen behind schedule, raising the possibility that imports from Russia will continue to dominate the Turkish market as the "Blue Stream" pipeline across the Black Sea moves toward completion. Michael Lelyveld, "Turkey: Iranian Gas Import Delays May Favor Russia," *RFE/RL*, July 10, 2001.

[23]Abeer Allam, "Regional Tensions Thwart Egypt's Hopes for Gas Sales," *New York Times*, August 17, 2001.

[24]"Cyprus/Lebanon: Talks on Oil-Gas Zone," *New York Times* (AFP), March 6, 2002.

of the supply network. But unlike oil, gas will never be an essentially fungible, global commodity. Gas use and transport infrastructure is relatively inflexible, and patterns of import dependence are structural, at least in the short term. As gas usage has increased in Europe, the perception of gas as a strategic commodity has also increased, and gas supply is now a significant factor in European views of Middle Eastern security. This has been particularly evident in French and southern European perceptions regarding the Algerian crisis. The potential for interruptions in gas production and transport has been among the leading concerns regarding the turmoil in Algeria since the early 1990s, alongside the fear of a refugee crisis and spillovers of political violence. Despite a decade of extraordinary violence, energy production and exports from Algeria have been unaffected by the crisis, which is a testimony to the security arrangements in energy producing areas in southern Algeria and at transport facilities in the north. It is also likely that Algeria's various violent factions have seen little strategic benefit in targeting the country's oil and gas industry. Nonetheless, future risks to gas supply from sources on the European periphery are probably more likely to arise from chaotic conditions in producing states than from deliberate cutoffs or interference with transport routes.

Some observers see this European stake in gas supply, and in the stability of key producers, as an important new source of interest in Middle Eastern affairs, and one that has little to do with American regional priorities in the Gulf and Arab-Israeli relations.[25] Indeed, this factor could help drive a more active European foreign and security policy in the Middle East, including but not limited to North Africa. With much Gulf energy production headed to Asia in the coming years, this could suggest a significant adjustment of Western thinking and planning on energy security, with greater emphasis on Europe's gas-rich "near abroad." Washington may feel, and Europe may prefer, that the European Union (EU) take the lead in defense policy in this area. It is also an area that Europe may be able to reach with its more limited power projection capabilities.

---

[25]See, for example, George Joffe, "The Euro-Mediterranean Partnership: Two Years After Barcelona," Chatham House, *Middle East Briefing*, No. 44, May 1998, p. 2.

New Lines of Communication for Oil

Over the next decade, Middle Eastern security may be affected by developments concerning existing and new lines of communication for oil. As noted earlier, the appearance of larger amounts of Caspian oil on world markets will be an important, but not a transforming development. The outlook for the Baku-Ceyhan pipeline, designed to bring Caspian oil across Turkey to the Mediterranean, has been hotly debated for almost a decade. Although Baku-Ceyhan has enjoyed strong diplomatic support from the United States, the prospects for implementation of the project have always turned, above all, on its long-term economic viability as seen by commercial investors.

Three key variables are at play. First, environmental risks may compel Turkey to limit the passage of very large and ultra large crude carriers through the Bosporus, constraining the existing Russian–Black Sea route for Caspian oil transport. It is unclear whether Ankara could impose such restrictions without renegotiating the Montreaux Convention governing passage through the Turkish straits. Second, U.S.-Iranian relations could evolve substantially over the next decade, opening the possibility of an end to American opposition to an Iranian route for Caspian oil. The shorter distances and existing pipeline infrastructure make this route attractive in commercial terms, and some in the international oil industry are known to favor this option. A route through Iran would, however, mean a substantial increase in the flow of tanker traffic through the vulnerable choke points of the Persian Gulf and through Hormuz. Third, the outlook for Baku-Ceyhan probably turns critically on the anticipated throughput of Caspian oil and gas. As exploration around the Caspian has accelerated, and with increased estimates of proven reserves, the project's viability has improved. The pessimistic discussion regarding Baku-Ceyhan, characteristic of most of the 1990s, has begun to change. Key agreements are now in place among Turkey, Azerbaijan, Georgia, and the consortium of companies involved in the project. Preliminary construction work is about to begin, and there is now a fair chance that Baku-Ceyhan will become a reality by 2010.[26]

---

[26]For a discussion of Caspian alternatives, including Baku-Ceyhan, see "Whose Game, How Great?" *Private View* (Istanbul), Autumn 2000; Jan H. Kilicki, "Caspian Energy at

If Baku-Ceyhan is built, it will deepen Turkey's role as an energy entrepot and will reinforce the position of the eastern Mediterranean in world oil trade. But the restoration of pre-1990 Iraqi oil shipments to terminals on Turkey's Mediterranean coast may be even more important in this regard. The two existing lines for the shipment of Iraqi oil across Turkey have roughly twice the capacity of the proposed Baku-Ceyhan line. Transport through Turkey may become increasingly attractive as Iraqi oil exports gradually return to their pre-1990 levels, since that would reduce exposure to potential Iranian interdiction. The end of oil-related sanctions on Iraq will therefore be a transforming development for Turkey and the Levant in energy security terms.

If Baku-Ceyhan is not completed, and the Iranian option becomes feasible, commercial benefits may conflict with strategic interests as greater amounts of oil flow through the Gulf to Hormuz headed mainly to Asian markets. Western strategists may be concerned about the security implications of even greater reliance on passage through Hormuz, although the political changes necessary to allow an Iranian route for Caspian oil would probably be accompanied by a reduction in concerns about Iranian behavior overall. This might also reinforce the Chinese interest in relations with Iran, both as a leading supplier of oil and gas and as a regional security actor. In recent years, there has also been some consideration of bringing Caspian oil to China overland, by pipeline through Afghanistan. The events of September 2001 and their aftermath make this an uncertain prospect at best. Over the longer term, however, and if a stable regime remains in place in Kabul, initiatives aimed at Afghan reconstruction might well include revenue-generating projects such as energy transport.

"Rogue" (or Isolated) States, Sanctions, and Energy Supply

Many recent analyses have questioned the efficacy of international and above all unilateral sanctions that regimes have imposed on "rogue" states.[27] The issue is also highly divisive on a transatlantic

---

the Crossroads", *Foreign Affairs*, Vol. 80, No. 5, September/October 2001, pp. 120–134; and Richard Sokolsky and Tanya Charlick-Paley, 1999.

[27]The term "rogue states" is inadequate and perhaps misleading but has become part of the general discourse on sanctions policy.

basis. European allies are particularly uncomfortable with the extra-territorial application of U.S. economic sanctions, since many European countries are looking to invest in the Iranian and Libyan oil sectors.

Ironically, the one area where economic sanctions have probably been effective has been in the energy sector. Most analyses agree that UN and U.S.-imposed sanctions have hindered energy exploration and the modernization of aging infrastructure in Iran, Libya, and Iraq (until 2003). The effect has been to keep several key producers from expanding production, contributing to a generally close relationship between current production and capacity. Western advocates for an end to sanctions—a mixed constituency, including but not limited to many in the energy industry—argue that energy-related sanctions actually jeopardize global energy security by keeping important new increments of supply off the market. It is also argued that energy trade can be a valuable vehicle for engaging regimes and moderating the behavior of otherwise isolated states.[28] The prospect of access to unfettered Western investment in energy production, especially at a time when producers are operating near capacity and the need for oil and gas revenue is high, should be an important "carrot" in relations with Iran and Libya.[29]

In the case of sanctions, arguments based on energy security may conflict with other strategic aims. Sanctions may or may not have changed the international behavior of Iran, Iraq, and Libya, but they have clearly affected the overall prosperity of the targeted states. Energy-related sanctions have probably played a key role in this regard, limiting revenues that might otherwise have bolstered the ability of "rogue" states to pay for conventional and unconventional arms, or to pursue regional initiatives of their own. As a matter of principle, some might argue that states that violate international norms and

---

[28]See *Thinking Beyond the Stalemate in U.S.-Iranian Relations, Volume I—Policy Review,* Washington, D.C.: The Atlantic Council of the United States, May 2001, pp. 6–7; *Strategic Energy Policy: Challenges for the 21st Century, A Task Force Report,* New York: Council on Foreign Relations, 2001, pp. 22–23; and Ray Takeyh, "The Rogue Who Came in from the Cold," *Foreign Affairs,* Vol. 80, No. 3, May/June 2001.

[29]Whether Iran itself is prepared to take full advantage of foreign participation in its energy sector is another matter and the source of active debate within Iranian policy circles.

pursue "revolutionary" objectives should not be rewarded with integration into the global economy. As a matter of practice, UN-imposed sanctions on Iraq between 1990 and 2003 became increasingly difficult to maintain.[30]

In the Iranian and Libyan cases, and barring new crises in relations with the West, the outlook is almost certainly for a weakening or disappearance of sanctions and a commensurate increase in foreign energy-related investment. Indeed, even without the participation of American companies, both Iran and Libya have remained well integrated in the world energy market (Iran, like Saudi Arabia, is experiencing its own debate about whether to allow increased foreign participation in the country's energy sector).[31] The U.S. Department of Energy estimates suggest that Iran will satisfy some 5 percent of global energy needs in 2005, a figure that could increase significantly with new exploration and investment.[32] Even more dramatically than in the case of Iran, the key variable affecting the weight of future American sanctions in the Libyan energy sector will be European behavior. Europe is Libya's leading trade partner and also the market for 90 percent of the country's energy exports. Without European compliance and support, future sanctions on Libya may prove largely symbolic.[33]

Arms and Oil

In the 1970s, Europe was often described as pursuing relations with key Middle Eastern energy producers—Iraq, Iran, and the Gulf monarchies—on the basis of "arms for oil." The term had a negative connotation, suggesting self-interested hedging against politically inspired oil boycotts, securing a preferred supply relationship regardless of the effect on regional balances. After 1973, large-scale Ameri-

---

[30]Starting in the late 1990s, Iraq steadily increased its economic relations with Europe and other regions. Syria and Jordan also maintained a significant trade in diesel oil and other products, despite the UN restrictions.

[31]Italy's ENI is among the most active investors in Iranian energy development, having recently signed a $920 million oilfield development agreement. "The Fight Over Letting Foreigners into Iran's Oilfields," *The Economist*, July 14, 2001, pp. 41–42.

[32]Cited in *Thinking Beyond the Stalemate*, 2001, p. 6.

[33]Takeyh, 2001, p. 71.

can arms transfers to the region made European patterns of arms trade less distinctive. In today's strategic environment, there may be new openings for the rise of closer economic and military ties, less "arms for oil" than "arms *and* oil," based on growing Middle Eastern energy exports to Asia.

China and North Korea (with Russia) have emerged as leading suppliers of components and technologies for weapons of mass destruction and the means for their delivery at longer ranges, including ballistic and cruise missiles. It is possible that as China imports greater amounts of oil from the Gulf and the Caspian, existing patterns of arms and technology transfers will deepen and perhaps become less amenable to suspension under Western pressure. The argument here is not that resource dependency itself will compel China or North Korea to transfer military technology and equipment as a form of strategic exchange (although this cannot be ruled out if Asian leaderships *perceive* themselves to be vulnerable to supply cutoffs). Rather, increased energy trade may facilitate more extensive political and security relations, which could, in turn, foster new defense trade.[34] The result could be an acceleration of troubling proliferation trends in the Middle East and a more dangerous strategic environment for the United States as well as for Middle Eastern states themselves.

Russian interests in the region also have an energy and arms dimension. Iran is now the third largest customer for Russia's arms industry, and Libya has also negotiated new arms purchases from Russia.[35] The destabilizing effects of such transfers could contribute to perceptions of regional risk and contribute to higher prices in periods of crisis from which Russia will benefit. This is not to suggest that Moscow pursues new arms transfers to the Gulf and North Africa simply to provoke instability among Middle Eastern energy producers; there are more prosaic and direct reasons for such transfers. But the benefits of higher oil prices might well keep Moscow from worrying unduly about the regional security consequences.

---

[34]The prospects for and implications of such developments are explored in greater detail in Chapter Nine.

[35]Amy Myers Jaffe and Robert A. Manning, "Russia, Energy and the West," *Survival*, Vol. 43, No. 2, Summer 2001, p. 145.

Energy Prices, Regime Stability, and Military Potential

For most Middle Eastern states, including the leading energy producers, security is largely a matter of internal security. Notwithstanding examples of conventional cross-border threats to the security of oil producers (e.g., the Iran-Iraq and Gulf Wars), the leading source of energy-related risk is probably internal instability and the precariousness of regimes. Demographic pressures, high defense expenditures, high levels of debt, and fairly low energy prices for much of the last decade have left Middle Eastern producers facing difficult social and political challenges.

Algeria is perhaps the most extreme case. Well over 100,000 people have been killed in political violence in Algeria since the early 1990s. The regime has survived a series of extraordinary and continuing challenges and has itself been implicated in much of the violence. It has survived, in large measure, because a period of higher oil prices beginning in the mid-1990s allowed the government to meet its staggering debt obligations and secure new loans. Lower energy prices leave the regime in Algiers little room for maneuver in meeting explosive social challenges in the midst of a continuing Islamic insurgency, Berber unrest, and chaotic conditions throughout the country. Algeria offers an example of how the demand for cheaper gas could jeopardize Europe's energy security if Algeria's political violence should begin to affect energy production (something that has not happened in a decade of conflict). Indeed, Algeria's president, Abdelaziz Bouteflika, has made the question of "equity" in energy trade a keynote of his conversations with European political leaderships.

In the Gulf, leading producers also face strong social and political challenges, and have relied on energy revenues to subsidize internal stability, as well as high levels of defense spending. There is no clear and definite linkage between oil revenues and internal stability, just as the Middle East offers few absolutely predictable links between economic reform and stability at least in the short term. Nonetheless, analysts of regional affairs tend to agree that energy revenues allow otherwise dysfunctional states to "cover a multitude of sins" in terms of governance and public policy. Lower revenues, against a background of social unrest and political turmoil across the region, could press some regimes past the breaking point. Regime change itself might not affect oil exports over the longer term, but internal instability might well interrupt production on a temporary basis, pushing up prices and discouraging foreign investment. One consequence of the events of September 2001 has been to increase Western scrutiny of the internal situation in Saudi Arabia and the Gulf monarchies. The potential for internal instability in Saudi Arabia, the key "swing producer," may well be the leading source of energy security risk over the next few years.

Iran is also not immune to the challenges posed by volatility in oil prices. As with Saudi Arabia, oil revenue may be a factor in its stability over the next decade, and it may affect Iranian procurement priorities and its ability to pursue WMD-related programs. It is often assumed that lower energy revenues, as a result of lower prices or sanctions, will have the salutary effect of limiting arms and technology purchases. In broad terms, this may be so. But lower oil revenues might also spur the acquisition of WMD in preference to more expensive conventional defense improvements, driving "rogue" regimes toward more asymmetrical forms of warfare.

Energy Denial as an Asymmetric Strategy

There is a long tradition of strategy aimed at denying an adversary access to vital resources as a mode of asymmetric warfare. To take just one example, with striking modern parallels, the French *jeune école* of naval strategists at the end of the 19th century saw brief, devastating attacks on British seaborne trade in the English Channel as a way of sending British financial markets into chaos. Such strikes could be carried out with light torpedo boats, or with mines, obviating the need for an expensive battle fleet with which to confront Britain in a symmetrical fashion. The notion of high-leverage interdiction of specific resources such as oil has been an important subset of economic warfare since the Industrial Revolution. As noted earlier, Cold War strategists considered the problem of Russian threats to key maritime choke points, especially for oil, and later the issue of strategic minerals.

Historically, most such concerns have been overblown, but the interest in resource denial as an adjunct to conventional warfare, or as an alternative to it, shows considerable durability. One recent analysis sees a coming clash over resources as an important facet of the strategic environment—"a reconfigured cartography in which re-source flows rather than political and ideological divisions constitute the major fault lines."[36] Whatever its shortcomings as an organizing principle for understanding future conflict, the rise of thinking along these lines, perhaps with a strong north-south flavor, could encourage consideration of energy denial as a strategy to be employed against the United States or the West.

Several risks are worth considering in this regard. First, states, or even terrorist groups, might attack or threaten to attack specific energy-related targets. In the calculus of the attacker, a sustained campaign or prolonged interdiction of supplies might not be necessary. It might, for example, prove difficult to close the Strait of Hormuz to tanker traffic for more than a few days. But the attacker might count on provoking chaos in world oil and financial markets. The September 11 terrorist attacks offer a reminder of the potential, and several press reports in 2002 suggested that terrorist networks have planned for attacks on shipping in the region. In May 2002, for example, Moroccan authorities disrupted an al Qaeda plot to attack ships in the Strait of Gibraltar with explosive-laden boats, which may still occur given al Qaeda's proclivity to revisit targets that it has previously failed to hit.[37] In another setting, interference with Algerian gas shipments to Europe, or an attack on Caspian pipelines, might have a brief disruptive effect on a regional basis. This is very much in the tradition of the *jeune école*, seeking disruption rather than destruction as a means of strategic leverage.[38] Persistent rather than temporary disruptions in energy and financial markets through

---

[36]Michael T. Klare, "The New Geography of Conflict," *Foreign Affairs*, Vol. 80, No. 3, May/June 2001, p. 52; see also by the same author *Resource Wars: The New Landscape of Global Conflict*, New York: Metropolitan Books, 2001.

[37]See Kim Sengupta, "Five Held in Morocco Planned to Strike Warships," *The Independent* (London), June 12, 2002; Peter Finn, "Arrests Reveal Al Qaeda Plans; Three Saudis Seized by Morocco Outline Post-Afghanistan Strategy," *Washington Post*, June 16, 2002.

[38]Key maritime energy choke points around the Middle East include the Strait of Hormuz (accounting for passage of roughly 30 percent of world exports in 2000, as much as 40 percent by 2020); Bab el Mandeb on the Red Sea; the Suez Canal (less important since very large and ultra large crude carriers cannot use the canal); the Bosporous; and the key off-loading ports in the Gulf, at Iskenderun in Turkey, Baku, and elsewhere. See *World Oil Transit Chokepoints*, Washington, D.C.: Energy Information Administration, 1998.

interdiction or sabotage would be far more difficult, perhaps impossible, to achieve.

Second, an adversary might attempt to seize oil or gas fields, or hold pipelines, as a vehicle for longer-term advantage, regionally and in relations with the West. This was perhaps part of the Iraqi rationale for invading Kuwait in 1990. When regime survival itself is in question, an adversary might even contemplate the destruction of energy infrastructure and the denial of resource-rich areas as a deterrent or as a means of revenge.[39]

Third, access to energy supplies might be threatened as a form of economic and political blackmail. This was the case during the Arab oil embargo of 1973–1974. Since that time, it has generally been assumed that a more globalized oil market and a weakened and diverse OPEC make new politically motivated supply restrictions unlikely. Some have, however, seen the potential for more subtle, politically driven behavior on the part of leading oil producers. Against a background of Arab-Israeli conflict and strong internal demand for energy revenue, key OPEC states may feel constrained in taking very public production decisions aimed at moderating prices for the benefit of Western consumers. With deep ambivalence in many quarters across the Arab and Muslim world regarding the events of September 11 and the war in Iraq, production decisions in the Western interest may also be problematic for insecure oil-producing regimes. In cases where regimes perceive themselves to be engaged in a broader geopolitical competition with the United States and West, these patterns of behavior may take on the characteristics of asymmetric strategy.

All of these examples, from the most direct to the most subtle, would pose problems of discrimination for the adversary, whether a state or a nonstate actor. In a globalized oil market, attacks or embargoes aimed at provoking price increases and financial instability would hurt all oil consumers. Less developed economies might actually be

---

[39]There is a long history of such attempts, though few have been successful. For example, the Dutch attempted to destroy oil wells and production facilities ahead of the Japanese occupation of Indonesia, and the Japanese, in turn, attempted the same during their withdrawal. Production was easily restarted. Iraqi forces blew up numerous wells in Kuwait during the Gulf War, with substantial economic and environmental consequences, but the effect on world oil markets was insignificant.

the leading victims, as they were in the early 1970s. Attacks conceived as symbolic blows against the West might well have a more far-reaching and counterproductive effect. Gas production and transport, with regional markets, might offer more promising targets for an adversary bent on using energy denial as a focused asymmetric strategy.

Transatlantic and Asian Perspectives

As both the United States and Europe come to be less dependent on oil imports from the Middle East, transatlantic differences on energy security matters may lose some of their traditional edge. That said, both the United States and Europe will retain a strong stake in Middle Eastern oil because of the influence of Gulf producers on oil pricing worldwide, and because of longer-term security commitments affecting the defense plans of the United States and to a lesser extent Britain, France, and others. Looking ahead, Europe will probably retain a strategy of access emphasizing economic and political engagement over the physical defense of oil resources, at least in the Gulf. A distaste for energy-related sanctions and the desire to construct a web of economic, political, and (where possible) security relations with key producers will be part of this equation. U.S. interests in regional counterterror cooperation and the reconstruction of Iraq might also push the United States in this direction.

At the same time, Europe may develop more powerful energy security interests of its own, centered on growing gas imports from around the Mediterranean. This could also be a focus of emerging European security and defense policy initiatives through 2010. Here, in contrast to the Gulf, political and economic engagement may be accompanied by planning for military intervention to protect gas production and transport infrastructure as well as large numbers of European personnel in Algeria and Libya. Intervention in North Africa is more likely to be within the capability of European defense establishments.

In Asia, growing reliance on Middle Eastern and Caspian energy sources may encourage importers to augment political and commercial ties with deeper security relationships and increased direct investment in regional energy projects. This could go well beyond existing arms transfer relationships. With China set to import ever-larger quantities of oil from the Gulf, it is not inconceivable that some form of Chinese naval presence in the region will be common-place by 2010.

CONCLUSIONS AND POLICY IMPLICATIONS

After a period of relative neglect, energy security questions are fash-ionable again and, as in the past, much of the new debate turns on developments in the Middle East. The analysis offered here suggests several conclusions regarding energy geopolitics and Middle Eastern security.

First, the consensus judgment among analysts of the energy scene suggests a world of moderate oil prices through 2010, with growing demand, above all in Asia, but also increasing supply. Outright scarcity of oil and gas resources, or a perception of looming exhaus-tion that might affect prices, is not likely to be a factor through 2010, or in all likelihood well beyond. A period of slow economic growth would naturally reinforce this outlook. Price volatility, driven largely by political and security risks, will nonetheless remain a factor, and could affect the internal stability of regimes and the policies of extra-regional powers toward the Middle East.

Second, the increasing globalization of the oil market (it was always globalized to a considerable degree) has contributed to energy secu-rity and has quickened the pace of exploration and production. Sub-stantial new reserves are being exploited worldwide, but much of the new production will be in the Middle East. Thus, the region's overall contribution to world energy supply is actually set to grow through 2010. Oil is a global and fungible commodity, but the overwhelming role of oil exports from the Gulf means that the price of oil is still de-termined largely by the behavior of Middle Eastern producers.

Third, patterns of energy trade are changing in ways that will alter but not eliminate Western concerns about the security of Middle Eastern supply. The United States and Europe are importing more oil, but they are importing it largely from Western Hemisphere sources and from West Africa. By 2010, the system of supply will be, above all, an Atlantic system. Russia is also likely to play a larger role in meeting Western demand and could emerge as a more significant player in energy geopolitics over the next decade. Most Middle Eastern and Caspian oil will go to Asia, driven by strong demand in China, India, and elsewhere. Gas will also loom larger in the energy picture worldwide. For Europe, this will mean closer energy ties to North Africa and producing and transit states around the Mediterranean and the Black Sea. Gas is increasingly a transregional commodity, but the system of supply for gas will always be less flexible than that for oil. Europe's focus on gas as a component of energy security is likely to grow, suggesting new security concerns and commitments on the European periphery.

Fourth, the proliferation of transport routes for oil and gas in and around the Middle East, from the Maghreb to the Caspian, will be an important new factor in the strategic environment. To an increasing extent, energy security in the region will be about the security of transport and transit states as well as the stability and policies of producers. In many cases, the "great game" model of competition over resources and lines of communication may not be appropriate. The complexity and redundancy of the emerging oil and gas infrastructure within the region, and between the region and adjacent areas, will also offer many opportunities for economic interdependence and increased stability. Commercial considerations aside, U.S. support for the Baku-Ceyhan pipeline across Turkey would contribute to energy security by promoting the diversification of export routes, avoiding even greater reliance on transit through the Gulf.

Fifth, the greatest risk to energy security emanating from the Middle East through 2010 is likely to arise from internal instability in key producing states—including Algeria, Iran, and Saudi Arabia, leading to periods of reduced production. In the case of gas, where there is little flexibility in supply arrangements, even a temporary cutoff of North African supply could pose a serious problem for some European importers. A sustained period of low energy prices could itself prove destabilizing for key producers facing the prospect of political opposition and social unrest. The U.S. intervention in Iraq places all of these open questions in sharper relief.

These realities suggest the opening of a period, spurred by the events of September 2001 and the war in Iraq, in which Western policies in the Gulf will be framed, first and foremost, with an eye to internal stability rather than territorial threats. We may also wish to loosen sanctions related to energy development, while tightening measures aimed at containing the spread of weapons of mass destruction and ballistic missiles. This tradeoff would greatly facilitate a concerted transatlantic policy toward Iran, Iraq, and Libya.

Finally, energy issues will interact in significant ways with other challenges, with implications for the future of the region in security terms. New patterns of oil exports, principally to Asia, could reinforce existing arms and technology transfer relationships, fueling a destabilizing regional arms race and complicating the outlook for Western intervention in future crises. Future adversaries, both states and nonstate actors, might attempt to use energy denial as a form of asymmetric economic warfare with global effects. In a less direct fashion, a deteriorating security environment in the Middle East could alter the outlook for dialogue and cooperation among producers and consumers, with lasting implications for energy security.

Chapter Seven

THE INFORMATION REVOLUTION AND THE MIDDLE EAST

Jon B. Alterman

In the last two decades, the information and media environment in the Middle East has changed dramatically. Partly through such recent high-tech advances as the Internet, and even more fundamentally through older technologies like satellite television, photocopiers, fax machines, and videocassettes, individuals and groups in the Middle East have far greater abilities to share ideas than ever before.

This change in the information environment has broad implications for the societies and politics of the region, and for U.S. policy. Increasingly informed public debate, the ability of actors living abroad to influence events in the region, and the spread of images from the West are challenging many long-held ideas and transforming the politics of the Middle East. These changes are likely to complicate U.S. policy and possibly military operations.

Yet limits to what is often termed "the information revolution" must also be recognized. Although more breathless proponents believe that advanced technologies such as the Internet will empower the poor and disenfranchised, in the Middle East those technologies are likely to be used only by the wealthy and well educated. Instead, "mid-tech" advances such as satellite television, videocassettes, and photocopiers are likely to have the most profound effect among broad populations.

This chapter analyzes changes in patterns of communication in the Arab world and their import for U.S. policy. It surveys how technology is changing the information environment in the region, drawing special attention to the effects of mid-tech technologies that are inexpensive, easy to use, and ubiquitous in much of the region. It then examines the probable effects of those changes on politics, governments, and societies in the region, and concludes with a consideration of the implications of those changes for U.S. policymakers.

A RICHER INFORMATION ENVIRONMENT

In the last decade, almost every media form found in the Middle East has improved in the quantity, quality, and variety of information it provides. Competition for audience has increased in recent years, forcing outlets in every medium to address the needs and desires of their consumers more effectively.[1]

Newspapers

In the not-so-distant past, same-day newspaper and magazine readership in the Middle East was restricted to domestic publications, many of which were controlled by individual states. Although Lebanon had a tradition of a diverse press, it was the exception. Lebanese papers were often available in other Arab capitals, but they arrived days or weeks after publication.

The nationalization of independent newspapers in the 1960s, and the establishment of government outlets, meant that Arab newspapers in that period were often shrill and ideological regime mouthpieces. Instead of intelligent debate on the news of the day, the print media often featured fawning coverage of national leaders. Political leaders' meetings with foreign dignitaries were a staple of news coverage,

---

[1]Most studies of technology and social and political change tend to be focused on wealthier countries, or suggest that technology will force poorer countries to follow the path of wealthier countries. The classic expression of this view is Thomas L. Friedman, *The Lexus and the Olive Tree*, New York: Farrar, Strauss and Giroux, 1999. A relatively early view of the role of computational power and the Internet in daily life is Nicholas Negroponte, *Being Digital*, New York: Knopf, 1995. A comprehensive view is Manuel Castells, *The Rise of the Networked Society*, 2d ed., Oxford: Blackwell, 2000. One essay collection that deals especially with media in the developing world is Lloyd S. Etheredge (ed.), *Politics in Wired Nations: Selected Writings of Ithiel de Sola Pool*, New Brunswick, N.J.: Transaction, 1998.

but newspapers only rarely gave even a flavor of what was discussed behind closed doors.

Starting in 1976, Saudi investors created *Asharq Alawsat*. Edited in London and printed around the Arab world using satellite technology similar to that employed by *USA Today*, the paper represented an important step in creating a vibrant and viable overseas Arab press. With time, other international Arabic papers emerged in London, the most prominent among them being a reinvigorated *al-Hayat* (originally out of Lebanon, and now Saudi-supported), and the independent, pro-Palestinian *al-Quds al-Arabi*. These papers published news that was generally accurate and offered selective criticism of regional governments and figures.

Current circulation and readership for the papers vary. *Asharq Alawsat*, whose outside pages are printed on eye-catching green newsprint, remains basically a Saudi paper. The vast bulk of its roughly 250,000 daily circulation is in Saudi Arabia,[2] and its editor is a Saudi. Its editorial lines are thought to reflect Saudi official thinking, albeit sometimes only its most liberal strain. Because it is written and edited outside of the Kingdom, however, the paper has broader freedom than domestic papers in its discussions of controversial issues. Still, it avoids criticism of Saudi leaders. It has extensive cooperative agreements with several leading American newspapers, and sometimes draws criticism for running others' reporting on its front page instead of its own reporters' work.[3] Seemingly alone among the international Arab papers, *Asharq Alawsat* is a money-maker, in part because of official Saudi encouragement of advertising

---

[2]Like all audience data from the Middle East, this number is difficult to verify. The problem has many parts: long-standing state sponsorship of media, lack of advertiser demand for accurate information, societal suspicions of poll-taking, poor demographic data necessary for accurate polling, especially weak data from the poorer and more populous countries in the region, and the lack of a large cadre of well-trained poll-takers. Beyond the question of raw audience numbers, the characteristics of audiences are also poorly understood. The huge gaps in our knowledge of audience data are outlined in Jon B. Alterman, "Counting Nodes and Counting Noses: Understanding New Media in the Middle East," *Middle East Journal*, Vol. 54, No. 3, Summer 2000, pp. 355–361.

[3]Author's interviews with Arab journalists, London, July 3, 2002, Washington, D.C., July 20, 2002, et al.

there.[4] The late Prince Ahmed Bin Salman, the son of the governor of Riyadh, was the principal owner until his early death in July 2002.

One counterpart to *Asharq Alawsat* is *al-Hayat*. Although its world-wide circulation is smaller—probably less than 125,000 per day—it enjoys broad readership among the intelligentsia throughout the Arab world and among Arab expatriate communities in the West. *Al-Hayat* has positioned itself as an intellectuals' paper, not only providing authoritative news coverage (often combining Western wire reports with local Arab reporting) and a variety of viewpoints but also covering the arts, poetry, and philosophy. The paper is owned by Khalid Bin Sultan, the son of the Saudi defense minister. The operation loses something on the order of $10 million/year, as neither advertising nor sales cover the costs of production.[5]

There are a variety of other expatriate papers. *Al-Quds al-Arabi* is an independent Palestinian paper with no visible means of support. It features some of the most critical reporting of Saudi Arabia to be found in the Arab world, and is thought to be funded through a wide range of subsidies from individuals and governments. *Azzaman* is published by former Iraqi information minister Saad al-Bazzaz, reportedly with Saudi support. *Al-Arab* is published by former Libyan information minister Ahmed Salhin al-Houni. The smaller papers all tend to be more ideological and more anti-American. They all operate on the basis of mysterious subsidies.[6]

Collectively, all the pan-Arab newspapers combined are unlikely to sell more than 400,000 copies a day worldwide (by comparison, *The New York Times* alone averages more than 1 million copies a day). But concentrating on raw numbers would be to miss their impact. The pan-Arab papers are a fundamental link between expatriate Arab communities in London, Paris, New York, Washington, and beyond,

---

[4]Author's interviews with Arab editors in London, March 1998.

[5]Jon Alterman, *New Media, New Politics: From Satellite Television to the Internet in the Arab World*, Washington, D.C.: Washington Institute for Near East Policy, 1998, p. 10.

[6]While the source and amount of subsidies for Middle Eastern papers is a mystery, their existence is clear. Many papers have little or no advertising. According to one source, "independence" in the Arab newspaper business means having several sources of subsidy, so that one need not be wholly dependent on any one source. Author interview in Beirut, May 2001.

and the Arab world itself. They represent a zone of freedom and intellectual innovation that is hard to find in many Arab countries. Because of their relatively elite audience, international publications often benefit from a more lax censorship regime than Arab governments are willing to extend to their own domestic products.

The Arab newspapers also represent a regional intellectual voice, as scholars and opinion leaders from around the world come together to discuss common issues on their pages. Finally, international Arab newspapers play a significant agenda-setting role for the Middle East. Newspaper editors are far more likely to read broadly in the international Arab press than is the general population, as are high governmental officials. The same is true of leading university professors and businessmen. If an idea is to gain currency around the Arab world, stating it in the pan-Arab press is a good place to start.

The pan-Arab press, then, serves as a forum for the discussion of ideas in a region in which such forums are rare. While not of a uniformly high quality, its status as a genuinely international forum for the exchange of ideas gives it an important role in the intellectual life of the region. As there are few quality journals in the region, newspapers have emerged as a more important locus for discussion than would be the case in other societies and remain an important outlet for elite political and social debates.

Television

As television came to the Arab world in the 1960s and 1970s, it fell into the drab mode of state-sponsored media. News broadcasts invariably began with a series of stories on the president's or king's activities of the day; the author witnessed one broadcast in Egypt in 1995 which began with a soundless 17-minute segment of the president greeting visiting Gulf dignitaries at the Cairo airport. When there was actual news, the media often did not report it. In one of the most egregious failings of journalistic integrity, Saudi television did not report the Iraqi invasion of Kuwait for three days because it was unsure what the official line would be.[7]

---

[7]See, for example, Abdelwahab El-Effendi, "Eclipse of Reason: The Media in the Muslim World," viewed at http://msanews.mynet.net/Scholars/Affendi/media.html.

The leap into Arab television began after the Gulf War, when CNN's coverage of the war created a thirst for timely, well-produced news of concern to an Arab audience. First into the fray was the Middle East Broadcasting Centre (MBC), which established operations in London in 1991. It is owned by Shaykh Walid al-Ibrahim, a brother-in-law of King Fahd.[8] MBC established a pattern for expatriate Arab broadcasters, broadcasting authoritative news by satellite to the Arab world. MBC also gave life to the idea of a pan-Arab newsroom, putting forth presenters and reporters from all over the Arab world. In addition to its news programming, MBC features music, Western comedies, and dramatic series.

Five years later, the network al-Jazeera took MBC's experimentation to another level. Established in Qatar with support from a dynamic new emir, al-Jazeera presented a combination of hard-hitting news coverage (boosted by an impressive network of local correspondents) and lively debate shows that became the talk of the Arab world. "Freed from the political constraints that often guide the Saudi-owned media, al-Jazeera pursued controversy with such programs as "The Opposite Direction" and "More Than One Opinion," which pitted secularists against Islamists, feminists against traditionalists, and even Israelis against Arabs.

Indeed, al-Jazeera's genesis was in part due to Saudi sensitivities. In 1994, a Saudi satellite service contracted with the BBC to produce Arabic television news, but the Saudis pulled the plug in 1996 after the BBC supplied content they found offensive. The operation shut down just as the Qataris were beginning to implement their plan for a regional television station, and many of the BBC veterans quickly shipped off to Doha where they reconstituted much of their organization.[9]

Al-Jazeera burst onto American consciousness in the fall of 2001, with its extensive (and sometimes frankly sympathetic) coverage of Taliban-controlled Afghanistan in the face of an American-led onslaught. Osama bin Ladin appeared to favor the station, which gave his statements extensive airtime. Indeed, most graphics of bin Ladin

---

[8]As stories circulated that the king himself sometimes called to request specific programming, some joked that MBC really stood for "My Broadcasting Center."

[9]See Alterman, 1998, pp. 27–28.

circulating since the September 11 attacks are taken from al-Jazeera video feeds and contain a graphic bar that says "al-Jazeera exclusive" in Arabic or English. Al-Jazeera's prominence brought increased scrutiny to the channel's overall tone, which many outside critics found wanting. As one wrote in the *New York Times Magazine,* "Although Al Jazeera has sometimes been hailed in the West for being an autonomous Arabic news outlet, it would be a mistake to call it a fair or responsible one. Day in and day out, Al Jazeera deliberately fans the flames of Muslim outrage."[10]

To be sure, al-Jazeera gives extensive coverage to the Palestinian intifada and provides ample platform for commentators (and sometimes reporters) who are skeptical of Western intentions. But al-Jazeera also takes seriously its slogan, "Opinion . . . and the other opinion." Despite its many shortcomings, al-Jazeera allows ideas to be aired that would have been immediately squelched in previous eras. Some of those are pro-Western, and some are anti-Western. Most significantly, al-Jazeera creates a marketplace for those ideas.

Although many of the most popular ideas on al-Jazeera are ones that are inimical to U.S. policy, the station has been notably willing to extend airtime to those with whom the bulk of their audience disagrees. For example, al-Jazeera does give extensive opportunities for American officials to speak directly to the Arab world, through both direct interviews and coverage of U.S. news. Secretary of Defense Donald Rumsfeld's address on the first anniversary of the September 11 attacks was carried live and unedited on al-Jazeera, for example, beaming it into millions of Arab homes during a prime viewing hour. Indeed, al-Jazeera featured extensive Washington coverage that day, bringing Americans to an Arab audience even when those Americans saw themselves speaking only to other Americans.

During coalition operations in Iraq, al-Jazeera joined most Arab stations in abandoning any pretense of objectivity. Presenters made asides, and reporters editorialized both through words and pictures. Debate on talk shows was most often deeply one-sided. But al-Jazeera also gave significant time to American views, covering coali-

---

[10]Fouad Ajami, "What the Muslim World Is Watching," *New York Times Magazine,* November 18, 2001.

tion press conferences in Doha and increasing its coverage of Washington events. Its defenders argued that al-Jazeera was merely doing for the Arab side what Fox News and other American outlets were doing for the American side; it is too soon after the conflict to assess the veracity of the observation.

Other stations have taken different approaches to programming. The Lebanese Broadcasting Corporation (LBC) and Lebanese Prime Minister Rafiq al-Hariri's Future Television generally present entertainment-oriented programming. They feature young and attractive presenters interacting in flirtatious ways, and they stress music and game shows. Abu Dhabi Television has recently revamped in an all-news format and is attempting to go head-to-head with al-Jazeera. To compete with al-Jazeera, MBC is also planning to launch a 24-hour news channel headquartered in Dubai and employing a veteran al-Jazeera news director. A new youth channel headquartered in Dubai, Zein, hit the airwaves in February 2001, and so on. In all, there are something over 200 Arab satellite stations, all seeking an audience among the Arab viewing public.[11]

Most of the Arab satellite broadcasters, like MBC and al-Jazeera, are free-to-air. That is to say, one only needs to buy a satellite dish and a television, and there are no ongoing subscription fees. The cost of dishes is going down, and is now less than $200 for a single unit. In addition, widely available technology allows several users to share a single dish. Public accommodations such as coffee shops can buy dishes, thereby creating far wider audiences than would be otherwise possible.[12]

---

[11]Although al-Jazeera has made a big splash and won accolades for its news coverage, viewers are clearly looking for something else from their programming. The most popular show in the Arab world today is an MBC-produced version of "Who Wants to Be a Millionaire?" produced out of the same studios as the original British production. The Arabic version has an Arab host, Arab contestants, and questions on Arab history and culture. It appears at the same time as al-Jazeera's flagship debate show, "The Opposite Direction," and has a decisive lead in viewership in that time slot, and it has spawned a host of imitators. Author interview in Dubai, February 2001.

[12]A recent shift toward digital broadcasting may be driving up the cost of watching while simultaneously lowering the cost of broadcasting. Digital signals require decoder boxes and proprietary "smart cards" to receive a signal, and although counterfeit versions of the latter can often be had at low cost, the former require an additional outlay. On the broadcasting side, digital signals mean multiple signals can use the

In the quest for an audience, channels have found that emotion is better than detachment. The Palestinian intifada is a staple of most Arab broadcasters, who report not from afar, but through field reporters and wire services to bring the violence into viewers' living rooms. The events of September 11 were another common theme, although much of the commentary focused on shifting blame rather than rooting out terrorists.

Precise details about who is watching satellite television are hard to obtain. Not much viewer polling is done, especially outside of the wealthy Arab Gulf, and even pollsters themselves warn that commissioned polling data often reflect the interests of the party commissioning the poll.[13] The stations themselves do not engage in organized viewer research, through either polling or focus groups, and new programming ideas appear to be the result of purely internal debate rather than research into viewers needs.[14] In addition, executives at leading satellite channels appear not to invest much energy into targeting specific segments of the overall audience. This situation is largely a result of the perception that advertising in the region is driven largely by political concerns rather than audience data.[15] Firms seeking the support of the Saudi government will support Saudi stations allied with the royal family and eschew advertising on al-Jazeera, for example. As a consequence, there is at least some self-censorship among broadcasters on matters of high interest to the Saudi government or other potential sponsors.

A Wide Spectrum of Content

Taken as a whole, there is no single perspective expressed in the Arab press. At one end of the spectrum are newspapers and television commentators that appear to be magically transported from the early 1960s. Beating their breasts, they rail against the United States and its client state, Israel. They talk of uniting the Arabs under a sin-

---

same satellite transponder, driving down the cost of access time and increasing the capacity of individual satellites.

[13]Every discussion I have ever had with anyone involved in media research in the region has confirmed this point.

[14]Author interview in Abu Dhabi, February 2001.

[15]Author interview in Doha, February 2001.

gle banner to resist the West and all that it stands for. This has been the general tone of the Syrian domestic press and the Iraqi domestic press under Saddam Hussein, although individual writers and commentators from throughout the region espouse a similar line.

At the other end of the spectrum are those who decry much of the Arab idea as a failure. Some urge a turn toward Islam, and some urge a turn toward democracy, but what is characteristic of both groups is a sense that the 20th century Arab experiment was a failure and that the Arab world needs to reinvent itself to escape from a dead end. No outlets wholly endorse such a view, but writers and commentators who embrace some part of it can be found at all the major international outlets in the region, from al-Jazeera to *Asharq Alawsat*. These world views are fundamentally inner-directed, and in them the United States remains mostly in the background, as neither a model of emulation nor an object of derision.

The largest bulk of opinion falls somewhere between these extremes. Most Arab commentators, especially those courting a regional audience, consider themselves in some way to be Arab nationalists. Few writers are defiantly secular and most agree on some role for Islam in public life. There is little support for overall U.S. government policy in the region, and even support for discrete U.S. actions, such as operations to protect Muslim Kosovars, can be grudging and difficult to come by. If there is an overall thrust to the vision, it is that the U.S. government is hopelessly biased toward Israel and completely indifferent to Arab suffering. On a broader level, there is considerable concern that American culture, with its corrupting sexual attitudes, its individualism, and its ruthless capitalism, is overwhelming the region. These concerns do not provoke a uniform response; in many cases, they do not provoke a response at all. There is periodic discussion of using "the oil weapon," but such calls appear to be signs of frustration rather than future intentions.

The Internet

The Internet gets a great deal of attention in the world media, but it is still quite rare in most parts of the Arab world. While more than one in five residents of the United Arab Emirates (and perhaps as many as one in three Emirati nationals) have Internet access, the ratio declines to perhaps one in 25 Jordanians and something like one in 100

Egyptians. Typical access rates in wealthier countries such as Kuwait or Bahrain is approximately 10 percent of the population, and about 23 percent in Israel.[16] The Internet is available in some form in every country in the Middle East, although access has been severely restricted in Libya, Syria, and Iraq.[17]

Most of the wealthier countries in the Middle East (with the exception of Israel) have some sort of government monopoly over Internet access, while many of the poorer countries have created a market of Internet service providers. World Trade Organization rules will open up telecommunications services down the road for members and aspiring members,[18] and monopoly providers are already beginning to plan for when they will need to find a new business model.

The level of censorship of the Internet or monitoring is not clear in many countries. Egypt and Jordan proclaim policies of free access to the Internet, whereas Qatar and Saudi Arabia attempt to force users to go through proxy servers that restrict access to objectionable sites. Evasion of restrictions is widespread. In the words of one Saudi interlocutor, "The authorities have created a nation of hackers. They don't want us to see anything related to religion, or sex, or politics. That's what people want to see, so everyone gets around the restrictions. Hackers must be a higher percentage of the population in Saudi Arabia than anywhere else in the world."[19] Surveillance of Internet communication and usage habits is fairly easy at the system administrator level. If domestic intelligence services have either the capability or desire to do so, they have not gone public with it.

---

[16]See http://www.itu.int/ITU-D/ict/statistics/at_glance/Internet01.pdf. The number for Bahrain is an estimate for Bahraini use; many Saudi subscribers access the Internet through Bahrain to avoid Saudi censorship, thereby inflating Bahrain's numbers.

[17]Presentation by Seymour Goodman, Georgetown University, April 21, 2001. The rates for the indigenous population versus expatriates is not known. In the Gulf, however, expatriates are typically more than half the countries' populations.

[18]Bahrain, Egypt, Jordan, Kuwait, Morocco, Oman, Qatar, Tunisia, and the United Arab Emirates are members of the WTO, and Algeria, Lebanon, Saudi Arabia, and Yemen are observer governments that are seeking admission. Membership entails the responsibility to change one's laws and domestic practices to comport with agreements reached within the WTO framework, although time is generally allowed to bring about such compliance.

[19]Author interview in London, February 2001.

The Rise of Mid-Technology

Many important technologies, like the satellite television phenomenon described above, might best be described as "mid-tech." These technologies are by no means new; in many cases, they are decades old. Examples of mid-tech devices are photocopiers (which have become ubiquitous even in villages), telephones, fax machines, and video and audiocassette players. Although many of these technologies do not require literacy, the general rise in Arab literacy of the last several decades increases the avenues for information distribution throughout the region. Because these technologies are so inexpensive and easily diffused, it is hard to get precise numbers for their prevalence. According to World Bank figures, in the Middle East and North Africa there are approximately 175 televisions per 1,000 people, making them seven times more common than personal computers.[20] The television advantage is even greater than it appears, since televisions and videocassettes are commonly viewed in coffeehouses and other public spaces.[21] Videocassettes of popular television programs are also a staple of regional video stores, providing low-cost rental programming and ensuring that programs have lives long after they have left the airwaves.

The mid-tech technologies described above are similar in that they all facilitate one-to-many communication. Many of them help reproduce a single message quickly and cheaply, which can then be distributed widely. Further, they are generally easily shared, inexpensive to use, and do not require a high degree of skill or training to operate. Another similarity is that they often operate completely beyond the control of an individual state. Mid-tech developments aid spreading messages across borders.

Mid-tech is a boon to those with attractive or memorable messages, from incendiary preachers to lascivious models. Groups that have exploited mid-tech range from such Western-based groups as Human Rights Watch to such violent Islamist groups as al-Qaeda. They have used the technology to communicate, to duplicate messages,

---

[20]World Bank, *2001 World Development Indicators*, Washington, D.C: World Bank, 2001, p. 308.

[21]Author observations in Egypt, Jordan, Yemen, Syria, and Kuwait, 1990–2001.

and to build a sense of group solidarity. On the grassroots level, however, Islamists have been far more successful integrating technology into mobilizing communities. To date, we have not seen populations use mid-tech to articulate their grievances nearly to the extent that was expected in the academic literature.

Greater Information Diversity and Access

The technologies described above have created a richer information environment. State information bureaucracies used to enjoy near monopolies on promulgating political and even economic information within their borders, but monopoly has eroded. In the modern Middle East, information on politics, religion, society, style, consumer products, and other topics is increasingly available from several viewpoints. Sharp increases in literacy in the last two decades accelerate the process of information exchange still further, although literacy as a whole in the region remains low by global standards.

It is impossible to characterize the information pool except by its diversity. Increasingly, individuals have to choose among an array of alternative narratives on an ever-widening variety of topics. Some of the information circulating is accurate, and some is inaccurate. Some constitutes efforts at incitement, while some appeals for reconciliation. Some is religious, and some is avowedly secular. Some is stridently political, while some has absolutely no political agenda whatsoever.

Because of technological change, government censorship of political information is eroding. Governments may be able to block a magazine from circulating, but it is much harder to block faxes or e-mails and innumerable photocopies of offending articles. They can ban a subject from terrestrial television, but they often have scant ability to influence what appears on satellite channels broadcasting from another country. They can work with commercial printers to control the printing of books, but they are powerless to prevent individuals from making photocopies on cheap machines and distributing handbills at rallies or even on the street. It is true that a repressive regime, through a combination of direct efforts and brutal intimidation, can provoke people to self-censor. But the costs of doing so are high in terms of direct effort as well as the inhibiting effect such repression has on investment and economic growth.

One exception to this trend is that the government of Saudi Arabia retains unusual control over what appears in the mass-market media. Because Saudi consumers represent the most attractive target for regional advertisers, and because Saudis connected to the royal family directly own so many of the regional advertisers, the Saudis have a unique ability to shape stories of high interest to them. This ability is not total, and al-Jazeera and *al-Quds al-Arabi* have often loudly tweaked the Saudis to demonstrate their independence. Osama bin Ladin finds an outlet for his anti-Saudi message on al-Jazeera, and *al-Quds al-Arabi* sometimes airs the views of dissident Saudi Prince Talal bin Abdelaziz, who muses on Saudi democracy in its pages. Still, offending Saudi sensibilities is a business decision that is not entered into lightly, whereas broadcasters and writers need not care nearly as much for the sensibilities of surrounding states.

LIMITED ASSIMILATION OF HIGH-TECH

While mid-tech is rampant, high-tech faces significant barriers to widespread adoption. In the first place, the educational systems in the region stress rote memorization rather than problem solving. As a result, they do not prepare their students for information-rich environments in which mental agility is more important than memorizing facts.[22] Private education in many countries provides an alternative, but it is restricted to those with considerable means.

A second problem is that many Arab countries have been slow to develop the technical skills that they would need to support a more developed high-tech infrastructure. Interlocutors in the region noted that many computers are glorified desk ornaments, as they are not connected to networks and their users do not know the capabilities of the software. Maintenance is also a problem, as there is not a base of highly trained personnel. In the absence of an educational system

---

[22]See UNDP, *Arab Human Development Report 2002*, chapters 5 and 6, and World Bank, *Claiming the Future*, Washington, D.C.: World Bank, 1995, especially pp. 38 and 40; also pp. 28, 72, 85.

that can turn out such personnel, or the economic resources to hire such personnel from abroad, technology efforts will falter.[23]

A third problem is the Middle East as a whole is a low-income region. Per capita incomes in the Middle East and North Africa are, on average, just over $2,000 per year, and in the most populous countries are scarcely more than half that. The United Arab Emirates has a per capita income nudging toward $20,000, but even mighty Saudi Arabia has a per capita income just under $7,000.[24] Despite falling prices, technology remains out of reach for many in the Middle East.

A final problem is that English-language literacy in the Middle East is limited. The Internet remains a largely English-based medium, and Arabic sites have been slow to take off, representing significantly less than one-tenth of one percent of all extant web sites.[25] It is hard to ascertain precisely how limited English-language proficiency is, in part because of the difficulty in defining what represents literacy in English, and in part because there are no good surveys that cover a broad spectrum of the region's population. While schools have inculcated a basic ability to recognize Latin characters among many in the primary grades, anecdotal observation confirms that only a small percentage of individuals have the level of English proficiency required to participate comfortably in language-intensive discourse.[26]

---

[23]One American technology company had to cut back its investment in Egypt because it was unable to find a sufficient number of properly trained engineers in country. Officers of another company asserted that the skills can be found among Egyptian workers, but that the most skilled are likely to work overseas for higher salaries rather than stay in the region. Author interviews in Washington, D.C., and Dubai, February 2001.

[24]2001 World Development Indicators Database, World Bank. The figures above are 1999 numbers based on the Atlas method (rather than purchasing power parity). Since the equipment involved in information technology is composed of internationally traded, foreign-produced commodities, the Atlas method gives a better measure of affordability.

[25]See http://cyberatlas.Internet.com/big_picture/demographics/article/0,1323,5901_408521,00.html. Although it is possible to send e-mail in Arabic, doing so requires that computers at each end of the transaction are similarly configured. To get around compatibility problems, many Francophone Arabs send messages in French, and others send messages in either English or in Arabic transliterated into English text.

[26]According to an informal conversation with a U.S. government source in April 2001, the percentage in Egypt is probably below 5 percent of the population, and Egypt's population alone represents 25 percent of the entire Arab world.

None of this is to suggest that nobody in the Arab world can profit from technological advances. Indeed, in absolute terms, many such individuals exist. Often, they have received private school educations, and many have received additional education abroad. They are more numerous in the wealthy countries of the Gulf. As a percentage of the population, however, these individuals represent only a small number, especially in the poorer yet more populous states of Egypt, Syria, and Yemen.[27]

Especially in the poorer countries in the Arab world, then, the society breaks down into two primary groups. The first are those with the education, training, language skills, and capital resources to take full advantage of the information revolution. This group is often technologically savvy, especially among the young. Travelers to the Middle East will recognize them for their pagers, cell phones, and e-mail addresses on their business cards, as well as their general fluency in English. For this small, elite group, the information revolution allows opportunities for profit and enrichment.

Although such a group exists in every Arab country (and, in fact, may represent the majority of contacts of most U.S. nationals in a given country), in relative terms the group is often a distinct minority. The overwhelming majority of the population in many Arab countries is technologically unsophisticated, has a fairly low level of education, and is unlikely to profit from technological innovation. Television and videos may alter their consumption patterns, but technology, especially high-tech, is unlikely to alter their production patterns.

As a result of this gap, social mobility—never easy—becomes even more difficult, especially if private school education remains far beyond the reach of most and public school education continues to lag in teaching advanced skills. The well-to-do begin assimilating technical skills earlier and earlier in childhood, get an increasingly distinctive education, and learn foreign languages earlier and better than their countrymen. By adulthood, the gap between the technologically sophisticated and the great bulk of the population can become insurmountable.

---

[27]Francophone North Africa is clearly an exception to this rule; whether the Francophone economy will prove large enough to carry along the countries that depend on it is unclear.

IMPLICATIONS

The changes in the information environment in the Middle East have broad implications for regional societies, regimes, and the United States. Publics' expectations of their governments may grow, while regime control of the public debate steadily erodes. To take advantage of these changes, the United States must anticipate changes in regional political dynamics and reconsider its tactics for swaying public opinion.

New Mass Politics

Elite politics have been unaffected by technological change. Politics relies on personal relationships, which are tied to regimes. Elites tend to be pro-regime in any event, and elites have long had access to alternative sources of information. Arab governments tend to seek to further coopt them through the new media, as when the government of Jordan seized on the advent of the Internet in the late 1990s to sponsor an "Ask the Minister" feature on NETS, a leading Internet service provider.

For most in the Arab world, technological change means that they are exposed to a broader variety of views than has ever been true before. As literacy and bandwidth both expand dramatically, publics are exposed to a broad, often unregulated, spectrum of views that range from secular to religious, from nationalist to global, and from material to spiritual. Under the new paradigm, information is demand-driven rather than supply-driven, and the universe of available views is far broader than ever before.

One consequence of this is greater political spontaneity. Whereas Arab politics have often been characterized by orchestrated demonstrations of solidarity, anger, sorrow, or joy, the regime's ability to orchestrate such demonstrations in the future will be greatly diminished. What we are likely to see is a more bottom-up expression of joy or rage. Arab leaders were caught unaware by the outpouring of public anger in October 2000, when satellite television stations repeatedly showed footage of the Israeli shooting of 12-year-old Palestinian boy Muhammad al-Durra. As demonstrators took to the streets not only in Cairo, but also in the normally quiescent Gulf region, governments had to move quickly to assuage public sentiment.[28] Unprecedented public protests erupted throughout the Gulf in March 2002, in response to Israel's reoccupation of parts of the West Bank, resulting in several attacks on U.S. embassies.

Another consequence of technological change is that consumption patterns among Arab publics are likely to shift toward Western products. Media penetration is likely to increase consumption of branded goods and boost demand for goods that were previously considered luxuries, such as consumer electronics, health and beauty aids, and packaged foods. Entertainment spending is also likely to increase as increased exposure leads to a greater demand for recorded products and licensed goods (as well as counterfeit copies of each). Such shifts are also likely to promote something of a backlash or, at the very least, calls for "authenticity." Many in the Arab world already believe that their way of life, their values and morals, are under Western assault through the media, and they are likely to use that same media to press their case for what they label "traditional values."

Indeed, there will be huge rewards in the next decade for those who use initiative, creativity, and innovation to seize control of the public discourse. As control of public opinion increasingly slips away from governments' grasp, those who can organize and mobilize will find a far more receptive environment than any time in the recent past. The information revolution presents new opportunities for individuals and groups with a good feel for the public mood to seize on these issues and promote political agendas independent of government wishes. Islamist groups in the Middle East are among the most modern of political organizations, both in their techniques of organizing and in the sophistication of their communications strategies. Two of the most popular clerics in the Muslim world, Sheikh Yusuf Qaradawi and the late Sheikh Muhammad Shaarawi, made their reputations not through dry scholarship but through their dynamic television personalities. In Egypt, the most popular religious personality, Amr Khalid, has little religious training. He has earned a wide following for his urging viewers to be sensitive to the spiritual in their everyday lives.

---

[28]Author interviews in Dubai, Abu Dhabi, and Doha, February 2001; conversation with Arab embassy official in Washington, D.C., May 3, 2001.

Challenges for Regional Governments

The most important consequence of the information revolution for Arab governments is that it removes some of their traditional advantage in the public realm. While governments remain an overwhelmingly powerful force in most countries, the information revolution allows new challenges to governmental dominance and frees an even larger sphere of activity from governmental control, influence, and even knowledge. Governments have lost the near monopoly they used to enjoy over certain kinds of information, and as a result they have less ability to direct domestic politics. The traditional tools of government information ministries, censorship and propaganda, are withering, and governments must create new strategies and tools to cope with the new environment.

Another important consequence of technological change is that expatriates can play a much more intimate role in domestic politics than was true heretofore. As Ayatollah Khomeini's supporters were able to slip his message into Iran in the 1970s by cassette tape, expatriate leaders now enjoy myriad avenues to influence politics at home, and to do so in real time. As Iranian oppositionists used audiocassettes, today's political activists have ready access to faxes, satellite television broadcasts, videocassettes, and photocopies.

London has emerged as a hub for opposition movements to regional governments. It offers a permissive political environment, good infrastructure and technical training opportunities, access to Western news agencies, and significant operations by all of the regional news outlets. Organizations as diverse as the Bahrain Freedom Movement, the Committee for the Defense of Legitimate Rights in Saudi Arabia, the Iraqi National Congress, Amnesty International, and the al-Khoie Foundation have found a home in London that allows them to monitor and often influence daily political developments in the Middle East.

What all of this means is that governments can take much less for granted. Whereas they used to be able to rely fairly on tight control of the political space in a country, they now face competition in many areas. As a consequence, they will come under pressure to be more supple. Because they will be less able to control public sentiment, they will become more responsive to it. This is not to say that electoral democracies will flourish in the Middle East because of technology. In fact, governments of some of the poorer countries may become more authoritarian in some regards, especially toward those who seek to use violence to displace the state. But governments will choose their battles with public opinion more carefully, and they will seek to integrate "bottom-up" influences where possible to prevent pressure from below from damaging the political system.

One example of this has been the Egyptian government's relative passivity in the face of some clerics' efforts to Islamicize Egyptian society and censor dissenting views. When religious students protested the government's reprinting of a novel some regarded as blasphemous in the spring of 2000, the government in the first instance used the uprising as a pretext to crack down on the pro-Islamist Labor Party but later fired the officials who had authorized the reprinting.[29] The signals are clearly intended to indicate responsiveness while delimiting political actions that go beyond acceptable behavior.

Finally, governments will come under increasing pressure to deliver economic goods to the broad population. Exposure to the international media, as well as to the advertising that sustains it, will induce many in Arab countries to demand better standards of living than they have enjoyed heretofore. As satellite television and videocassettes present vivid examples of living in material abundance, Arabs will increasingly blame their governments if the world gets richer but the Arab public does not.

In the longer term, technological change is unlikely to force a deep restructuring of Arab governance patterns. Authoritarianism has predominated in the region for decades, and seems poised to do so for the years to come. Indeed, much of the enthusiasm for technology sweeping away authoritarianism is based on a flawed understanding of authoritarianism as a simple top-down process rather than a delicate mix of cooptation and coercion applied by governments to their subjects.

---

[29]See, for example, "Cultural Ambush," *Cairo Times*, Vol. 4, No. 43, January 2001, pp. 11–17.

Because of technological developments, states have lost many of the tools that had helped them lead public opinion in the past, and thus coopt their populations. States still hold the vast preponderance of power in the public sphere, but they have far less ability to define what happens in that sphere than at any time in the last century. In meeting this new kind of challenge, governments in the Gulf are in a somewhat better position than the governments of the Levant and North Africa. In general, they have emphasized cooptation over co-ercion, and they retain the deep pockets to make cooptation work. Also, with their smaller populations, they have found it easier to edu-cate their citizens, and their ability to import labor for menial jobs has helped prevent the development of a large underclass. Conse-quently, Gulf states retain the potential to grow their way out of many of these issues, using the distributive power of the state to keep people vested in the system and to constantly improve the human capital within their borders.

At the other end of the spectrum, the governments of poorer and more populous states face new challenges. They lack the ability to coopt their citizens through money, and as they lose control of the media environment, their ability to coopt slips still further. Some regimes may respond by ceding public space to loud voices that do not immediately threaten the regime. Such a move could kick off a noisy debate between secularists and Islamists, for instance, while still keeping democratic change at arm's length. In addition, regimes that have relied on moderate repression in the past may feel com-pelled to use more repression and to act especially swiftly and strongly against groups that could potentially affect their hold on power. In this scenario, regimes may react to their declining control of the public sphere by taking harsh action against groups and indi-viduals who present alternatives to the status quo.

Implications for the United States

The most important implication of the technological revolution is that the U.S. government should devote far more attention to moni-toring mid-tech developments in the Arab world. Government translating efforts currently focus on national broadcasts and news-paper reports that enjoy a dwindling audience at home. It is impera-tive that the U.S. government have a good idea of what is happening "on the street," actively obtaining and translating handbills and pamphlets, understanding what is rented in video stores, and closely monitoring what millions watch on satellite television.

Another imperative is that the U.S. government remain alert to the possibility of new political actors arising, especially outside of the elite circles in which many officials circulate. Non-elites are likely to continue to use technology to disseminate new kinds of messages to new audiences. Indeed, one should expect an almost Darwinian sort of experimentation on the popular level, as a bewildering number of groups resort to an array of strategies to see what works.

Politics will also become increasingly transnational, partly through expatriate participation in domestic politics and partly through an increase in transborder movements based on religion, ethnicity, or other factors. This is not all bad news. Many expatriate Arabs in the West are strong supporters of liberalization and pluralism in their home societies. Others, of course, capitalize on Western freedoms to agitate for less liberal societies back home.

Some allied governments may face unaccustomed difficulties in the new political environment, and instability may increase. Much of the leadership in many Arab countries has been in power for decades, and a combination of the duration of their rule, arrogance, age, and indifference may allow one or more of these regimes to be surprised by developments from below. While some of the new leaders like King Mohamed in Morocco and King Abdullah in Jordan have exhibited a keen understanding of how to use the media in new ways, many of their older counterparts have exhibited less skill in the new environment. Egypt's Information Ministry continues to seek to dominate the public space partly through its sheer size and partly through monopolizing the tools for creating media content, but informal discussions with Egyptians suggest that it is losing more and more of its audience every day.

The revamping of Voice of America's programming to become "Radio Sawa" is an important experiment, the results of which are too early to judge. Radio Sawa's music-oriented programming appears to have won a substantial audience among young people curious about Western music and culture. Radio Sawa has, until now, limited almost all of its news coverage to straightforward newscasts for a few minutes of every hour. It is too early to tell if those broadcasts come to be seen as authoritative, or if they inspire others to greater journalistic responsibility. At the same time, questions remain if Sawa will remain popular if it expands its news envelope beyond its current limited scope.

The United States must recognize the limits to the assimilation of technology. Technological sophistication of a broad level is likely to remain low among most Arab nationals. If U.S. defense operations depend on counterparts with high levels of technological sophistication, they are likely to face continued difficulties. Although there will certainly be pockets of well-trained engineers and technical professionals, those skills are unlikely to be highly diffused among the general population in the near future.

For political leaders and rulers in the region who seek to work closely with Washington, a freewheeling press contributes to creating hostile publics who will increasingly hem them in. The rise of mid-tech is likely to be accompanied by a rise in anti-American rhetoric in the region, especially if current conflicts in the Arab-Israeli arena and in occupied Iraq persist. This is partly because opposition forces will seek to paint governments as American toadies and rally support behind nationalist slogans that reject foreign interference. It is also because calls for cultural authenticity will seek to reject Western cultural influence. Governments are increasingly unlikely to censor anti-U.S. protests, partly because doing so would be ineffective and inflame passions still further.

It will also be far more difficult for regional governments to engage in tacit cooperation with the United States. Increased flows of information will make arrangements for basing and access, traditionally kept secret and given little publicity, better known to regional publics. Long-standing but low-profile U.S. basing in Egypt and implicit security guarantees to the Gulf states are likely to come under more fire domestically. Behind-the-scenes support for the peace process or other unpopular U.S. initiatives also will be harder to secure.

Public reaction to the U.S. assault on the Taliban, as well as Israel's "Operation Defensive Shield," are instructive in many respects. In the former case, Arab anger was controlled, and it dissipated considerably when images of celebrating Afghans filled the airwaves. Mitigating the Arab public's response was the short duration of hostilities, the fact that much of the fighting was carried out by Afghan troops and not American ones, that Afghanistan is not an Arab country, and an understanding that the United States had been attacked and lost more than 3,000 civilian lives. In contrast, Israel's incursion into the West Bank in March 2002 received extensive negative news coverage. Boycotts of American products quickly gained public support through newspaper ads, photocopies, and the Internet, especially among such nontraditional political actors as women and children. Although the results of such a boycott might be managed, it portends a broader politicization of the public that could pose a new kind of problem if the United States were directly involved in hostilities against an Arab country. Perhaps equally important, we can count on an Arab adversary seeking to appeal for Arab public support much more actively than has ever been the case in the past.

In the presence or absence of hostilities with the Arab world, the United States should increase its outreach to the Arab media. A cadre of well-trained Americans who can explain U.S. government positions and assessments cannot eliminate the potential difficulty of restive publics, but they can certainly help give allied governments far greater freedom of action with their own publics than they would otherwise enjoy. Although satellite television attracts huge and growing audiences throughout the region, only one U.S. official has been willing to appear on Arab satellite television, speaking in Arabic, to explain U.S. positions. Military action in Iraq produced more up-close images of warfare than we have seen in some time. Pictures from those embedded with coalition troops, combined with Arab networks' images from the Iraqi side, gave viewers on each side an idea of how the other side was covering the war. Still, this was a story told in pictures, and the images on each side were starkly different. In conflict situations such as this one, it is not clear how the United States might better influence the pictures and stories Arab viewers are watching.

In more placid times, managing Arab reactions remains an afterthought to many in Washington, partly because of an uncertainty as to *how* and *when* Arab public opinion matters. Budget cuts in the 1990s led many U.S. public diplomacy programs to shift their emphasis almost entirely to small elite audiences, leaving embassies unconnected to and unaware of broader public trends except as expressed in local newspapers. Rather than simply assert a need to abandon elite audiences for a mass public, U.S. public diplomacy needs to differentiate between audiences and determine what is needed from each. In some cases, the goal is likely to be to persuade; in others, it will be merely to mute criticism. Rather than prescribe a single outcome or process for every situation, missions and services need to revisit the ways in which public opinion can shape or constrain host government action. The process is not a straightforward one, but one that must bring political officers and political advisers together with public diplomacy officers in the first instance to define targets and goals, direct state-of-the-art market research, and then feed the results back to the policy process. Any effort to persuade that neglects audience feedback is doomed to fail.

We are at a fascinating juncture in Arab history. Nations and populations remain distinct, but information flows across borders as never before. More than ever, publics themselves decide what they see, read, and hear. We cannot control what they think, but we can compete for their attention, and we should.

WEAPONS OF MASS DESTRUCTION IN THE MIDDLE EAST: PROLIFERATION DYNAMICS AND STRATEGIC CONSEQUENCES

Ian O. Lesser

The proliferation of weapons of mass destruction (WMD) and the means for their delivery at longer ranges has been an important part of the debate about security in the Middle East since at least the 1970s. The 1991 Gulf War brought these concerns to the forefront, especially among Western observers. The post–September 11 environment, the subsequent debate over the "axis of evil," and the 2003 war against Iraq have strongly reinforced these concerns, as a matter of national security strategy, but also in a regional setting.[1] Indeed, the perceived nexus between weapons of mass destruction, terrorism, and global reach has made developments in the Middle East a matter of homeland as well as regional security.

Why do WMD play such a prominent role in the contemporary Middle Eastern calculus? Throughout the Cold War, strategists accepted the risk of nuclear Armageddon as a "permanently operating factor" and discussions of regional security acknowledged the possibility of escalation and the potential for nuclear or chemical use. Nuclear weapons and missiles have been part of the regional equation at least since the 1956 Suez crisis, during which Russia threatened (albeit not very credibly) nuclear strikes against Britain and France in response to their intervention in Egypt. In 1967 and again in 1973, the specter

---

[1]See Henry Sokolski, "Post 9/11 Nonproliferation," *E-Notes*, Foreign Policy Research Institute, January 25, 2002.

of a nuclear-armed superpower confrontation loomed over Arab-Israeli conflict. Israel's own nuclear deterrent has been a factor in regional security for decades, and Israel has acted to preserve its nuclear monopoly in the region, destroying the Iraqi Osirak reactor in 1981.

The end of the Cold War broke the accepted link between regional conflict and the prospect of escalation, superpower involvement, and possible use of WMD. The post–Cold War era offered all actors, regional and extraregional, greater freedom of action. It lowered the risks associated with intervention but also removed many of the previous constraints on behavior within the region. Moreover, in a world in which extraregional actors might hope to insulate themselves from the consequences of Middle Eastern frictions, suppliers of military technology, including WMD-related items and technology, were now less careful about such transfers. The Soviet Union was a major strategic patron and supplier of conventional military hardware during the Cold War, but it was reluctant to transfer technology that might prove escalatory and complicate its own security planning.[2] The economic and political incentives for Russia and other extraregional actors to make WMD-related transfers to the Middle East may now outweigh the perceived risks.

Several factors contribute to the prominence of WMD and ballistic missiles in Middle Eastern security today. First, the Middle East is the place where unconventional weapons and missiles have been used, at least in a limited, tactical fashion, in modern conflict. Egypt employed chemical weapons in Yemen in the 1960s, and Libya is alleged to have used them in Chad. They were reportedly employed in Afghanistan and, more recently, in Sudan.[3] Iraq used them against the Kurds, and they were employed on a large scale by both sides in the Iran-Iraq war. Missiles were used in the 1973 Arab-Israeli war

---

[2]As an example, Moscow refused to sell SS-23 missiles with a range of 500 km to Syria in the early 1980s. Dore Gold, "Middle East Proliferation, Israeli Missile Defense, and the ABM Treaty Debate," *Jerusalem Letter*, Jerusalem Center for Public Affairs, No. 430, May 15, 2000, p. 2; and conversation with the author.

[3]See Gordon M. Burck and Charles C. Flowerree, *International Handbook on Chemical Weapons Proliferation*, New York: Greenwood Press, 1991, pp. 221 and 341–355; and Sterling Seagrave, *Yellow Rain*, New York: Evans, 1981. Cited in Geoffrey Kemp and Robert Harkavy, *Strategic Geography and the Changing Middle East*, Washington, D.C.: Brookings Institution Press, 1997.

(Egyptian Scuds and Syrian Frog-7s), in the "war of the cities" between Iran and Iraq, in the civil war in Yemen, and during the 1991 Gulf War. They have been fired, ineffectively, at Italian territory by Libya. Threats to employ these systems are a regular feature of confrontation in the region, and on its periphery.

Second, even without use, the Middle East is a leading area of proliferation. Most of the world's leading WMD proliferators are arrayed along an arc stretching from North Africa to Pakistan (and nuclear and missile tests in South Asia may affect proliferation norms in the Middle East). The presence of active conflicts and flashpoints across the region means that the possession of WMD is not just a matter of national prestige and strategic weight, but a very real factor in military balances and warfighting.

Third, the prominence of WMD in the Middle Eastern security environment is accompanied by great uncertainty about the motivations and strategic culture of regional actors. The ways of thinking about WMD, especially nuclear weapons and missiles, developed during the Cold War, are often assumed to have less relevance in a Middle Eastern setting. The question of whether "rogue" proliferators will act rationally and can be deterred in the conventional sense is unclear. In this and other contexts, the prospect of conflict involving WMD in the Middle East raises a variety of uncomfortable issues for Western strategists, and presumably for regional actors themselves. The ongoing Palestinian-Israeli confrontation, with the risk of regional escalation, lends greater weight and immediacy to these issues.

Fourth, the pace and character of WMD proliferation in the Middle East is of intense interest to extraregional actors. Russia, China, North Korea, and potentially others are leading suppliers of weapons, materials, and the technological know-how for developing indigenous capabilities. Pursuit of Middle East peace and access to the region's energy supplies are extraordinarily prominent issues in international affairs, and will compel continued American and Western attention. For these and other reasons, the region is demanding of Western military presence and intervention. Proliferation can interact with the Middle East peace process and stability in the Gulf and the Mediterranean. The potential for new nuclear powers in the region, coupled with the deployment of missiles of increasing range, could profoundly alter the calculus of Western intervention and engagement in the Middle East. So, too, could a shift to a "world of defenses," operationally and strategically. And as the 2003 war against Iraq shows, the issue of WMD possession and potential use can be a *casus belli* in its own right.

Finally, and to a growing extent, American concerns about WMD capabilities in the Middle East reflect a more profound concern about the security of the U.S. homeland itself, especially after September 11.[4] The prominence of international terrorism with ties to the Middle East together with the growing lethality of the "new terrorism" pose the risk of terrorist use of WMD on American territory.[5] The easy mobility of people, materials, and technology means that proliferation in the Middle East is not a remote phenomenon for the United States and its allies. Whether delivered by missiles or couriers, highly destructive weapons are the most dramatic illustration of the transregional character of the new security environment. The growing reach of these weapons challenges traditional notions of regional security. Asia, the Middle East, Europe, Eurasia, and the Western Hemisphere are now far more interdependent in security terms. The spread of WMD in the Middle East affects security on a global basis, and developments far afield can influence patterns of proliferation inside the region.

Taken together, these factors explain the growing prominence of WMD in Middle Eastern security. They also illustrate the issue's increasing linkage to developments outside as well as within the region. This chapter surveys the many excellent open source assessments of proliferation trends and WMD programs. It focuses on the analysis of proliferation developments and their meaning for regional security and strategy and then assesses recent trends and their effect on the proliferation debate. An examination is made of the *internal* dynamics of WMD proliferation in the Middle East. This

---

[4]Although one could also argue that September 11 demonstrated the potential for mass destruction and disruption without the use of WMD per se.

[5]Some of the most prominent terrorist incidents of recent years have a Middle Eastern connection, but historically the Middle East is not the leading venue for such incidents, including attacks on Americans. See Bruce Hoffman, "Terrorism Trends and Prospects" in Ian O. Lesser et al., *Countering the New Terrorism*, Santa Monica, Calif.: RAND, MR-989-AF, 1999.

chapter then addresses WMD-related *regional* dynamics in the Maghreb, the Levant, and the Gulf and discusses the role of *extraregional* actors and developments. Finally, conclusions and policy implications are offered for the United States and its allies.

The term "weapons of mass destruction" is used frequently in strategic debates, often in reference to limited, tactical uses that may not imply mass destruction or mass casualties. Similarly, the numerous instances of ballistic missile use in the Middle East have involved conventional warheads. In principle, it would be more accurate to distinguish between the tactical use of chemical, biological, radiological, and nuclear (CBRN) weapons and their employment as true weapons of mass destruction against military or civilian targets. For the purposes of this analysis, the question of the proliferation of these unconventional weapons is taken as a whole but with the recognition that, ultimately, the ability to threaten large-scale destruction and casualties is of central significance. Ballistic missiles also figure prominently in the discussion, with a focus on their role as potential delivery systems for WMD. Other delivery systems, such as artillery, cruise missiles, and covert means, although potentially important, are not discussed in a systematic fashion here.

ASSESSING RECENT TRENDS

Western assessments of proliferation trends in the Middle East often assume a faster pace of acquisition and deployment than recent experience would justify. For decades, analysts have predicted the emergence of a new nuclear power in the region "within a decade."[6] Iran's nuclear ambitions were a subject of speculation even prior to the Iranian revolution. The deployment of ballistic missiles of transregional (1,000-km-plus) range has similarly lagged somewhat behind the most alarmist predictions. Such countries as Algeria, a focus of Western proliferation concern a decade ago, have not developed significant programs. By contrast, the resilience of Iraq's capacity for WMD development, even under intense scrutiny and sanctions, would have surprised analysts in the early 1990s, and revelations about apparent Iraqi development of a radiological weapon

---

[6] I am grateful to Daniel Byman for this observation.

in the late 1980s underscore the potential for proliferation even short of a true nuclear capability.[7] Indeed, judgments about how fast the nuclear clock was ticking in Iraq became central to the international debate about intervention and regime change before the 2003 war. Iran's nuclear and missile programs have evolved in a steady fashion. But even here, judgments about when Iran could produce nuclear weapons or field intercontinental missiles vary widely. All of these questions are sure to attract closer scrutiny in the wake of the 2003 war in Iraq and continuing uncertainty regarding the extent of Iraq's WMD holdings.

WMD capabilities in the region have expanded and have proven highly resistant to nonproliferation regimes. The pace, especially in the case of nuclear weapons, may be slower than predicted, but the trends are alarming nonetheless. Even without further development and deployment, the WMD capacity of many states in the region is substantial. The resources devoted to WMD programs underscore the importance of these weapons to many states in the region. It is worthwhile surveying, briefly, the state of WMD capabilities in certain countries, and to provide a "snapshot" of current judgments, highlighting programs of special concern.[8] (In light of the occupation of Iraq, that country's WMD programs and ambitions are not

---

[7]See William J. Broad, "Document Records 1987 Bomb Test by Iraq," *New York Times*, April 29, 2001.

[8]This discussion focuses, in each case, on nuclear, chemical, and biological programs, and ballistic missiles. In terms of delivery systems, it can be argued that missiles are the most significant and "transforming" in strategic terms. But obviously WMD can be delivered using more prosaic means, including aircraft, increasingly widespread cruise missiles, artillery, and other unconventional or covert means. This section relies heavily on several excellent open-source surveys, including Gerald Steinberg, *Arms Control and Non-Proliferation Developments in the Middle East: 1998–99*, Ramat Gan: BESA, 2000; *Proliferation Threat and Response*, Washington, D.C.: Office of the Secretary of Defense, 2001; Justin Anderson, *Ballistic Missile Arsenals in the Middle East*, Washington, D.C.: The Carnegie Non-Proliferation Project, 2001; *Foreign Missile Developments and the Ballistic Missile Threat to the United States Through 2015*, Washington, D.C.: National Intelligence Council, 1999; The International Institute for Strategic Studies, *The Military Balance 1999–2000*, Oxford: IISS, 1999; Anthony Cordesman, *Weapons of Mass Destruction in the Middle East*, Washington, D.C.: Center for Strategic and International Studies, 1996; Kemp and Harkavy, Appendix 4; and the summary of regional capabilities prepared by Ashley Tellis for Ian Lesser and Ashley Tellis, *Strategic Exposure: Proliferation Around the Mediterranean*, Santa Monica, Calif.: RAND, MR-742-A, 1996, p. 7.

discussed in the following survey of current WMD-capable Middle Eastern states.)

Algeria

Before the outbreak of violent turmoil in 1991, Western analysts were focused on Algeria's nascent nuclear program, test reactors, and a substantial power reactor (Ain Oussera) developed largely with Chinese assistance. Algeria also reportedly received nuclear materials from Iraq at the time of the 1990–1991 Gulf crisis. The circumstances and extent of the Algerian program raised suspicions in the West about Algeria's nuclear ambitions. Algerian officials were also quite outspoken about the geostrategic value of a nuclear capability, even a civil power program alone.[9] Algeria has a substantial technical capability for chemical and biological weapons research, but there is little evidence that this is a priority for the regime. Algiers has reportedly explored purchases of ballistic missiles from China and North Korea and is known to deploy Scud-Bs (300-km-range) of Russian manufacture.

As the violence in Algeria has abated, the country has begun to explore a more active foreign policy, including overtures to Western security institutions (Algeria is now a member of NATO's Mediterranean Dialogue). With the improvement of relations with the country's main geopolitical competitor, Morocco, and much reduced investment in nuclear technology, the prospects for an ambitious Algerian WMD program are much reduced.

Libya

Libya has been a leading focus of proliferation concern, with an emphasis on its chemical and missile capabilities. Libya has a long-standing effort to acquire or develop a nuclear weapon but has apparently made little progress. However, the regime's interest in

---

[9]In 1992, for example, a senior Algerian official told the author that "in ten years time, there will be two countries in Africa that the U.S. takes seriously—South Africa and Algeria; both will be nuclear powers." The official in this case was probably referring to civilian nuclear development, but the statement was intentionally ambiguous. See Lesser and Tellis, 1996, p. 7.

purchasing a weapon, as opposed to developing the capacity for indigenous manufacture, means that the threshold question for Libya is ongoing, and the possibility exists for a "surprise" covert acquisition of a weapon. In areas where Libya might more credibly seek to sustain its own development efforts, including biological and chemical programs, the suspension of UN sanctions in the wake of the Lockerbie trial may facilitate Libyan access to dual-use technology. For the moment, Libya is believed to have a modest biological weapons research program, and a more extensive chemical program that has produced quantities of blister and nerve agents. The Rabta and Tarhunah plants—the subject of much scrutiny and threats of American intervention in the mid-1990s—are believed to be inactive.

Libya's missile program is arguably the leading North African proliferation concern for both American and European governments and is prominent in a regionwide context. Libya deploys aging Russian-supplied Frog-7 and Scud-B missiles. Since the early 1990s, Libya has explored the purchase from North Korea of Scud-C and intermediate-range systems capable of reaching 1,000 km or more. The increasing range of missiles tested by North Korea in recent years, including the 1,300-km-range No Dong and the 2,000-km Taepo-Dong 1, suggests that the components and technical assistance for such systems are on the market, and Libya would be a potential purchaser. Libya fired Scud missiles at a US LORAN station on the Italian Island of Lampedusa in 1986 and has repeatedly threatened to strike targets in southern Europe. Libyan deployment of missiles with trans-Mediterranean range could sharply increase the sense of risk among NATO allies and might play a part in evolving European approaches to missile defense.

Libya retains a strong rhetorical commitment to acquiring weapons of mass destruction as a "deterrent force," and presumably to enhance its regional weight. Most recently, it has been reported that Libya has helped Iraq to circumvent UN resolutions and international scrutiny of its WMD programs by allowing the transfer of some missile-related material and technicians to Tripoli.[10] Looking ahead,

---

[10]Ray Takeyh, "Libya: Opting for Europe and Africa, Not Ties with Washington," *Policywatch* No. 486, Washington, D.C.: Washington Institute for Near East Policy, September 21, 2000.

Libya could face new scrutiny, and perhaps be inhibited in its WMD ambitions, as a result of the 2003 war in Iraq.

Egypt

Egypt has been a leading critic of Israel's unannounced nuclear posture and has made this issue central to its multilateral diplomacy in the Middle East, within the Nonproliferation Treaty review framework, at the UN and in other settings. At the same time, Egypt has long-standing WMD capabilities of its own. Egypt is often described as having chosen to pursue chemical capabilities—"the poor man's bomb"—in lieu of a more expensive and difficult nuclear program. Egypt has had a chemical weapons manufacturing capability for decades and actually employed chemical weapons in Yemen in the 1960s. Egypt is also reported to have collaborated with Iraq on the development of chemicals before the Gulf War.[11] The Egyptian interest in chemical weapons may stem, in part, from the influence of Soviet doctrine on Egyptian planning and procurement from the 1960s through the 1973 war.

In terms of the capacity for indigenous manufacture, perhaps even without imported precursor chemicals, Egypt's chemical weapons capability is among the most advanced in the region. Although Egypt's chemical capability is not symmetrical with Israel's nuclear capability, either as a deterrent or as a warfighting weapon, the two arsenals have been played against each other in multilateral arms control talks.[12] Egypt is not normally cited as having a serious biological weapons program, although it clearly has the capacity to move in this direction quickly should it choose to do so (some sources do refer to modest Egyptian biological warfare efforts).[13]

Egypt has a ballistic missile capability in the form of Scud-Bs (and possibly Scud-Cs or variant), which were acquired from North

---

[11]Geoffrey Kemp and Robert E. Harkavy, *Strategic Geography and the Changing Middle East,* Washington, D.C.: Brookings Institution Press, 1997, pp. 393–394.

[12]This comparison figured prominently in the Arms Control and Regional Security (ACRS) negotiations, part of the multilateral track of the "Madrid" process between Israel and its Arab neighbors. It contributed to the failure of the talks in the context of the NPT review debate in the mid-1990s.

[13]See Lesser and Tellis, 1996, p. 61.

Korea.[14] The North Korean connection could facilitate the purchase of more capable systems in the future. Egypt was also a participant in Argentina's now-defunct Condor program for the production of intermediate-range missiles. An increase in regional tensions with Israel could spur Egyptian interest in deepening the country's chemical and missile arsenal and complicate American efforts to slow this trend.

Israel

Excluding Pakistan (arguably part of the Middle Eastern WMD equation, but not discussed here) Israel is the region's sole nuclear power. Estimates of Israel's nuclear arsenal range as high as 300 warheads, possibly including thermonuclear weapons.[15] Even accounting for disputes in the open source literature, it is a formidable "assumed" arsenal that has profound effects on the strategic calculus. Israel also has a large chemical weapons capability and biological weapons research program concerned, above all, with research on chemical and biological warfare defenses. These capabilities were developed after Israel's acquisition of nuclear weapons and probably reflect concerns about the credibility of a deterrent based overwhelmingly on nuclear forces and the demonstrated interest in biological and especially chemical weapons on the part of some of Israel's neighbors. It may also reflect a sense that Israel's nuclear weapons might ultimately be traded away for an "end of conflict" settlement with Arab neighbors and Iran, a remote but not impossible scenario.

Israel also has one of the longest-range, and probably the most effective, missile arsenal in the region, with well-tested, indigenously developed Jericho I (500 km) and medium-range Jericho II (1,500 km) systems. The country's advanced space launch capability also suggests that Israel could rapidly field multistage missiles of much longer range, capable of reaching Pakistan or Russia. As with Egypt,

---

[14]See Justin Anderson, "Ballistic Missile Arsenals in the Middle East," *Carnegie Proliferation Brief*, Vol. 4, No. 3, March 15, 2001.

[15]The higher estimates were offered by Seymour Hersh in his now somewhat dated book *The Samson Option: Israel's Nuclear Arsenal and American Foreign Policy*, New York: Random House, 1991. See also Yair Evron, *Israel's Nuclear Dilemma*, Ithaca, N.Y.: Cornell University Press, 1994.

the lack of confidence in an "end of conflict" in relations with the Arab world deepens the Israeli stake in retaining a potent WMD and missile capability.

Syria

Syria is generally not judged to be pursuing a nuclear capability, although it has a test reactor built by China. The country is reported to have only a modest biological program. Nonetheless, the steady erosion of Syria's conventional military capability, at least in relative terms, over the past decade has reinforced the Syrian interest in other WMD and the means for their delivery, principally in a tactical setting. Syria is a good example of a regime that has opted for WMD as a cost-effective path to maintaining its regional weight in the face of a growing conventional gap with Israel—an asymmetric strategy in-region.

By all accounts, Syria has an extensive chemical weapons program, which remains dependent on imports of precursor materials. Unlike Egypt, Iran, and Iraq, Syria has no history of employing chemical weapons but has built substantial stockpiles of a nerve agent (Sarin) capable of delivery by aircraft or missiles. In the future, Syria is expected to devote considerable resources to the improvement of its already significant chemical weapons capability.[16]

Syria has an arsenal of several hundred mobile Scud-B, Scud-C, and (Russian) SS-21 missiles. North Korea, China, Iran, and Russia are suppliers of ballistic missiles and missile technology to Syria, and the country possesses a capacity for domestic production. Syria is reportedly looking to develop more modern, solid-fueled short-range missiles and has also tested a longer-range Scud-D.[17] These systems are capable of reaching Israel as well as much of Iraq, Jordan, and Turkey. The war in Iraq has cast a spotlight on Syrian behavior on several fronts, not least its WMD programs. Like Libya, Syria may now find it more difficult to pursue its WMD interests against a backdrop of heightened U.S. and international scrutiny.

---

[16]*Proliferation Threat and Response, 2001*, Washington, D.C.: Office of the Secretary of Defense, p. 45.

[17]See Anderson, 2001.

Iran

A state of particular concern with regard to WMD, Iran possesses substantial chemical and biological capabilities, a large missile arsenal and development program, and a very active nuclear program. The country employed tactical chemical weapons during the Iran-Iraq war and has large stocks of weaponized chemicals. Iran has adequate national infrastructure to develop biological weapons and may already have modest amounts of usable agent. Iran is known to be seeking fissile material and nuclear technology and is engaged in extensive nuclear cooperation with Russia, including construction of a power reactor at Bushehr. The country has made extensive efforts in recent years—most thwarted—to acquire nuclear materials and precision engineering equipment important to the manufacture of nuclear weapons. There is considerable uncertainty about materials and technology Iran may have succeeded in acquiring covertly.[18] Recent International Atomic Energy Agency (IAEA) revelations regarding previously unrecognized Iranian nuclear facilities reinforce these concerns, and EU as well as U.S. policymakers are increasingly focused on exposing and constraining Iran's nuclear ambitions. Broadly, Iran may be seen as a threshold or near-threshold nuclear state.

Iranian missile forces include Scud-B and -C, as well as Chinese-made CSS-8 short-range missiles. Notably, Iran is producing Scud missiles itself. A 1300-km (intermediate) range Shahab-3 missile was flight-tested in 1998 and again in 2000. This system is based on the North Korean No-Dong and is being pursued with considerable Russian and Chinese assistance. Iran is reportedly seeking to develop longer-range missiles (Shahab-4 and -5), possibly including ICBMs capable of reaching North America.[19] Even in the near term, the deployment of missiles based on the Taepo-Dong 1 (2,000 km) or 2 (5,000–6,000 km) would enable Iran to target Europe and Eurasia. Iranian Scuds were employed extensively during the war with Iraq. Coupled with Iran's advanced nuclear program, the pursuit of longer-range and more effective missiles gives Iranian proliferation

---

[18]See Michael Eisenstadt, "The Armed Forces of the Islamic Republic of Iran: An Assessment," *Middle East Review of International Affairs*, Vol. 5, No. 1, March 2001, p. 10.

[19]*Proliferation Threat and Response*, 2001, p. 35.

special relevance to the strategic calculus of the GCC states, Israel, and the West, including Turkey.[20]

Saudi Arabia

Saudi Arabia is not normally characterized as a state of proliferation concern. The country's WMD capabilities and ambitions are generally thought to be limited, with the important exception of ballistic missiles. In fact, Saudi Arabia deploys the longest-range missile system in the Middle East, the Chinese supplied CSS-2 missile purchased in 1987. Saudi Arabia reportedly possesses several dozen of these medium-range missiles, whose reach of over 2,000 km is sufficient to reach much of Europe, Eurasia, and the subcontinent.[21] At least one recent assessment points to Saudi Arabia's technical potential, and possible motivations, for pursuing a clandestine nuclear program in the future.[22]

Transforming Developments and Synergies

Despite the diversity of WMD programs under way in the region, two thresholds are of potentially transforming importance for the strategic environment. The first concerns the likelihood and timing of the emergence of one or more new nuclear powers in the region. Judgments about when Iran or (less likely) Libya or Syria could acquire a useable nuclear weapon vary widely. In general, nuclear proliferation in the region has not kept pace with the most alarmist predictions of the past decade. But Iran is clearly capable of a nuclear breakout in the medium term, perhaps even the near term. In 1993, published CIA estimates suggested that Iran could develop a nuclear development in eight to ten years. More recent estimates are in the

---

[20]In addition to Iranian longer-range missiles, Turkey has expressed concern about tests of Iran's solid fueled Fateh-110 system. "Turkey Concerned Over Iran's Guided Missile Test," *Turkish Daily News*, June 3, 2001. See also "Iran's Weapons: A Bigger Punch," *The Economist*, May 26, 2001.

[21]The operational state of these missiles is questionable. See Anderson, 2001, p. 2.

[22]See Richard L. Russell, "A Saudi Nuclear Option?" *Survival*, Vol. 43, No. 2, Summer 2001, pp. 69–79.

range of five to ten years.[23] Attempts to estimate the time required
for nuclear development tend to assume a linear progression toward
nuclear capability. But nuclear expertise in the leading states of
concern is probably sufficiently advanced to make the deployment of
some minimal nuclear arsenal quite rapid if they can access
fissionable material. The potential for a surprise breakout toward
nuclear capability is therefore substantial.

The second transforming threshold concerns the deployment of reasonably accurate ballistic missiles of intercontinental range (i.e., over
5,500 km). The progress toward this kind of capability is probably
more linear, and less contingent on the acquisition of a single,
critical technology or material (i.e., in contrast to the threshold posed
by the need for sufficient fissionable material in the case of a nuclear
weapons program). It is also based on the development of progres-
sively longer-range systems elsewhere, especially among suppliers
such as North Korea. The technology and components for these
systems have found their way to world markets in short order.

Recent estimates suggest that Iran could test an ICBM capable of delivering a payload of several hundred kilograms to the United States
"in the last half of the next decade." It might be able to test an ICBM
with a lighter payload in the next few years. Overall, the first test of
an Iranian ICBM is judged "likely before 2010 and very likely before
2015."[24] The availability of Russian technology and assistance would
clearly quicken the pace of development. The spread of interest in,
and expertise for, the development of space launch vehicles (SLV)
provides another route to the acquisition of systems capable of delivering warheads to the United States from launch sites in the Middle
East. Iran is thought likely to test an SLV in the next few years. An
active international market for missile technology outside the Missile
Technology Control Regime (MTCR), and sometimes even by signa-

---

[23]See Thanos Dokos, "The Proliferation of Weapons of Mass Destruction in the
Mediterranean: The Threat to Western Security," *Mediterranean Politics*, Vol. 5, No. 3,
Autumn 2000, p. 102. As with Iraq, there have also been periodic reports of Iran having acquired functioning nuclear warheads from abroad. A 1992 report cited a purchase from Kazakhstan. See James Wyllie, "Iran's Quest for Security and Influence,"
Jane's Intelligence Review, July 1993, pp. 311–312. Analysts have generally treated such
reports with skepticism.

[24]National Intelligence Council, *Foreign Missile Developments and the Ballistic Missile
Threat to the United States Through 2015*, September 1999, p. 2.

tories, means that the assessment of prospective capabilities in the Middle East cannot be undertaken on a regional basis alone. Developments in Asia and elsewhere are highly relevant. Indeed, much concern about regional missile proliferation "futures" has been fueled by recent North Korean tests.

Nuclear and ICBM programs in the Middle East are closely linked in strategic and quite probably in developmental terms. From the perspective of the West, the deployment of missiles capable of reaching European and eventually North American targets takes on far greater significance if coupled with new nuclear arsenals. Under these conditions, even with limited numbers and accuracy, the potential for damage would be enormous, and the potential for political blackmail commensurately great. From the perspective of a Middle Eastern proliferator, it would be difficult to justify the enormous investment in multistage, intercontinental missiles merely to deliver conventional warheads. A truck bombing would be easier and cheaper to organize and certainly more accurate (the September 11 terrorist attacks on the World Trade Center and the Pentagon point to what can be accomplished even without resort to true weapons of mass destruction). The addition of chemical or biological warheads would increase the system's value as a terror weapon but would require great sophistication in the case of a biological weapon. Given their more limited lethality, weaponizing chemicals for such a purpose might not make sense at all.

Ultimately, the possession of ICBMs might only be "cost-effective" in the context of a nuclear capability. Certainly, the combination of nuclear and ICBM technology would confer enormous advantages in holding at risk high-value targets such as cities. The synergy of these two capabilities would contribute to national prestige and strategic weight, within and outside the region, in ways that would be difficult to duplicate by other means.

Longer-range missiles may be an advantageous delivery system for WMD, but they are hardly the only option available to Middle Eastern states. Virtually every state in the region, and all of the countries of special proliferation concern, possesses tactical aircraft capable of delivering nuclear, chemical, or biological weapons. Many states have cruise missiles that could be configured to carry unconventional warheads, and such systems, as well as a variety of unmanned aerial vehicles (UAVs) are increasingly available on the international market. Nuclear devices might also be employed using a variety of forward-based techniques, including civilian aircraft, submarines, merchant ships, or barges or containers moved into place covertly, and even couriers. These approaches to the employment of WMD might prove effective under certain conditions and could be attractive to the extent that more capable ballistic missile defenses are developed and deployed. But for Middle Eastern states looking to the possession of WMD as a contribution to power and prestige, covert approaches may be less attractive. Covert employment is more likely to be a vehicle of terror and revenge, rather than deterrence and warfighting.

PROLIFERATION MOTIVES AND INTERNAL DYNAMICS

Broadly, the motivation for the acquisition of WMD and ballistic missiles in the Middle East consists of several elements that, taken together, contribute to the dynamics of proliferation in the region. These elements include the search for regional and global weight, the desire for a counterweight to Western military superiority, and domestic interests and incentives.

The Search for Weight and Prestige

Insecurity is a common denominator across the Middle East. Borders are, in many cases, artificial affairs, and the risk of conventional aggression is tangible. The relationship between Israel and its Arab neighbors and frictions in the Persian Gulf are the most obvious examples of regional insecurity and threats to the territorial status quo. But there are many others, including historic tensions between Morocco and Algeria, Libya and Tunisia, Libya and Egypt, Egypt and Sudan, and the complex of tensions between Turkey and its neighbors. Beyond the defense of borders, security in the Middle East is, above all, a matter of internal security. The nature of governance, the prevalence of totalitarian regimes, precariously balanced monarchies, separatist forces, and unrequited nationalism all contribute to a pervasive sense of insecurity. Under these conditions, regional tensions threaten to interact with internal vulnerabilities. A wide range of risks can take on an existential character in the eyes of those threatened. Regime survival, regional stability, and coexistence and confrontation with extraregional actors form a continuum with considerable potential for escalation. The fact that Middle Eastern states perceive a range of threats to their *existence* and not just to their *interests* provides a strong motivation to acquire WMD for purposes of deterrence, coercion, and prestige.

The quest for weight and prestige is heightened by the circumstances of state creation in the Middle East. The experience of decolonization, often after violent struggle, has left a legacy of pronounced nationalism from North Africa to the Persian Gulf. Even in states such as Iran and Turkey with long traditions of independence and national identity, the more recent experience of sovereignty compromises imposed by the West has given the modern state a strong sense of international "place" and prerogative. WMD, and especially nuclear weapons and ballistic missiles, have become important symbolic as well as tangible measures of state power and modernity. Even in the West, the existence of second-tier nuclear arsenals in France and Britain owes as much to considerations of national independence and prestige as to strategic utility. In the far more insecure and uncertain environment of the Middle East, these factors take on greater significance.

Beyond their military utility, WMD and especially proven capabilities are demonstrations of technological accomplishment. Images of ballistic missiles appeared on Iraqi billboards under Saddam Hussein, and missiles are paraded in central Tehran.[25] The prestige factor is an important part of the rationale for the high expenditure involved in some forms of WMD. The choice of ballistic missiles as a delivery system similarly contributes to national prestige. It also keeps costly and highly escalatory capabilities under central control, as these systems tend to be deployed by elite units close to the national leadership.

Considerations of prestige and control also argue against the use of terrorist proxies as delivery systems for WMD. Given the enormous effort and cost associated with WMD development, Middle Eastern regimes, however revolutionary, will probably not wish to place weapons symbolic of national power and prestige in the hands of

---

[25]Gold, 2000, pp. 5–6.

nonstate actors. In the case of nuclear weapons, regimes are probably least likely to relinquish control. A decision to offer nationally developed WMD capabilities to proxies as a form of state-sponsored terror, or to carry out a clandestine or symbolic attack against a Western target, is more likely to be an act of desperation than a deliberate "asymmetric" strategy.

September 11 and the wars in Afghanistan and Iraq have focused Western and regional attention on the issue of nuclear command and control among active proliferators. Pakistan, with its existing nuclear arsenal, political instability, and troubling links between nuclear technicians and Islamic radicals, presents the most obvious problem case. A nuclear Iran could pose similar risks to the control of WMD. Even short of nuclear proliferation, there is a risk of biological, chemical and radiological leakage, or rogue use. Where the command and control of WMD are weak or disrupted, dangerous weapons and materials will have a greater risk of falling into the hands of nonstate actors.

In the post–Cold War environment, the quest for WMD as a vehicle for strategic weight has taken on new significance for several regional states as other sources of weight have declined. Algeria, Libya, Syria, and Iraq (and for a time, Egypt) all acquired an additional increment of diplomatic and military weight from their Cold War relationship with the Soviet Union. Algeria and Egypt also sought regional influence through Arab nationalism and leadership in the nonaligned movement. These connections no longer count for a great deal, although the link to Russia retains its importance for access to WMD technology. Even American patronage, important for Israel, Egypt, and Saudi Arabia, among the states under discussion here, has a different and less automatic quality in the post–Cold War setting.

In short, some important alternative sources of geostrategic weight have evaporated or declined, increasing the value of proliferation as a way of being taken seriously on the international scene. When Algeria's nuclear program was active in the early 1990s, Algerian officials were clear about this linkage, at least in terms of nuclear development. Iranian nuclear and missile ambitions predate the Islamic regime and reflect the view that such weapons are appropriate to the country's defensive needs and regional status. Even in Western security debates, it is possible to hear the idea that Iranian (as opposed to Iraqi, Libyan, and Syrian) nuclear ambitions are, at some level, legitimate; they reflect Iran's desire to be taken seriously as a regional power. Whereas during the Cold War, actors in the south, including Arab states in North Africa and the Middle East, were inclined to argue that the WMD arsenals of the superpowers should be limited through arms control and kept out of regional balances, their approach today stresses their own right to possess such systems.

Countering Western Superiority

The experience of Western intervention in the Middle East and the emergence of a seemingly unassailable gap in conventional military capability without any tangible counterbalance offer a strong rationale for proliferation for such states as Libya and Iran that have been in a prolonged state of confrontation with the West. This is, above all, an argument about the need to counter the military superiority and U.S. post–Cold War freedom of action. In the absence of any real transparency in the military doctrine of confrontation states, it is also, at base, an approach imputed by Western strategists: a deductive argument about "what rogues would do if they were clever," rather than an empirical judgment. With a more pervasive American and coalition presence in the region following the intervention in Afghanistan and the war in Iraq, such leading proliferators as Iran may see even more reason to acquire an effective deterrent while they can.

The argument about asymmetric strategies also applies to the strategic relationship with Israel and, to some extent, Europe. In the case of Iran, it may even apply to the military balance with Russia. In the Western strategic debate, this quest for alternatives to hopeless conventional confrontation has been described as the search for "asymmetric strategies." Such strategies might range from terrorism at the low end, to WMD and missile threats at the high end. The discussion of asymmetric strategies is largely a product of the 1991 Gulf War, but it has many historical antecedents and is imbedded in the process of strategic innovation. Asymmetric conflict has been a frequent occurrence in the Middle East. The wars of decolonization were essentially asymmetric, pitting insurgent forces against conventional armies. Arab states have sought to overcome Israel's technological edge through mass and vice versa. Successive Palestinian intifadas and the use of terrorism for Middle Eastern causes are essentially attempts to circumvent the conventional strength of adversaries.

Israeli analysts have often portrayed the Iraqi, Syrian, and Iranian quest for missiles coupled with WMD as a counter to Israel's air power. This may be true even in the context of a conventional military confrontation, in which missile attacks could be used to disrupt the mobilization of Israeli ground forces.[26] The presence of WMD in the Middle East can interact with conventional warfare in ways that reinforce rather than supplant the utility of regular armies and traditional objectives—for example, by breaking tactical or operational deadlocks.[27]

The 1991 Gulf War gave impetus to the search for asymmetric strategies, including the use of WMD, a quest imputed to "rogue regimes" by Western analysts but also observable in regional debates and procurement. One of the lessons of that war for adversaries of the United States (and Israel) was summarized neatly in the phrase of a senior Indian military officer: "Don't fight the United States unless you have nuclear weapons."[28] At the time, there was also considerable concern that Iraq would mobilize terrorists, possibly armed with biological or chemical weapons, as a means of striking at targets in the United States or Europe. For a variety of reasons, including the lack of a sympathetic terrorist infrastructure, this threat did not materialize in a serious fashion during the 1990s.[29] As of May 2003, it has also not materialized in the context of the war with Iraq, or the subsequent occupation of the country.

---

[26]See Gold, 2001, p. 6; and Yitzhak Rabin, "Deterrence in an Israeli Security Context," in Ahron Kleiman and Ariel Levite (eds.), *Deterrence in the Middle East*, Tel Aviv: Jaffe Center for Strategic Studies, 1993.

[27]Barry Rubin, "The Military in Contemporary Middle East Politics," *Middle East Review of International Affairs*, Vol. 5, No. 1, December 2000; see also George Tenet, "Weapons of Mass Destruction: A New Dimension in U.S. Middle East Policy," *Middle East Review of International Affairs*, Vol. 4, No. 2, June 2000.

[28]See Patrick J. Garrity, *Why the Gulf War Still Matters: Foreign Perspectives on the War and the Future of International Security*, Los Alamos, N.M.: Center for National Security Studies, 1993.

[29]See Lesser et al., *Countering the New Terrorism*, p. 108.

The threat of WMD use may deter Western intervention, either in the context of a direct confrontation or by preventing Western action in support of a regional state. Even where it does not deter intervention, as in the case of the 2003 American action in Iraq, it may well influence the timing and character of military operations. The threat to use WMD, and even the possession of a WMD "arsenal in being" without an explicit threat of use, can complicate or disrupt deployments to the region and can place troops and facilities at risk. Regimes possessing WMD may also exaggerate the sensitivity of the United States and its allies to military casualties. Indeed, the active debate on this topic in the United States, Europe, and Israel may well fuel these perceptions and reinforce the interest in WMD as a deterrent and as a psychological weapon in war. Societies that appear to be "de-bellicized," as Edward Luttwak asserts, may well encourage asymmetric approaches to warfare, with WMD as a leading vehicle. The proliferation of missiles of increasing range also creates the opportunity to threaten use of WMD strategically against population centers, for deterrence and to foster the view that intervention in far-flung places is not worth the risk. Even short of being able to reach American territory, proliferators in the Middle East can already credibly threaten the territory of America's allies in Europe and around the region, complicating the formation of coalitions and the projection of power.

The prospect of overwhelming retaliation, even national annihilation, makes the actual employment of WMD in this manner a questionable proposition for Middle Eastern regimes in conflict with the West. In the case of very small arsenals (e.g., of nuclear weapons or even well engineered chemical and biological warheads), systems hidden and retained may confer more advantages than systems used, even in the midst of conflict. This reality may well have influenced Iraqi behavior in the final weeks and days before the fall of the regime.

Indigenous Development and International Trade

The spread of WMD and more capable delivery systems has been accompanied by the spread of the capacity for indigenous development and production. To be sure, this process has been uneven, and the expertise and infrastructure to develop WMD varies widely among proliferators. Some have a fairly large and sophisticated technical base. Others are much less well developed. Broadly, Middle Eastern states may be divided into two categories in terms of their WMD-related interest and indigenous capacity (really three categories, if one includes an additional group of states with no apparent WMD interest or capability). In the first category are those states that possess or seek to acquire WMD and longer-range delivery systems but have no real capacity for indigenous development and manufacture, or even modification of systems purchased abroad. Algeria, Libya, and Syria fall into this category and are commensurately reliant on external assistance for their WMD programs. Even here, however, there may be specific areas of higher capability, as in the Syrian capacity for indigenous manufacture of chemical weapons. Overall, the WMD infrastructure of such states may be characterized as highly dependent on continued access to international trade and imported expertise.[30]

A second category of proliferators comprises states that not only possess WMD and are seeking to expand the size and sophistication of their arsenals but also have a considerable capacity for domestic development, manufacture, and modification. Egypt, Iraq under Saddam Hussein, Iran, and of course Israel all fall into this category. In each case, the state's technical base is substantial and institutionalized. The states also possess the expertise and material wherewithal to participate in collaborative programs, with partners in the region or further afield. But their indigenous capabilities are not symmetrical. Only Israel possesses a high degree of capability across all areas of WMD development, even if some areas (e.g., nuclear and missile development) have received greater attention than others. A large technical base may also permit such states as Iran to rapidly exploit access to critical materials from abroad, and to field WMD quickly, with little warning.[31] Thus, one of the important advantages such "category two" states enjoy is the ability to domesticate technologies obtained elsewhere.

Even with the existence of indigenous capabilities in the region, access to international trade in expertise and WMD-related materials,

---

[30]Lesser and Tellis, 1996, pp. 36–37.

[31]Lesser and Tellis, 1996, pp. 38–39.

even entire weapons systems, remains a critical part of the proliferation equation. Without WMD-related commerce from China, Russia, and North Korea, the proliferation potential of even capable and committed states would almost certainly be much reduced. If one adds the far-larger trade in "dual-use" technology and materials, most of Western origin, it becomes clear that the development of an indigenous WMD capability is closely intertwined with access to external trade and assistance.

Institutional and Domestic Factors

In addition to the desire for regional weight and prestige and military utility, WMD programs in Middle Eastern states may also be affected by bureaucratic and economic factors. Civilian and military institutions may be given control of WMD programs for political reasons, because they are trusted by the regime, or as a privilege to secure their trust. Along with other large military and civilian programs, the infrastructure and expense associated with nuclear, chemical, biological, and missile research provide ample opportunities for corruption and patronage. The institutionalized "benefits" of such programs may help to explain sustained, large-scale expenditures on nuclear infrastructure, sometimes with no long-term commitment to completion. Once decisions regarding WMD-related procurement are made, it is likely that substantial bureaucratic interests come into play, making these decisions hard to reverse. Thus, WMD-related programs can gain momentum and acquire a life of their own. This was probably a factor in Algeria, where the nuclear test and power reactor programs became a leading source of prestige and patronage for the ruling National Liberation Front.[32]

The institutionalization of WMD development programs may also impede attempts by proliferators to reassess their requirements and to stop or limit programs that no longer serve national interests. Even if the security environment or attractive arms control arrangements suggest the abandonment or limitation of nuclear, chemical, biological, or missile arsenals—a possible outcome of a comprehensive Arab-Israeli peace—it is unclear that proliferators will be able to

---

[32]Lesser and Tellis, 1996, p. 16.

take advantage of such opportunities. Internal politics and delicately poised civil-military relations may stand in the way.

The sustained insecurity, both internal and external, of most Middle Eastern regimes gives military and defense-industrial establishments considerable weight. In a region characterized by strong centralized states, nuclear, chemical, and biological research programs with WMD application offer vehicles for bureaucratic politics and even the promotion of key individuals. WMD programs are also not immune to the more general phenomenon of Middle Eastern arms procurement driven by the preferences of senior military commanders, often without regard to the country's ability to maintain and employ sophisticated systems.[33] As an example, analysts have voiced doubts about whether Saudi Arabia's Chinese-supplied medium-range missiles, acquired in the 1980s, remain operational.

Some forms of WMD development may be relatively modest in cost—for example, the production of chemical weapons in a state with a well-developed chemical industry. Other programs, above all nuclear development, can be extraordinarily costly, although their cost must be weighed against the expense of building larger or more sophisticated conventional forces. Of course, a regime may have a transcendent interest in possessing WMD and longer-range delivery systems that is not amenable to rational cost-benefit analysis. But in many cases, cost is likely to be a factor in the extent and pace of proliferation. Defense budgets in many Middle Eastern states are high relative to GNP, and WMD-related spending may be hidden amid other national research and infrastructure spending.

For Algeria, Libya, Iran, and to some extent Egypt (with its growing gas exports), energy prices have an important influence on state revenue and the resources available for research and procurement. Higher energy prices in recent years have boosted the otherwise troubled economies of key states in the region and may have contributed to WMD proliferation. It can also be argued that low energy prices might increase the attractiveness of WMD to the extent that

---

[33]For more on this point, see Chapter Three of this volume; Rubin, 2000, p. 3; and V. J. Parry and M. E. Yapp (eds.), *War, Technology and Society in the Middle East*, London: Oxford University Press, 1975.

they are seen as a inexpensive alternative to the expansion of conventional forces.

For states under economic sanctions of varying stringency and effectiveness, including Libya and Iran, trade restrictions may have some effect on the capacity for WMD-related spending. Given the demonstrated ability of regimes to move forward with WMD programs despite economic sanctions, however, the focused denial of materials and technology is probably a greater impediment to proliferation than generalized embargoes.

REGIONAL DYNAMICS

The strategic environment in the Middle East influences, and is in turn influenced by, the proliferation of weapons of mass destruction. The growing range of delivery systems also raises the important question of the region's boundaries. Clearly, discussion of the Middle East as a zone of proliferation cannot be limited simply to the Levant and the Gulf. North Africa and the Mediterranean are part of the equation, as are Turkey, the interaction between north and south on Europe's southern periphery, and developments in South Asia. Geography and demographics also play a role in proliferation motivations and consequences.

Geography Matters

Compared with the intercontinental competition of the Cold War, or the strategic environment in Asia, the Middle East is a fairly compact region. It is also heavily urbanized. Both factors have implications for WMD possession and use. The small distances between the population centers of potential adversaries mean that a wide range of systems may be used to deliver WMD within the region, including tactical aircraft, cruise missiles, artillery, even barges or torpedoes. In the case of ballistic missiles, the short distances translate into extensive "reach" and very short warning times. With the most sophisticated detection methods, an ICBM launch from Russia would afford the United States perhaps 20 minutes of warning, much more with manned bombers, less with submarine-based systems. In the context of missile launches in the Gulf or against Israel, warning time would be measured in minutes. Given the absence of accurate space-based detection systems in the region (Israel is a likely exception, along with Turkey through its NATO link), there is a possibility of complete surprise.[34]

All of the region's leading adversaries can reach targets of value in each other's territory with weapons of mass destruction and a reasonable prospect of success. They can already reach the periphery of the Middle East, to Turkey, Europe, and Eurasia, with implications for the freedom of action of extraregional powers. Eventually, at least some regional states will be able to reach much further, to northern Europe, and ultimately North America. The result will be a far greater degree of exposure and interdependence among the Middle Eastern, Eurasian, and Atlantic security environments. Within the Middle East, proximity, urbanization, and the lack of strategic depth give rise to a "hair trigger situation of mutual vulnerability" in which existential threats abound. The use of nuclear weapons against any of a small number of critical urban targets (Tel Aviv, Amman, Cairo, Baghdad, Tehran, etc.) would be tantamount to national destruction.[35]

The problem of the conventional defense of borders and the potential use of WMD are closely linked in the Middle Eastern setting where national survival has often been threatened by invasion. The problem of WMD use in this context is perhaps most akin to the role of nuclear and missile forces in European defense during the Cold War. But unlike the situation in Cold War Europe, there is no prospect that a WMD-armed war in the Middle East will be fought by superpowers over the heads of other combatants. In the Middle East, the territory of the regional combatants will be the battlefield. Short warning time also makes the maintenance of a secure second-strike capability (and even the development and deployment of WMD systems without a risk of preventive attack) more difficult in the Middle East unless considerable effort is devoted to hardening and mobility. Geography and the delicately poised nature of the strategic environment make arguments about the stabilizing affects of nuclear proliferation unconvincing.

---

[34]Kemp and Harkavy, 1997, p. 286.

[35]Kemp and Harkavy, 1997, p. 286.

Middle Eastern demographics also impose some constraints on WMD use. The proximity of Israeli and Arab populations inside Israel, and in the West Bank and Gaza, might complicate the calculus for adversaries looking to use nuclear or biological weapons against Israel. Conventional and perhaps chemical warheads might be used with less risk, especially with more accurate delivery systems. If Syria were to use WMD-armed missiles in a confrontation with Turkey, the city of Iskenderun might be an attractive target in the south, but much of the population is Arab. Seasonal weather patterns across this compact and densely populated region could produce casualties far afield from the target, and possibly across borders, especially in the case of nuclear weapons.

North-South Frictions and Regional Balances

As a general proposition, proliferation dynamics are more heavily influenced by south-south than north-south tensions in and around the Middle East.[36] Libya's interest in WMD has much to do with the regime's quest for regional weight in the Maghreb, Africa, and the Middle East, although Libyan proliferation is of concern to the West. Egypt clearly views its capabilities in terms of its strategic relationship with Israel and its prestige in the Arab world. Iraq and Iran have been concerned with acquiring leverage over each other, Israel, and the Gulf monarchies. Deterring Europe and the United States is often an additional part of the calculus, although it can emerge as a dominant consideration in the midst of a confrontation with the West. Israel's WMD capabilities have regional application, first and foremost, although the ability to reach Russia or Pakistan is useful. The pattern and frequency of regional conflict suggest that states in the "south," within the region, are the most likely targets of weapons of mass destruction.

Less plausibly, proliferation and the threat of WMD use might take on a more explicit south-north flavor. Samuel Huntington's provocative (and, in the opinion of this author, far too deterministic) notion of the "clash of civilizations" suggested the potential for WMD

---

[36]See Dokos, 2000, pp. 95–116; and Lesser and Tellis, 1996.

cooperation along religious lines—an "Islamic Bomb."[37] September 11 and its aftermath have revived the fear of a clash along civilizational lines, despite bin Ladin's failure to inspire a wider confrontation between the Muslim world and the West. The idea of chemical and biological weapons as a "poor man's nuclear weapon" implicitly points to deterrence among haves and have-nots. More realistically, the deterioration of relations within the south (e.g., between Israel and its neighbors) could affect the relationship between the Arab world and the West. Indeed, this is already visible in the context of numerous Mediterranean security initiatives. But it is most unlikely to fuel the proliferation of weapons aimed explicitly at the north as a whole.

The security of areas on the periphery of the Middle East can, of course, be affected by the growth of WMD arsenals within the region. In particular, the increasing range of ballistic missiles deployed in the Middle East has implications for the security of Europe and defense cooperation with the United States in the context of Middle Eastern crises. Southern Europe is already within range of some existing systems, and within a decade, all Western European capitals will probably be exposed to the retaliatory consequences of involvement in North Africa and the Middle East. This could have important implications for American access to European bases for Middle Eastern contingencies. In the past, Qadhafi has threatened to strike Italian, Spanish, or Greek territory if these countries facilitate an American attack on Libya. If Iraq had been able to reach Europe with ballistic missiles during the 1991 Gulf War, it might well have done so. Against this background, the price of cooperation with the United States might well increase and could include demands for effective, rapidly deployable defenses.

Regional proliferation can affect adjacent regions in other ways. A nuclear Iran, for example, might encourage Turkey to consider the development of a national deterrent, especially if Ankara loses confidence in the NATO security guarantee. There is already an active debate in Turkish defense circles on how to respond to the missile arsenals on Turkey's borders, and Turkey is exploring the production

---

[37]See Samuel P. Huntington, "The Clash of Civilizations?" *Foreign Affairs*, Summer 1993.

of short-range missiles. The procurement of deterrent systems in Turkey would surely affect strategic perceptions and balances in the Balkans and the Aegean and around the Black Sea. Proliferation around Russia's southern periphery must ultimately affect that country's strategic calculus (a reality that successive American administrations have tried to impress on Moscow). In short, the spread of WMD in the Middle East affects security across a much wider area.

The Arab-Israeli Conflict

The deterioration of the Middle East peace process and the escalation of violence between Israel and the Palestinians could greatly affect proliferation dynamics in the region. Four observations are relevant.

First, the current confrontation and the absence of effective negotiations are likely to reinforce the leading, explicit motivation for proliferation in the Arab world and in Iran. The ongoing conflict with a nuclear-armed Israel can be used to justify the continuation of existing WMD programs and the exploration of new ones. Even if other subregional competitions and, perhaps, the desire to hold the United States and the West at bay are part of the calculus, countering Israel is a potent rationale. It is also closely bound up with the quest for prestige and regional weight noted earlier. Heightened tension with Israel places these interests in sharper relief.

Second, Palestinian-Israeli confrontation and the failure of negotiations with Syria raise the specter of escalation and regionalization of the conflict. Syria in particular will have a stake in building its WMD capabilities, principally chemical weapons and ballistic missiles, as a deterrent and as an asymmetric instrument in war. Renewed confrontation also gives greater prominence to the ability of "second-tier" states that do not border Israel—Iran, but also perhaps Libya and Pakistan—to participate in the conflict with Israel from afar. This over-the-horizon participation has been a leading consequence of the spread of longer-range missiles across the region. Current circumstances underscore this trend and have opened opportunities for the proxy deployment of systems capable of reaching Israeli territory, not unlike the Soviet deployment of missiles in the early 1960s. There is already an example in the form of Iranian-controlled rockets of 70-km range, reportedly deployed in Lebanon and capable of reaching Haifa.[38]

Third, the combination of longer-range missile systems, threshold nuclear programs in Iran, and a heightened rationale for WMD use will increase Israel's perception of existential risk. It will also stimulate the Israeli debate about deterrence, defense, and strategy in a WMD environment. In many respects the Israeli debate on these issues mirrors the discussion in the United States and elsewhere, but with a greater sense of urgency. Missile defense (for Israel, theater and national missile defense are essentially synonymous), with a focus on Israel's Arrow program and possible cooperation with such allies as Turkey and the United States, is receiving even greater attention than in the past. Long-range strike, WMD-related intelligence and surveillance and the ability to attack mobile targets are obvious priorities. Israeli strategists are also wrestling with the problem of inevitably imperfect defenses in a WMD-laden region. Thus, alongside defensive, preemptive, and deterrent measures, there is interest in taking a more comprehensive approach, including efforts to "immunize" Israeli society against unavoidable risks. This is partly a matter of passive defenses (civil defense) and partly a matter of perception management. The idea is to keep the threat of WMD attack from interfering with quality of life and destabilizing policymaking, consequences that could encourage adversaries to acquire and use WMD.[39]

Fourth, the existence of WMD may influence the nature of Arab-Israeli confrontation short of WMD use and outside conventional war. The increased potential for escalation inherent in regional WMD arsenals may actually encourage a reversion to low-intensity forms of conflict, the use of proxies, and terrorism. Urban warfare is likely to be a hallmark of this type of confrontation. This trend is already observable in southern Lebanon, the West Bank, and Gaza. It is also evident in the confrontation between nuclear-armed adver-

---

[38]Interview with Dore Gold, now national security advisor to Israeli Prime Minister Ariel Sharon, January 2001.

[39]Yehezkel Dror, "Systems Perspective: The Dangers of Fragmented Thinking," in Arieh Stav (ed.), *Ballistic Missiles: The Threat and the Response*, London: Brassey's, 1999, p. 198.

saries in the subcontinent.[40] Regional states may pursue WMD for reasons of prestige and strategic weight but may also seek lower intensity and lower risk alternatives to their use.

Gulf Security

Subregional frictions in the Persian Gulf are a continuing stimulus to proliferation. Competition between Iran and Iraq, the vulnerability of Saudi Arabia and the smaller GCC states, the Pakistani nuclear capability, and the U.S. military presence have been key variables in the proliferation equation in the Gulf, and the aftermath of the U.S.-led invasion of Iraq may become a key factor as well.[41] Moreover, the existence of longer-range missiles capable of reaching Israel and further afield means that systems acquired with Gulf adversaries in mind inevitably affect the regional balance in the Levant and vice versa.

The Iran-Iraq war saw the extensive use of WMD including protracted ballistic missile exchanges and the tactical use of chemical weapons. The friction between Iraq and Iran has contributed substantially to proliferation dynamics. However, Iran has been a beneficiary of the military containment of Iraq during the 1990s. The reduction of Iraq's formidable conventional capability improved Iran's security situation and arguably reduced, although clearly not eliminated, the incentives for acquiring WMD. At a minimum, the containment of Iraq probably allowed a slower pace of nuclear and missile development. The current occupation of Iraq further reduces the risk to Iran from this quarter but also introduces a new challenge in the form of an American presence of uncertain duration on Iran's doorstep.

In the case of Iran, the quest for high-prestige weapons and strategic weight predates the revolutionary regime and is likely to continue regardless of the outlook for reform and moderation. That said, improved Iranian relations with Europe and potentially the United States may impose a degree of restraint in acquiring the most lethal

---

[40]*Global Trends 2015,* 2001, p. 58.

[41]I am grateful to Daniel Byman for his identification of several of the issues discussed in this section.

and longer-range technologies.[42] Pakistan's emergence as a nuclear weapons state could place new pressures on Tehran to keep pace, and further erode the nuclear taboo.

Saudi Arabia is implicitly threatened by Iranian WMD as well as Israeli arsenals. Under conditions of conflict in the Gulf, or between Israel and its neighbors, Saudi Arabia might be tempted to invest in more modern missiles and, in the most extreme case, nuclear weapons. This scenario could be made more likely should Iran "go nuclear," if a new Middle East conflict saw the extensive use of WMD, or if the United States disengaged from Gulf defense. The durability of the Saudi regime is another important variable. The advent of a more radical (revolutionary rather than status quo) regime could spur Saudi acquisition of WMD.

The presence of American forces in and around the Gulf raises the cost of conventional aggression for Iran and probably stimulates the search for asymmetric alternatives, from subversion to possession of WMD. A reduction in the American commitment to Gulf defense, the transformation of American relations with Iran, or a long-term occupation of Iraq could all affect proliferation trends. But regional competitions are likely to remain and provide their own rationale for the development of WMD capabilities at some level.

North Africa

Proliferation in North Africa has been more modest than many analysts envisioned ten years ago. Libyan programs continue in uneven fashion, but the overall sense of WMD risk emanating from Libya has waned as the regime has moderated its rhetoric and behavior. To the extent that Libya's WMD ambitions appear bound up with Qadhafi's highly personalized approach to the region and the world, the outlook for Libyan programs is likely to depend critically on the potential for leadership change in Tripoli. New crises in relations with neighbors, especially Egypt, might reinvigorate Libya's WMD efforts.

---

[42]German intelligence and defense circles have become increasingly concerned about the prospect of Iranian missiles capable of reaching European targets.

After a decade of turmoil, Algeria is rediscovering its foreign policy activism. So far this reassertion of Algeria's regional role has taken the form of diplomatic initiatives and tentative security dialogue with Europe and the United States. These trends should discourage a revival of Algeria's nuclear and missile interests. The potential for a radical Islamic regime in Algiers—a development that might have raised serious concerns about the country's nuclear potential—has clearly receded and is unlikely to reemerge. Geopolitical competition with Morocco and Algeria's interest in recovering its leadership position in the Third World provide some continuing but weak incentives to seek strategic weight through prestigious technical programs. Algeria's latent WMD potential is important because, if developed, it is likely to spur a strong reaction in France and elsewhere in Europe. That, in turn, could kindle European interest in missile defense.

EXTRAREGIONAL DYNAMICS

States outside the Middle East can influence proliferation dynamics within the region in a variety of ways. They can do so through their foreign policies, security strategies, and, not least, transfers of WMD technology and expertise.[43] It is also useful to consider differences in perspective on proliferation, and the effect of evolving Western approaches to deterrence and missile defense on the Middle Eastern environment. Thus far, there is little to suggest that Russian and Chinese cooperation with Washington in the post–September 11 struggle against terrorism will translate into improved cooperation in limiting WMD-related transfers to the Middle East. Moscow and Beijing, and many of America's allies, simply view the terrorism and proliferation issues as separate problems, as demonstrated by the diplomatic friction in the run-up to the 2003 war in Iraq.

---

[43]Western suppliers can also play a role, especially in the area of dual-use technology and materials. See, for example, Stephen Grey, "French 'Weapons Grade' Exports to Iraq Blocked," *London Sunday Times*, April 22, 2001.

The Russian Factor

Analysts observe little in the way of a coherent post–Cold War Russian strategy toward the Middle East.[44] Moscow's approach appears to build on a tradition of concern about insecurity on Russia's southern periphery, primarily in relation to Turkey. In the wake of the Cold War, Russia has inherited a series of lapsed relationships from North Africa to the Levant, including arms supply connections with Algeria, Libya, Syria, and Iraq. In recent years, and despite some divergent interests, Russia has developed a more far-reaching relationship with Iran, which has elements of a strategic partnership.[45] Russian-Libyan cooperation also shows signs of revival.[46] Moscow's engagement in the Middle East may appear to lack coherence as a result of competing commercial and political interests and, in some instances, a lack of full state control over bureaucratic actors with a stake in arms and technology transfers. Nonetheless, Russian behavior displays some disturbing characteristics that could deepen if the overall relationship between Russia and the West becomes more competitive.

Russia has emerged as a leading supplier of WMD to the region, including chemical, nuclear, and missile technology. Russia is the leading foreign participant in Iran's civil nuclear program and almost certainly contributes, if indirectly, to Iran's covert nuclear weapons program.[47] Russian companies have supported Iran's Shahab-3 medium-range missile program and are leading purveyors of missile systems and expertise to others, including Syria and Libya. In recent years, Russia has actively marketed ballistic missiles (notably the Iskander-E) with ranges and payloads just limited enough to comply with the rules of the Missile Technology Control Regime (MTCR). The country's long-standing expertise in chemical and biological weapons has supported the development of these capabilities in

---

[44]See, for example, Eugene Rumer, *Dangerous Drift: Russia's Middle East Policy,* Washington, D.C.: Washington Institute for Near East Policy, 2000.

[45]See Galia Golan, "Russia and Iran: A Strategic Partnership?" *Discussion Paper No. 75,* London: Royal Institute for International Affairs, 1998. See also Michael Wines, "Putin to Sell Arms and Nuclear Help to Iran," *New York Times,* March 13, 2001.

[46]"Russia, Libya Determined to Revive Cooperation," *Interfax* (Moscow), November 15, 2000.

[47]*Proliferation Threat and Response,* 2001, p. 58.

Iran, Iraq, Egypt, and Syria. The problem of Russian nuclear and other WMD-related engineers, in search of employment and available on the world market, further contributes to proliferation potential in the Middle East. Since the breakup of the Soviet Union, much attention has been devoted to the problem of "loose nukes," nuclear arms and materials that could find their way to world markets.[48] Middle Eastern proliferators with limited access to fissionable material could take this covert route to nuclear status.

Russia's role as a leading supplier of WMD and missile technology appears to represent a triumph of shortsighted commercial gain over longer-term strategic interest.[49] Given the multiple flashpoints along Russia's southern periphery and the potential for friction with nearby Muslim states, Russia is itself a potential target of WMD-armed missiles based in the Middle East. American policymakers have attempted to engage Russian officials in a dialogue about this shared exposure with limited success. Under conditions of heightened competition between Russia and the West, the problem of Russian arms transfers to the Middle East could deepen. This is especially worrisome given the lack of opportunities for Russia in Europe, with the possible exception of the Balkans. Renewed friction with the United States and its allies is much more likely to take the form of competition in peripheral but strategic areas such as the Persian Gulf and the eastern Mediterranean, where Russian arms and technology transfers can have a marked effect on military balances and American freedom of action. Thus, the outlook for Russian-Western relations emerges as a key variable in the WMD proliferation equation in the Middle East. Indeed, Russian WMD transfer policies in the region are a leading source of U.S.-Russian friction in their own right.[50]

---

[48]Some recent incidents of nuclear theft and attempted sales are detailed in James Risen, "Nuclear Items Sold by Russia to Iran Pose an Obstacle, Panel Finds," *New York Times*, January 11, 2001.

[49]See Oksana Antonenko, "Russia's Military Involvement in the Middle East," *Middle East Review of International Affairs*, Vol. 5, No. 1, December 2000.

[50]See Patrick E. Tyler, "Moscow Says Remarks by U.S. Resurrect 'Spirit of Cold War,'" *New York Times*, March 21, 2001.

China and North Korea

In a similar fashion, WMD suppliers in Asia are important contributors to proliferation in the region.[51] Both China and North Korea continue to play a particularly important part in the spread of longer-range ballistic missiles and support the development of indigenous capacities for manufacture and modification. Neither China nor North Korea is a member of the MTCR, although China asserts that it will not transfer MTCR-class systems.[52] Examples of Chinese missile transfers to the region include the sale of CSS-8 missiles to Iran, contributions to Pakistan's Shaheen (ranges up to 2,000 km) and shorter-range Hatf systems, and assistance to Libya.[53] China has made modest contributions to Iran's nuclear program and was heavily involved in Algeria's nuclear program until the early 1990s when political violence against foreigners made the presence of Chinese technicians untenable. Thus far, Chinese WMD-related transfers to the Middle East are probably motivated by commercial interest and a generalized desire to consolidate political relationships across the region.

North Korea has a remarkable record of WMD-related transfers to the region and is a leading engine of missile proliferation.[54] Over the past decade, the country has transferred improved Scuds to Egypt and Syria and variants of its No-Dong medium-range missile to Iran and Pakistan. Both Algeria and Libya have expressed interest in acquiring North Korean systems of No-Dong or longer range. The scope and intensity of North Korea's own missile and space-launch vehicle programs, and its pattern of transfers to the region, suggest that North Korea is a likely source of technology for intermediate- and intercontinental-range systems appearing in the Middle East

---

[51]Recent transfers of technology related to nuclear-capable missiles are summarized in International Institute for Strategic Studies, *Strategic Survey 1999/2000*, Oxford: Oxford University Press, 2000, pp. xxviii–xxix.

[52]See Jim Mann, "US Takes New Tack on China Arms Exports," *Los Angeles Times*, October 5, 2000.

[53]China is also an important supplier of WMD-capable cruise missiles in the Middle East.

[54]North Korean transfers continue, ostensibly for economic reasons, despite periodic commitments to limit such exports. See Doug Struck, "North Korea Insists on Missile Sales," *International Herald Tribune*, May 5–6, 2001.

over the next decade. Pakistan or Iran could, in turn, transfer North Korean missile systems elsewhere in the region. North Korea's own October 2002 revelations about its continued nuclear program also reveal the supporting role played by Pakistan, perhaps in exchange for access to missile technology, a two-way street in WMD-related trade.

Asian involvement in arms transfers of all kinds to the Middle East could take on greater geostrategic importance as a result of developments in energy markets. Many analyses point to Asia's, and especially China's, growing energy demands. These demands are likely to be met in large measure by imports from the Persian Gulf and perhaps the Caspian, as discussed in Chapter Six. This would create conditions for deeper "arms for oil" relationships between Asia and the Middle East, on the pattern of arrangements between Europe and Arab oil producers in the 1960s and 1970s. Higher oil prices might encourage such arrangements. The combination of larger oil revenues and more eager suppliers prepared to offer WMD and other technologies on a concessionary basis could introduce a new and dangerous dynamic on the proliferation scene. Such considerations are more likely drivers of WMD-related cooperation than the notion of an "Islamic-Confucian alliance" against the West suggested by Samuel Huntington.

India, Pakistan, and Proliferation Alliances

WMD capabilities in South Asia may influence proliferation in the Middle East, but the influence is likely to be marginal. It can be argued that India and Pakistan are, effectively, part of the region in proliferation terms, despite the distinctive character of their geopolitical competition. Tests of Indian and Pakistani nuclear devices and their deployment of nuclear-capable missiles set a standard of strategic weight and prestige that others, such as Iran, might wish to emulate. At a minimum, nuclear weapons on the subcontinent may fuel a sense of nuclear entitlement among regional actors. The sophistication of their WMD arsenals also makes India and Pakistan potentially important sources of WMD technology. With its closer ties to the Middle East, Pakistan has shown a greater interest in playing such a role, and the availability of

Pakistani technology figures prominently in the idea of nuclear cooperation among Muslim states.

The motivations of proliferators within the Muslim world remain largely regional and secular. Pakistan's nuclear development has had India as a reference point. Iran's nuclear ambitions predate the revolution, and the Islamic inclinations of such states as Libya and Syria are weak. WMD-related cooperation tied explicitly to Muslim interests would require a common sense of threat, going beyond the current state of confrontation with Israel or the fear of Western intervention.[55] Strategic weight in a regional setting is, again, a factor. States that have managed, at great economic and diplomatic cost, to acquire transforming capabilities (i.e., nuclear weapons, ICBMs) will be most unwilling to dilute this achievement through transfers to state or nonstate actors within the region (the very different risk of Pakistani loss of control over nuclear weapons and expertise, and possible transfers by this route to state and nonstate actors in the Middle East, has been mentioned earlier). Nuclear states in the West have shown very little willingness to share these capabilities, even in an alliance context.[56] India, with its strategic concern about competition with Muslim states to the north and west, is most unlikely to seek proliferation alliances in the Middle East. The country's only viable regional partner, Israel, already has well-developed capabilities of its own.

South Asia has also been a very discouraging test of nonproliferation efforts, with possible implications for the Middle East. Decades of diplomatic pressure and, later, sanctions proved quite ineffective in constraining nuclear proliferation on the subcontinent. In the wake of September 11 and the intervention in Afghanistan, the sanctions-based approach to nonproliferation in South Asia was abandoned altogether to consolidate the strategic relationship with both India and Pakistan. Proliferators in the Middle East may well draw lessons from this experience, leading them to (further?) discount the credibility and effectiveness of proliferation-related sanctions. In

---

[55]For a critical discussion of this concept, see Graham E. Fuller and Ian O. Lesser, *A Sense of Siege: The Geopolitics of Islam and the West,* Boulder, Colo.: Westview/RAND, 1995, pp. 64–68.

[56]U.S.-UK nuclear cooperation is a leading exception; and NATO has its "dual key" arrangements regarding nuclear systems deployed in Europe.

some instances, they may judge that the United States may tolerate WMD proliferation provided that there is an overriding interest in strategic cooperation.

Implications for European Security

The deployment of missile systems of trans-Mediterranean range in the Middle East will eventually increase Europe's exposure to risks emanating from the south. For the moment, this exposure to missile attack is largely confined to Turkey and southern Europe, accounting for the higher degree of attention to WMD risks in NATO's south. Indeed, Turkey displays an approach to WMD and missile defense issues most closely resembling that of the United States within NATO. European policymakers and strategists generally take a more relaxed attitude toward WMD and missile proliferation in the Middle East. To some extent, this may be a matter of strategic culture and differing notions of acceptable risk.

European analysts emphasize that although the United States places a premium on capabilities as a measure of risk (and these capabilities are, objectively, growing), Europe is more concerned with intentions. North African and Middle Eastern states may be able to reach European population centers with modern missiles, perhaps armed with WMD. But why would they wish to do so?[57] In light of the 1991 Gulf War experience, many Europeans would also argue that the most serious risk to Europe in this regard may actually flow from U.S.-led intervention in the Middle East, possibly in cooperation with European allies. Regimes in conflict with the West may not be able to reach North America, but they may be in a position to retaliate against targets in Europe. This exposure is also likely to complicate strategies for power projection to the Gulf or elsewhere in the region that rely on European bases and forces (and, in terms of Egyptian vulnerability, the Suez Canal).

Europeans have been skeptical of approaches to Middle Eastern proliferation that have become more central to American security

---

[57]See Joachim Krause, "The Proliferation of Weapons of Mass Destruction: The Risks for Europe," in Paul Cornish, Peter van Ham, and Joachim Krause (eds.), *Europe and the Challenge of Proliferation*, Paris: WEU Institute for Security Studies, 1996, pp. 5–21.

thinking. Broadly, European allies tend to favor diplomatic approaches to nonproliferation over military counterproliferation strategies.[58] That said, developments over the next decade may well increase the European stake and interest in missile defense oriented toward Middle Eastern risks. First, the proliferation of delivery systems of ever increasing range suggests that, eventually, missile exposure will be an issue for London, Paris, and Berlin, and not just the less influential allies in NATO's south. At that point, pressure for some form of deployable theater defense may increase.

Second, the current approach to transatlantic cooperation in support of American power projection for the Middle East may not be sustainable as Europe is more fully exposed to the retaliatory consequences of intervention. If Saddam Hussein had been able to reach European territory in response to U.S. use of bases in Spain, Italy, Greece, and Turkey, he might well have done so. The "sanctuarization" of European territory is waning, and this implies an expansion of Article Five threats (to members' territory) calling for a collective NATO response.

Third, Europe has ambitions of greater diplomatic and security engagement in the Middle East. It is likely to be one of the first areas affected by the EU's emerging foreign policy and defense capabilities. In a decade, the pretexts for Middle Eastern strikes against European territory will very likely not all be related to U.S. action. Europe may face challenges of its own, and the interest in defenses against WMD will increase. To the extent that Arab-Israeli relations continue to worsen, and perhaps move toward broader confrontation, Europe's concern about its own exposure will be reinforced.

---

[58]A distinctive European approach is suggested in Camille Grand, "The European Union and the Non-Proliferation of Nuclear Weapons," *Chaillot Paper No. 37,* Paris: WEU Institute for Security Studies, January 2000, pp. 4–5. For a contrasting American perspective, see Jan Lodal, *The Price of Dominance: The New Weapons of Mass Destruction and Their Challenge to American Leadership,* New York: Council on Foreign Relations, 2001. For a more general discussion of U.S. and European foreign policy differences, see Robert Kagan, *Of Paradise and Power,* New York: Knopf, 2003.

A WORLD OF DEFENSES: IMPLICATIONS FOR THE MIDDLE EAST

Although the scope and pace of U.S. missile defense efforts is in flux, the first effective capabilities to be put in place will probably be oriented toward the theater defense of allies and U.S. forces deployed in and around the Persian Gulf. These might include land- or sea-based systems deployable to the Gulf and the eastern Mediterranean. For reasons noted above, Europe is more likely to participate in theater systems, including defenses that would be "strategic" from its perspective. Germany and Italy are already participants in the U.S.-led Medium Extended Air Defense System (MEADS) program with application to missile risks emanating from the south. Demands for improved defenses based on Patriot or Russian SA-10 systems can be expected across the region. Israel, of course, has its own missile defense effort based on the Arrow 2, developed jointly with the United States. A minimal system has already been deployed, and the wider system is expected to be fully operational by 2005. It will operate in conjunction with Israel's lower-altitude Patriot air defenses.[59] Within the region, Turkey is exploring participation in the Arrow program. Egypt, Jordan, Israel, and Turkey are possible participants with the United States in regional missile defense for the Levant.

The movement toward a "world of defenses," an environment with more capacity for missile defense and greater relevance of defenses in strategy, would have some important implications for the Middle East. In operational terms, it would reinforce the utility and credibility of existing military capabilities and strengthen the position of actors with the most sophisticated conventional forces. Because WMD-armed missiles can be employed as an asymmetric counter to modern air power as a vehicle for strategic attack, regional missile defenses would enhance the security of states that have relied on advanced Western air platforms for their defense, including Israel, Turkey, Saudi Arabia, Jordan, Egypt, and the United Arab Emirates.[60]

By reinforcing the role of conventional forces, regional missile defense would probably have a stabilizing effect, reducing the potential

---

[59]International Institute for Strategic Studies, 2000, pp. 127–128.

[60]Gold, 2000, p. 7.

for political intimidation and escalation, and lengthening warning times. Effective defenses might also dampen proliferation trends by raising the cost to proliferators. States determined to possess a credible delivery system might need to invest in expensive countermeasures (e.g., penetration aids), larger arsenals, or both. Uncertainties surrounding the ability of missiles to penetrate defenses might also dampen enthusiasm for nuclear weapons if their employment could not be assured.

The consequences for regional arms control are less clear. By complicating WMD employment and "raising the bar" for effective systems, defenses might encourage some Middle Eastern states to explore arms control as an alternative method of achieving parity with regional competitors. This might be the case between Israel and Egypt. At the same time, the deployment of theater defenses, possibly in parallel with strategic defenses, might complicate the arms control issues. It is unclear whether the linkage of regional defense systems (e.g., Arrow) to strategic early warning radars—an approach that could increase the effectiveness of both—would violate provisions of the 1972 Antiballistic Missile (ABM) Treaty.[61] In light of the U.S. withdrawal from the treaty, however, this issue may have little relevance for the future.

Russia might find itself similarly limited in its ability to help develop regional defenses among its Middle Eastern partners. Interest in acquiring missile defenses among some of the current states of proliferation concern such as Iran might be revealing with regard to their strategic thinking. A move toward defenses coupled with continued WMD development could indicate a more rational approach to missile use than is sometimes assumed. It might also suggest the depth of their commitment to acquiring survivable WMD capabilities.

Regional defenses would reduce the potential for political blackmail of allies and would help to neutralize weapons that might otherwise severely limit Western freedom of action in the Middle East. Effective strategic defenses (a national missile defense) capable of "deterrence by denial" would also contribute to freedom of action in

---

[61]The treaty forbids, among other things, the transfer or international deployment of treaty-limited components. Gold, 2000, p. 7.

the widest sense, helping to keep homeland defense considerations from dominating regional policymaking. This would allow for more vigorous coercive strategies in dealing with "rogue" or revolutionary regimes. At the same time, effective defenses might actually increase the exposure of states left out of a defensive architecture in the Middle East (this was one of the European criticisms of American plans for a "national" missile defense). Given the extent of American alliance relationships across the region, there would therefore be considerable pressure to make any ballistic missile defense architecture as comprehensive as possible, so that some states are not left exposed.

Finally, a shift toward missile defense is likely to stimulate a more searching debate on strategy, deterrence, and rationality in a Middle Eastern context. Much Western thinking about the problem of "rogue" states and WMD has turned on the problem of rationality in regime behavior and assumptions about whether and how such states can be deterred.[62] The problem of deterrence in the Middle East underscores the ethnocentrism of much strategic thought. Quite apart from the dilemmas posed by "crazy states," leaderships whose worldview and objectives are at variance with international norms, or loose weapons in Middle Eastern arsenals, there is probably a useful distinction to be made between WMD-armed states with status quo as opposed to revolutionary aspirations.[63] It might be argued, for example, that Iran's more advanced nuclear and missile programs are ultimately less worrisome for the United States than is the prospect of continued WMD development in Iraq, based on regime behavior and the essentially conservative character of Iranian decisionmaking.[64]

The missile defense issue has revived the classic Cold War debate between "existentialists" and "extenders."[65] The former emphasized

---

[62]For a classic treatment of the problem, see Yehezkel Dror, *Crazy States: A Counterconventional Strategic Problem*, Lanham, MD: Lexington Heath, 1980; Thomas C. Schelling, *The Strategy of Conflict*, Cambridge, Mass.: Harvard University Press, 1960; and Dean Wilkening and Kenneth Watman, *Nuclear Deterrence in a Regional Context*, Santa Monica, Calif.: RAND, MR-500-A/AF, 1995.

[63]As suggested by Gerald Steinberg in discussion with the author.

[64]Gold, 2000, discussion with author.

[65]As suggested by Robert Levine.

the apocalyptic nature of assured destruction and saw stability in minimal or "existential" deterrence. The latter sought stability through the survivability of nuclear arsenals, making nuclear use more plausible by a variety of means, including defenses (or "extended" deterrence). In a Middle Eastern context, the increasing availability of technologies for both WMD attack and defense might eventually pose this same dilemma for states in the region and those within range outside the region. The issue would acquire greater salience if Israel loses its regional monopoly on nuclear weapons, and those with active programs are compelled to decide on minimal or larger arsenals, more or less accuracy, hardening versus mobility, the extent of their own defenses, etc. In all likelihood, these choices will be more limited by cost than was the case for adversaries at the height of the Cold War. If longer-range ballistic missiles and nuclear warheads are primarily vehicles for national prestige, such complex calculations may be unnecessary. If regional proliferators view these systems as weapons of active deterrence and even warfighting, the introduction of defenses will compel a more sophisticated approach.

CONCLUSIONS AND POLICY IMPLICATIONS

In a period of continued tension in the Persian Gulf, renewed Palestinian-Israeli confrontation, and significant frictions elsewhere in the Middle East, the proliferation of weapons of mass destruction and the means for their delivery at longer ranges is troubling. For the United States, the events of September 11, the tendency to treat WMD proliferation and international terrorism as linked phenomena with increasingly global reach, and the 2003 war against Iraq reinforce an already serious concern in the minds of policymakers.

Libya and Algeria are now less of a concern, while proliferation dynamics in the Levant and the Gulf and influences from South Asia darken the picture. In sum, the context for regional proliferation is in flux, even if the pace of proliferation continues. The emergence of a new nuclear power in the region, coupled with programs for the development of missiles capable of reaching Western Europe and ultimately North America, would be a transforming development in strategic terms. Short of this, even existing capabilities have important implications for regional stability and U.S. strategy. Some more specific policy implications also flow from this analysis.

First, the expansion of WMD and missile capabilities in the Middle East constrains the United States' freedom of action in several ways. Operationally, it increases the vulnerability of deployed forces and complicates military presence. Over the horizon, strategies for reassurance and intervention can reduce this exposure but may not be appropriate in many cases where deployments on the ground are required. Strategically, the exposure of European bases and population centers to longer-range missiles means that Middle Eastern proliferation is also a problem of European security. The end of European sanctuarization means that defensive systems aimed at neutralizing the missile risk must be multiregional to make power-projection arrangements predictable. If North America comes within range of Middle Eastern missiles, presumably WMD-armed, American strategy and diplomacy in the Middle East will acquire even greater significance. An arms-length approach toward the Arab-Israeli conflict or security in the Gulf will be much more difficult to the extent that developments in the Middle East directly influence the security of U.S. territory.

Second, a reasonably effective missile defense in and around the Middle East will be important to address the exposure of allies and deployed forces under current conditions. It will also be a hedge against more dangerous proliferation scenarios that could result from a widening of Arab-Israeli confrontation or the emergence of a new nuclear power in the region. Missile defense can help to offset any erosion of the advantage U.S.-supplied systems, principally modern tactical aircraft, have given key regional allies such as Israel, Egypt, Saudi Arabia, and Turkey. To the extent that their conventional edge declines, only American forces in the region can compensate for this. The design of a regional missile defense architecture must also take account of the perception of increased risk among those who may be left out. There are now promising opportunities to develop missile defenses based in, or deployable to, such areas as the eastern Mediterranean, where they might reassure NATO as well as Middle Eastern allies. The allied dimension in missile defense and counter-WMD strategy is essential if these efforts are to reinforce American freedom of action in and around the Middle East.

Finally, the two most prominent influences on the supply and demand side of the proliferation problem are transfers from Russia and China, respectively, and the course of the Middle East peace process.

These are also the sources of greatest uncertainty for the future. Preventing new transfers to the region should be a core aim in U.S. relationships with Russia and China. The United States may also need to adjust its approach to the peace process to recognize the potentially profound effect WMD proliferation can have on the "end of conflict" objective that has always been critical to the process. The ability of rejectionist states to carry on the confrontation with Israel from over the horizon suggests, among other things, that bilateral negotiations may not be sufficient in an increasingly multilateral conflict, and that a "settlement" may only imply a state of peaceful coexistence and acceptable risk.

Chapter Nine

CONCLUSIONS

Nora Bensahel, Daniel L. Byman, and Negeen Pegahi

The Middle East in the coming decade is likely to experience a range of challenges that will demand creative, and at times difficult, responses from the United States and its partners. The spread of WMD, potential leadership changes, and increased Russian and Chinese activism in the region could complicate U.S. attempts to engage friendly states in the region and deter hostile ones. Continued violence in Israel and the Palestinian territories could further destabilize the region, strain U.S. relations with its closest regional ally, and make it more difficult to achieve other U.S. regional objectives. Even progress on some U.S. goals, such as democratization and economic liberalization, could increase instability in the region and lead friendly regimes to turn away from Washington.

This final chapter reviews the implications of the previous chapters. It emphasizes three related issues: tensions already affecting the formulation of U.S. foreign policy, emerging challenges that are likely to further complicate U.S. decisionmaking, and key uncertainties that could considerably affect regional developments.

TENSIONS AFFECTING U.S. FOREIGN POLICY

The chapters in this volume demonstrate that U.S. policy toward the Middle East often faces contradictory pressures. One tension involves promoting stability versus encouraging political reform. A second involves whether to focus policies on regimes or on populations.

Stability Versus Political Reform

U.S. decisionmakers have often faced a choice between promoting a stable Middle East versus promoting a democratic one. As discussed in Chapter Two, although the United States has a broad interest in political reform throughout the region, there are equally important strategic concerns over the short-term implications of increased popular participation. High levels of anti-American sentiment throughout the region—discussed in the following section—mean that any opening of the political systems in the region could result in policies that reflect popular preferences for a more distant relationship with the United States. Any moves in this direction could complicate U.S. regional goals, including the rebuilding of Iraq and mediating the Arab-Israeli conflict, as well as broader U.S. goals such as counterterrorism and counterproliferation.

Increased political reform could also increase regional instability. As discussed in Chapter Seven, individuals throughout the region are now exposed to a wider range of viewpoints through new media outlets. These ideas are also more widely disseminated given the proliferation of mid-tech distribution outlets, including photocopiers, fax machines, and audiocassettes. Liberalization has increased the range of viewpoints expressed in the Middle East; democratization could potentially allow some of these new voices to become integrated into the government. Greater prominence of nationalists and/or Islamists in individual governments could alarm other regimes and precipitate interstate tensions. Further, states undergoing dramatic political changes often become involved in international conflict: States undergoing democratic transitions are more likely than others to initiate wars,[1] and they are also at risk of appearing weak and inviting aggression from their neighbors.

As decisionmakers struggle to find the right balance between stability and democracy, U.S. policy toward the region has often seemed contradictory. Rhetorical support for political reform in the region has coexisted with an acceptance of nondemocratic policies of U.S. partners while often overlooking democratic developments in potential U.S. adversaries. When the United States has had to choose

---

[1]Edward D. Mansfield and Jack Snyder, "Democratization and the Danger of War," *International Security*, Vol. 20, No. 1, 1995, pp. 5–38.

between democracy and regional stability, it has almost invariably chosen stability. This choice has had implications for both regional regimes and populations. Authoritarian regimes may have been further emboldened, secure in the belief that the United States would not press for democratic reforms, while populations—as discussed below—have increasingly viewed the United States as at least partially responsible for their own repressive regimes.

Regimes Versus Populations

The preference for stability over democratization has effectively aligned the United States with the interests of Middle Eastern regimes rather than those of their populations. Anti-American sentiment in the region is not a new phenomenon, but there are indications that it is on the rise. According to a world public opinion survey released by the Pew Global Attitudes Project in June 2003, 83 percent of those surveyed in Jordan reported a "very unfavorable" opinion of the United States, up from 57 percent in the summer of 2002, and the comparable figures in Lebanon rose from 38 to 48 percent. The 2003 data include very high percentages of people reporting either a "somewhat unfavorable" or "very unfavorable" opinion of the United States, which totaled 66 percent in Morocco, 71 percent in Lebanon, 98 percent in the Palestinian Authority, and 99 percent in Jordan.[2] Those believing that the United States factors their own countries' interests into policy decisions either "not too much" or "not much at all" was 63 percent in Morocco, 80 percent in Jordan (up from 71 percent in 2002), 81 percent in Lebanon (up from 77 percent), and 92 percent in the Palestinian Authority.[3] The percentage of people reporting that U.S. policies in the Middle East make the region less stable is also quite high, reaching 56 percent in Lebanon, 63 percent in Morocco, 85 percent in the Palestinian Authority, and 91 percent

---

[2]Kuwait, which has consistently been one of the most pro-U.S. states in the region, totals 32 percent on this question. "Views of a Changing World 2003," The Pew Global Attitudes Project, data available at http://people-press.org/reports/pdf/185topline. pdf, question Q.8 on pp. T-133 and T-134. The polling was done in the wake of the U.S.-Iraq conflict, but before the Bush administration began a major push on the Middle East peace negotiations.

[3]Pew Global Attitudes, Question Q.10 on pp. T-135 and T-136.

in Jordan.[4] While this survey indicates quite high, and in some places increasing, levels of anti-American sentiment, it did not include some important regional countries, such as Saudi Arabia and Iran. Reliable public opinion data are extraordinarily difficult to attain in these countries because of repressive governmental policies. Anecdotal reports suggest that anti-Americanism is also quite high in these countries, but it is difficult to determine how widespread it is and whether it cuts across all layers of society.

The September 11 attacks have made the U.S. decisionmakers more sensitive to popular perceptions of the United States and U.S. policy in the region. In October 2001, former advertising executive Charlotte Beers was appointed Undersecretary of State for Public Diplomacy and Public Affairs, to head the government's effort to reduce anti-American sentiment in the Middle East and beyond. During her 17 months at the post, she oversaw a campaign of U.S government-sponsored publications and programs that sought to explain the American way of life and to showcase the lives of American Muslims.[5] This strategy contained an implicit assumption that the main U.S. obstacle in the region is a lack of understanding of U.S. values and identity. In short, if Arabs and Muslims would only get to know us, they would like us, or at least dislike us less.

The main flaw in this assumption is that the central problem seems to be disagreement with U.S. policies, not a lack of information about the United States.[6] However, misperception does make problems much worse. The very worst motives are often imputed to the United States, and Washington seldom receives credit for policies, such as intervention in the Balkans, that save the lives of Muslims or otherwise should receive the approval of citizens in the region. To reduce misperceptions, U.S. public diplomacy efforts should focus on explaining the reasons behind U.S. policy and should acknowledge that these efforts will be limited by policy disagreements as well as a basic lack of knowledge.

---

[4]Pew Global Attitudes, Question Q.28 on pp. T-150 and T-151.

[5]Mark Leonard, "Velvet Fist in the Iron Glove," *The Observer* (London), June 16, 2002.

[6]James Zogby, "It's the Policy, Stupid!" *Media Monitors Network*, April 15, 2002, available at www.mediamonitors.net/zogby49.html, accessed June 17, 2003.

EMERGING CHALLENGES

A range of problems may exacerbate these tensions and make the decisions facing U.S. policymakers even more complex in the coming decade. The politics of the region remain volatile, and the military picture, while in many ways better than in past decades—remains challenging.

Political Challenges

Regional leaders face a range of challenges to their rule and, more specifically, to their ability to maintain or improve ties to the United States. As discussed in Chapter Two, nascent political parties, a freer press, and other elements of a growing civil society are reducing many governments' once total domination of politics. As a result, leaders will have less flexibility in their foreign policy and may have to respond to public pressures in ways that they never have before. Moreover, even limited power sharing measures have the potential to increase anti-regime organization and dissent, raising the risk of regime change or at least increased instability. However, if leaders crack down, do not tolerate more dissent or make concessions, they risk even greater unpopularity, which may endanger them in the long run.

In countries with pro-U.S. governments, such as Egypt and Saudi Arabia, liberalization and democratization have profound security implications. Although precise data are lacking, the Pew poll suggests that many citizens in the region are hostile to U.S. policies. Greater popular input into decisionmaking will enable them to press their governments to limit cooperation, particularly with regard to policies that are interpreted as pro-Israel.

The spread of accessible and affordable information technologies, such as satellite television and videocassettes, poses an additional challenge. As discussed in Chapter Seven, these technologies expose Arab publics to a range of new opinions and unprecedented criticism of their governments. Expatriate opposition figures of all political stripes also can play a greater role in national politics. The Arab public now has more information available to it than ever before. As a result, it will be more difficult for governments to have extensive but quiet links to U.S. military forces even as their capitals publicly denounce U.S. policy on a range of issues.

Economic problems facing many governments magnify these challenges. Chapter Three discusses the economic difficulties faced by Egypt, Jordan, Saudi Arabia, and other states in the region, and the prognosis for reform is gloomy. In many countries, demographic trends will exacerbate these economic difficulties as large numbers of young people demand social services and enter the workforce. Regimes will confront painful tradeoffs between politically difficult reform measures and the risks inherent in continued economic stagnation.

Civil-military relations may also pose a challenge to many Middle Eastern regimes. Chapter Four argues that new leaders, including Syria's Bashar al-Assad and Jordan's King Abdullah, will have to forge new agreements with power brokers in their countries, particularly the military and the security services. However, placating the military may be difficult for some leaders. Almost all the countries in the region face at least limited austerity measures, making it difficult to engage in massive weapons purchases or otherwise devote resources to the military—a traditional means of ensuring military quiescence in the past.

If successful bargains are not struck, military preferences and actions may diverge from those of the regime in general. This may make coordination with such regional partners as Jordan, Egypt, and Morocco more difficult, as bargains struck with political leaders are not honored or only grudgingly accepted by military officials. U.S. engagement efforts also will become more difficult if regimes do not devote the necessary resources to ensuring the modernization of their forces and military interoperability with the United States. Even more troubling, limited regime military spending may be skewed politically, with only a few loyal units receiving the latest equipment and training while regular military capabilities erode.

Despite these challenges, sustained instability seems unlikely because regional leaders have proven skilled at mixing cooptation and repression to stay in power. The Gulf ruling families have weathered the storms of Arab nationalism, leftist agitation, and Islamism, emerging stronger as a result. Egypt, Syria, Iraq, and Jordan have also had remarkably stable regimes in the face of daunting political and economic challenges. Popular pressure may force leaders at times to make decisions that are against U.S. interests, such as Jordan's 1990 refusal to work with the United States against Iraq, Egypt's subsequent condemnation of many aspects of the U.S. containment of Iraq, and Turkey's last-minute refusal to allow the United States to conduct offensive operations from its territory in 2003. Such decisions are not necessarily precursors to dramatic shifts in regime policy.

Military Challenges

The conventional military picture in the region is far more favorable than the political picture. In general, the gains in the 1990s are not likely to disappear, placing the United States and its friends in the region at a considerable advantage. Israel and Turkey will remain the region's dominant military forces. The improvements in the equipment (though not necessarily the skills) of Egyptian, Saudi, and other friendly military forces also augur well for the United States. Iraq's once hostile military has been devastated and presumably will become more pro-Western as part of an overall U.S. rebuilding effort. Perhaps more important, the military forces of Libya, Iran, and Syria face an array of staggering difficulties. Their officer corps are highly politicized, and morale is probably poor in general. Moreover, their equipment is largely obsolete, their training is poor, and their supplies are in disarray. With the exception of Iran, these forces are far less capable in absolute terms than they were a decade ago.

Regional militaries are also limited by a host of socioeconomic, political, and cultural barriers that inhibit their ability to engage in effective modern warfare. Regional militaries continue to face problems in operations that require initiative, advanced technology, or maneuver warfare. They are unlikely to practice effective combined arms, let alone joint operations. Although these problems plague friendly countries as well as foes, they are particularly a concern for militaries seeking to engage in rapid offensive operations. Those problems are more troubling for potentially aggressive states such as Iran than for Saudi Arabia, Jordan, or other friendly governments.

Darkening this bright picture is the shadow of WMD and ballistic missiles. Large chemical arsenals are already present among a wide range of Middle Eastern states and, as discussed in Chapter Eight, long-range missiles are proliferating and several states are seeking biological and nuclear capabilities. Although past warnings that these weapons will be widespread have proven false, Iran could possess chemical and biological weapons, and perhaps a nuclear weapon, in the coming decade. Any future confrontation between hostile states in the region and U.S. partners may plausibly involve chemical, biological, and nuclear threats, or even attacks, at both a strategic and a tactical level.

Ballistic missiles pose a range of new risks. Even if the United States enjoys overwhelming air supremacy, adversary missiles may be able to strike deep within friendly territory. U.S. bases, ports, and rear operating areas are no longer sanctuaries. Ballistic missiles also change the strategic equation. Europe is increasingly vulnerable to Iranian missiles. The spread of long-range ballistic missiles enables a range of new players to threaten Israel. As Iraq demonstrated during the first Gulf War, states do not need to be contiguous to Israel to strike Israeli territory. Iran's development of long-range missiles enables Tehran to threaten Israel as well. By the end of the decade, Iran may even be able to strike the continental United States with ballistic missiles.[7] The defense of Israel may therefore become an important concern, if the continuing violence escalates beyond the Palestinian territories or if there are other conflicts in the Gulf.

Extraregional dynamics will play a key role in determining the pace of regional WMD and missile programs. The willingness of Russia and China to provide assistance to nuclear and biological programs will affect the pace of proliferation in the region. In addition, the programs of such nearby states as Pakistan may spur regional states such as Iran to acquire WMD. Russian and Chinese assistance could also help regional states extend the range and increase the accuracy of their ballistic missiles.

The U.S. military presence also may spur regional states to seek WMD. As noted above, regional adversaries face considerable difficulties employing conventional forces for offensive purposes even

---

[7]Regional states, however, can use forces other than ballistic missiles to strike outside the immediate theater. Iran in particular has skilled special operations forces and could use these to deploy WMD.

without the U.S. military presence. Given the significant U.S. regional presence, which may be even higher than historic levels because of the possibility of a long-term U.S. occupation of Iraq, WMD may be seen as an attractive means, or perhaps the only means, of deterring U.S. intervention.

In the aftermath of September 11, counterterrorism has become a top strategic priority of the United States. Military operations have succeeded in removing the Taliban from power, but it still remains unclear whether they have also succeeded in destroying al Qaeda's organizational structure. Many al Qaeda leaders remain unaccounted for, as do the tens of thousands of people who were trained in Afghanistan camps during the past decade. The war on terrorism will certainly continue for the foreseeable future, though it may not always include high-profile military action. It will require the active cooperation of traditional regional partners, such as Saudi Arabia and Egypt, and new partners, such as Pakistan and Uzbekistan. Yet the increased U.S. activity and presence in the region may fuel criticism from those who believe the United States is using the counterterrorism campaign to consolidate its influence over the region, or those who see it as further evidence of a Western campaign against Islam.

KEY UNCERTAINTIES

Although the spread of long-range missiles and increased access to information technologies are probable, other important possible trends are difficult to determine with any degree of certainty. Five developments are of tremendous importance but are difficult to predict: the price of oil, the future of Iraq, the future of the Arab-Israeli conflict, the policies of Russia and China, and the nature of regime change.

The Price of Oil

The security dynamics of the oil market are often contradictory.[8] A higher oil price will enable possible aggressors to purchase more

---

[8]This report does not address the impact of low or high oil prices on the economy of the United States or other countries outside the Middle East. Clearly, a low price of oil

weapons and sustain their regimes in the face of domestic discontent. However, a low oil price would hurt regimes friendly to the United States as well as adversaries, increasing the risk of political instability in the region.

By 2010, oil prices are predicted to be (in 2001 dollars per barrel) between $19.04 and $32.51, with the expected price at approximately $23.99 a barrel.[9] However, the track record of experts predicting oil prices is poor. During the 1970s, the U.S. Department of Energy expected oil to reach $250 a barrel by the year 2000. Similarly, few in early 1999 believed that oil prices would more than triple in the coming year, even temporarily. Thus, the $19.04–$32.51 estimated range must be viewed with caution.

Low prices could have the following implications:

- Internal unrest among states in the region. Almost all regional states' economies depend on oil. Even Egypt and Jordan, which have little or no oil reserves, rely on the income from expatriate workers living in oil-rich states. A low price of oil would decrease regimes' ability to buy off popular dissent but would probably not greatly lower popular expectations of government. Regimes seeking to avoid unrest may be forced to privatize state assets, reduce the size of the safety net, limit subsidies to businesses, cut largesse to ruling family members, and otherwise take politically difficult steps. In addition, they might seek assistance from the International Monetary Fund and the World Bank, enabling the United States to exercise a different form of influence in this region.

- Tension among states in the region. States facing discontent stemming in part from low oil prices may threaten force to influ-

---

in general would benefit oil-consuming nations, while oil producers would benefit from higher prices.

[9]Oil price predictions for 2025 are remarkably similar to the predictions for 2010, with an estimated range of $19.04 to $33.05, with the expected price at $26.57. See Energy Information Agency, *International Energy Outlook 2003*, available at http://www.eia.doe.gov/oiaf/ieo/tbl_15.html, accessed June 17, 2003.

ence other states' production decisions, to divert domestic discontent, or to conquer other states' reserves.[10]

- Hinder efforts to rebuild militaries. Libya, Iran, and Syria need
both qualitative and quantitative improvements in their military
forces if they are to regain past levels of effectiveness, a low bar
by any measure. This will require large amounts of money for
purchases and to maintain large numbers of men at arms.[11]

High oil prices, of course, would have the opposite implications.
Area regimes will simply have more: more to spend on government
services, more to pass on to bolster local economies, and more to
buy off dissent should it arise. If they choose to restructure their
economies—a sensible long-term decision, but one that regional
states have consistently avoided when oil prices have been high—
they will be able to cushion many of the negative effects, such as
higher initial unemployment. Militarily, however, high prices will
enable Iran, Syria, Libya, and Iraq to rebuild their militaries more
quickly and to acquire more sophisticated equipment.

The Future of Iraq

The United States is currently leading an ambitious effort to rebuild
Iraq's battered infrastructure, reform its military, revive its economy,
and establish a democratic political system. Success would have
profound implications for the region, as well as for Iraq itself. Iraq
would go from one of the world's most aggressive and anti-Western
states to a more peaceful, pro-Western polity. It could be a source of
basing for the U.S. military, a partner in counterterrorism, and a
voice for moderation in the Israel-Palestinian dispute. It is even

---

[10]Use of oil pricing and production as means to influence regional states is a common
practice. In 1997, Saudi Arabia pushed OPEC to increase production in part to punish
Iran for its cheating on its oil quota. See James Richards, "New Cohesion in OPEC's
Cartel?" *Middle East Review of International Affairs*, Vol. 3, No. 2, June 1999, pp. 18–23.
After the May 1997 election of Mohammad Khatami in Iran, Saudi Arabia and Iran
worked together to coordinate their policies within OPEC.

[11]U.S. allies, of course, will also spend less on defense. When oil prices fell in 1998,
Saudi Arabia cut defense spending by 22 percent. However, given the limited capabilities of allied forces, this reduced spending may have only a marginal impact on the
overall military balance of the region. See Steve Liesman, "Low Oil Prices Pressure
Saudi Economy," *Wall Street Journal*, March 1, 1999.

possible that Iraq might become a beacon of democracy for other Middle Eastern states, inspiring their citizens and providing a model for reform.

However, a collapse of Iraq's democracy, or a failure to establish democracy in the first place, could shake the region. Ethnic, tribal, or sectarian conflict could sweep the country, creating widespread suffering and generating massive refugee flows. Iran, Turkey, and other states might intervene to secure their interests or bolster their preferred proxies. Instability could also make Iraq a terrorist swamp, enabling groups to recruit, train, and plan with relative impunity. If the government in Baghdad became hostile, Iraq might again seek WMD or threaten its neighbors.

Even success has its risks. A sizable U.S. military presence for many years appears necessary, but this will inevitably act as a magnet for al Qaeda and other terrorist groups. The United States will inevitably be accused of imperialism, and radical voices will use the occupation to recruit for their cause. In addition, if democracy in Iraq does inspire democrats elsewhere in the region, it might destabilize key countries, at least temporarily.

The Arab-Israeli Conflict

The failure of the Camp David peace summit in July 2000 and the violence that broke out in September 2000 set back almost ten years of progress between Israel and the Palestinians. The situation remains extraordinarily tense as of this writing, with continued suicide bombings throughout Israel leading to a heavily militarized response in the Palestinian territories. President Bush's recent road map for peace marks yet another U.S. attempt to mediate the conflict, but the ongoing violence diminishes its prospects for success. Spoiler groups such as Hamas will have many opportunities to disrupt moves toward peace.

The Palestinian-Israeli conflict, and the hostility that it generates toward the United States in Arab and Muslim countries, may also pose a range of domestic political problems for Middle East regimes. Regimes have in the past used anti-Israel hostility as a safety valve for political expression, allowing demonstrations against and criticism of Israel as one of the few forms of political expression. Such demonstrations have often spilled over into anti-regime protests, either because the regime is perceived as insufficiently hostile to Israel or because the organization for the protests was captured by anti-regime voices. Both Arab nationalists and Islamists have long exploited Arab-Israeli tension to criticize pro-Western regimes and their cooperation with the United States, and in the 1960s, tension arising from the Arab-Israeli issue led to military coups against pro-Western governments. Military forces have been, and may again, be called on to repress popular discontent, testing their loyalties.

Such problems have spilled over into U.S. relations with the region. As a result, in the past even friendly Arab governments have cut back military ties with the United States, opposed U.S. political initiatives, and reduced the overall supply of oil to demonstrate their support for the anti-Israel cause. Israel has also used its political influence in the United States to block arms sales to friendly Arab states in the Gulf.[12]

Even more ominously, as long as the Arab-Israeli conflict remains unresolved, a major military confrontation remains a possibility. The most likely avenue for such an explosion is the volatile triangle of the Syrian-Lebanese-Israeli border region. A major regional confrontation could erupt in the Shebaa Farms area or the Golan, through an accident, a miscalculation by Hezbollah or Syria, domestic Syrian pressure to support the Palestinian struggle by opening up a second front, or domestic Israeli pressure for retaliation against sponsors of terrorist acts.[13] As long as there are no peace negotiations to sacrifice, the danger of such escalation is that it could draw

---

[12]See Zalmay M. Khalilzad, David A. Shlapak, and Daniel L. Byman, *The Implications of the Possible End of the Arab-Israeli Conflict for Gulf Security* (Santa Monica, Calif.: RAND, MR-822-AF, 1997, pp. 11–24 for a review.

[13]The Lebanese Hezbollah gained significant standing throughout the Arab world, but most notably among Palestinians, after the Israeli withdrawal from southern Lebanon in May 2000. So far, Hezbollah has chosen to sustain its domestic support in Lebanon by restricting its anti-Israel activities to the Shebaa Farms area in the Golan foothills. But the current stasis in the triangle rests on a very delicate balance. Hezbollah is (with input from both Iran and Syria) calculating its activity so as to sustain its reputation without provoking an Israeli reaction. Israel, increasingly under threat of a two-front guerrilla war (in the territories and on the Lebanese border), may be less and less willing over time to absorb Hezbollah attacks with impunity. And should the Israelis retaliate, given their insistence on holding Syria responsible for Hezbollah activity, the targets would probably include Syrian positions inside Lebanon as well as Lebanese civilian infrastructure.

Israeli and Syrian troops into their first direct confrontation since 1982. Given the unconsolidated and untested nature of the Bashar al-Assad regime, such a confrontation could overheat into a wider regional conflict.

At best the coming decade might witness the creation of a region-wide "cold peace." The populations of the Levant Arab states are at best unsympathetic to Israel and at worst highly hostile to the Israeli presence in the region. Thus, Arab public opinion will probably remain belligerent toward Israel for a long period following a full diplomatic peace. In such an environment, Arab governments might feel pressured to slow or avoid normalization of economic relations, security cooperation, and other steps necessary to solidify regional peace and stability. If Arab governments are faced with domestic problems (such as economic crisis or political protest) that demand an aggressive response, they will have little or no political capital remaining to invest in Arab-Israeli rapprochement. Similarly, the new leaders of the Middle East, such as Bashar al-Assad and King Abdullah, may seek to shore up their power base at home before engaging in risky diplomacy with Israel. The result could be that a comprehensive Arab-Israeli peace would not, in practice, reach much beyond the diplomatic level and would not further such broader American interests as regional stability, a decline in terrorism, or liberalization of politics or economics. Additional regional military cooperation involving Israel would be particularly difficult for regional states to support.

The Policies of Russia and China

Whether Russia and China become more hostile to the United States in the coming decade and whether their perceived interests in the Middle East increase beyond their current limited levels will affect the security balance of the region. Russia and China might assist Iran or other states hostile to the United States in order to counter U.S. dominance in the region or simply to increase their own influence in a critical region. Russia's role is currently far more important than that of China given its historical ties to several regimes and its superior military technology; by the end of the decade, however, increases in China's economic, technological, and military strength may make Beijing the more important extraregional player of the two.

If Russia and China became more active in the region, it could greatly complicate U.S. policy and military operations in the following ways:

- Russia and China could offset U.S. efforts to bring about peace between Israel and its neighbors. Russia and China could oppose international mediation efforts and provide military and political support to rejectionist states and Palestinian factions.

- Russia and China could also offset attempts to isolate Iran, Libya, and other potential aggressors. By using their vetoes at the United Nations, these countries could block efforts to extend restrictions on military sales or punish countries for developing WMD programs. They could also establish direct political and economic ties, encouraging these regimes in their intransigence.

- On a conventional military level, Russia and, to a lesser degree, China could provide regional aggressors with a range of sophisticated systems, such as advanced air defense or anti-ship cruise missiles, which would greatly complicate U.S. military operations in the region. In addition, Russian training could increase the skill levels of regional states.

- Russian and Chinese assistance is particularly important for the future of the region's WMD and ballistic missile programs. So far, a lack of fissionable material has stymied regional states' efforts to gain a nuclear capability, a situation that Russia or China could remedy if they so chose. Russia and China could also help regional countries develop their industrial infrastructure to improve their own capabilities for producing WMD and missiles.

- Russia or China might also hinder efforts to resolve ongoing conflicts in the region, or perhaps stir up new conflicts, to distract or bog down the United States, allowing them greater freedom of action in other regions.

A more positive stance from Russia and China could produce several benefits:

- Sustained pressure on regional aggressors. Several regional states have demonstrated that they will respond to concerted international pressure. Iran and Libya, for example, have both reduced their support of terrorism to cultivate the goodwill of European states. If Russia and China became more favorable to U.S. views, regional states would have additional disincentives to proliferate or attack their neighbors.

- Reduced military effectiveness of aggressors. Even if area regimes do not respond to Russian and Chinese political pressure, decreased military assistance will reduce the potency of their conventional and WMD arsenals.

- Greater potential for progress on an Arab-Israeli ceasefire or settlement. Although the settlement of the Arab-Israeli dispute depends largely on the immediate players involved, a concerted international effort might be able to reduce regional tensions and encourage all sides to sit at the negotiating table.

- Improved anti-terrorism cooperation. Russia and China have considerable influence with governments in the region and strong ties to many local factions, making them important partners in the effort to prevent future terrorist attacks against the United States.

The Nature of Regime Change

Individual leaders have shaped their countries' policies to a remarkable degree in the past, influencing the choice of allies, economic policies, and their willingness to cooperate with the United States, among other factors. Leaders have often done so in the face of populaces that are opposed to their policies. In Egypt and Saudi Arabia in particular, the popular resentment of the United States may, in the future, lead a different leader or regime to curtail ties to Washington to gain or bolster public support for the government.

Even new leaders who are not hostile pose risks. Untested leaders may overreact during a crisis, enabling problems to spin out of control. Inaction is also a risk. Many Middle East countries face a daunting array of social and economic problems. These cannot be put off indefinitely, but the risks of dramatic reform may persuade many leaders to delay change until it is too late.

The outlook is not all bleak. Many of the hostile and despotic regimes in the Middle East are under siege or could face dramatic change. Iran and Libya are two of the countries that could see a new leadership, and dramatically new policies, in the coming decade. Indeed, in both countries it is possible that a new leadership could emerge that would completely reorient the country's foreign policy in general and its relationship with the United States.

FINAL WORDS

Although the Middle East will remain a turbulent region, the nature of the danger has changed dramatically. Traditional concerns such as a conventional military attack from an aggressive state remain plausible, but they are of far less importance than new challenges such as WMD and terrorism. U.S. policy must also recognize that the lack of democratic institutions and the individual-dependent nature of many regimes may lead to sudden and profound changes in the region's politics.

Not only has the region changed, but so too has the American role. The United States is perhaps more influential in the Middle East than at any other time in its history. U.S. involvement in postwar Iraq and in the ongoing struggle against terrorism requires close cooperative relationships with many countries in the region. Yet threats to the United States seem likely to continue as long as the United States is perceived as upholding the regional status quo. Efforts to reconstruct Iraq and mediate the Arab-Israeli conflict therefore take on particular importance.

Because of this turbulence, U.S. policy must be flexible and robust. Years of relying largely on military power to achieve interests may have to give way to a wider array of tools, ranging from economic restructuring to counterterrorism training to encouraging the rule of law. Unless it pursues a multidimensional and coordinated policy approach, the United States will be confined to reacting to crises rather than preventing and managing them.

Ahrari, M. Ehsan, "Political Succession in Saudi Arabia: Systemic Stability and Security Implications," *Comparative Strategy*, Vol. 18, No. 1, 1999.

Ajami, Fouad, "What the Muslim World Is Watching," *New York Times Magazine*, November 18, 2001.

al-Gamasi, Mohamed Abdel Ghani, *The October War: Memoirs of Field Marshal el-Gamasy of Egypt*, Cairo: The American University in Cairo Press, 1993.

al-Haj, Abdullah Juma, "The Politics of Participation in the Gulf Co-operation Council States: The Omani Consultative Council," *Middle East Journal*, Vol. 50, No. 4, 1996.

Ali, Ali Abdel Gadir, "The Behavior of Poverty in the Arab Region," in *Preventing and Eradicating Poverty*, New York: United Nations Development Program, 1996.

Allam, Abeer, "Regional Tensions Thwart Egypt's Hopes for Gas Sales," *New York Times*, August 17, 2001.

Alnajjar, Ghanim, "The Challenges Facing Kuwaiti Democracy," *Middle East Journal*, Vol. 54, No. 2, 2002.

al-Rasheed, Madawi, "God, the King, and the Nation: Political Rhetoric in Saudi Arabia in the 1990s," *Middle East Journal*, Vol. 50, No. 3, 1996.

al-Sayyid, Mustapha K., "A Civil Society in Egypt?" in A. R. Norton (ed.), *Civil Society in the Middle East, Volume 1*, Leiden, Netherlands: E. J. Brill, 1995.

al-Sayyid, Mustapha Kamel, "The Concept of Civil Society and the Arab World," in Rex Brynen, Baghat Korany, and Paul Noble (eds.), *Political Liberalization & Democratization in the Arab World: Volume 1, Theoretical Perspectives*, Boulder, Colo.: Lynne Rienner, 1995.

Alterman, Jon B., "Counting Nodes and Counting Noses: Understanding New Media in the Middle East," *Middle East Journal*, Vol. 54, No. 3, Summer 2000, pp. 355–361.

Alterman, Jon B., "Egypt: Stable, but for How Long?" *The Washington Quarterly*, Vol. 23, No. 4, Autumn 2000.

Alterman, Jon, "The Gulf States and the American Umbrella," *Middle East Review of International Affairs*, Vol. 4, No. 4, December 2000, electronic version.

Alterman, Jon B., *New Media, New Politics? From Satellite Television to the Internet in the Arab World*, Washington, D.C.: The Washington Institute for Near East Policy, 1998.

Aly, Abdel Monem Said, "Egypt-U.S. Relations and Egyptian Foreign Policy," *Policywatch* 448, Washington, D.C.: The Washington Institute for Near East Policy, March 24, 2000, electronic version.

Amouzegar, Jahangit, *Iran's Economy Under the Islamic Republic*, London and New York: I. B. Tauris, 1993.

Amouzegar, Jahangit, "Khatami and the Iranian Economy at Midterm," *Middle East Journal*, Vol. 53, No. 4, Autumn 1999.

Anderson, Justin, "Ballistic Missile Arsenals in the Middle East," *Carnegie Proliferation Brief*, Vol. 4, No. 3, March 15, 2001.

Antonenko, Oksana, "Russia's Military Involvement in the Middle East," *Middle East Review of International Affairs*, Vol. 5, No. 1, December 2000.

"AQUASTAT: Saudi Arabia," Food and Agriculture Organization, 1997, http://www.fao.org/waicent/faoinfo/agricult/agl/aglw/aquastat/sauarab.htm.

"Are Khaddam, Hariri and Jumblatt on Damascus's Corruption Hit List," *Mideast Mirror*, Vol. 14, No. 108, June 8, 2000.

Assaad, Ragui, Alan Richards, Charles Schmitz, and Michael Watts, "Human Security of the New Millennium: Poverty and Sustainable Livelihoods in the Arab Region: Elements for a Poverty Alleviation Strategy," New York: United Nations Development Program, 1997.

Ayyoubi, Nazih, "Arab Bureaucracies: Expanding Size, Changing Roles," Department of Politics, University of Exeter, England, unpublished manuscript, 1985.

Baaklini, Abdo, Guilain Denoeux, and Robert Springborg, *Legislative Politics in the Arab World*, Boulder, Colo.: Lynne Rienner, 1999.

"Bahrain: First Parliament Session in Three Decades," *New York Times*, December 14, 2002.

Baktiari, Bahman, *Parliamentary Politics in Revolutionary Iran*, Gainesville, Fla.: University Press of Florida, 1996.

Bank of Beirut and the Arab Countries, *Economic Report*, 3rd Quarter, Beirut: BBAC, 2000.

Barraclough, Steven, "Al-Azhar: Between the Government and the Islamists," *Middle East Journal*, Vol. 52, No. 2, Spring 1998.

"Bashar Assad First Six Months: Reform in a Dangerous Environment," *Mideast Mirror*, January 26, 2001.

"Bashar's World," *The Economist*, July 17, 2000, electronic edition.

"Bashar Assad: No Change in Syria's Peace Terms, and Its 'Doors Are Open' to Saddam and Arafat," *Mideast Mirror*, February 9, 2001.

Be'eri, Eliezer, "The Waning of the Military in Coup Politics," *Middle Eastern Studies*, Vol. 18, No. 3, January 1982.

Bensahel, Nora, *The Counterterror Coalitions: Cooperation with Europe, NATO, and the European Union*, Santa Monica, Calif.: RAND, MR-1746-AF, 2003.

Berenson, Alex, and Jonathan Fuerbringer, "Oil and Gas Prices Tumble, but Sticks Soar Worldwide," *New York Times*, September 25, 2001.

Biddle, Stephen, "Victory Misunderstood: What the Gulf War Tells Us About the Future of Conflict," *International Security*, Vol. 21, No. 2, Fall 1996.

Biddle, Stephen, and Robert Zirkle, "Technology, Civil-Military Relations, and Warfare in the Developing World," *Journal of Strategic Studies*, Vol. 19, No. 2, June 1996.

Boyne, Sean, "Inside Iraq's Security Network: Part One," *Jane's Intelligence Review*, July 1991.

BP Amoco Statistical Review of World Energy 2001, available at http://www.bpamoco.com/centres/energy/index.asp, accessed March 28, 2002.

Brand, Laurie, "'In the Beginning Was the State . . .': The Quest for Civil Society in Jordan," in A. R. Norton (ed.), *Civil Society in the Middle East, Volume 1*, Leiden, Netherlands: E. J. Brill, 1995.

"Britain Makes New Delivery of Tanks to Jordan," *Agence France Presse*, September 1, 2001.

Broad, William J., "Document Records 1987 Bomb Test By Iraq," *New York Times*, April 29, 2001.

Bronson, Rachel, "Syria: Hanging Together or Hanging Separately," *The Washington Quarterly*, Vol. 23, No. 4, Autumn 2000.

Brooks, Risa, *Political-Military Relations and the Stability of Arab Regimes*, International Institute for Strategic Studies, Adelphi Paper 324, Oxford University Press, December 1998.

Brown, Michael E., Sean Lynn-Jones, and Steven E. Miller (eds.), *Debating the Democratic Peace*, Cambridge, Mass.: MIT Press, 1996.

Brown, Nathan J., *The Rule of Law in the Arab World*, Cambridge, UK: Cambridge University Press, 1997.

Brynen, Rex, "The Politics of Monarchical Liberalism: Jordan," in Baghat Korany, Rex Brynen, and Paul Noble (eds.), *Political Liberalization & Democratization in the Arab World: Volume 2, Comparative Experiences*, Boulder, Colo.: Lynne Rienner, 1998.

Brynen, Rex, Bahgat Korany, and Paul Noble, "Introduction: Theoretical Perspectives on Arab Liberalization and Democratization," in Rex Brynen, Bahgat Korany, and Paul Noble (eds.), *Political Liberalization & Democratization in the Arab World: Volume 1, Theoretical Perspectives*, Boulder, Colo.: Lynne Rienner, 1995.

Buchta, Wilfried, *Who Rules Iran?* Washington, D.C.: The Washington Institute for Near East Policy and the Konrad Adenauer Stiftung, 2000.

Bulatao, Rodolfo A., and Gail Richardson, "Fertility and Family Planning in Iran," Middle East and North Africa Discussion Paper Series, No. 13, Washington, D.C.: The World Bank, November 1994.

Bulliet, Richard, "Twenty Years of Islamic Politics," *Middle East Journal*, Vol. 53, No. 2, Spring 1999.

Burck, Gordon M., and Charles C. Flowerree, *International Handbook on Chemical Weapons Proliferation*, New York: Greenwood Press, 1991.

Byman, Daniel L., "Explaining Ethnic Peace in Morocco," *Harvard Middle Eastern and Islamic Review*, Vol. 4, Nos. 1–2, 1997–1998.

Byman, Daniel L., Shahram Chubin, Anoushiravan Ehteshami, and Jerrold Green, *Iran's Security Policy in the Post-Revolutionary Era*, Santa Monica, Calif.: RAND, MR-1320-OSD, 2001.

Byman, Daniel L., and Jerrold L. Green, *Political Violence and Stability in the States of the Northern Persian Gulf*, Santa Monica, Calif.: RAND, MR-1021-OSD, 1999.

Byman, Daniel, and Kenneth Pollack, "Let Us Now Praise Great Men: Bringing the Statesman Back In," *International Security*, Vol. 25, No. 1, Spring 2001.

Byman, Daniel L., and Matthew C. Waxman, *Confronting Iraq: U.S. Policy and the Use of Force Since the Gulf War*, Santa Monica, Calif.: RAND, MR-1146-OSD, 2000.

"Can Crown Prince Abdullah Lead His Desert Kingdom into the 21st Century?" *Business Week*, May 21, 2001, available at http://www.businessweek.com:/2000/00_30/b3691008.htm, accessed on May 19, 2001.

Castells, Manuel, *The Rise of the Networked Society, 2d ed.*, Oxford: Blackwell, 2000.

Center for Nonproliferation Studies, Monterey Institute of International Studies, "Nuclear, Biological, Chemical, and Missile Capabilities in the Middle East," available at http://cns.miis.edu/research/wmdme/egypt.htm.

Central Intelligence Agency, *The World Factbook 2001*, Washington, D.C.: 2001.

Champion, Daryl, "The Kingdom of Saudi Arabia: Elements of Instability Within Stability," *Middle East Review of International Affairs Journal*, Vol. 3, No. 4, December 1999.

Chaudhry, Kiren Aziz, *The Price of Wealth: International Capital Flows and the Political Economy of Late Development*, Ithaca, N.Y.: Cornell University Press, 1997.

Chesnot, Christian, "Drought in the Middle East," *Le Monde Diplomatique*, February 2000.

Clawson, Patrick L., "Oil Resources: Markets, Politics and Policies," in Richard Kugler and Ellen L. Frost (eds.), *The Global Century: Globalization and National Security*, Vol. 2, Washington, D.C.: Institute for National Strategic Studies, 2001.

Cockburn, Andrew, and Patrick Cockburn, *Out of the Ashes: The Resurrection of Saddam Hussein*, New York: HarperCollins, 1999.

Collier, David, and Steven Levitsky, "Democracy with Adjectives: Conceptual Innovation in Comparative Research," *World Politics,* Vol. 49, No. 3, 1997.

Collier, Robert, "Saudis Take Small Step Towards Political Reform; Conservative Monarchy Opens Ears for Criticism," *San Francisco Chronicle,* January 28, 2003.

Cordesman, Anthony, *Perilous Prospects: The Peace Process and the Arab-Israeli Military Balance,* Boulder, Colo.: Westview Press, 1996.

Cordesman, Anthony, *Saudi Arabia,* Boulder, Colo.: Westview Press, 1997.

Cordesman, Anthony, *Weapons of Mass Destruction in the Middle East,* Washington, D.C.: Center for Strategic and International Studies, 1996.

Cordesman, Anthony H., *Iraq and the War of Sanctions,* Westport, Conn.: Praeger Publishers, 1999.

Cordesman, Anthony H., and Abraham R. Wagner, *The Lessons of Modern War, Volume 2: The Iran-Iraq War,* Boulder, Colo.: Westview Press, 1990.

Crystal, Jill, "Civil Society in the Arabian Gulf," in A. R. Norton (ed.), *Civil Society in the Middle East, Volume 2,* Leiden, Netherlands: E. J. Brill, 1996.

Crystal, Jill, "Negotiating with the State: Political Dialogue in the Arabian Gulf," in P. Salem (ed.), *Conflict Resolution in the Arab World: Selected Essays,* Beirut: American University of Beirut, 1997.

Crystal, Jill, and al-Shayeji, "The Pro-Democratic Agenda in Kuwait: Structures and Context," in Baghat Korany, Rex Brynen, and Paul Noble (eds.), *Political Liberalization & Democratization in the Arab World: Volume 2, Comparative Experiences,* Boulder, Colo.: Lynne Rienner, 1998.

CSIS Panel Report, *The Geopolitics of Energy into the 21st Century: Volume 2—The Supply-Demand Outlook 2000–2020*, Washington, D.C.: CSIS, 2000.

"Cultural Ambush," *Cairo Times*, Vol. 4, No. 43, January 11–17, 2001.

"Cyprus/Lebanon: Talks on Oil-Gas Zone," *New York Times* (AFP), March 6, 2002.

Dahl, Robert A., *Polyarchy*, New Haven, Conn.: Yale University Press, 1971.

Danziger, Sheldon H., and Daniel H. Weinberg, "The Historical Record: Trends in Family Income, Inequality, and Poverty," in Sheldon H. Danziger, Gary D. Sandefur, and Daniel H. Weinberg (eds.), *Confronting Poverty: Prescriptions for Change*, Cambridge, Mass.: Harvard University Press, 1994, pp. 18–50.

Davis, Lynn, Steve Hosmer, Sara Daly, and Karl Mueller, *The U.S. Counterterrorism Strategy: A Planning Framework to Facilitate Timely Adjustments*, Santa Monica, Calif.: RAND, DB-426-AF, 2003.

Dekmejian, R. Hrair, "The Rise of Political Islam in Saudi Arabia," *Middle East Journal*, Vol. 48, No. 4, 1994.

Dekmejian, R. Hrair, "Saudi Arabia's Consultative Council," *Middle East Journal*, Vol. 52, No. 2, 1998.

Denoeux, Guilain, "The Politics of Morocco's 'Fight Against Corruption,'" *Middle East Policy*, Vol. 7, No. 2, 2000.

Diamond, Larry, Juan J. Linz, and Seymour Martin Lipset, "Introduction: Comparing Experiences with Democracy," in J. J. Linz and Seymour Martin Lipset (eds.), *Politics in Developing Countries*, Larry Diamond, Boulder, Colo.: Lynne Rienner, 1990.

Dobbs, Michael, "Reform with an Islamic Slant," *Washington Post*, March 9, 2003.

Dokos, Thanos, "The Proliferation of Weapons of Mass Destruction in the Mediterranean: The Threat to Western Security," *Mediterranean Politics*, Vol. 5, No. 3, Autumn 2000.

Dror, Yehezkel, *Crazy States: A Counterconventional Strategic Problem*, Millwood: Kraus, 1980.

Dror, Yehezkel, "Systems Perspective: The Dangers of Fragmented Thinking," in Arieh Stav (ed.), *Ballistic Missiles: The Threat and the Response*, London: Brassey's, 1999.

Drummond, James, and Roula Khalaf, "Unity Hides Hope Saddam Will Leave and Spare Area a War," London: *Financial Times*, March 3, 2003.

Drysdale, Alisdair, "The Asad Regime and Its Troubles," *MERIP Reports*, No. 110, November–December 1982.

Dupuy, Trevor N., *Elusive Victory: The Arab Israeli Wars, 1947-1974*, New York: Harper and Row, 1978.

"Egypt: Talking About a Vice President," *Mideast Mirror*, September 5, 2001.

Eisenstadt, Michael, "The Armed Forces of the Islamic Republic of Iran," *Middle East Review of International Affairs*, Vol. 5, No. 1, March 2001.

Eisenstadt, Michael, *Arming for Peace? Syria's Elusive Quest for Strategic Parity*, Washington Institute Policy Paper 31, Washington, D.C.: Washington Institute for Near East Policy, 1992.

Eisenstadt, Michael, "Who Rules Syria? Bashar al-Asad and the 'Alawi 'Barons,'" *Policywatch 472*, Washington, D.C.: The Washington Institute for Near East Policy, June 21, 2000, electronic version.

El-Effendi, Abdelwahab, "Eclipse of Reason: The Media in the Muslim World," viewed at http://msanews.mynet.net/Scholars/Affendi/media.html.

El Sarafy, Salah, "The Proper Calculation of Income from Depletable Natural Resources," in Y. J. Ahmad (ed.), *Environmental Accounting for Sustainable Development*, Washington, D.C.: World Bank, 1993.

Energy Information Administration, *International Petroleum Monthly Assessments; Strategic Energy Policy: Challenges for the 21st Century*, New York: Council on Foreign Relations, 2001.

Energy Information Agency, *International Energy Outlook 2003*, available at http://www.eia.doe.gov/oiaf/ieo/tbl_15.html, accessed June 17, 2003.

Energy Security: Evaluating U.S. Vulnerability to Oil Supply Disruptions and Options for Mitigating Their Effects, Washington, D.C.: General Accounting Office, December 1996.

Esposito, John L., and John O. Voll, *Islam and Democracy*, New York: Oxford University Press, 1996.

Etheredge, Lloyd S. (ed.), *Politics in Wired Nations: Selected Writings of Ithiel de Sola Pool*, New Brunswick, N.J.: Transaction, 1998.

Evron, Yair, *Israel's Nuclear Dilemma*, Ithaca, N.Y.: Cornell University Press, 1994.

"Exit of Syria's Military Intelligence Chief Leaves Assad's Son-in-Law as De Facto Boss," *Mideast Mirror*, Vol. 14, No. 30, February 14, 2000.

Fandy, Mamoun, *Saudi Arabia and the Politics of Dissent*, New York: St. Martin's Press, 1999.

Fandy, Mamoun, and Dana Hearn, "Egypt: Human Rights and Governance," in P. J. Magnarella (ed.), *Middle East and North Africa: Governance, Democratization, Human Rights*, Aldershot, UK: Ashgate, 1999.

Farrell, Theo, "Transnational Norms and Military Development: Constructing Ireland's Professional Army," *European Journal of International Relations*, Vol. 7, No. 1, March 2001.

"The Fight Over Letting Foreigners into Iran's Oilfields," *The Economist*, July 14, 2001.

Finn, Peter, "Arrests Reveal Al Qaeda Plans; Three Saudis Seized by Morocco Outline Post-Afghanistan Strategy," *Washington Post*, June 16, 2002.

Food and Agriculture Organization, *The State of Food and Agriculture, 2001*, Rome: Food and Agriculture Organization, 2001.

Foreign Missile Developments and the Ballistic Missile Threat to the United States Through 2015, Washington, D.C.: National Intelligence Council, 1999.

"Former Syrian Chief of Staff Is Next on Anti-Corruption Hit-List," *Mideast Mirror*, Vol. 14, No. 106, June 6, 2000.

Freedom in the World 1999–2000. New York: Freedom House, 2000.

Friedman, Thomas L., *The Lexus and the Olive Tree*, New York: Farrar, Strauss and Giroux, 1999.

Fuller, Graham E., and Ian O. Lesser, *A Sense of Siege: The Geopolitics of Islam and the West*, Boulder, Colo.: Westview/RAND, 1995.

Garrity, Patrick J., *Why the Gulf War Still Matters: Foreign Perspectives on the War and the Future of International Security*, Los Alamos, N.M.: Center for National Security Studies, 1993.

Gas Daily, Financial Times Energy Section, May 3, 2001.

Gas in the CIS and Europe, London: Petroleum Economist/Ruhrgas, 2000.

Gause, F. Gregory III, *Oil Monarchies: Domestic and Security Challenges in the Arab Gulf States*, New York: Council on Foreign Relations, 1994.

Gergez, Fawaz, "The Decline of Revolutionary Islam in Algeria and Egypt," *Survival*, Vol. 41, No. 1, Spring 1999.

Gergez, Fawaz, "The End of the Islamist Insurgency in Egypt? Costs and Prospects," *Middle East Journal*, Vol. 54, No. 4, Fall 2000.

Global Trends 2015: A Dialogue About the Future with Nongovernment Experts, Washington, D.C.: National Intelligence Council, 2001.

Golan, Galia, "Russia and Iran: A Strategic Partnership?" *Discussion Paper No. 75*, London, UK: Royal Institute for International Affairs, 1998.

Gold, Dore, "Middle East Proliferation, Israeli Missile Defense, and the ABM Treaty Debate," *Jerusalem Letter*, Jerusalem Center for Public Affairs, No. 430, May 15, 2000.

Grand, Camille, "The European Union and the Non-Proliferation of Nuclear Weapons," *Chaillot Paper No. 37*, Paris, France: WEU Institute for Security Studies, January 2000.

Green, Jerrold, *Leadership Succession in the Arab World: A Policymakers Guide*, Center for Policy Options, Los Angeles, Calif.: University of Judaism, Summer 2000.

Gresh, Alain, "The World Invades Saudi Arabia," *Le Monde Diplomatique*, April 2000.

Grey, Stephen, "French 'Weapons Grade' Exports to Iraq Blocked," *London Sunday Times*, April 22, 2001.

Gumbel, Andrew, "The Iraq Conflict: Arab Governments Struggle to Control Protests Against Us," *The Independent* (London), March 26, 2003.

Hammond, Andrew, "Egypt Gains Another Political Party, Which Looks More Like the Government Than the Opposition," *The Washington Report on Middle East Affairs*, Vol. 19, No. 4, 2000.

Hammond, Andrew, "Though Nominal Winner, Egypt's Ruling NDP Party Embarrassed in Parliamentary Elections," *The Washington Report on Middle East Affairs*, Vol. 20, No. 1, 2001.

Harris, Martha Caldwell, "The Globalization of Energy Markets," in Stephen J. Flanagan, Ellen L. Frost, and Richard L. Kugler (eds.), *Challenges of the Global Century*, Washington, D.C.: National Defense University, 2001.

Hashim, Ahmed S., "Civil-Military Relations in the Islamic Republic of Iran," in Joseph Kechichian (ed.), *Iran, Iraq, and the Arab Gulf States*, New York: Palgrave, 2000.

Hawthorne, Amy B., "Egyptian Elections: Rumblings of Change, But NDP Dominance Maintained," *Policywatch* 506, Washington, D.C.: The Washington Institute for Near East Policy, 2000.

Heller, Mark, "Iraq's Army: Military Weakness, Political Utility," in *Iraq's Road to War*, Amatzia Baram and Barry Rubin (eds.), New York: St. Martin's Press, 1996.

Hendawi, Hamza, "Hussein's Long Years in Power Not So Unusual in Arab Politics," *The Associated Press*, February 9, 1999.

Henderson, Simon, *After King Fahd: Succession in Saudi Arabia*, Washington, D.C.: The Washington Institute for Near East Policy, 1994.

Heper, Metin, "Islam and Democracy in Turkey: Toward a Reconciliation?" *Middle East Journal*, Vol. 51, No. 1, 1997.

Hersh, Seymour, *The Samson Option: Israel's Nuclear Arsenal and American Foreign Policy*, New York: Random House, 1991.

Hicks, Neil, and Ghanim al-Najjar, "The Utility of Tradition: Civil Society in Kuwait," in A. R. Norton (ed.), *Civil Society in the Middle East, Volume 1*, Leiden, Netherlands: E. J. Brill, 1995.

Hinnebusch, Raymond, *Authoritarian Power and State Formation in Ba'athist Syria*, Boulder, Colo.: Westview Press, 1990.

Hinnebusch, Raymond, *Peasant and Bureaucracy in Bàthist Syria: The Political Economy of Rural Development*, Boulder, Colo., and London: Westview Press, 1989.

Hirst, David, "Egypt Stands on Feet of Clay," *Le Monde Diplomatique*, October 1999.

Hoffman, Bruce, "Terrorism Trends and Prospects," in Ian O. Lesser et al., *Countering the New Terrorism*, Santa Monica, Calif.: RAND, MR-989-AF, 1999.

Honig, David, "A Mighty Arsenal: Egypt's Military Build-Up, 1979–1999," *Policywatch* 447, Washington, D.C.: The Washington Institute for Near East Policy, March 21, 2000.

Hufbauer, Gary, *China, the United States and the Global Economy: Trends and Prospects in the Global Economy*, Washington, D.C.: Institute for International Economics, November 1999.

Huntington, Samuel P., "The Clash of Civilizations?" *Foreign Affairs,* Summer 1993.

Huntington, Samuel P., *The Third Wave: Democratization in the Late Twentieth Century,* Norman, Okla.: The University of Oklahoma Press, 1991.

Ibrahim, Saad Eddin, "Civil Society and Prospects of Democratization in the Arab World," in A. R. Norton (ed.), *Civil Society in the Middle East Volume 1,* Leiden, Netherlands: E. J. Brill, 1995.

Ibrahim, Youssef M., "The Saudi Who Can Speak Our Language," *Washington Post,* February 24, 2002 (electronic version).

International Energy Outlook, Paris: International Energy Agency, 2000.

International Institute for Strategic Studies, *Strategic Survey 1999/2000,* Oxford: Oxford University Press, 2000.

International Institute for Strategic Studies, *The Military Balance 2000–2001,* Oxford: Oxford University Press, 2000.

International Monetary Fund, *Building on Progress: Reform and Growth in the Middle East and North Africa,* Washington, D.C.: International Monetary Fund, 1996.

"Iran's Liberal Culture Minister Is Out, Dealing Blow to Reform," *New York Times,* December 15, 2000.

"Iran's Weapons: A Bigger Punch," *The Economist,* May 26, 2001.

"Iraq's Army: The Lessons from the War with Iran," *The Economist,* January 12, 1991.

"Is Syria Really Changing?" *The Economist,* November 18, 2000.

Jaffe, Amy Myers, and Robert A. Manning, "The Shocks of a World of Cheap Oil," *Foreign Affairs,* Vol. 79, No. 1, January–February 2000.

Jaffe, Amy Myers, and Robert A. Manning, "Russia, Energy and the West," *Survival,* Vol. 43, No. 2, Summer 2001.

Joffe, George, "The Euro-Mediterranean Partnership: Two Years After Barcelona," Chatham House, *Middle East Briefing*, No. 44, May 1998.

"Jordan's Predicaments," *Strategic Comments*, International Institute of Strategic Studies, Vol. 7, No. 7, 2001.

"Jordan's Street Moves Again," *Mideast Mirror*, July 26, 2002.

Kagan, Robert, *Of Paradise and Power*, New York: Knopf, 2003.

Kanofsky, Eliyahu, *The Middle East Economies: The Impact of Domestic and International Politics*, Begin-Sadat Center for Strategic Studies, Bar-Ilan University, Israel, 1998.

Karl, Terry Lynn, "Dilemmas of Democratization in Latin America," *Comparative Politics*, Vol. 23, No. 1, 1991.

Karsh, Efraim, *The Iran-Iraq War: A Military Analysis*, Adelphi Paper 220, International Institute for International Studies, Oxford: Oxford University Press, 1987.

Kazemi, Farhad, and Augustus Richard Norton, "Hardliners and Softliners in the Middle East: Problems of Governance and the Prospects for Liberalization in Authoritarian Political Systems," in H. Handelman and M. Tessler (eds.), *Democracy and its Limits: Lessons from Asia, Latin America, and the Middle East*, Notre Dame, Ind.: University of Notre Dame Press, 1999.

Kechichian, Joseph A., *Oman and the World*, Santa Monica, Calif.: RAND, MR-680-RC, 1995.

Kechichian, Joseph, *Political Dynamics and Security in the Arabian Peninsula Through the 1990s*, Santa Monica, Calif.: RAND, MR-167-AF/A, 1993.

Kemp, Geoffrey, and Robert E. Harkavy, *Strategic Geography and the Changing Middle East*, Washington, D.C.: Brookings Institution Press, 1997.

Kessler, Martha Neff, "Syria, Israel and the Middle East Peace Process: Past Success and Final Challenges," *Middle East Policy*, Vol. 7, No. 2, February 2000.

Khajehpour, Biijan, "Domestic Political Reforms and Private Sector Activity in Iran," *Social Research*, Summer 2000.

Khalaf, Roula, "Bashar Steps Out of His Father's Shadow," *Financial Times*, January 16, 2001.

Khalilzad, Zalmay M., David A. Shlapak, and Daniel L. Byman, *The Implications of the Possible End of the Arab-Israeli Conflict for Gulf Security*, Santa Monica, Calif.: RAND, MR-822-AF, 1997.

Kienle, Eberhard, "More Than a Response to Islamism: The Political Deliberalization of Egypt in the 1990s," *Middle East Journal*, Vol. 52, No. 2, 1998.

Kilicki, Jan H., "Caspian Energy at the Crossroads," *Foreign Affairs*, Vol. 80, No. 5, September/October 2001.

Klare, Michael T., "The New Geography of Conflict," *Foreign Affairs*, Vol. 80, No. 3, May/June 2001.

Klare, Michael T., *Resource Wars: The New Landscape of Global Conflict*, New York: Metropolitan Books, 2001.

Korany, Baghat, "Monarchical Islam with a Democratic Veneer: Morocco," in Baghat Korany, Rex Brynen, and Paul Noble (eds.), *Political Liberalization & Democratization in the Arab World: Volume 2, Comparative Experiences*, Boulder, Colo.: Lynne Rienner, 1998.

Korany, Baghat, "Restricted Democratization from Above: Egypt," in Baghat Korany, Rex Brynen, and Paul Noble (eds.), *Political Liberalization & Democratization in the Arab World: Volume 2, Comparative Experiences*, Boulder, Colo.: Lynne Rienner, 1998.

Korany, Bahgat, and Paul Noble, "Introduction: Arab Liberalization and Democratization—The Dialectics of the General and the Specific," in Baghat Korany, Rex Brynen, and Paul Noble (eds.), *Political Liberalization & Democratization in the Arab World: Volume 2, Comparative Experiences*, Boulder, Colo.: Lynne Rienner, 1998.

Krause, Joachim, "The Proliferation of Weapons of Mass Destruction: The Risks for Europe," in Paul Cornish, Peter van Ham, and

Joachim Krause (eds.), *Europe and the Challenge of Proliferation*, Paris: WEU Institute for Security Studies, 1996.

Krimly, Rayed Khalid, "The Political Economy of Rentier States: A Case Study of Saudi Arabia in the Oil Era: 1950–1990," Ph.D. dissertation, Department of Political Science, George Washington University, 1993.

"Kuwait: Women's Rights Case Rejected," *New York Times*, January 17, 2001.

Lamb, David, "Arab Leaders May See Iraq as a Wakeup Call," *Los Angeles Times*, April 30, 2003.

Lelyveld, Michael, "Turkey: Iranian Gas Import Delays May Favor Russia," *RFE/RL*, July 10, 2001.

Leonard, Mark, "Velvet Fist in the Iron Glove," *The Observer* (London), June 16, 2002.

Lesser, Ian, *Oil, the Persian Gulf and Grand Strategy: Contemporary Issues in Historical Perspective*, Santa Monica, Calif.: RAND, R-4072-CENTCOM/JS, 1991.

Lesser, Ian O., *Resources and Strategy*, New York: St. Martin's Press, 1989.

Lesser, Ian, and Ashley Tellis, *Strategic Exposure: Proliferation Around the Mediterranean*, Santa Monica, Calif.: RAND, MR-742-A, 1996.

"Lessons from Syria's Experiment with Democracy," *Mideast Mirror*, July 5, 2001.

Liesman, Steve, "Low Oil Prices Pressure Saudi Economy," *Wall Street Journal*, March 1, 1999.

"Like Father, Like Son," *The Economist* (U.S. edition), June 2, 2001.

Lipset, Seymour Martin, *Political Man*, Garden City, New York: Doubleday, 1960.

Lodal, Jan, *The Price of Dominance: The New Weapons of Mass Destruction and Their Challenge to American Leadership*, New York: Council on Foreign Relations, 2001.

Long, David E., *The Kingdom of Saudi Arabia*, Gainesville, Fla.: University Press of Florida, 1997.

Lynch, Marc, *State Interests and Public Spheres*, New York: Columbia University Press, 1999.

"Major Personnel Changes Expected in Baghdad," *Mideast Mirror*, Vol. 11, No. 130, July 8, 1997.

"Make Haste Slowly," *The Economist*, June 16, 2001.

MacFarquar, Neil, "Arab Protesters Focus Ire on U.S.," *New York Times*, April 6, 2002.

MacFarquhar, Neil, "Egypt Sentences Sociologist to 7 Years in Quick Verdict," *New York Times*, May 22, 2001.

MacFarquhar, Neil, "Egyptian Court Frees Rights Advocate and Orders Retrial," *New York Times*, December 4, 2002.

MacFarquhar, Neil, "Syria Reaches Turning Point but Which Way Will It Turn," *New York Times*, March 12, 2001.

MacFarquhar, Neil, with Nazila Fathi, "Iran's President Wins a New Mandate to Promote Reform," *New York Times*, June 9, 2001.

Mainuddin, Rolin G., "Democratization, Liberalization, and Human Rights: Challenges Facing the Gulf Cooperation Council," in P. J. Magnarella (ed.), *Middle East and North Africa: Governance, Democratization, Human Rights*, Aldershot, UK: Ashgate, 1999.

Makovsky, Alan, "Syria Under Bashar al-Asad: The Domestic Scene and the 'Chinese Model' of Reform," *Policywatch* 512, Washington, D.C.: The Washington Institute for Near East Policy, January 17, 2001, electronic version.

Mann, Jim, "US Takes New Tack on China Arms Exports," *Los Angeles Times*, October 5, 2000.

Mansfield, Edward D., and Jack Snyder, "Democratization and the Danger of War," *International Security*, Vol. 20, No. 1, 1995.

Ma'oz, Moshe, *Syria Under Hafiz al-Assad: New Domestic and Foreign Policies*, Jerusalem Policy Papers, 15, Jerusalem: Hebrew University of Jerusalem, 1975.

Martin, Paul, "Qataris Vote for Greater Freedom," *Washington Times*, April 20, 2003.

McKee, E. S., "Still Waters on the Nile," *The Jerusalem Report*, November 8, 1999.

Meital, Yoram, "Domestic Challenges and Egypt's U.S. Policy," *Middle East Review of International Affairs*, Vol. 2, No. 4, November 1998, electronic version.

Menashri, David, "Whither Iranian Politics? The Khatami Factor," in P. Clawson, M. Eisenstadt, E. Kanovsky, and D. Menashri, *Iran Under Khatami*, Washington, D.C.: The Washington Institute for Near East Policy, 1998.

Middle East Watch, *Syria Unmasked: The Suppression of Human Rights by the Asad Regime*, New Haven, Conn.: Yale University Press for Middle East Watch, 1991.

Millett, Allan R., Williamson Murray, and Kenneth H. Watman, "The Effectiveness of Military Organizations," in Allan R. Millett and Williamson Murray (eds.), *Military Effectiveness: Volume 1: The First World War*, Boston: Allen & Unwin, 1988.

Monterey Institute of International Studies, Center for Nonproliferation Studies, "Syria's Scuds and Chemical Weapons," available at http://cns.miis.edu/research/wmdme/syrscud.htm.

Morello, Carol, "Saudis Free Prominent Critic After 8 Years," *Washington Post*, March 26, 2003.

Morello, Carol, and Emily Wax, "Hussein's Fall Bolsters Middle East Reformers," *Washington Post*, April 13, 2003.

Morse, Edward L., and James Richard, "The Battle for Energy Dominance," *Foreign Affairs*, Vol. 81, No. 2, March/April 2002, pp. 16–31.

Mottahedeh, Roy P., and Mamoun Fandy, "The Islamist Movement: The Case for Democratic Inclusion," in Gary G. Sick and Lawrence G. Potter (eds.), *The Persian Gulf at the Millennium*, New York: St. Martin's Press, 1997.

Moussalli, Ahmad S., "The Geopolitics of Syrian-Iraqi Relations," *Middle East Policy*, Vol. 7, No. 4, October 2000.

Murphy, Kim, "Saudis Take the Slow Road," *Los Angeles Times*, April 9, 2003.

Murphy, Richard W., and F. Gregory Gause III, "Democracy and U.S. Policy in the Middle East," *Middle East Policy*, Vol. 5, No. 1, January 1997.

Nakhoul, Samia, "Egyptian Militants Aim to Infiltrate Armed Forces," *Reuters*, August 23, 1993.

National Intelligence Council, *Foreign Missile Developments and the Ballistic Missile Threat to the United States Through 2015*, September 1999.

A National Security Strategy for a Global Age, Washington, D.C.: The White House, December 2000.

Negroponte, Nicholas, *Being Digital*, New York: Knopf, 1995.

Norton, Augustus Richard, "Introduction," in A. R. Norton (ed.), *Civil Society in the Middle East, Volume 1*, Leiden, Netherlands: E. J. Brill, 1995.

Ochmanek, David, *Military Operations Against Terrorist Groups Abroad: Implications for the U.S. Air Force*, Santa Monica, Calif.: RAND, MR-1738-AF, 2003.

O'Donnell, Guillermo, and Philippe C. Schmitter, *Transitions from Authoritarian Rule: Tentative Conclusions About Uncertain Democracies*, Baltimore, Md.: The Johns Hopkins University Press, 1996.

Olstead, Thomas, "A New Generation of Leaders Will Shake Up the Mideast," *U.S. News and World Report*, February 22, 1999.

"Paper Controlled by Uday Notes 'Absurd' Report on Qusay's Powers," Babil,' Baghdad in Arabic, August 5, 1999, reported in *BBC Monitoring Middle East—Political, BBC Worldwide Monitoring*, August 7, 1999.

Parry, V. J., and M. E. Yapp (eds.), *War, Technology and Society in the Middle East*, London: Oxford University Press, 1975.

Penn World Tables 5.6, available at http://datacentre.chass.utoronto.ca:5680/pwt/index.html, accessed June 2003.

Perthes, Volker, *The Political Economy of Syria Under Asad*, London: I. B. Tauris, 1995.

Perthes, Volker, "The Political Economy of the Syrian Succession," *Survival*, Vol. 43, No. 1, Spring 2001.

Pew Research Center for People and the Press, Year-After 9/11 Poll, available at http://people-press.org/reports/print.php3?PageID=639.

Piore, Michael J., *Birds of Passage: Migrant Labor and Industrial Societies*, Cambridge and New York: Cambridge University Press, 1979.

Pollack, Kenneth M., *The Influence of Arab Culture on Arab Military Effectiveness*, Ph.D. dissertation, Massachusetts Institute of Technology, 1996.

"Poverty in the Mashreq Region," United Nations Development Program, unpublished report, 1995.

Proliferation Threat and Response, Washington, D.C.: Office of the Secretary of Defense, 2001.

"Qatar: Vote on Constitution," *New York Times*, April 29, 2003.

Quandt, William B., *Saudi Arabia in the 1980s: Foreign Policy, Security, and Oil*, Washington, D.C.: Brookings, 1981.

Quilliam, Neil, *Syria and the New World Order*, Reading, UK: Garnet Publishing, 1999.

Quinlivan, James T., "Coup-Proofing: Its Practice and Consequences in the Middle East," *International Security*, Vol. 24, No. 2, Fall 1999.

Rabin, Yitzhak, "Deterrence in an Israeli Security Context," in Ahron Kleiman and Ariel Levite (eds.), *Deterrence in the Middle East*, Tel Aviv: Jaffe Center for Strategic Studies, 1993.

Rathmell, Andrew, "Iraqi Intelligence and Security Services," *International Defense Review*, Vol. 24, No. 5, May 1991.

Reiter, Daniel, and Allan C. Stam III, "Democracy and Battlefield Military Success," *Journal of Conflict Resolution*, Vol. 42, No. 3, June 1998.

Richard, James, "New Cohesion in OPEC's Cartel?" *Middle East Review of International Affairs*, Vol. 3, No. 2, June 1999.

Richards, Alan, "The Political Economy of Dilatory Reform: Egypt in the 1980s," *World Development*, Vol. 19, No. 12, December 1991.

Richards, Alan, and Nirvikar Singh, "No Easy Exit: Property Rights, Markets, and Negotiations Over Water," *Water Resources Development*, Vol. 17, No. 3, 2001.

Richards, Alan, and John Waterbury, *A Political Economy of the Middle East*, Boulder, Colo., and London: Westview Press, 2nd ed., 1996.

Risen, James, "Nuclear Items Sold by Russia to Iran Pose an Obstacle, Panel Finds," *New York Times*, January 11, 2001.

Rivlin, Paul, *Economic Policy and Performance in the Arab World*, Boulder and London: Lynne Rienner, 2001.

Robinson, Glenn E., "Can Islamists Be Democrats? The Case of Jordan," *Middle East Journal*, Vol. 51, No. 3, 1997.

Robinson, Glenn E., "Palestine After Arafat," *The Washington Quarterly*, Vol. 23, No. 4, Autumn 2000.

Rochin, Gene I., and Chris C. Demchak, *Lessons of the Gulf War: Ascendant Technology and Declining Capability*, Policy Papers in

International Affairs, No. 39, University of California at Berkeley: Institute for International Studies, 1991.

Rosen, Stephen Peter, *Societies and Military Power*, Ithaca, N.Y.: Cornell University Press, 1996.

Rouleau, Eric, "Iran's 'Referendum for Democracy,'" *Le Monde Diplomatique*, June 2001.

Roy, Sara, "Civil Society in the Gaza Strip: Obstacles to Social Reconstruction," in A. R. Norton (ed.), *Civil Society in the Middle East, Volume 2*, Leiden, Netherlands: E. J. Brill, 1996.

Rubin, Barry, "The Military in Contemporary Middle East Politics," *Middle East Review of International Affairs*, Vol. 5, No. 1, December 2000.

Rumer, Eugene, *Dangerous Drift: Russia's Middle East Policy*, Washington, D.C.: Washington Institute for Near East Policy, 2000.

Russell, Richard L., "A Saudi Nuclear Option?" *Survival*, Vol. 43, No. 2, Summer 2001.

"Russia, Libya Determined to Revive Cooperation," *Interfax* (Moscow), November 15, 2000.

Sachs, Susan, "Leaders of Syria Building Support for Son of Assad," *New York Times*, June 12, 2000.

Sachs, Susan, "Saudi Prince Urges Reform, and a Move from Shadow," *New York Times*, December 4, 2000.

"Saddam's Second Son Gets Succession Boost," *Ha'aretz*, May 20, 2001.

Safran, Nadav, *Saudi Arabia: The Ceaseless Quest for Security*, Ithaca, N.Y.: Cornell University Press, 1988.

Salameh, Mamdouh G., "A Third Oil Crisis?" *Survival*, Vol. 43, No. 3, Autumn 2001.

Samii, A. William, "Iran's Guardians Council as an Obstacle to Democracy," *Middle East Journal*, Vol. 55, No. 4, Autumn 2001.

Sands, David R., "Qatar Says Iraq Will Be Democracy Test Case," *Washington Times*, May 10, 2003.

Schelling, Thomas C., *The Strategy of Conflict*, Cambridge, Mass.: Harvard University Press, 1960.

Schmitter, Philippe C., "Civil Society East and West," in L. Diamond, M. F. Plattner, Y.-h. Chu, and H.-m. Tien (eds.), *Consolidating the Third Wave Democracies: Themes and Perspectives*, Baltimore, Md.: The Johns Hopkins University Press, 1997.

Schmitter, Philippe C., "Still the Century of Corporatism?" *Review of Politics*, Vol. 36, No. 1, 1974.

Schmitter, Philippe C., and Terry Lynn Karl, "What Democracy Is . . . and Is Not," *Journal of Democracy*, Vol. 2, No. 3, 1991.

Schneider, Howard, "Bahrain's New King Sets Date for Vote," *Washington Post*, February 15, 2002.

Schneider, Howard, "Court Hands Scholar Jail Term for Defaming State; Pro-Democracy Think Tank Broken Up," *Washington Post*, May 22, 2001.

Schumpeter, Joseph A., *Capitalism, Socialism, and Democracy*, 3rd ed., New York: Harper & Brothers, 1950.

Sciolino, Elaine, *Persian Mirrors*, New York: The Free Press, 2000.

Seagrave, Sterling, *Yellow Rain*, New York: Evans, 1981, cited in Geoffrey Kemp and Robert Harkavy, *Strategic Geography and the Changing Middle East*, Washington, D.C.: Brookings Institution Press, 1997.

Seckler, David, David Molden, and Randolph Barker, "Water Scarcity in the Twenty-First Century," *International Journal of Water Resources Development*, March 1999.

Sengupta, Kim, "Five Held in Morocco Planned to Strike Warships," *The Independent* (London), June 12, 2002.

Seznec, Jean Francois, "The Perils of Privatization in the Gulf," Lecture at Center for Contemporary Arab Studies, Georgetown University, Washington, D.C., March 19, 2001.

Sicherman, Harvey, "Hafez al-Assad: The Man Who Waited Too Long," *Peacefacts,* Foreign Policy Research Institution, Vol. 7, No. 1, July 2001, electronic version.

Siegman, Henry, "Being Hafiz al-Assad: Syria's Chilly but Consistent Peace Strategy," *Foreign Affairs,* Vol. 79, No. 3, May/June 2000.

Simons, Geoff, *Iraq: From Sumer to Saddam,* London: Macmillan Press, 1994.

Sipress, Alan, "Jordan Breathes Sigh of Relief After Iraq War," *Washington Post,* May 6, 2003.

Sokolski, Henry, "Post 9/11 Nonproliferation," *E-Notes,* Foreign Policy Research Institute, January 25, 2002.

Sokolsky, Richard, and Tanya Charlick-Paley, *NATO and Caspian Security: A Mission Too Far?* Santa Monica, Calif.: RAND, MR-1074-AF, 1999.

Springborg, Robert, *Mubarak's Egypt: Fragmentation of the Political Order,* Boulder, Colo.: Westview Press, 1989.

Stam, Allan C. III, *Win, Lose, or Draw: Domestic Politics and the Crucible of War,* Ann Arbor: University of Michigan Press, 1996.

State Failure Task Force Report: Phase II Findings, Science Applications International Corporation: Washington, D.C., July 31, 1998.

Steinberg, Gerald, *Arms Control and Non-Proliferation Developments in the Middle East: 1998-99,* Ramat Gan: Begin-Sadat Center for Strategic Studies, 2000.

Strategic Energy Policy: Challenges for the 21st Century, a Task Force Report, New York: Council on Foreign Relations, 2001.

Struck, Doug, "North Korea Insists on Missile Sales," *International Herald Tribune,* May 5–6, 2001.

Susser, Asher, "The 'Alawis, Lords of Syria," in Ofra Bengio and Gabriel Ben-Dor (eds.), *Minorities and the State in the Arab World,* Boulder, Colo.: Lynne Rienner, 1999.

Susser, Asher, "The Palestinians in Jordan: Demographic Majority, Political Minority," in Ofra Bengio and Gabriel Ben-Dor (eds.), *Minorities and the State in the Arab World*, Boulder, Colo.: Lynne Rienner, 1999.

"Syria Now," *Middle East Economic Digest*, May 16, 1997.

"Syria's Assad Sees Little Cause for Optimism," *Mideast Mirror*, July 1, 2002.

Takeyh, Ray, "Libya: Opting for Europe and Africa, Not Ties with Washington," *Policywatch*, No. 486, Washington Institute for Near East Policy, September 21, 2000.

Takeyh, Ray, "The Rogue Who Came in from the Cold," *Foreign Affairs*, Vol. 80, No. 3, May/June 2001.

Taylor, Catherine, "Saudi Arabia's Quiet Voices of Reform Start to Speak Up," *Christian Science Monitor*, January 15, 2003.

Tenet, George, "Weapons of Mass Destruction: A New Dimension in U.S. Middle East Policy," *Middle East Review of International Affairs*, Vol. 4, No. 2, June 2000.

Tétreault, Mary Ann, *Stories of Democracy*, New York: Columbia University Press, 2000.

Tétreault, Mary Ann, "Women's Rights in Kuwait: Bringing in the Last Bedouins?" *Current History*, Vol. 99, No. 633, 2000.

Thinking Beyond the Stalemate in U.S.-Iranian Relations, Volume I— Policy Review, Washington, D.C.: The Atlantic Council of the United States, May 2001.

Tripp, Charles, *A History of Iraq*, Cambridge: Cambridge University Press, 2000.

"Turkey Concerned Over Iran's Guided Missile Test," *Turkish Daily News*, June 3, 2001.

Tyler, Patrick E., "Moscow Says Remarks by U.S. Resurrect 'Spirit of Cold War,'" *New York Times*, March 21, 2001.

Tyler, Patrick E., "Saudis Plan to End U.S. Presence," *New York Times*, February 9, 2003.

United Nations Develoment Program, *Arab Human Development Report 2002*, available at http://www.undp.org/rbas/ahdr/, accessed June 2003.

United States Department of Energy, Energy Information Administration, *OPEC Revenues Fact Sheet*, at http://www.eia.doe.gov/emeu/cabs/opecrev.html, accessed June 2003.

United States Embassy in Riyadh, "Saudi Arabia: 2001 Economic Trends," May 2000.

Van Dam, Nikolaos, *The Struggle for Power in Syria: Politics and Society Under Asad and the Ba'th Party*, New York, London: I. B. Tauris, 1996.

van Eeghen, Willem, "Poverty in the Middle East and North Africa," World Bank, unpublished, 1995.

"Views of a Changing World 2003," The Pew Global Attitudes Project, data available at http://people-press.org/reports/pdf/185topline.pdf.

Vogel, Frank E., "Islamic Governance in the Gulf: A Framework for Analysis, Comparison and Prediction," in Gary G. Sick and Lawrence G. Potter (eds.), *The Persian Gulf at the Millenium*, New York: St. Martin's Press, 1997.

Waterbury, John, *Exposed to Innumerable Delusions: Public Enterprise and State Power in Egypt, India, Mexico and Turkey*, Cambridge: Cambridge University Press, 1993.

Weaver, Mary Ann, "Egypt on Trial," *New York Times*, June 17, 2001.

Wege, Carl Anthony, "Assad's Legions: The Syrian Intelligence Services," *Intelligence and Counterintelligence*, Vol. 4, No. 1, Spring 1990.

Weymouth, Lally, "Mubarak: 'Jerusalem Can Stop Everything,'" *The Jerusalem Post*, April 3, 2001.

Whitaker, Brian, "Saudi King Agrees to Human Rights Panel," *The Guardian* (London), May 8, 2003.

White House, *A National Security Strategy for a Global Age*, Washington, D.C.: December 2000.

"Whose Game, How Great?" *Private View* (Istanbul), Autumn 2000.

Wilkening, Dean, and Kenneth Watman, *Nuclear Deterrence in a Regional Context*, Santa Monica, Calif.: RAND, MR-500-A/AF, 1995.

"Will the Oil Run Out?" *The Economist*, February 10, 2001.

Williamson, Jeffrey G., and Tareq Yousef, "Demographic Transitions and Economic Performance in MENA," unpublished paper, Harvard University, 1999.

Wilson, Peter W., and Douglas F. Graham, *Saudi Arabia: The Coming Storm*, New York: M. E. Sharpe & Co., 1994.

Wines, Michael, "Putin to Sell Arms and Nuclear Help to Iran," *New York Times*, March 13, 2001.

World Bank, *2001 World Development Indicators*, Washington, D.C.: World Bank, 2001.

World Bank, *Claiming the Future: Choosing Prosperity in the Middle East and North Africa*, Washington, D.C.: The World Bank, 1995.

World Bank, *Egypt: Social and Structural Review*, Social and Economic Development Group, Middle East and North Africa Region, Report No. 22397-EGT, June 20, 2001.

World Bank, *Middle East and North Africa Environmental Strategy: Towards Sustainable Development*, Washington, D.C.: The World Bank, 1995.

World Bank, *World Development Report 2000*, New York and Oxford: Oxford University Press, 2000.

World Oil Transit Chokepoints, Washington, D.C.: Energy Information Administration, 1998.

World Report 2001, New York: Human Rights Watch, 2000.

Wyllie, James, "Iran's Quest for Security and Influence," *Jane's Intelligence Review*, July 1993.

Zeidan, David, "Radical Islam in Egypt: A Comparison of Two Groups," *Middle East Review of International Affairs*, Vol. 3, No. 3, September 1999, electronic version.

Zimmerman, Ekkart, "Toward a Causal Model of Military Coups d' État," *Armed Forces and Society*, Vol. 5, No. 3, Spring 1979.

Zisser, Eyal, "The Renewed Struggle for Power in Syria," in Moshe Ma'oz, Joseph Ginat, and Onn Winckler (eds.), *Modern Syria*, Brighton, UK: Sussex Academic Press, 1999.

Zogby, James, "It's the Policy, Stupid!" *Media Monitors Network*, April 15, 2002, available at www.mediamonitors.net/zogby49.html, accessed June 17, 2003.